Date Due

FEB 21-2002 NOV 15 2006			
No	DISCARDED		
Wh			
to Ev			

Copyright © 1993 by Wm. B. Eerdmans Publishing Co.
255 Jefferson Ave. S.E., Grand Rapids, Michigan 49503
Paperback edition 1993
Published jointly in the United States by Wm. B. Eerdmans Publishing Co.
and in the U. K. by Inter-Varsity Press
38 De Montfort Street, Leicester LE1 7GP, England

Printed in the United States of America

00 99   9 8

Library of Congress Cataloging-in-Publication Data

Wells, David F.
No place for truth, or, Whatever happened to evangelical theology? /
David F. Wells.
p.   cm.
Includes bibliographical references and index.
ISBN 0-8028-0747-X
1. Evangelicals — United States — History — 20th century.
2. Christianity and culture. I. Title. II. Title: No place for truth.
III. Title: Whatever happened to evangelical theology?
BR1642.U5W45   1992
230'.046 — dc20   92-41322
CIP

British Library Cataloguing in Publication Data

A catalogue record for this book is available from the British Library
Inter-Varsity Press ISBN 0-85111-163-7

Cover photo: B. H. Conant Photo #0675 —
Courtesy of the Wenham Museum, Wenham, MA.

No Place for Truth

or

Whatever Happened to Evangelical Theology?

David F. Wells

William B. Eerdmans Publishing Company
Grand Rapids, Michigan

Inter-Varsity Press
Leicester, England

To Jane

To whom I have been married
for only twenty-seven years

Contents

THE CIRCUMSTANCE OF FAITH

Preface

OF THE WRITING OF BOOKS, the sage said, there is no end, and there might have been no end in sight to the writing of this particular book had I not received considerable help from others. First and foremost, I wish to thank the Pew Charitable Trusts for an extraordinarily generous grant which enabled me to take off the necessary time to think about the disappearance of theology and to commit these thoughts to paper. This also required that I be loosed from my teaching responsibilities. Gordon-Conwell was most accommodating and co-operative. I am also grateful to all of those who filled in in my absence. They did this so well that I began to fear that the Seminary might decide to make my leave of absence permanent!

During this leave, I received a number of invitations to give lectures in various places. Some of these I felt that I had to decline, but I did accept several which I thought might enable me to get my own ideas clear on the disappearance of theology. I was correct. It was very helpful to receive responses to my ideas as I was going along. I therefore wish to thank the Southern Baptist Theological Seminary in Louisville for the opportunity to lecture and debate on this subject in 1990; the Coalition for Christian Outreach, the Christian College Coalition, and the Christian Higher Education Commission of the National Association of Evangelicals for their invitation to address this theme and to engage in discussion on it in 1991; the Board of Wheaton College, who invited me to think with them about college education in the future, given the changes in the evangelical world that I sought to describe; the Archdiocese of Sydney, Australia, for the kind invitation to speak to the clergy of the region on how modernity colors our perception of the uniqueness of Christ; and to Trinity Evangelical Divinity School for the honor of being asked to deliver the Kenneth Kantzer Lectures in 1991 on the theme of the disappearance of theology. And in the summer of 1992, after the manuscript had been completed and was lost to sight somewhere in the labyrinth of the publisher, I gave two addresses at Biola University and a series at the Francis A. Schaeffer Institute, Covenant Theological Seminary, on some of the themes in this book. It was, at that time, too late to make changes. The dice were in the air but had not yet landed on the table. I was, however, grateful for the interest in the issues I had raised.

In addition, I am indebted to a number of people who, at my request, read portions of this manuscript. I am grateful for their judicious comments. These include Thomas Askew, Stanley Gaede, T. David Gordon, Os Guinness, Nathan Hatch, James Hunter, Garth Rosell, Mark Noll, John Stott, Douglas Stuart, and Ken Swetland. Naturally, I alone am responsible for the book as it now stands. I am also grateful for the comments and critiques that were offered to portions of this manuscript at two conferences on "theology and modern consciousness" held at Rockport in 1990 and 1991. Finally, for the chapter on Wenham, I was given every assistance possible by the staff at Wenham Museum, for which I am grateful; I quote from materials under their care with permission.

Finally, I cannot but express my indebtedness to all of those who, over the years, have enriched my understanding by their faithful preaching of the Word of God, by their examples of principled living, and by their spiritual authenticity — those whose friendship has constantly provoked me into doing better myself. They have helped me to see that those who are most relevant to this world are those who are judged most irrelevant.

Introduction

I HESITATED BRIEFLY as I entered the large, inhospitable lecture hall to which my beginning class in theology had been assigned. My hesitation had little to do with the room, though that does leave something to be desired. Not only is the professor's desk remote from the students, who are banked away in ascending tiers to the point of dim visibility at the back, but the heating system often goes into reverse. From time to time in winter, the bonhomie is rudely broken, with little warning and less reason, by a merciless, icy blast as this rogue system suddenly begins to suck air in from the outside instead of warming and circulating it from within. Here, indeed, is a parable of modern existence: a machine that no one can tame, intended for the comforting of human life, working its wreckage on the best laid plans of the institution.

That, however, was not why I hesitated, for I had learned to protect myself against this temperamental monster by having an over-coat at hand when things got really bad. Nor was it the palpable quietness that I knew would suddenly overcome this class as I began my descent toward the front. Many of these students, if they were like their predecessors, would be scared stiff. First, there was my reputation to be considered: more alarming than Ivan the Terrible, I am told, especially at exam time. And second, there was the subject. Theology is so remote from anything that many had thought about, or considered important, that the first encounter was always quite puzzling and often threatening.

All of that was simply part of the situation, the "given," as they say. But I hesitated that day for another reason. I really had no great

1

certainty as to how I was going to circumvent their fear and make some connections with the curiosity that surely had to be lurking somewhere in each of these men and women. It was important that I do that early in the going.

But before I could attempt this tricky venture, there was the introduction to the course to be taken care of. Now, I had the great advantage of knowing one of the questions that would later appear on the student evaluation form — the consumers' report — which each would be asked to fill out at the end of the course: "Was the course adequately introduced?" And after the question there follow numbers from one to five, from superior to poor, for grading the professor. The problem is that I have never understood the question. Is it not enough that the catalog describes the content of the course? Or am I expected to read this to them? Elaborate on it? Give a potted version of what lies before them? Talk in vague but reassuring ways about life to give them time to get acclimated to me and to start feeling comfortable with the course of studies into which they were entering? My confusion on this point is amply attested by the low grades I always garner. After these student evaluations have passed before my eyes, heavy with their somber scoring, they go to the dean's office and then into some wretched file, a permanent and damning testimony to the fact that I have not yet learned how to introduce my courses well. And who knows when they will be dragged out and unleashed upon me with a pointed finger? He is the one who knows not how to introduce his courses adequately.

So, on this particular day, once the quietness had settled over the class, I quickly completed the opening rituals and got down to business. What better way to introduce the course and, at the same time, dispense a bit of paternal comfort than to deal head-on with their fears? I knew, I said, that some of them would be beginning a long walk into unknown territory and one that they might not be taking had the faculty in its wisdom not required it of them. Warming to my theme, I said that I understood the reluctance that they might be feeling, for theology has not always commended itself to people. Certainly, I conceded, theologians themselves have not always adorned the subject which they love and, in the modern period, off which they have lived. Theologians can be argumentative, though I doubted that they had a monopoly on that particular vice. Not only so, but sometimes they have been known to impose their ideas upon the Bible, though I added quickly that they are hardly different from many other scholars in this respect. For these and a number of other reasons upon which I touched briefly, it might not seem to be a subject that would naturally hold their attention.

By now I could see I had made some connections. And it occurred to me how fortunate I was to have students who were so genuinely anxious to do the right thing, to give themselves to the matter at hand despite the reluctance that some undoubtedly experienced. And part of this reluctance no doubt arose from the minimal preparation that they had received prior to coming to seminary. Students who want to learn can find ways to surmount what they encounter at an undergraduate level, and many of these students had done that. But the innocents, those whose minds had been upon other matters in their collegiate years, were now discovering that they had been quietly defrauded. It is not impossible for a student in today's university to wend his or her way through all of the requirements, ending in a blaze of glory and relief in the graduation ceremonies, without having received an education. This happens even in the best universities. Somehow they manage to graduate students who have no mental connections with the past, little knowledge of its literature, less of its great thinkers, scant ability to think for themselves, and for whom the prospect of writing a research paper is a matter for great consternation. As I looked out on that class, I guessed that at least some of these victims of the educational system were present. Yet here they were, gamely exposing themselves to what must have seemed to them like grave peril. Their desire to be in seminary was a powerful compensation for — indeed, a counterforce to — the habits and disposition they had brought with them.

So I continued, now becoming more assertive. Let us not think, I said, that we really have a choice between having a theology and not having one. We all have our theologies, for we all have a way of putting things together in our own minds that, if we are Christian, has a shape that arises from our knowledge of God and his Word. We might not be conscious of the process. Indeed, we frequently are not. But at the very least we will organize our perceptions into some sort of pattern that seems to make sense to us. The question at issue, then, is not *whether* we will have a theology but whether it will be a good or bad one, whether we will become conscious of our thinking processes or not, and, more particularly, whether we will learn to bring all of our thoughts into obedience to Christ or not. The biblical authors had a theology in this sense, after all, and so too did Jesus. He explained himself in terms of biblical revelation, understood his life and work in relation to God, and viewed all of life from this perspective. He had a

worldview that originated in the purposes and character of his Father
and that informed everything he said and did. Clearly I had precedent
— important biblical precedent — for what I was about to attempt in
this course. It was, I thought, a tour de force as introductions go.

I later discovered that my audience did not share my opinion.
When the dreaded evaluation sheets were duly returned, they conveyed the same dismal judgment on my introduction, another marker
on the path of bad beginnings. But at the moment it seemed to me
that I had made a minor conquest. Before I could gather my belong-
ings, a circle of students quickly accumulated around me. Is it not odd
how inconsequential remarks have a way of sticking in the mind like
burrs? That day, an obviously agitated student who had come forward
told me how grateful he was for what I had said. It was as if I had
been reading his mind. He told me that he was one of those I had
described who felt petrified by the prospect of having to take this
course. As a matter of fact, he said, he had had a mighty struggle with
his conscience about it. Was it right to spend so much money on a
course of study that was so irrelevant to his desire to minister to people
in the Church? He plainly intended no insult. As a matter of fact, this
confession, which I rather think he had not intended to blurt out, had
begun as a compliment. That was the day I decided that I had to write
this book.

What I had intended to write then, however, was just a modest
introduction for a small audience, perhaps entitled, without much
originality, *A Little Encouragement for Young Theologians*. It was to be a
little offering simply designed to get students launched into orbit. That
was then. What I have written now is not only much larger than what
I had originally envisioned but is also intended for a much broader
audience. In the intervening years I have watched with growing disbelief as the evangelical Church has cheerfully plunged into astounding
theological illiteracy. Many taking the plunge seem to imagine that they
are simply following a path to success, but the effects of this great
change in the evangelical soul are evident in every incoming class in
the seminaries, in most publications, in the great majority of churches,
and in most of their pastors. It is a change so large and so encompassing
that those who dissent from what is happening are easily dismissed as
individuals who cannot get along, who want to scruple over what is
inconsequential, who are not loyal, and who are, in any case, quite
irrelevant. Despite this, the changes that are now afoot are so pregnant
with consequence that it becomes, for me, a matter of conscience to
address them. Conscience, I have learned, is a hard taskmaster, and I

have not the slightest doubt that my attempt at doing this will appear quite ridiculous. I will look to some like the foolish dog that squats on the front lawn and, to everyone's displeasure, bays at the moon. But bay I must.

The change in the nature of this book from what I originally had in mind does not reflect simply a change of intention. It actually grows out of deepening convictions about the nature of theology, about its proper audience, and about the principles of its construction. Despite these origins, however, I say nothing in this book about its principles of construction and little about its nature; almost everything is directed to its audience, to addressing how the condition of the audience affects the very possibility of any theology being done at all and why this is so.

The question of the proper method of doing theology is, to be sure, a matter of large importance to which the scholarly community is giving considerable attention these days, and it is a bit risky to pass it all by so blithely. The premise of much of the work that is being done, though, seems quite wrongheaded to me. Much of it looks on theology as if it were a machine. The presumption is that, like the old family lawn mower, it should start with one or two good pulls, and if it does not, then a little tinkering will probably remedy the problem. To put the matter a little differently, the assumption is that if theology is in decline, which few doubt is the case, the reason is that it is not tapping its own sources of healing. Unfortunately, despite all of the tinkering that is going on with this ancient discipline, despite all of the new proposals about ways in which to remake it, and despite a mass of new correctives from a growing number of fields, the melancholy conclusion that now seems inescapable is that something is so seriously amiss that no amount of tinkering is going to suffice.

So I am striking out in a different direction in this book. I do so on the assumption that theology is a knowledge that belongs first and foremost to the people of God and that the proper and primary audience for theology is therefore the Church, not the learned guild. Whatever this guild might contribute to the life and construction of theology is to be gratefully received, but the university fraternity is not its primary auditor. I say this because theology is not simply a philosophical reflection about the nature of things but is rather the cogent articulation of the knowledge of God. Its substance is not drawn from mere human reflection, no matter how brilliant, but from the biblical Word by which it is nurtured and disciplined. And its purpose is not primarily to participate in the conversation of the learned but to nurture the people of God. That is its nature and that is its purpose. It is here in the Church that the circle of knowing — the kind of knowing that has Christ as its object and his service as its end — is to be found. It is here, then, that the audience for theology is to be found. And so it is the community of faith that the theologian addresses fundamentally, because it is only by faith that the knowledge of God is first arrived at and only by faith that it is sustained.

Without question, theology that is constructed in this way has a powerful intellectual relevance to society and a legitimate place in discussions of our public square. Nevertheless, because the locus of the work is in the Church, the locus of our contemporary failure will almost inevitably be seen to lie there too. If the learned guild stands apart from its primary audience, it will have at most only a secondary significance in the apportioning of blame for what has gone wrong. And the truth is that adjustments in the doing of theology, even adjustments of large methodological magnitude, are not going to repair the damage that has been done, because the problem is less intellectual than spiritual. The reason that theology is disappearing has little to do with the technical skills of the fine-tuners and much to do with the state of the Church. So it is not with the technicians that I begin but with the Church. It not with the professionals in the learned guild that I start but with the whole people of God. And it is not to methodology that I look for a recovery of this fallen art but to a reformation in the way that Christian people go about their business of being Christian in the midst of the extraordinary changes that modernity has wrought in our world.

Already, then, it is plain that I am thinking of theology as taking place at the point where several different worlds intersect. First, there is the world of learning into which theology taps; second, there is the Church for whom theology is constructed; and, third, there are the intermediaries who, in the modern context, often become small worlds unto themselves but who must work within this matrix — the scholars who mediate the world of learning and the pastors who broker what results to the churches. What I shall argue in this book is that this intersection is now sundered and that these worlds are not only disengaging from one another but even breaking down within themselves. Many of the scholarly disciplines, such as Old and New Testament study, that once fed into theology now assail it in the interests of asserting their own independence; many of those whose task it is to broker the truth of God to the people of God in the churches have now redefined the pastoral task such that theology has become an embarrassing encumbrance or a matter of which they have little knowledge; and many in the Church have now turned in upon themselves and substituted for the knowledge of God a search for the knowledge of self. There can be little doubt that if the capacity to think Christianly about this world is eroding in the churches, so too will the propriety of doing theology, both in the pulpit and in the academy. The propriety of this kind of knowledge will disintegrate as certainly as would the propriety of a novelist continuing to work when it was discovered that the culture in which he or she was living had gradually lost the ability to read.

Those who are conversant with the ways in which the modern world has been analyzed will recognize, even in this brief sketch, themes that are all too familiar. Whatever else one may say about modernization, one of its principal effects has been to break apart the unity of human understanding and disperse the multitude of interests and undertakings away from the center, in relation to which they have gathered their meaning, pushing them to the edges, where they have no easy relation to one another at all. It has done this by breaking down the central core so that there is nothing to which thought and life returns. It has eroded those ideas and convictions, that truth which, precisely because it arose in God and was mediated by him, stood as an unchanging sentinel amid changing circumstances. And it is this flight to the edges, this dispersion from the center, that has intruded on evangelical faith even as it has disordered the warp and woof of contemporary life. In the one it leaves a faith denuded of theology and in the other a life stripped of absolutes.

It is not difficult to trace out the path this cultural decay has taken, nor is there much disagreement about its passage when the matter is discussed in the abstract. After all, is there not wide agreement that the effect of secularization has been to marginalize God, to make what is absolute and transcendent irrelevant to the stuff of everyday life? Has it not supplanted interest in the supernatural with interest in the natural? Surely our everyday language betrays us in this matter. When we want to suggest that a statement is incontrovertible, we punctuate the assertion with the words "It's a fact!" — not "It's a truth!" Just give me the facts, and I'll make up my own mind about what constitutes the truth. And are we not consumed with what is changing in cultural and personal circumstance rather than with what is unchanging about life, the great universal truths about God, the world, and human nature? Have we not substituted the relative for the absolute, the Many for the One, diversity for unity, the human for the divine, our own private religious experience for truth that was once also public and universal in its scope?

On these changes in the topography of our contemporary perception, there is little dispute. But the dynamic that accomplishes all of this is not seen so easily. For lying beneath these changes, and coursing through them, is a force that flings all of the components of life away from every center that we once had to a periphery that is often quite distant and even unknown. We thus lose our bearings, for we lose that truth, that divine order to which in mind and spirit we could always return, the divine order by which we understood our world, the order for which we looked in life's dark moments to re-establish our bearings. This has all broken apart. The many parts of life are scattered, its many interests and activities broken apart from one another. They have become small private worlds of special interest presided over by specialists of one sort or another. In other words, gone is the possibility that there can be in culture men and women of broad understanding who, standing at the center that God has given in his Word, can understand life's diversity in the light of its unity, can see its multiplicity in the light of the overarching themes that are common to all of it. This unity is lost. The diversity of cultures, religions, professions, and personal circumstances is triumphant. More than that, this diversity is all we have. And, as the center has collapsed, our psyches have become more and more strained, even fractured.

Those who see so plainly the effects of modernization do not, however, always see so well how this fragmentation has been loosed in the Church. Though largely unnoticed, the same dynamic is also at work here. In the Church, too, the center has been fractured, and the fragments of belief are scattered to the edges. Here, too, the person of understanding has been supplanted by the specialist.

As elsewhere in the Church, the effects of modernization are evident in what has incorrectly been identified as the evangelical movement. I say *incorrectly* because, however evangelical it may once have been, it never managed to become a movement. Movements must exhibit three characteristics: (1) there must be a commonly owned direction, (2) there must be a common basis on which that direction is owned, and (3) there must be an *esprit* that informs and motivates those who are thus joined in their common cause. What has been missing most obviously from evangelicalism is the direction, despite the best efforts by such leaders as Carl Henry in the earlier years of its current growth to provide one (see issues of *Christianity Today* from the late 1950s through the early 1970s). To be sure, there was the semblance of common direction every time churches were rallied to the call of world evangelization, but that focus always proved too narrow to provide a lasting sense of a common direction in a culture now adrift from its moorings. Unity must be built on more than a shared desire to evangelize; it has to grow out of a broad cultural strategy, the implementation of a broad biblically worked-out view of the world. And that was never there.

As the sense of direction faded, so too did the *esprit*. Like the ancient Israelites in uncertain times, evangelicals took to their tents, each to his or her own. The enormous numerical growth of the past three decades spilled out in all directions, and the telltale signs of modernization were on every hand. Those who had marched gladly under the banner of evangelicalism and had affirmed the truths of historic Protestant orthodoxy now began to look sideways. As the theological center began to give way, there arose a multitude of evangelical amalgams with, among other things, Catholicism, Eastern Orthodoxy, special interests such as feminism, the pieties of the World Council of Churches, and radical politics. The most important thing that this potential movement needed — theological unity — grew ever thinner and more insubstantial. And as this common basis wore thin, whatever semblance of common direction there may have been dissipated with it, and the *esprit* then vanished like the morning mist.

As this fragmentation has progressed, both in culture and in Christian faith, and the center has given way, one might think that people would believe in less and less. But the reverse has happened. A culture for whom God is no longer present believes everything. Who would have imagined that as we became more and more technologically oriented, for example, millions of people would also become more and more devoted to astrology, directing their lives by what the planets were doing? Who would have expected that some of the most secularized cities, such as Los Angeles and Amsterdam, would become hosts to a growing array of bizarre cults, many of which reek of primitive superstition? Who would have thought that after two awful world wars and many subsequent conflicts, Western thought would still be indulging in the myth of inevitable progress with a devotion that makes most believers look like pikers? When we believe in nothing, we open the doors to believing anything. And the same is true within the precincts of Christian faith. As the body of common belief has shrunk and the importance of that belief has diminished within the evangelical world, there have arisen advocates for almost everything within the larger religious world. Who would have thought, for example, that *Christianity*

Today would carry a proposal for the remaking of evangelical faith that scuttled one of the cardinal beliefs of the Protestant Reformation — justification by faith?

And so I came to write this book both as a believer and as a disbeliever. I should say that immediately. Anyone who believes in God and accepts the transcendent character of biblical revelation, as I do, must reject belief in all of those myths that the modern world has fostered about itself. Indeed, I find on the one hand that I believe more than many other evangelicals and on the other hand that I believe a great deal less than most of them do — more in the center, less in the periphery; more in the importance of truth, and not at all in the fabric of modern life.

To assert my disbelief in much that the modern world holds so dear is, I know, an uncommonly pugnacious way to begin a book, but I intend no disrespect either for the reader or for the modern world. After all, I work for the one and must live with the other. The pugnacity is only in the appearance, not in the intention. The problem is that even the mildest assertion of Christian truth today sounds like a thunderclap because the well-polished civility of our religious talk has kept us from hearing much of this kind of thing. A person who enters the room by leaning on an infirm door may get a reputation for violence, John Kenneth Galbraith has said, but the condition of the door did have something to do with his precipitous entry. So it is here.

In saying that I am a staunch disbeliever in the modern world, I do not wish to appear immodest, as if I come flushed with the knowledge of a new discovery. In fact, I do not. In this connection, I well remember G. K. Chesterton's story about the restless yachtsman who set sail from England with the intention of arriving at an exotic South Sea island. After many days, he sighted land and, as soon as he could, beached his boat and ventured inland. Before him stood a dreadful pagan temple. Undaunted, he decided to claim it for England. He scaled its walls and bravely planted the Union Jack at its pinnacle. Only then did he realize that what he had scaled was the Brighton Pavilion on England's south coast! He thought that he had sailed in a straight line, but, because of an unfortunate miscalculation, he had actually traveled in a circle. He imagined that he was first in the land, but it turned out that he was the last.

I come to the subject of this book like this yachtsman, a late arrival, scaling what others have diligently built. The thought that the world takes refuge in myths and rationalizations should astonish only those who are disinclined to think of them as myths and rationalizations, those who want to hide beneath them and are dead set against being dislodged. Even those who have followed modern discussions about Western culture from afar know that I have said nothing that is new, even if it seems to have the appearance of being outrageous.

Yet I would be remiss if I failed to point out that while the angle from which I approach culture may be commonplace among some of its interpreters, it is not common among evangelicals. Evangelicals are antimodern only across a narrow front; I write from a position that is antimodern across the entire front. It is only where assumptions in culture directly and obviously contradict articles of faith that most evangelicals become aroused and rise up to battle "secular humanism"; aside from these specific matters, they tend to view culture as neutral and harmless. More than that, they often view culture as a partner amenable to being coopted in the cause of celebrating Christian truth. I cannot share that naivete; indeed, I consider it dangerous. Culture is laden with values, many of which work to rearrange the substance of faith, even when they are mediated to us through the benefits that the modern world also bestows upon us. Technology is a case in point. While it has greatly enhanced many of our capabilities and spread its largess across the entirety of our life, it also brings with it an almost inevitable naturalism and an ethic that equates what is efficient with what is good. Technology per se does not assault the gospel, but a technological society will find the gospel irrelevant. What can be said of technology can also be said of many other facets of culture that are similarly laden with values. It is the failure to see this and to see how, in consequence, evangelical faith is being transformed that is now greatly straining its connections to historic Protestant orthodoxy. It is precisely because I reject belief in the modern world that I am able to believe in the truth that this orthodoxy seeks to preserve. It is because many evangelicals believe in the innocence of modern culture and for that reason exploit it and are exploited by it that they are unable to believe in all of the truth that once characterized this Protestant orthodoxy. In the current typology, evangelicals are typically moderns in their orientation; this book is insistently antimodern.

This difference in orientation to modernity leads to a stark difference in faith. The stream of historic orthodoxy that once watered the evangelical soul is now dammed by a worldliness that many fail to recognize as worldliness because of the cultural innocence with which it presents itself. To be sure, this orthodoxy never was infallible, nor was it without its blemishes and foibles, but I am far from persuaded that the emancipation from its theological core that much of evangelicalism is effecting has resulted in greater biblical fidelity. In fact, the result is just the opposite. We now have less biblical fidelity, less interest in truth, less seriousness, less depth, and less capacity to speak the Word of God to our own generation in a way that offers an alternative to what it already thinks. The older orthodoxy was driven by a passion for truth, and that was why it could express itself only in theological terms. The newer evangelicalism is not driven by the same passion for truth, and that is why it is often empty of theological interest.

Let me explain how I am going to develop this case. My central purpose is to explore why it is that theology is disappearing. (This task is substantial enough in its own right that I will have to leave to another volume assessments about what can be done to reverse it.) It is already clear, however, that my approach in this book is going to be broad rather than narrow. It is not theology alone in which I am interested but theology that is driven by a passion for truth; and it is not evangelicalism alone in which I am interested but evangelicalism as the contemporary vehicle for articulating a historical Protestant orthodoxy. Why has this linkage between the past and the present broken down? Why has the passion for truth diminished? Why is it that contemporary evangelicals suppose their faith will survive intact without this passion and this theology?

I know that finding the answers to these questions may well be as complex as finding the causes of cancer. In both, there are many potentially plausible and fruitful lines of inquiry that do not seem to converge. Indeed, though they seem to be related, they often *diverge*. As in the search for a cure for cancer, so in the search for a cure for disintegrating theology and contemporary evangelicalism: there are many possible lines of inquiry, many possible solutions, but they do not always point back to the same root causes. I do not claim to have found these lines of inquiry in any complete or exhaustive way, but it has become clear to me that the disappearance of theology, in both Church and academy, is itself one of the fruits of modernization and that it has little to do with the way that theology is being constructed per se. Furthermore, the unraveling of the ties between contemporary evangelicalism and historic orthodoxy is not the result of a deliberate strategy but is rather one of the effects of modernity that evangelicals have unconsciously accepted.

The first two chapters of this book constitute a prologue in which I try to get at the essence of modernity so that we might more easily discern its intrusion into the mind of the Church and the minds of its scholars. I begin by reconstructing the life of a small New England town, a town with which I have become quite familiar. As I have thought about its inner life, it has become obvious to me that about a century ago a divide was crossed, and those who live in the town today simply would not be able to recognize the town as it was then — and this not because of changes in the physical topography, the buildings and streets. Something much more profound is afoot than that. It is that, in this town as elsewhere, the entire social organization has changed and with it the very way that we are able to look at life and what we look for in life. After having documented these changes with respect to this small town, I move on to try to explain them in terms of the emergence of a new world culture that has intruded upon and enveloped this town over the past century or so, as it has every other town in America. What is this world culture like, and what does it do to the way in which we see our own world, how we think, what we want? More importantly, how has its intrusion into our psyches affected our capacity for truth, our desire to know God, and the ways in which we pursue these matters?

I begin the main part of the book with a chapter in which I lay out the problem, as I see it, in the inner life of the evangelical world. In this chapter, "Things Fall Apart," I try to explain why the sense of truth is disappearing and what has happened to the ligaments that once held this world together. But this discussion dwells only on the dynamic of the fragmentation of evangelicalism. That itself does not provide the answer I am seeking; it simply states the problem. The explanation of this problem lies in the three chapters that follow. In two of these, I try to explain how the current expression of the American character has affected the ability of evangelicals to think in ways that are cogently biblical. In the last of these three chapters, I look at the way in which the pastorate has become professionalized, how the central function of the pastor has changed from that of truth broker to manager of the small enterprises we call churches. To the extent that this tendency has taken root, I have concluded that it is producing a new generation of pastoral disablers. At this point, I suggest a contrast between the contemporary evangelical world and the world in biblical times. This chapter, entitled "The Habits of God," is followed by a concluding chapter in which I present a plea for a new kind of evangelical, one who is much more like the old kind used to be.

I think back now to that introductory lecture in my beginning class in theology and the student who wondered about how right it was to spend a lot of money on a course in theology given that it was so irrelevant to his desire to minister to people in the Church. Such a concern would have been incomprehensible to most generations of Christians that have preceded us. What has happened in our world that can explain a transformation so large, so deep, in the evangelical soul? The place where we will begin trying to find the answer is in a quaint New England town that you might even have seen yourself. It is called Wenham, and it is situated in Massachusetts.

PROLOGUE

CHAPTER 1

A Delicious Paradise Lost

Those who labor in the earth are the chosen people of God, if ever He had a chosen people, whose breasts He has made his peculiar deposit for substantial and genuine virtue.

Thomas Jefferson

History is a constant tragedy in which we are all involved, whose key note is frustration and anxiety, not progress and fulfillment.

Arthur Schlesinger, Jr.

THE MAIN STREET in Wenham, Massachusetts, has witnessed the most astounding revolution that has occurred in this or any other century. This street, which is built on an old stagecoach route and today is graced by the presence of old trees and antique houses from the seventeenth and eighteenth centuries, is actually more of a vantage point than a witness. It is from here, and from within these houses, that families have looked on a world that has changed before their eyes.

Revolution is not, of course, the word that naturally comes to mind when one walks through Wenham today, unless perhaps one should glance along Larch Row, which turns off Main Street, where Ezra Lummus's old tavern still stands. The tavern has long since abandoned its trade, but during the past century it was an important stopping place for stagecoaches along the Newburyport Turnpike,

17

which, Adeline Cole tells us, "shot a straight line" from Boston, "over hill, brook and ravine to its destination, Newburyport."[1] At this tavern, horses were changed and travelers wondering about the hills and ravines ahead could revive themselves with a shot of West Indian rum, for which the tavern was well known. Down the street that bounds the north side of the old tavern, Larch Row, one is greeted by the sight of European larches, twisted and gnarled by many a wintry storm and said by old-timers to have been planted during the Revolution. But that was a long time ago, and most people do not know that. What they see is simply a quaint New England town that is now fiercely protective of its heritage. If the hamburger merchants want to service the good people of Wenham, they must do so from a distance, and those who own the antique houses on this street can make changes only with permission. The townsfolk see the evening news on television and learn about the day's crime, but it mostly happens in Boston, seldom in Wenham. Here the cops seem to have so little to do that they can give their undivided attention to careless motorists. In Wenham, inattention to posted speed limits is never wise. Wenham is a decent, solidly middle-class town, an enclave of civility in the midst of a nasty world, a town with old families, old money, and still quite a few old ideas. The more one knows about this little town, the more incongruous the idea of revolution seems.

But the truth is that few of the townsfolk would even remotely recognize the world of 1870 if we could take them back to it. Though they are often traditional people, they, like everyone else, are now part of the modern world. Since that time the country's industrial output has increased almost 5,000 percent. It has created the material basis for what utopians used to dream about — and, paradoxically, it has also brought a world of despair and complexity that few fully understand. In its multiple daily assaults upon the individual, it is rending the fabric of private consciousness.

Wenham is not a "typical" town today, nor, indeed, has it ever been. Occupying seven square miles and with boundaries that have never changed, it was in the eighteenth and nineteenth centuries part of a line of farming towns that had trading links with and were serviced by such seaports as Beverly, Salem, and Gloucester. The farming towns produced grain crops, livestock, and poultry; the seaports offered the services that these small agricultural communities needed, such as facilities for ship-

1. Cole, *Notes on Wenham History, 1643-1943* (Wenham, Mass.: Wenham Historical Association, 1943), p. 82.

ping, warehouses, and fish markets. Their economies, social organization, and existence differed, and no one town was exactly like another. Furthermore, America in the nineteenth century, to which we need to look back in particular, was bursting with new life, ideas, inventions, and disagreements, all of which affected each town and city differently. It is, therefore, impossible to find a single paradigm for understanding the American experience, one place that might serve as a crucible in which these changes could be examined in ways that would be applicable to everyone else. That, as a matter of fact, is why Wenham is so interesting. While the rest of America was being roiled by change, Wenham was an astonishing island of tranquillity, a little town that seemed to have its own internal gyroscope, that seemed to treasure its capacity for being oblivious to the outside world, even though it is situated only twenty-five miles north of Boston. It is because Wenham has not been typical of other towns and its residents have not been typical of other Americans that it provides a fascinating aperture through which to observe some of the great changes that have engulfed our world.

The Delicious Paradise

Wenham was Salem's "little sister," a spur of civilization that was inspired by a sermon. The preacher was Hugh Peters, first pastor in Salem, and the sermon was delivered just eighteen years after the Pilgrims had landed in Plymouth. At the time, Oliver Cromwell was still just a farmer. In due course, Peters was to return to England and become one of Cromwell's chaplains. While he was still in Salem, however, in 1638, he led a small group of people to the Great Pond, now known as Wenham Lake, to view the land with the idea of increasing the settlements there. He preached on the text "in Aenon, near to Salim, because there was much water there . . . they came, and were baptized." The sermon had its effect, and a village was started, which was first known as Enon, until its incorporation as Wenham in 1643. A short while after, in 1686, John Dunstan, Esq., came visiting from England and must have pleased the settlers by describing their small town as "a delicious paradise." He added that "it abounds with all rural pleasures, and I would choose it above all towns in America to dwell in."[2]

2. Dunstan, quoted by Myron O. Allen in *The History of Wenham: Civil and Ecclesiastical from Its Settlement in 1639 to 1860* (Boston: Bazin & Chandler, 1860), p. 22.

The words of Peters's text were obviously chosen because of their seeming appropriateness to the geographical situation in Massachusetts, not in order to draw attention to a figure especially revered by the Baptists, John the Baptist, whose baptizing is recorded in the text. Peters had no intention of using the waters of the Great Pond to baptize, much less to establish a Baptist settlement. He was a Puritan and, like the early Puritans, had little patience for Baptist sensibilities. Baptists, as a matter of fact, did not settle in the town until the 1790s. Among them and probably the first was Rebecca Goldsmith, a schoolteacher, who was described by one of the townsfolk as being not only "an active and zealous worker in the 'vineyard of the Lord'" but also "an ardent lover of the sect then so universally opposed."[3] Wenham Baptists, perhaps with good reason, began meeting outside the town, and the first Baptist church was not built in the town until 1831, some two centuries after its incorporation. The old Puritan ideals lived on in Wenham, but their principal channel of transmission was not the Presbyterians, and certainly not the Baptists, but the orthodox Congregationalists. It was through them that the Puritan ideals flourished well into the nineteenth century, imparting to the town some of the uniqueness of its character.

Wenham's character was also formed from the kind of people who were drawn to it. The original settlers were English, many of them apparently from Wenham in Suffolk, which probably accounts for the change in name from Enon. They seem to have been prosperous people in England, and they apparently brought with them that sense of deference toward the aristocracy that their class often had. This sense was tested during the Revolution, and it had to be transformed subsequently into something more obviously American. In the first half of the nineteenth century, however, the steady transformation of Wenham society in this direction increased: 31 percent of the men were classified in court records as "gentlemen," as opposed to professionals, tradesmen, artisans, or maritime or agricultural workers — up from 14 percent for the comparable period in the previous century. This was a designation more of class than of occupation. So it is, perhaps, no accident that today Wenham bounds the Myopia Hunt Club. On occasion, one can still hear the sound of the bugle and the baying of the hounds as horses, red-coated riders, and dogs race along the town's

3. Louise A. Dodge, "The Rise of Little Jacob: An Historical Sketch of the Wenham Baptist Church, 1831-1931," n.d., "Wenham: Churches: Baptist" file, Wenham Museum, Wenham, Mass.

trails and through its fields. It is one of the very few places in America where this remnant of British aristocratic life is preserved. And to the sense that the well-bred English gentleman brought to life were joined the values that were part and parcel of being well-to-do farmers and prosperous landowners, which is what most of the settlers rapidly became, the one then merging into the other. Thus the character and outlook of the townsfolk were formed.

Wenham remained a small town in a rural setting, even into the nineteenth century, when it seemed that every other town was abuzz with change. Boston was the recipient of waves of immigration in the century past, mostly Catholics, from Britain, Ireland, and other European nations. Between 1825 and 1875, its population grew six-fold, from 58,000 to 340,000. During the same period, the population of the whole United States tripled. By 1850, Catholics were the largest religious body in America, and at about this time in New England the Methodists were gathering strength and had become the second largest body.[4] Though Wenham farmers took their produce into Boston (they could make the round trip in one day by horse and cart), Wenham itself stood entirely aloof from these changes. Its population grew only a little in the first half of the century and then dropped off in the second half. In 1800, its population was 476; in 1850, it was 977; by 1900, it had fallen back to 847. The great swelling tide of immigrants that flowed into Boston in this time did not produce so much as the smallest eddy twenty-five miles north in Wenham, and to this day the town has neither a Catholic nor, for that matter, a Methodist church. It is true that during this time a significant number of migrant workers visited the town looking for work, and an increasing number of tramps passed through, but few outsiders managed to establish a foothold in Wenham unless they did so through the bonds of marriage.[5] The truth

4. Sidney E. Ahlstrom, *A Religious History of the American People* (New Haven: Yale University Press, 1972), p. 437.

5. I am indebted to Douglas Lamar Jones for his careful work in establishing the movement of people in and around Wenham due to population growth and economic mobility (Jones, *Village and Seaport in Eighteenth-Century Massachusetts* [Hanover, N.H.: University Press of New England, 1981). His book does show that the escape valves for a growing population — the frontier and the city — operated in Massachusetts before the pattern was evident more widely, the frontier being to the north rather than to the territories of the west. The migrant workers, however, typically arrived in the summer, seeking employment during the crop season. Tramps became more common later on in the century, and Wenham eventually elected to require their nightly incarceration in the lower reaches of the Town Hall. In 1875, no fewer than 250 were thus locked up.

is that Wenham's capacity to change was limited. There were complaints that the town was getting crowded. Certainly its economic prospects as a farming community were frustrated as land became scarce. Some of the town's sons were forced to seek better prospects elsewhere because land could not be had. But these limitations also served to insulate the community from a changing world.

If Wenham stood splendidly isolated from the surrounding demographic changes, it also stood aloof from the extraordinary industrial transformation that was happening. With the invention of power looms, carding machines, and new technology for the production of metals, factories were springing up everywhere. Along rivers, the new mill towns were coming into being. Consider Lowell, for example. Located some twenty-five miles northwest of Boston at the confluence of the Concord and Merrimac rivers, it was once known as "the Spindle City." In a very short span of years it was transformed into the one of the leading textile centers in New England; business was so substantial and thriving there that workers had to be imported from Europe constantly to keep the mills running. In 1900, almost half of its population of 95,000 was made up of immigrants — Canadians (both French and English), Irish, Greeks, and Britons.

But Wenham had neither the natural resources to exploit the new industrial climate nor, what is as important, the inclination to do so. It steadfastly eschewed any of the newfangled ways of making a living. The sole exception to this was, on the face of it, a highly implausible scheme, though it turned out to be quite a success.[6] Between 1844 and 1873, ice was carved out of Wenham Lake and shipped off in huge blocks to countries as far away as India and Scandinavia. So pure was the lake then, before dirty rivers were diverted into it, that it was said that newsprint could be read through two feet of its ice, and "Wenham Lake ice" in Europe became a byword for purity. In 1873, a disastrous fire put a stop to this brief experiment with modern industry, and Wenham reverted to what it had always been: a quiet, undisturbed town, a town of rural tranquillity and beauty that was not "modern" in any discernible sense.

Not only did it cease any further involvement with the industrial age, but it continued its cottage industries, shoe and boot-making and

6. Wenham did also see a brief excursion into the corporate world following a decision by the Massachusetts General Court in 1870 that allowed cooperatives to be organized through the sale of stock certificates. Thus began the Wenham Cooperative, a drug and grocery store that was bought out in 1880 by the Trowt brothers. "Trowt's Store" remained in that family until 1943.

lace-making, long after factories and efficient machinery had supplanted the old ways everywhere else. As a matter of fact, in 1930 there were still some eighty shoe-making shops in operation! Most of them were run out of residences, either in the house itself or in an adjoining barn. Artisans continued to make shoes, boots, and other leather goods, such as harnesses and saddles, for the most part in the old way.

It is no surprise, then, that Myron Allen, the town's first historian, wrote in 1860 that Wenham was "a small country town" that was in "no way conspicuous among its neighbors."[7] Still later, in 1929, a reporter called it a "drowsy little town." This reporter was giving an account of a Wenham concert featuring descant singing — something he viewed as very strange in a town whose "Main St. has a single car track and, most of the way, just one side-walk."[8] But if Wenham gave the appearance of having slept through the century's great developments — and it did because it had — it nevertheless was a town of exquisite charm and character, a town whose boundaries were clear and whose citizens were undoubtedly the citizens of *Wenham*. We need to think a little more fully about their life in this town, because it was destroyed by modernity with the suddenness of the executioner's sword — and as irreversibly. What was it like, then, to be a Wenhamite?

A Puritan Town Revisited

Harriet Spofford, in writing about the childhood of the remarkable Gail Hamilton in the early nineteenth century, observed that to the New England farmers in places like Wenham, "the Church was a central point, the orthodox Congregational Church, which had much of the authority still that it had in the days of the Puritans. The subjects of conversation were its articles of faith, and the Bible was its literature."[9] As a matter of fact, Congregationalism remained the established religion in Massachusetts until 1833, some time after established reli-

7. Allen, *The History of Wenham*, p. iii.
8. Boston *Sunday Globe*, 10 November 1929, p. 64.
9. Spofford, "Biographical Sketch," in *Gail Hamilton's Life in Letters*, 2 vols., ed. H. Augusta Dodge (Boston: Lee & Shepherd, 1901), 1: x. The most innovative work on the early Congregationalists is to be found in Perry Miller's *Orthodoxy in Massachusetts, 1630-1650* (Cambridge: Beacon Press, 1933) as well as more generally in his *New England Mind*, 2 vols. (Cambridge: Harvard University Press, 1953). For a general survey which, though a little dated, is still useful, see Verne D. Morrey, "American Congregationalism, 1900-1952," *Church History* 21 (1952): 323-39.

gion had fallen on hard times elsewhere in America. And even after disestablishment, Wenham retained the ethos of the Puritan town it had once been.

The Congregational church was visually the town's center.[10] One of the first things the Puritans had always done when building a new town was to establish the church in a position of prominence, at the center of the community. The same kind of thing can still be seen in many British and European towns with their magnificent cathedrals and churches. But the Puritans were not interested simply in a visual eminence and certainly not in aesthetic extravaganzas. Their churches were plain in looks and design. They saw the town's church as both the place where God addressed his people through the preached Word and as the knot that bound society together, the hub into which all of life's spokes were fixed by covenant. Even though much water had passed beneath the bridge since the days of Hugh Peters, the spiritual and social outlook of the citizens of Wenham in these respects had changed little. The church was the town's center, spiritually and socially. In the first part of the century, all important social occasions took place there. The minister was the town's First Citizen. Christian faith — more particularly, evangelical Christian faith in a Congregational form — permeated all of the town's life.

The first real challenge to the church's centrality in Wenham came about almost inadvertently with the proposal to build a town hall, the hope being that it would serve as an expanded forum for some of the town's activities. The proposal was bitterly fought by some of the townsfolk, but it passed by a vote of 79 to 61, and in 1854 the town hall was built across the street from the church. Perhaps no one really saw in this vote the straw that was blowing in the wind, but it was not long before the change extended not just to social activities but to the entire way in which Wenham's citizens understood life and valued it. It was an initial evidence of how all aspects of life were being reordered around secular structures, not simply within the town but within the larger society to which, in the later part of the twentieth century, the town's citizens have almost inevitably belonged psychologically. Thus emerged in Wenham two centers of social life, standing on opposite sides of Main Street, symbols of that much greater sundering of the old order that would soon take place, a sundering that would leave

10. The first church in Wenham was built in 1640, but I am here referring to the present church building, First Congregational, which was built in 1843. Its fine tower and three-faced clock were added in 1870.

behind, seemingly forever, the older view of life that had been framed by Christian certainties and replace it with a way of life that, in its secularity, would make those "certainties" seem highly implausible.

The True Woman

But our attention must now be given to an imaginary Wenham citizen, a woman who was first sent to school in 1836. This is the year from which a firsthand report of a teacher in the Red Schoolhouse has survived. And it is the time in which the New England school system was considered the best in the nation, by 1850 producing a 95 percent literacy rate, which far exceeds what prevails in the nation as a whole today. The particular school of which the report spoke and in which, the teacher said, "many prominent citizens were attendant"[11] was a brick building measuring 16' by 25' and heated by a stove. Girls sat in three rows on one side of the building's single room, and boys on the other side. In the winter term of 1836-37, seventy-one young pupils were enrolled in the school. The cramped quarters might have given a new meaning to the word *bedlam* but for the fact that iron discipline was maintained. "How they sat," the teacher said, "I hardly know, it seems almost impossible when I think of it, but so it was." And then she added philosophically, "Little folks are small."

In Wenham, there were two terms for school children, the summer term running about four and a half months for older children, and the winter term running three months. The town determined that it was necessary to have their children taught for ten years, until they reached the age of fifteen. In the country as a whole the campaign to secure free, universal education was gathering momentum,[12] but the age of progressivism, perhaps most widely associated with the name of John Dewey, had not yet set in.[13] In the latter part of the nineteenth century, under the progressives, schools became instruments for social transformation. They broadened their curricula to include matters of vocation, health, and community involvement, and they taught from an entirely new set of educational premises that were sociological and psychological in nature. In the 1830s, however, the curriculum was very simple: arithmetic, geography, reading, and writing. The subject

11. "Wenham: Schools: Neck" file, Wenham Museum, Wenham, Mass.

12. See Frederick M. Binder, *The Age of the Common School, 1830-1865* (New York: John Wiley, 1974).

13. See Lawrence A. Cremin, *The Transformation of the School: Progressivism in American Education, 1876-1956* (New York: Alfred A. Knopf, 1969).

matter was learned by rote. This was true not only in a school such as this, but also in church, where, for example, Gail Hamilton had learned the Lord's Prayer by heart at the age of two and then moved on to the church's teachings. And it was also true in the colleges, where lectures were frequently dictated and students were expected to take down most of what was said verbatim and then memorize it.[14]

A parting of the ways between boys and girls took place at an early age. Each prepared for life in a very different way because each had a very different role to fulfill. British visitors to America around mid-century, as well as many preachers here, frequently marveled at how wild American children were, especially the boys, characterizing them as willful and rude, disobedient and undisciplined, and prone to use foul language.[15] But Alexis de Tocqueville had quite a different perspective on this. As he observed American families, he noted that the effect of democracy was to eliminate the halfway-house of adolescence; here one went from being a boy to being a man without any intermediate apprenticeship. This situation eliminated the painful struggles between fathers and sons seen elsewhere,[16] but it also pitched the children into the world early and unceremoniously. Wenham boys began their adult life at the age of fifteen.

Throughout his discussion of the American family, Tocqueville noted that society's mores were determined by women. This was a widely apprehended fact in America. Moralists and campaigners in the nineteenth century almost invariably addressed their pleas and admonitions to women, to the hands that rocked the cradles. Men, it seemed, were beyond redemption unless their womenfolk could get to them. Carousing and cavorting were accepted as an inevitable part of being male, but it was felt that if women were in some way to fall

14. An interesting example of this type of lecturing style has been preserved in the student notes that remain from Nathaniel William Taylor's discourses at Yale Divinity School. A comparison of the notes taken on "mental philosophy," for example, which were given to different classes, shows striking similarities. In the definitions and in many of the important points, there is often verbatim agreement. Apart from revealing how Taylor apparently taught, these student notes also show that over the eight-year period during which they were produced, Taylor seems not to have revised his own notes at all. These handwritten notes are deposited in the Manuscript Library, Yale University, under the names of Solon C. Avery, James R. Mershon, S. W. S. Dutton, L. A. Saxton, W. D. Ely, and S. J. M. Merwin and in the Library of Yale Divinity School under the name of Eliza Hallock Belden.

15. See Richard L. Rapson, "The American Child as Seen by British Travellers, 1845-1935," *American Quarterly* 17 (Summer 1965): 520-34.

16. Tocqueville, *Democracy in America*, book 2, ed. J. P. Mayer, trans. George Lawrence (Garden City, N.Y.: Doubleday, 1969), p. 585.

as well, the very fabric of society would be rent. For this peculiar role in the world, women were not sequestered away from wickedness, as was often the case in Europe, but, as Tocqueville noted, were encouraged to develop the strength of mind and independence of thought without which their innocence would soon be overcome. The American woman avoided evil, he said, not because she was ignorant of it, as were her European sisters, but because she knew what it was.[17] And so perhaps we may assume that our imaginary pupil was thus prepared in home, school, and in "Sabbath school."

We will have occasion shortly to visit her church, which presumably would have contributed much to her understanding of the world, but it would probably not be amiss to suppose that, like other women of her time, she had in mind a model of womanhood to which she aspired. It was commonly referred to during the middle years of the nineteenth century as "True Womanhood." It was one of those bits of cultural shorthand for which definitions were unnecessary.

The cultural differences between men and women, as a matter of fact, were becoming sharper at this time, honed on both sides of the gender divide by the rapidity of change in the world. With industrialization came new ventures, new opportunities, new ways of thinking about life. These were the changes into which men, whether they wished it or not, were plunged. Women, on the other hand, remained at home, the repository of faith, of the values of the past with which contact needed to be kept. Perhaps by default, certainly because of the shifting social terrain, they often seemed to be the last and only thread that remained linking the traditional past to the turbulent present, anchoring the changes and providing some certainty and order amid the excitement and chaos. Thus were juxtaposed two sides of life, the home and the world, the field of experience for

17. Tocqueville, *Democracy in America*, book 2, pp. 590-92. Lyman Beecher, for one, does not seem to have believed that these American women had much success in conveying their virtues to the next generation, however. He complained in a sermon that from "various causes the ancient discipline of the family has been extensively neglected. Children have been neither instructed in religion, nor governed in early life, as they were in the days of our fathers. The imported discovery, that human nature is too good to be made better by discipline, that children are enticed from the right way by religious instruction, and driven from it by the rod, and kept in thraldom by the conspiracy of priests and legislators, has united not a few in the noble experiment of emancipating the world, by the help of an irreligious, ungoverned progeny" (*A Reformation of Morals, Practical and Indispensable: A Sermon Delivered at New-Haven on the Evening of October 27, 1812* [Andover, 1814], p. 15).

women and the field of experience for men, and the contrast between the two was rendered more extreme by the new circumstances. The world into which men now entered was dominated by the procurement of life's goods; the world in which women largely remained was devoted to the preservation of what was right.

According to Barbara Welter, in order to be a True Woman, one had to master four principal virtues. First, there was piety. It was frequently assumed that by nature women were more pious, that they found believing in and submitting to the divine will easier than did men, and that this was part of the divine governance of society. Men were under God, and women under men, and the female ability to submit to God made it easier for them to submit to men. Furthermore, religion did not take women away from their "proper sphere," the home. To the contrary, church work enhanced caring skills and domesticity. The second virtue was purity — principally sexual purity — which constituted a significant part of a woman's femininity. A woman's modesty was viewed as a sort of barrier reef against which the waves of male sensuality crashed with predictable regularity. Male weakness was expected in this regard, but the fall of a woman was simply not tolerable. Stories abounded of how innocent women had lost their innocence to "city slickers" and then had to be taken off to the madhouse shortly after the illegitimate baby was born. The third virtue was submission to men. In keeping with the context of a society in which egalitarian impulses ran very deep, this submission did not entail a theoretical understanding of the genders as being inherently unequal; it simply assigned different roles to equal partners. Finally, there was the virtue of domesticity. A woman was expected to be able to produce a warm and cheerful home to which the husband, father, brother, or son would return naturally and from which wandering would not seem desirable. The woman was expected to be able to cook, manage her home, be accomplished in needlework and flower arrangement, and to serve as nurse and doctor when gout, fevers, indigestion, or any of a host of other maladies struck. Guidance in these domestic skills was freely offered in a variety of advertisements in newspapers and cookbooks.

When Philip Schaff wrote back to his learned friends in Germany in 1855, trying to explain to them what America was like, he said that "America's profound respect for the female sex is well known." Indeed, he said, America is "sometimes called woman's paradise" because the woman was spared the hard drudgery common in Europe, was so regarded by men as to be able to travel freely without molestation, and "she has the precedence in every company." In Europe, a speaker addressing a mixed crowd would begin, "Gentlemen and Ladies"; in America, speakers addressing the same crowd would say, "Ladies and Gentlemen."[18]

To be sure, not all women subscribed to these ideals in the nineteenth century, and fewer did so as the decades rolled by; moreover, there would certainly have been those who would have taken issue with Schaff's portrait of conditions. Some tried to redefine the ideal. Others tried to redefine themselves. And still others, having made the effort, concluded that they had come close enough to attaining the ideal. That this ideal was around in Wenham when our representative young woman would have been growing up is evident from a poem written by Francis Whiting Hatch during the time when ice was being shipped from Wenham Lake. Entitled "Love's Labor Found (and Bound)," it concerned the inner thoughts of a young woman called Hester Price who lived "by the famous lake in Wenham":

> Pies she baked were straight from Heaven,
> Every cookie, every tart,
> Was an arrow shot by Cupid
> Piercing stomach, piercing heart.
>
> "When it comes my time to marry,"
> Hester said, "I'll have you know,
> That my Bible and my Cook Book
> Are the books to make things go."[19]

The poetic merit of these lines may be questionable, but there can be no doubt that Hester knew what it was to be a True Woman. And the disintegration of this understanding in the twentieth century, the supplanting of the True Woman by the New Woman, is "a transformation as startling in its way," says Barbara Welter, "as the abolition of slavery and the coming of the machine age."[20]

18. Schaff, *America: A Sketch of Its Political, Social, and Religious Character*, ed. Perry Miller (Cambridge: Harvard University Press, 1961), pp. 55-56. On the attitude of the clergy to women, see Gordon A. Riegler, *The Socialization of the New England Clergy, 1800-1860* (1945; reprint, Philadelphia: Porcupine Press, 1979), pp. 39-54.

19. Hatch, "Love's Labor Found (and Bound)," in "Wenham Poems" file, Wenham Museum, Wenham, Mass.

20. Welter, "The Cult of True Womanhood: 1820-1860," *American Quarterly* 18 (Summer 1966): 174.

From about the 1880s onward, the regnant model of family life came under assault with increasing frequency by writers of the period. The fathers were presented as tyrannical absentee landlords, the mothers as dominated, frustrated, and stifled human beings. What is remarkable is that, far from reducing the irritations on the young that the old family order imposed, the disintegration of that order seemed only to excite them to new levels of outrage. The more lightly family expectations and responsibilities rested on them, the more egregious their behavior became. The impatience with the structure of the family implicit in such behavior has had large cultural consequences. The transmission of values and moral understanding in our own time has been significantly changed by the fracturing of the family, which has served for centuries as the principal means by which values, wisdom, and moral knowledge have been passed from one generation to another.

The young woman whose life we are following was fortunate that she had not been born in the previous century, when the education of women was considered dangerous and those who did manage to attain it were derided as "bluestockings." By the nineteenth century, education for women was often encouraged, so long as marriage was still the goal toward which they were moving. After completing her schooling in Wenham, then, the young woman might very well have responded to what Mt. Holyoke Female Seminary had to offer. The Seminary's 1839 catalog promised an education that would render women handmaidens to the gospel and provide them with tools they could use "in the great task of renovating the world." Mt. Holyoke retained its evangelical outlook for some years before becoming a secular college, and during that time might well have produced a number of missionaries from among the daughters of Wenham. But it will not serve our purposes here to suppose that our representative woman would have left her home to join them, so let us say that she returned home after graduating from the Seminary. And, that granted, let us proceed to retrace our steps and see her from another angle as she grew up in the church in Wenham.

A Quiet and Staid Revival

Ministers and moralists at the turn of the nineteenth century may have exaggerated the state of decline in the nation, as well as in the church and home. Perhaps congregations were not as small, as elderly, as somnolent as ministers thought. Perhaps children did not scurry for cover as often as these ministers supposed when they came calling to discharge their pastoral responsibilities. Perhaps there was more praying and piety than they saw. And perhaps the rising tide of intellectual "infidelity" that they feared so much was less widespread, less effective, and less socially pernicious than they imagined. But there is no question that Christian faith was in a state of considerable disrepair as the century began.[21]

But beginning in 1792, the breath of revival was experienced in the towns and villages along the Connecticut River valley.[22] The initial gust eventually grew into a storm in the 1820s and 1830s, and though it tapered off later, it continued to blow in different places and times all the way down to the end of the century. This Second Great Awakening ushered in the new Age of Protestantism.[23] The age was new not only in the extent to which Protestant belief affected the nation but in its theological temper as well. The Puritan establishment had been formed around Calvinistic beliefs, and it was these, *sans* their political outworkings, that were given new life under Jonathan Edwards in the

21. The target of much concern in the pulpit was "infidelity," both the general sort of unbelief that undoubtedly was rooted in the Enlightenment and the more organized expressions of free-thinking. At the same time, however, it was also recognized that these adversaries would not have posed such a threat had the Christian faith not been in so parlous a state. See, for example, Joseph Lathrop, *A Sermon, on the Dangers of the Times, from Infidelity and Immorality; and Especially from a Lately Discovered Conspiracy against Religion and Government, Delivered at West Springfield* (Springfield, Mass.: Francis Stebbins, 1798); Timothy Dwight, *The Nature and Danger of Infidel Philosophy, Addressed to the Candidates for the Baccalaureate, in Yale College* (New Haven: George Bunce, 1798); and [Luther Hart], "A View of the Religious Declension in New England, and of Its Causes, during the Latter Half of the Eighteenth Century," *Quarterly Christian Spectator* 5 (June 1833): 207-37. On free-thinking, see Albert Post, *Popular Freethought in America, 1825-1850* (1943; reprint, New York: Octagon Books, 1974). The account is brought forward by Sidney Warren in *American Freethought, 1860-1914* (New York: Columbia University Press, 1943).

22. On the 1792 revival, see [Edward N. Packard,] *Sermons and Addresses Commemorative of the Seventy-Fifth Anniversary of the Second Church, Dorceter* (Boston: Alfred Mudge, 1883), p. 24. A mass of firsthand accounts of this revival are included in Tyler Bennet's *New England Revivals, as They Existed at the Close of the Eighteenth, and the Beginning of the Nineteenth Centuries* (Boston: Massachusetts Sabbath School Society, 1846). On the subsequent revivals, see Martin Moore, *A Brief History of the Evangelical Churches of Boston, together with a More Particular Account of the Revival of 1842* (Wheaton, Ill.: R. O. Roberts, 1980). For a general account of the revival in Connecticut, see Charles Roy Keller, *The Second Great Awakening in Connecticut* (New Haven: Yale University Press, 1942).

23. See Sidney Mead, *The Lively Experiment: The Shaping of Christianity in America* (New York: Harper, 1963), p. 55.

First Great Awakening of the eighteenth century. The second half of
the nineteenth century, by contrast, saw the emergence of a pervasive
Arminianism, which, as George Marsden has noted, was a way of
thinking that was thoroughly in step with the active, confident, and
democratic mood in the country.[24] Achieving a perfect embodiment in
Charles Finney, this revivalistic Arminianism eventually stifled, if not
supplanted, the older form of Reformation thinking, and it has continued to flow through our own century, losing depth as it has gained
breadth, finally spilling out over most of contemporary evangelicalism.

But this is, of course, a story that is far broader in its scope than
the one that we are presently following, for here in New England there
was a stubborn resistance to new ways of doctrinal reasoning. It is true
that Nathaniel Taylor and his Arminian friends at Yale Divinity School
did manage to effect some changes in the 1830s, the upshot being that
in 1837 the Congregationalists and Presbyterians, who had been in
union since 1801, were sundered down the middle and went into
schism. But the success of the Yale divines created great dismay among
those whose way was being unsettled. In 1829, Ebenezer Porter wrote
to Lyman Beecher to say that "not an Arminian candidate has been to
be found [sic], or has been wanted in New England for many a year."[25]

The best-known churchman to come out of the Wenham church
was Adoniram Judson, the first missionary doctor sent to Burma. His
father had been the Wenham church's pastor, but he chose to leave in
1799 after his regular pleas for an increase in salary to offset the ravages
of inflation were turned down by the town. But we are concerned here
with four of his successors: Ebenezer Sperry (1820-37), Daniel Mans-
field (1837-47), Jeremiah Taylor (1847-56), and John Sewall (1859-67).

The early years of the century brought a spiritual drought to this
little church as they did throughout New England. Between 1810 and
1825, only thirteen people were added to the church. But then, under
the leadership of Sperry (who, in his spare time, took out a patent for
a "wind wheel," which appears never to have been built), the church
found itself being driven by a wind of an entirely different kind.
According to a parishioner, the church held "a day of fasting and

24. Marsden, *The Evangelical Mind and the New School Presbyterian Experience:
A Case Study of Thought and Theology in Nineteenth-Century America* (New Haven: Yale
University Press, 1970), pp. 293-94. Cf. Winthrop S. Hudson, *Religion in America:
An Historical Account of the Development of American Religious Life*, 4th ed. (New York:
Macmillan, 1987), p. 179.
25. Porter, quoted in *The Autobiography of Lyman Beecher*, 2 vols., ed. Barbara
Cross (Cambridge: Harvard University Press, 1961), 2: 123.

prayer," and during the next year, fifty-nine people were converted.[26] This revival was the talk of the town for a long time. In fact, some forty years later John Sewall apparently still had these events in mind, for a parishioner reported that he "used often to express regret, his regret, and the sadness he felt that no large number had been led during his ministry to an open and decided entrance upon a Christian life."[27] To be sure, Wenham was not without its unbelievers, nor was the church entirely unaware of what was happening in other towns. One notes, for example, the wry comment of Jeremiah Taylor, given in the elegy he preached for a ship's captain who had been lost at sea, that happily this man, a Christian believer, had not considered it "a sufficient reason for rejecting an opinion" that "the pastor of the church had advocated it, as is too often the case in the present day."[28] And, as noted by Reuen Thomas, who preached at Taylor's own funeral, the Wenham minister had always found his intellectual anchorage in the teachings in which he had been schooled "in his younger days," the teachings of orthodoxy from which he had never strayed. Orthodox evangelical faith was believed and practiced and apparently considered normative in the town during this time.

During the pastorate of Ebenezer Sperry, the "Sabbath school" was started. There may be more to this than meets the eye. When the Congregational church was still established, ministers were legally responsible for the schooling of the children in the town. Indeed, John Fiske, the very first minister in Wenham, himself taught the children to read and write. With disestablishment, the pastor's potential to influence the children was greatly reduced. The pastor was removed from the schools even as later on town activities were removed from the church and shifted over to the town hall. Sabbath school was a context in which to make up for any loss in the children's education. In any case, it seems to have been a remarkable success. At the end of his pastorate, Jeremiah Taylor had two hundred "scholars" in Sabbath school instructed by twenty-four teachers, and the interesting thing about this is that there were only about two hundred children living

26. See "Wenham: Churches: Congregational Ministers Notes" file, Wenham Museum, Wenham, Mass.

27. See "Wenham: Churches: Congregational Ministers Notes" file, Wenham Museum, Wenham, Mass.

28. Taylor, "The Shipmasters Monument: A Brief Discourse Occassioned by the Death, at Sea of Capt. William Hadley, Delivered in Wenham, Mass., Nov. 28, 1850," in the "Wenham: Churches: Congregational Ministers Notes" file, Wenham Museum, Wenham, Mass.

in town at this time! Either the teachers ran a very compelling program or social custom made the attendance of the young inescapable. The young woman whose progress we have followed, then, would undoubtedly have attended regularly and would have been taught from some of the materials that have survived, which were put out by the American Tract Society. This Society was the fruit of the Second Great Awakening and produced a wide range of materials that explained evangelical conversion, offered selections of hymns suitable for young people, published missionary stories, and produced tracts on Christian character and living.

During the period when these pastors were preaching, great uncertainty about the minister's status began to surface. This was a time of transition in the nation from an older order to an order in which the principle of liberty was lifted from the political domain and applied to the rest of life in what some viewed as alarmingly gratuitous ways. It was also a time when the New England Congregationalists were having to reckon with the fact that their position of privilege in society was over. And yet the Puritan soul lived on homiletically in little towns like Wenham. The ministers were men of stature and learning, their sermons still held the town's attention, salvation and moral reform were still preached, and thus human life was still interpreted and corrected by God's Word. These discourses seldom made any self-conscious transition from the biblical text to life; rather, they were addresses distilled from Christian understanding in which text and life were interwoven with one another — and in this they reflected both how the people thought and how life was. Divine revelation was no stranger in their town. It needed no justification before the townsfolk who assembled weekly to hear it unfolded and applied. The painful and contorted maneuvers that preachers and theologians must now undertake in order to "contextualize" biblical revelation is no small reminder of how alien and incomprehensible it has become in the modern world. It was not so then. At least, these preachers assumed that it was not so then. They acted as if God's truth was accepted in the town as naturally as a piece of furniture would be in one of the houses.[29]

So it was that this graduate of the Red Schoolhouse, and later of

---

29. On the role and nature of Puritan preaching, see the excellent analysis by Harry S. Stout in *The New England Soul: Preaching and Religious Culture in Colonial New England* (New York: Oxford University Press, 1988). Stout's analysis features important modifications of Perry Miller's thesis, in part because Stout drew on thousands of unpublished sermons and the notes of those who heard them preached, whereas Miller based his analysis solely on available published materials.

Mt. Holyoke Female Seminary, would have experienced a total coherence to life provided by a set of influences at one with each other in home, in school, and in church. Between private ideas and public life there would have been no chasm to pass over, for the one simply gave accord and plausibility to the other. Things domestic and things vocational were cut from the same piece of cloth. Those with whom one traded were those with whom one lived in a town as transparent as glass. Those whose lives intersected with one's own during the week were those with whom one worshiped on the Sabbath. Character and work were thus joined, as were the home and the world, and personal relations governed the whole of it. Evangelical faith gave force, meaning, and linkage to a transcendent order the presence of which in the town was as tangible and obvious as the wheels on the stagecoach.

The True Woman about Town

The young graduate from Mt. Holyoke, having returned to Wenham, would have expected to marry, and it would have been a sore embarrassment to her parents if she had not. The pool of young men from whom she had to select would not, however, have been large. In Wenham at mid-century, every marriage had at least one partner who was born in the town, and of those who were not, nine out of ten came from one of the contiguous towns. Travel is the lubricant of a diversified social life, and in the first half of the century Wenhamites would barely have given a thought to what lay over the horizon. Edmund Batchelder, a captain in the Revolutionary War, kept a diary in which he made daily entries from 1794 to 1865.[30] While this document is regrettably bereft of a single thought about the meaning of life, it does nevertheless provide a microscopic, if cryptic, account of what each day held for the Captain. What one notices is the regular travel to nearby towns — Ipswich, Hamilton, Salem, Topsfield, Beverly, Marblehead, and Andover — even in the dead of winter. But always it was travel within this small world. This was entirely typical for the townsfolk of the time, and no doubt would have been for the woman whose life we are following. She would have married locally, and, even if marriage brought her sorrow and disappointment, almost certainly she would not have sought divorce. A few citizens from Massachusetts who were

---

30. Three volumes of Batchelder's handwritten entries, dated April 15, 1794, to April 27, 1865, are among the holdings of the Wenham Museum, Wenham, Mass.

unhappy in marriage did journey out to Ohio, where the binding vows could be unbound in a day, but this was not a common route for the unhappy to take. Even though a little later the Civil War and its aftermath produced a bountiful harvest of bruised marriages, divorce remained uncommon. Indeed, as late as 1880 only 5 percent of marriages ended in divorce.[31]

Our townswoman would have settled down to home life, rearing as many children as she was able and managing her household with cheer and fortitude without the benefit of either refrigeration or central heating; neither was widely available until the early years of our own century.

Society women, some of whom lived in Boston, often feigned delicacy and would scarcely ever venture outdoors. Many considered it improper to be seen in the markets. But this was changing generally, and it was probably changing in Wenham, too. Miss Paloa, principal of the School of Cooking in Boston, advised women to gain practical knowledge of what was available in the markets by shopping themselves. "Many think that the market is not a pleasant or proper place for ladies. The idea is erroneous. My experience has been that there are as many gentlemen among marketmen as are to be found engaged in any other business."[32]

And so our subject would have gone forth to gather supplies. She probably would have purchased mainly pork, which the surviving account books indicate was raised and slaughtered in the town, and of course fish; beef was eaten but was not a major part of the diet. In all likelihood, she would have kept and slaughtered her own chickens, geese, and ducks, too, in addition to growing her own vegetables, some of which she would have preserved, since there was no commercial canning at the time. She probably would have kept her own bees. So many people in Wenham kept bees that for a while it became hazardous to travel the streets, and the selectmen had to be called upon for remedial action! And she might even have begun to develop some novel ideas about nutrition. In 1839, Mrs. S. J. Hale published what she claimed was the first book on nutrition and cooking based on Christian ideas. She noted that foreigners had concluded that because Americans have "thin forms, sallow complexions and bad teeth," the

    31. See William L. O'Neil, "Divorce in the Progressive Era," *American Quarterly* 17 (Summer 1965): 203-17; and William E. Bridges, "Family Patterns and Social Values in America, 1825-1875," *American Quarterly* 17 (Spring 1965): 3-11.
    32. Paloa, *Miss Paloa's New Cook Book: A Guide to Marketing and Cooking* (Boston: Estes & Lauriat, 1881), p. 5.

climate must be bad. There was nothing wrong with the climate, she said. The problem lay with the typical eating habits, of which she singled out three for rebuke: "using *animal food* to excess," "eating *hot* bread," and "swallowing our meals with steam-engine rapidity."[33]

Less adventurous than Mrs. Hale's excursion into nutritional virtues, and of more consequence to the town, would have been our subject's involvement in the temperance movement. The movement was organized in Wenham in the year that our subject went to the Red Schoolhouse, and it was still flourishing at the beginning of the twentieth century. It was part of a network serviced in the Boston area by the *New-England Temperance Journal,* a publication that, by its own reckoning, endorsed "Teetotalism, Good Morals, Education, and Humanity."

In 1812, Ebenezer Porter, a prominent pastor in Connecticut, observed that the question of temperance was "but rarely made the theme of the pulpit."[34] About three decades later, in 1844, William Sprague, a prominent pastor in Albany, New York, declared in a sermon that "meetings without number" had been organized, "speeches without number" had been delivered, "societies without number" had been created, and the result, when the sermon was preached, was that "an extensive and benign reformation in almost every part of the land" had been effected.[35] And therein lies the story of the beginnings of the temperance crusade that in the end produced the Eighteenth Amendment and an entirely "dry" country, legally speaking, between 1920 and 1932.

The temperance movement was born in the evangelical Awakening, although it gathered strength from many other adherents and advocates along the way. In Wenham, however, as in the country as a whole, temperance was not necessarily a popular cause. It was true, as one anonymous tract informed its readers, that there were alternatives to warming oneself from "ardent spirits," such as "hot broth, soup, chocolate, milk porridge," but apparently not all were taken with the author's claim that by these means "you will be supported against the cold most astonishingly." For the disbelievers in 1830s, one of the two

33. Hale, *The Good Housekeeper; or, The Way to Live Well and to Be Well While We Live, Containing Directions for Choosing and Preparing Food, in regard to Health, Economy and Taste* (Boston: Weeks, Jordan, 1839), p. vii.

34. Porter, *The Fatal Effects of Ardent Spirits: A Sermon* (Middlebury, Vt.: T. C. Strong, 1812), p. 3.

35. Sprague, "Character to Which Young Men Should Aspire, to Meet the Demands of the Age," *American Pulpit* 2 (July 1846): 51-70.

taverns in town offered the opportunity to try out any alternative theses the townspeople might have had in mind.

A local poet, Allen Peabody, contrasted the two tavern owners as "King Richard" and "King Alcohol." "Richard" was actually John Thorne Dodge; the other king was Ezra Lummus, whose tavern, on the corner of Main and Larch, had been built in 1826 on the site where the stage horses were changed. King Richard was praised by the poet for having taught the people of Wenham to drink their water without rum. "King Alcohol's" establishment, on the other hand, was

> The only dwelling built of brick or
> Where hay teamsters stopped for liquor;
> Friend Ezra then kept grog for sale,
> And thereby doth hang a tale
> For years and years, town meeting days
> Were in excitement and Amaze.

Why so? we may ask. And the answer is that it was there that "drunken rowdies met to prance/Three cents for toddy, three for dance."[36] So there was much to do in Wenham in those days by those who believed, as our good townswoman probably would have, that "ardent spirits" were becoming the ruin of the country.[37]

Besides support for this voluntary association, there was also the work of the women from the Congregational Church who first organized themselves as the Female Reading Society of Wenham in 1823, which we may presume our True Woman would have joined. The society met monthly and imposed a fine on those not present, the proceeds going toward the society's good works. These were principally three. First, they began a collection of books which they purchased and circulated among themselves, thus laying the foundations for the present town library. Second, their earlier practice of listening to the

36. Peabody, *Poems by Allen Peabody, Bard of Enon: A Humorous and Historical Collection, Giving the Jokes, Experiences, and Characters of Many Citizens of Wenham, Thirty Years Ago and the People of the Present Time* (Salem, Mass.: E. H. Fletcher, 1868), p. 5.

37. It was estimated that in 1810, thirty-three million gallons of hard liquor was being distilled or imported into the United States annually. This official estimate did not take account of any quantities that might have been smuggled in or otherwise illegally produced. But even the officially acknowledged supply was large enough to provide every man, woman, and child with five gallons each. By 1829, the quantity was calculated to have doubled. These figures formed the bases of a great many sermons during this period and set the stage for the subsequent temperance movement.

reading of "uplifting" books when they gathered to sew was expanded to include listening to public lectures and other entertainments. Third, they made financial contributions to missionary societies and in support of Christian relief in counties as far away as China and Poland. They also supported students preparing for the ministry by making regular contributions to the American Educational Society, another organization that came out of the Awakening.[38]

Among all of the students in American educational institutions, the number preparing to become ministers had been declining proportionately for a long time. In 1820, Ebenezer Porter preached a sermon in Boston in which he noted that between 1620 and 1720, about one out of every two students attending Harvard and Yale was training for the ministry. During the next fifty years, 1720 to 1770, he calculated that the proportion in these and other colleges had dropped to one in three. In the next forty years, it fell to one in five, and between 1800 and 1810 it had fallen further to one in six.[39] The American Educational Society declared in 1828 that of the three thousand students "enjoying public education," only six or seven hundred "are on the Lord's side."[40] That same report indicated that of the 1,880 Presbyterians churches, 679 were without ministers, and of the 960 Congregational churches, 240 were vacant. The following year, Charles Hodge, the great Princeton theologian, lamented not only that the proportion of ministers was declining relative to the general population but also that men of piety and character who were fit for the ministry could not be found in sufficient numbers to reverse the trend, and among those who might well have sought training, not a few could not afford to do so.[41] The result was that the church was suffering acutely. And still the problem was unsolved twenty odd years later when the American Home Missionary Society issued a "loud call" for men to go West and serve the Lord in the territories that were opening up, listing the needs by state. The women in Wenham responded. They contributed to the education of "pious youths" and, in some of their meetings, they knitted "socks and cravats" for the students.

38. Olive Irene Tracy, "History of the Ladies Society of the Wenham Congregational Church, from 1823-1923," in the "Wenham: Churches: Congregational Ladies Society" file, Wenham Museum, Wenham, Mass.

39. Porter, *A Sermon Delivered in Boston, on the Anniversary of the American Education Society* (Andover, Mass.: Flagg & Gould, 1821), p. 10.

40. *Quarterly Journal of the American Education Society*, January 1828, p. 342.

41. [Hodge], "The General Assembly's Board of Education, and the American Education Society," *Biblical Repertory*, n.s., 1 (1829): 351.

What in retrospect does seem astonishing is that women, with all of their accomplishments, to whom moralists appealed for the sake of the society and upon whom preachers counted both to be in church and, so to speak, to man the ramparts of righteousness, were denied a vote in their nation's affairs. That, of course, was not remedied until 1920.

Perhaps the most striking fact about life in Wenham then was the clear sense of geography that the people had. It was akin to the peasants' bonding to their land, to a particular piece of land, with the corresponding uneasiness about other places, which always seemed strange and unfriendly. Wenham had its bounds which defined its place as a town — bounds that were not only geographical but psychological, economic, and organizational. They were the channel markers of their collective life, lining the passage within which the concourse of daily events took place, defining the social expectations of that life, and, at the same time, establishing the town's independence from the outside world. It was here that many of the families had lived for generations, handing on from parent to child the gathered folklore, the possessions, and a sense of who they were and what it meant to live in Wenham. They scarcely thought about the larger happenings in the world, nor did they experience the consequences of those happenings.[42] The Wenham community had not stayed entirely static, of course. Some of the sons had to seek better prospects and moved north to New Hampshire or Maine. Others who had done well in Wenham were lured away by the hope of even greater prosperity elsewhere. But for those who stayed, there was a strikingly undisturbed order, a stability to their world. The old ways changed very little in the first half of the nineteenth century. The outside world rarely intruded on their local circumstances, and when news from the outside did arrive, at least in the antebellum years, it was often already old.

Small-town life undoubtedly had two sides to it, and both are evident in the ambiguity with which small towns are often viewed today.

---

42. The first time it occurred to Arnold Toynbee, the philosopher of history, that the West might be mortal was in 1912. He found the ruins of a country house built in the baroque style on the island of Crete. At this time all such houses in England were not only preserved but in many cases were still inhabited by the families in whose possession they had remained, sometimes for hundreds of years. That this was not so in the case of the house on Crete suggested to Toynbee that a change had been loosed that might be of sufficient force and scope to render the whole of the West obsolete. It is precisely the unfolding of this reality that I am exploring first with respect to Wenham in this chapter and then more widely with respect to the West in the next.

On the one hand, the townspeople grasped the wholeness of life, the interconnections of its parts, their dependence upon one another in the community — all matters that have largely been lost today and about which we are often wistful. Our experience of "community," unlike theirs, is usually not connected to a particular place. It is made artificially, through voluntary association. And because the associations are voluntary, they are also fragile and often impermanent. Something intrinsic to human relating was made far more difficult and complex when the town began to disappear. On the other hand, small towns had their flaws and problems. They were places of low horizons and endemic parochialism, places that were always ready to believe myths about strangers, "old wives' tales," and gossip. And forgiveness for transgressions committed could be hard to obtain, public forgetfulness even harder. Moderns often feel a sense of relief that their flaws and transgressions are now, happily, concealed beneath a shroud of anonymity.

Even given the changes that have occurred, however, it seems odd that modern writers and movie makers should have shown such an interest in visiting a little revisionist history on the small town, apparently with the intent of demonstrating the innocence and desirability of the modern city by comparison. In 1882, Ed Howe's *Story of a Country Town* seems to have begun the tradition of debunking small-town parochialism, a task to which many skilled writers, such as Sinclair Lewis in his *Main Street,* have subsequently turned their hand. And the darker passions that flow beneath the orderly and respectable surface of small towns have also been frequent themes, as in Sherwood Anderson's *Winesburg, Ohio* and even John Steinbeck's *The Winter of Our Discontent.*

Hypocrisy was hardly unique to small towns, however, and while it is true that their soil did seem especially likely to encourage the growth of gossip and parochialism, this was but the other side of what was, in fact, their great virtue — the community that they provided. The losses we have experienced in moving from these small, personal worlds into the large and impersonal world of the modern city may not have sufficient compensations. Indeed, Erich Fromm argued that even preliterate villages, where there are bonds of community, contain more of the ligaments of a genuine culture than are present in the steel and glass edifices that are now home to millions and in which the fragmentation of life is inescapable.[43] It is this loss that has preoccupied

43. Fromm, *The Sane Society* (New York: Holt, Rinehart & Winston, 1976), pp. 544-45.

social scientists throughout the twentieth century as they have tried to measure its effects on human behavior and consciousness. And these effects provide the backdrop for this book, too, for the inescapable fact is that the structure of Christian belief must now wander the modern, fragmented world like an abandoned waif, and that was not true in towns like Wenham prior to the advent of modernity.

Perhaps the most obvious contrast between Wenham and our world is the sense of permanence that they had and that we lack. The loss of that sense is the most painful aspect of the transition between the two worlds. This sense of permanence was the result of many causes, too numerous and complex to examine here, and it produced a mass of outworkings that I can only begin to suggest here. That world prized permanence; ours knows that change is irresistible and has come to need it. They made houses and shoes to last; we build obsolescence into many of our products, and our houses last only about forty years. The deluge of new products that our productive economy has spewed forth itself generates a need that advertisers say will be satisfied only by a fresh purchase. The words *improved* and *new* and the like have been used with such frequency by the various marketers as to have lost their meaning entirely, but they nevertheless remain the code words of purchase.

It is this kind of change that is engulfing almost every aspect of our lives and is contributing to the deep sense of impermanence that we so often experience, in marked contrast to the sense of permanence that prevailed in the little town we have visited. This has changed our attitude toward life in many ways. Consider for instance our attitudes toward the things that surround us in everyday life. There was a time when artistry and craft often coincided in the making of furniture that was not only useful but also beautiful. It would be kept and handed on from parent to child. Today, the mechanized production line has often sundered this relationship, not only robbing the workers of the satisfaction of making furniture that contains an expression of their own aesthetic sense but also delivering products that are all too often simply utilitarian. Nor does a second generation typically express much interest in inheriting this sort of furniture. Today we look on many of our things simply as throwaway items. Indeed, much of what we produce is not meant to have anything but the briefest use, from paper plates to disposable diapers, from plastic knives to plastic milk bottles. We know that appliances will be with us for only a short time because many of them are not worth repairing when the first sign of trouble appears. The efficiency of the factory means that buying a replacement is less expensive than paying someone to repair the original. Men's socks used to be darned and shirt collars and cuffs turned to make them last longer. Now we simply replace them. And we exchange our homes on the average of once every seven years. We are an astonishingly mobile people. In any given year, about 20 percent of Americans move somewhere. Built into the high tempo of modern life, then, is an inescapable instability in which only a few (excepting those who are too impoverished to escape their surroundings) manage to sink roots in a particular place. We can no longer assume that knowing where someone lives, be it in New York or Boston or Chicago, will tell us much about that person, since in all likelihood he or she will be a relatively new arrival in that place; to have known that a person came from Wenham last century would have provided a foundational knowledge of that person.[44]

Place has never been less consequential. And the reasons are all too obvious. Not only are we impermanent residents in the towns or cities where we live, but modern transportation and television have shrunk space and time. Jet travel can move us from one city to another in less time than it would take to drive from a suburb into a major city and find a parking place. Teachers are able to commute weekly between cities to offer courses. Professional investors can work in the financial world of New York by computer hookup while they enjoy the Florida sunshine. And television has extended this transcendence of space mentally and psychologically, making us contemporary observers of the entire world. We become vicarious participants in all of its great events instantaneously. We are everywhere and we have access to everything. The transition from Wenham to our modern world, then, is a transition from a life that was bounded and limited to a life that knows few bounds and in which the citizens, cut loose from place and time, have to carry the awful load of being omniscient and omnipresent.[45] It is these two features — the extent of our mastery over

44. In this section I am indebted to and providing a summary of Alvin Toffler's *Future Shock* (New York: Random House, 1970), especially the first two parts, entitled "Impermanence" and "Transience." I have attempted to check Toffler's statistics independently. Although the book contains useful insights, they are found cheek by jowl with other assertions that can only be described as fatuous. Perhaps most troubling is the complete absence of any moral considerations in his analysis; he seems to assume that whatever is is good and whatever will be will be good. His remedy for the disordering of life that drastic change has brought is simply to urge that we learn to adapt! It seems rather clear that there are utopian assumptions behind his understanding of human nature.

45. I am indebted in this summary for the account of this massive shift in American life given by Daniel Boorstin in *The Americans*, vol. 2: *The Democratic Experience* (New York: Random House, 1973), pp. 358-448.

nature and the speed of change — for which there are no precedents in what Arnold Toynbee has identified as the nineteen civilizations that preceded our Western civilization.[46]

But if we are taking on divine attributes, it is not because we have a greater sense of the divine than was the case in Wenham. Quite the opposite. The sense of permanence then was framed by, if not explicitly linked to, a divine and supernatural order. That order has disappeared in public life and in much private life today, and where it still lingers in the latter it is usually accommodated to the expectations of the former. There is a sense of impermanence above our lives even as there is within our lives. The norms, values, and principles that were once seen to be enduring absolutes, along with the knowledge of God in which they were grounded, now seem quite uncertain and perishable, anything but the markers that once provided safe moral passage through life. The world that God was believed to have created then was easy to understand; the world that we have created out of our technological and marketing genius is dark and confusing — although one thing about it is quite certain: if God could be blamed for that world (and he was), he cannot be blamed for this one, since everyone from the most muddle-headed secularists to the most intractable Marxists insist that he has had nothing to do with it. We have created it, and we stand judged by our creation.

This same impermanence characterizes our relationships. Our mobility means that most of our friendships are quite fleeting. Christmas cards may tentatively renew the links once we have moved, but any such renewal is brief and insubstantial. It is simply a part of the reality of moving that we will have to make a new set of friends. And we may have to find fresh spouses as well, for the bonds that are formed with such high hopes at the beginning of the marriage often turn out to be impermanent. In 1880, only one in twenty marriages dissolved; today it is one in two.

This comparison might seem to suggest that the decaying of family life and the serious, even devastating, increase in divorce is a phenomenon of very recent vintage. That is not the case. Throughout this century, the divorce rate has risen steadily, fueled by the stress, anxiety, and uncertainty of modern life.[47] Today's climate of marital

46. Toynbee, *A Study of History*, 10 vols. (London: Oxford University Press, 1935-54), 9: 465-72.
47. On the growing difficulties that the family has encountered, see Christopher Lasch, *Haven in a Heartless World: The Family Besieged* (New York: Basic Books, 1979).

impermanence has not developed overnight. Since the beginning of this century, sociologists, psychologists, and moralists have given this institution concerted attention because of the widely held perception that in the modern world it is in serious danger of collapsing.

The explanations of why the model of enduring marriage has not been able to sustain itself in the modern world are numerous and complex, but there can be no doubt that part of the explanation lies in the fact that modern people have had to become amphibious, to belong to many worlds, many places, many institutions. As spouses begin to direct their energy, attention, and commitment to an increasing number of worlds, among ever more centers of responsibility, they will inevitably be prevented from focusing on marriage as much as they once did. The New Woman has traded the idealized social eminence of the True Woman for social opportunity that the True Woman neither sought nor was offered. The life of the True Woman, by contrast, was focused and undivided by opportunity. It had clear boundaries and expectations. The life of the New Woman is diffuse, and so her expectations and responsibilities clash and often become mutually incompatible. Given the many demands that are placed on her, life often becomes a balancing act of considerable ambiguity.[48] And with the loosening of the marriage bond, the genie of sex has escaped the bottle. Once the symbol, means, and expression of permanent union, sex is now all too often a matter of impermanent and transitory encounters.[49]

And so we have come into the modern world. We have left behind a predominantly agricultural and rural age for an urban and mechanized culture. The farmers in Wenham once resisted the introduction of mowers. They said the terrain was too stony, and perhaps it was.

48. The complexity of the transition that women have made in moving from the old model to the new model has been recognized even by Betty Friedan. In *The Feminine Mystique* (New York: W. W. Norton, 1963), she stood on its head the ideal of the True Woman and argued that it should be replaced by that of the New Woman. Twenty years later in *The Second Stage* (New York: Summit Books, 1981), she acknowledged that while women have been emancipated from old expectations, variously refusing to marry, refusing to remain chaste, refusing to have children, and demanding equal time and pay on the job, fulfillment has nevertheless proved to be more elusive than had been expected.

49. The change referred to here is part of a much broader and more complex set of changes related to family structures, roles, and social expectations. For a brief introduction to these broader issues, see Arlene Skolnick and Jerome H. Skolnick, *Family in Transition: Rethinking Marriage, Sexuality, Child Rearing, and Family Organization* (Boston: Little, Brown, 1980), pp. 127-274.

But one also suspects that they resented and feared the intrusion of a device that would change the patterns of centuries. We have no such patterns and no such fears. We have adapted to our technological world so completely that sometimes we seem to be little more than psychological components in it. The balance between what is familiar and what is new has been drastically changed. They had little that was new; we have little that has persisted. This is true of things, relationships, and values. That was a tranquil world. To be sure, they had their tragedies and sorrows, but they did not have the world's sorrow, from country after country, spilling nightly into their living rooms, their homes becoming places "where anguish comes by cable," to use W. H. Auden's words. They were permanent residents. We are nomads, perpetual immigrants, condemned to move from place to place in our own country until finally, if the sinews do not crack, we are allowed to pass into the forgetfulness of retirement.[50] Their needs were simple and related to survival; our needs are complex because our horizons are multiple and our possessions must serve many functions besides those related to survival. They were attached to place, even if they had to move from the towns of their birth and settle elsewhere, and they had a sense of time; we have neither. Their world was permanent because they knew God to be unchanging; ours is impermanent and God seems largely to have disappeared. Perhaps when our Wenham townswoman became depressed she would have gone into the church to pray; her counterpart today would probably go to the mall to shop. Therein lies the difference between these two worlds, worlds that are so close in time but so far apart in mentality.

A Small Town in a Big World

Driving north from Boston today, one passes through mile after mile of urban sprawl, a sprawl that does not cease even at Wenham but now surrounds and engulfs it. The development appears to have been entirely haphazard. The old and new are mixed indiscriminately. Interspersed along the way are garish billboards, parking lots, commercial enterprises, factories belching foul fumes, slick "modern" architecture, churches (quite a few of which are gasping for breath), and high-tech industry. There is no longer a rural divide between Wenham

50. This theme of rootlessness is explored tellingly by Vance Packard in *A Nation of Strangers* (New York: David McKay, 1972).

and Boston as there was in the nineteenth century, an interlude of trees and fields between city and town life. Nor are there any of the other interludes of a more psychological nature that stood between Wenham then and the modern world as it was rapidly developing. As Wenham was absorbed into the greater Boston area, it was also absorbed into the modern world. Then Wenham stood aloof from developments in Boston demographically, industrially, and even theologically, but today Wenhamites have become citizens in a larger society and within a larger world the presence of which is inflicted on them twenty-four hours a day through television. Whether they know it or not, they are part of an enjoined march to the city, a march that is national and even global in scale. In 1820, only one in thirteen lived in a city.[51] In each of the decades that followed, the general population grew by about 30 percent, but urban population grew by about 90 percent. The result was that in 1870, for example, one in four lived in an urban area; in 1970, it was three out of four; and the projection is that in the year 2000, it will be nine out of ten. And along with this incorporation has come an absorption into — or, to speak more accurately, a disappearance in — the modern world. From one angle it is true to say that Boston moved north to Wenham as industrial expansion occurred, but from another angle, Wenham made its own passage into the modern world principally through the channels of travel and communication.

Reaching Out to America

Communication between towns and with the larger world was slow at the beginning of the nineteenth century, and sometimes even impossible, but it was swift by the end of the century. The postal service played a part in this, but not the most dramatic part. A post office was established in Wenham in 1809. But the place where mail was deposited moved around a lot, taking up residence in the taverns, stores, a wheelwright's shop, a harness shop, and a private residence. There was not a post office building in Wenham until 1937. In 1863 mail carriers were first employed in America for towns of requisite size,

51. Statistics related to percentages of those living in cities are not altogether transparent. The problem is that the Bureau of Census has changed its mind with respect to what constitutes a city. In 1870, for example, it held that 8,000 people living in proximity to one another constituted an urban area. Between 1900 and 1950, it lowered the figure to 2,500. After 1950, it raised the figure to 50,000.

and in 1918 air mail first arrived in this town, thus establishing the arteries of written information that would make a place within the world even for this small town.

The more dramatic development was the telegraph, which in 1861 linked Europe to the Americas. This meant that the newspapers were able to make their readers aware of the world's events within hours of their occurrence, rather than days or weeks or even months. Seven times as many messages were being sent at the end of the last quarter of the century as had been sent at the beginning of that quarter. America had begun to shrink.

It shrank still more in 1877, when the first telephone line was strung between Boston and Somerville. During the next twenty-five years, the number of telephones in the country increased four hundredfold to 1.3 million. Though it took some time for this innovation to reach Wenham, the transcendence of place was becoming a reality.

It was not until the 1950s, when television sets began to enter American homes in significant numbers, that the transformation was completed, however. The great power that television exercises over its viewers, as Daniel Boorstin and many others have observed, is its ability to present events from anywhere in the world as they happen. We no longer have to wait for photographs to be developed. We no longer have to depend simply on voices transmitted over the radio, or the telephone, to be deprived of the sights the speakers are seeing. Now we can see and hear the event as it unfolds. Indeed, now we can see it even better than a witness at the scene, as multiple cameras give us views from different angles, from above, from the other side of the street, from behind, and up close. The picture can be switched from one view to another at the scene and, indeed, even from scenes in one country to another with the utmost rapidity. Radio produced its own kind of drama as the imagination of the listener filled in the events it transmitted, but television provides the more immediate drama of showing live events as they are unfolding. And yet with this omniscience, with this superhuman capacity to transcend place and time, has come loneliness. Given the increasing number of television sets in American homes and the divergent tastes of viewers, Americans more frequently watch their sets alone. As television discloses its intimacies and drama to these viewers, inviting a response, they are left to sigh or laugh or shout or cry alone in the company of the nonresponsive machine.

The first train to steam into nearby Beverly in 1840 was watched with awe by crowds of amazed townspeople, among whom were some

Wenhamites. Trains were still a relative rarity at this time, but by 1850 some 9,000 miles of line had been laid in America, and by 1860 there were 21,000 miles, putting this country at the fore of railway development in the world. In 1869, the completion of the transcontinental railroad bound America into a single country stretching from the Atlantic to the Pacific.

But in Wenham, a greater excitement was caused by the arrival of streetcars in 1885. These public conveyances were open horse-drawn carriages, lit by kerosene lamps and, in the winter, warmed by stoves. Although the comforts were not great, they increased travel for many people and were more versatile than the trains could be. They were partially superseded, a little later, by electric streetcars. But all such public transportation was eclipsed by the arrival of the automobile.

Although the first internal combustion engines were operating in Europe in the 1870s, Henry Ford's cars did not enter the streets of Detroit until 1896. And yet, despite its later introduction, Ford's auto, inexpensively mass produced, won the day and proceeded to transform the shape of American civilization completely.[52] It covered the terrain between the rivers and train tracks along which towns had been built, it closed the gaps between places not located on the rail line, it speeded up industry by providing swift delivery, it personalized travel, and in an unprecedented way it offered the individual new freedom from the community. It has, in fact, helped to supplant community life with patterns of life tailored to individual needs and preferences. It has opened up the entire country, but it has hastened the disappearance of ties to place.

These new forms of communication and transportation and the developments they have spawned have created the beginnings of a world civilization in which Americans, including the heirs of nineteenth-century Wenham, participate. It is a culture that belongs to no country in particular. It is not an American culture, though American movies and rock music are important purveyors and retailers of it. It is not European, though Europeans are a part of it. It has not arisen in the cities of the Third World, though increasingly they, too, are participants in it. It is simply modern, a culture located in no particular place but transcending all places, a culture that is the rich recipient of the past but has little recollection of that past.

It is in this global culture that Wenham and all of America's small

52. See George Rogers Taylor, *The Transportation Revolution, 1815-1860*, ed. H. David et al. (New York: Harper, 1968).

towns now live, and from it there now oozes the psychology associated
with the impermanence that is its centerpiece. In this culture of con-
temporaneity, for example, publicity takes the place filled by public
monuments and state edifices in the old culture. Such monuments
were once the permanent records of individual achievement or the
declarations of official function, but they belonged to time and place,
and the new culture transcends both. In the new culture it is publicity,
not perception or knowledge, that reveals the new achievement and
in some cases creates mythical achievements. And, says Christopher
Lasch, because "publicity is only the generalized gossip of the in-group,
the solidarity it creates is only synthetic."[53] Publicity created the myth
of Marilyn Monroe. Publicity transformed Truman Capote from an
author of some initial repute into a personality. It was as a personality
that he lived during the latter part of his life, not as a writer, his abilities
having long since been destroyed by drugs and inward decay. His
reputation was manufactured by the media more than it was established by his published works. He bonded briefly with his devotees,
but the bond was synthetic. In this new world, the statues are made
of celluloid, not of stone; here the achievements are those of personality, seldom of character; here the clicking of the cameras and the lights
of the television crew are the tip-off that a Big Event is underway, even
if it is only a brief shot of Zsa Zsa Gabor leaving the courtroom after
having been convicted for slapping a policeman.

This is experience without community. It is the experience of
mankind in the mass, bereft of the forces that once drew it into centers
of human fraternity and organization. From the impersonal mass, small
groups fly off and fashion their own small worlds: the beatniks, the
teddy boys, the skinheads, the molls, the hipsters, the inner-city gangs,
the metalheads, the drugged-out offspring of an affluent age. They
are rebels, Christopher Lasch argues, whose cultural amnesia deprives
them of the one thing they want most: the experience of being able to
revolt. In these ad hoc cultural protuberances there is nothing to revolt
against; there is only the contemporary moment dislocated from the
past and the future and stripped of parents, community, values, and
beliefs. And yet these small worlds are so light, so weightless, that even
the most fractured and fragile individual can feel safe and make connections, even if it is only with those who are equally fractured and
fragile. In these psychological environments, a fraternity of the

---

53. Lasch, *The New Radicalism in America, 1889-1963: The Intellectual as a Social
Type* (New York: Alfred A. Knopf, 1965), p. 73.

wounded, the frightened, the bored, and the disoriented typically develops, and with it comes an illusion of therapy.

Modern experience differs from the older kind of experience in that it is more attenuated, argues Boorstin, because modern experience democratically reduces all times and places to a common denominator, to a sameness.[54] Life in the past followed the rhythms of the seasons, he says; now it does not have to, for we have heat in winter and air conditioning in summer. Then, fresh meat could be purchased only when the local butcher made it available, and fresh fruits and vegetable were available only during the local season; now every variety of food is available in every season in endless variety. Then, there were visual boundaries between the inside of a house and what was outside, between one town and another. Now, glass and plastics blur the boundary between interior and exterior landscapes, and travel and communications link one town seamlessly with another.

As these many distinctions have fallen, the stream of information, the succession of new environments, and the number of new experiences have accelerated to the point sometimes of becoming unbearable. Our experience is now universal, not local. It is broad, not deep. It is multifaceted, not focused. It is boundless, not personal. As experience became attenuated, Daniel Boorstin has written, life grew "thinner, more diluted, its sensations . . . weaker and less poignant. It was a life punctuated by commas and semicolons rather than by periods and exclamation marks."[55]

The Wenham woman whose life we tried to reconstruct lived in a little town that might easily have been recorded on a Pieter Brueghel canvas. What is most notable about his paintings today is not their exaggerated perspective or the dramatic curves that are so often prominent in his work but that the dozens of people who are scattered around his towns, almost haphazardly, seem to be completely at home in their environment. His people, who are symbolically engaged in every kind of human activity that would go on in a town, and are doing so simultaneously, overwhelm the viewer with their humanness. They are in scale with their surroundings; they belong in their town; you feel that you could know them. What is most remarkable about modern people is that they are not in scale with the world they inhabit informationally and psychologically. They are dwarfed. And they have been emptied of their metaphysical substance; more precisely, it has been

54. Boorstin, *The Americans,* pp. 316-32, 336-58.
55. Boorstin, *The Americans,* p. 51.

sucked out of them. There is nothing to give height or depth or perspective to anything they experience. They know more, but they are not necessarily wiser. They believe less, but they are not more substantial. They are attuned to experience and to appearances, not to thought and character. And that is what it has meant to move from the kind of life represented by early Wenham to what we today encounter in the modern world.

Wenham was not a "typical" town, but it serves to illustrate, in its own way, how modernization has worked to bring about, in this small corner of the country, the intrusion of the gigantic world outside. It shows the marks of a revolution in which much has been born and much has perished. That something as momentous as this should have occurred would seem to require that someone did an inordinate amount of planning and preparation. One only has to think, for example, of how the Marxists have planned and plotted over the years to bring into being the "New Man," but despite all of that planning have failed so miserably. Think what plans and tests went into the first moon landing. Normally, the smallest breakthroughs happen only on the back of enormous human industry and application. But in this case, a truly momentous transformation of the human landscape took place without having been planned at all. The individual parts of the process were planned — the factories, the technological gadgets and devices, to some extent the cities, the system of manufacturing and distribution we know as capitalism — but the way in which these factors relate together and the way in which they are rewriting the human script are beyond the control of any mere mortal. Thus it can rightly be characterized as an "accidental revolution," to use Michael Harrington's term, a revolution with its own internal dynamic. It is an engine for change the operator of which heeds no human signals. So large, so overpowering is this set of unleashed forces that it has demolished the Berlin Wall, penetrated the Bamboo Curtain, and is accomplishing in Communist countries what forty years of Cold War failed to do. It has invisibly invaded the most closed of Marxist societies, instilling unwanted appetites in their citizens and focusing their attention on horizons that now appear all too clearly beyond the walls of their enclosure. And the fact that its presence has been felt there as well as in Wenham is a compelling indication of the global quality of this new order that we call modernity. It is on this new order of life that we must concentrate next.

CHAPTER II

World Cliche Culture

Why does man feel so sad in the twentieth century? Why does man feel so bad in the very age when, more than in any other age, he has succeeded in satisfying his needs and making the world over for his own use?

Walker Percy

We can shoot rockets into space but we can't cure anger or discontent.

John Steinbeck

Uneasy Rests the Spirit

LYING BETWEEN THE MIDDLE of the nineteenth century and the middle of our own century is a historical divide.[1] On the one side

1. Identifying the West's exact moment of transition into the modern world has proved to be notoriously difficult. Paul Johnson has argued for an early date, the period between 1815 and 1830. This period begins with the victory of Andrew Jackson over the British in New Orleans and of the British over the French at Waterloo, and it was during this time that the English-speaking nations increased their dominance in the world. At the same time, the Spanish empire in South America was breaking up, the Industrial Revolution was getting under way, and something like an international culture was beginning to emerge. Geoffrey Barraclough argues for a later period, roughly 1890 to 1900, when the scientific revolution began its transformation of life through advances in medicine, transportation,

is the Age of the West and on the other is an Age yet to be named. We know it already, however, for it is Our Time. On the other side of this divide, Europe was at the world's center politically and economically. On our side of the divide, the center is in America. On the other side of the divide, Judeo-Christian values were central to Western culture, even if they were not always believed personally. On our side of the divide, such values have been dislodged and replaced with a loose set of psychological attitudes that we now know as modernity.

A new civilization is, in fact, arising, and these changes are the markers along the road to its ascendancy. Unlike the kingdoms and empires of the past, it is not centered in a particular people or rooted in a particular place on earth. It is not political in nature. The soil in which this civilization flourishes is that which democracy and capitalism produce, to be sure, and it depends for its survival on technology and urbanization. But where these are present, it is able to transcend boundaries and place, languages and customs, for it is carried by democracy and capitalism, technology and cities, and these are all rapidly becoming universal phenomena. They are the Esperanto of the modern world, the language that belongs to everyone because it belongs to no one in particular.

And what is even more remarkable is that this civilization is not arising from the ashes of another, at least not deliberately. Behind it lies no conqueror; beneath it lie none of the crushed bones on which other civilizations and empires have rested; and within it the ligaments of power are not held by any particular ruler or dictator. This civilization has conquered silently, painlessly. It is thus the most benign civilization ever to have dawned. And yet, despite its many oddities, it has all of the marks of a new civilization, as clearly differentiated from what preceded

---

and generally accelerated technological change. David Bebbington cites a view that also has currency — namely, that the beginnings of the modern world were visually signaled with the first exhibition of post-impressionist art in London in 1910, though it was only in the 1920s that this new age really took root in Britain, Europe, and America. The options range over roughly a century, then, from the 1820s to the 1920s. The different views that have emerged seem to be explicable largely in terms of the different criteria that are applied. What one takes to be "modern" will determine when one sees the modern era as having begun. The criteria that are applied in this chapter lead me to think that this time is roughly in the third quarter of the nineteenth century, though the full shape of modernity was not apparent until the early part of the twentieth. See Paul Johnson, *The Birth of the Modern: World Society, 1815-1830* (New York: HarperCollins, 1991); Geoffrey Barraclough, *An Introduction to Contemporary History* (Harmondsworth: Penguin, 1967); and David Bebbington, "Evangelical Christianity and Modernism," *Crux* 26 (June 1990): 2.

it as were the Enlightenment, the Renaissance, and the Greek from what preceded them. What is now dawning, what is now intruding upon the world and beginning to forge links between peoples who do not share the same languages, ethnicity, religion, or social customs, is modernity.

The story of these two ages, Western civilization and modernity, is not quite as simple as this narrative suggests, of course. Life is seldom as simple as its retellings. In this case, these two cultures are not contiguous but continuous with one another. More than that, they often appear indistinguishable from one another. It is not as if the Age of the West ended when Our Time began. Rather, this new age is borne aloft on the achievements of the West and, in many ways, continues to be identical with the West. The emergence of America as the focus of Our Time does not mean that Europe is now so enfeebled as to be irrelevant; it only means that a shift in power has occurred within the West. And the ascendancy in Western cultures of a new set of values in place of the old does not mean that these cultures see themselves as being less Western. It is interesting to observe, however, how many think that the dawning of modernity is a sign that we are now in the late evening of Western civilization.

Even in the nineteenth century, sociologists after Comte began to listen for the death throes of the West, to look for signs of the demise of an order that did not seem then as if it would be able to survive its own enormous complexity. They thought it would fall a victim at its own hand. Thus it was that Ernst Troeltsch spoke of the "sunset of Western culture." Others were sensing the stretched fabric of society as well. Evelyn Waugh spoke of the "tumbling decadence of European civilization." George Eliot and Matthew Arnold bade Western culture adieu, too, the one with tears and the other with relief, on the assumption that its demise would mean the liberation of the hidden, instinctual regions of the human spirit that had been imprisoned by conventional Western morality. And earlier in the twentieth century, Oswald Spengler warned of the West's "decline," arguing that the culture of the past was being replaced by a machine age that would seal the destruction of the old.[2]

The cause of alarming the complacent has always been a lonely one, and those raising the alarm always appear to be malcontents whose disposition is not to enjoy what is set before them. Those who have

2. The view I am associating here with Spengler was actually articulated by many others who feared that progress would entail the uprooting of much that had given life its stability and meaning. For more on this, see Christopher Lasch, *The True and Only Heaven: Progress and Its Critics* (New York: W. W. Norton, 1991), pp. 135-47.

wondered about the survival of the West have seemed to be turning their backs on it with ingratitude, as if all of its rich bounty were a matter of no interest, its great achievements matters of no consequence. In the twentieth century, however, these lonely voices have become less lonely. Perhaps it is that the sense of foreboding about life, the sense of dis-ease, has become more widespread, and this has given plausibility to the concerns of these cultural critics. The triumphs of science and technology, after all, are never without their costs. Those who can harness the atom can also use it to split apart the human race. Those who can manufacture such abundance are not immune from the moral corruption that multiplies in the abundance. Genius is never antiseptic. No matter how brilliant the Western achievements are — and they have been brilliant — like all other human achievements, they, too, serve as vehicles for the vices to which fallen human nature is constantly prone. The values that often accompany Western plenty are not made hygienic by the genius whose company they keep. On the contrary, they have become the acid that is eating at the Western soul. The hand that gives so generously in the material realm also takes away devastatingly in the spiritual.

So it was that Solzhenitsyn described Our Time as "a world split apart." The split of which he spoke was not primarily ideological, between the communist and the Western countries, nor yet the split that industrial categories yields — a planet divided into First, Second, and Third Worlds; rather, he was thinking of the split between the best values of the West and the modern values of materialism that now threaten it with extinction. The new civilization could not have been born without the extraordinary achievements of Western democracy, commerce, and ingenuity, but the West, Solzhenitsyn believes, may not survive what it has brought forth.[3] And his is only one voice in a growing chorus of alarm. Jacques Ellul has spoken of the "betrayal" of the West by a corrupted intelligentsia; Philip Rieff has spoken of the "elaborate act of suicide" carried out by intellectuals as they have mutilated the workings of culture by destroying the possibility of authority; Carl Henry has spoken of the "end" of the West; Richard Weaver has spoken of its "dissolution"; Emil Brunner has spoken of its "progressive estrangement" from its Christian base and its movement toward nihilism; Robert Heilbroner has spoken of the "indefinable unease" that haunts the modern spirit as the realization sets in that all of the material and technological gain of recent years leaves

---

3. See *Solzhenitsyn at Harvard: The Address, Twelve Early Responses, and Six Later Reflections*, ed. Ronald Berman (Washington: Ethics and Public Policy Center, 1980).

the self empty; Graham Greene has spoken of the disintegration of spiritual values in the "sinless, graceless, chromium world" in which modern people live; Pope John Paul II has spoken of the "anticivilization" and "anticulture" that modernity nurtures in those blessed by its material abundance; and Bryan Wilson has spoken of the few small "rags and tatters" that now remain from this great civilization — rags and tatters with which we must try to cover ourselves in the winter chill that has fallen over Western societies as they have abandoned the best of what used to bond people together in community.

Most periods of history, undoubtedly, have provoked at least some melancholic pronouncements about the prospects of survival, the more so if these periods are roiled by change, when what is familiar is swept away and replaced too quickly. Some of these predictions have been wrong and others have been right. That is what one would expect. These are, after all, exceedingly difficult judgments to make, for in any culture there are always forces of decay at work alongside those of renewal, and it is no easy matter to be able to see how they are balanced with respect to one another. Those who see only the decay become alarmed and in their alarm offer broad, sweeping indictments; those who see only the forces of renewal become exultant and in their exultation make projections as broad and as sweeping. They are often just as wrong.

And all such assessments are complicated by the extent to which our perspective colors our view of what constitutes decay and what constitutes renewal. For example, those who operate from an Enlightenment perspective typically associate progress with renewal and view disillusionment as a symptom of decay. Those who operate within a framework of Judeo-Christian values, on the other hand, characteristically view a belief in progress as a symptom of decay and a sense of disillusionment the first step toward a realistic appraisal of the world without which renewal is impossible. It is important that these quite different ways of looking at the world be drawn out a little further, for they hold the key not only to understanding the constant collisions that occur between the competing agendas for society today but also to the strange ambiguities that now infest the modern soul. They are the threshold over which we enter the modern world.

Decay and Renewal

The Enlightenment world liberated us to dream dreams of the world's renovation and of ourselves at its center, standing erect and proud, recasting the whole sorry scheme of things bare-handed, as it were, leaning only on our own reason and goodness. It also liberated us to perceive illusion as reality. The illusion was that the forces at work within human life were benign, that life was bound and moved by the hidden purposes of an impersonal Good that would, in the end, serve only the high purposes the Enlightenment had imagined.

The real outcome of the Enlightenment, however, has not been the preservation of noble values but their collapse into complete relativism. The proud and erect shaper of life first remakes reality and then finds that what has been remade has no existence outside his or her private consciousness. Not only that, but it now begins to look as though this world, at first filled with such exhilarating freedom, has lost all of its benign good intent. There is violence on the earth. The liberated search only for power. Industry despoils the earth. The powerful ride roughshod over the weak. The poor are left to die on street grates. The unborn are killed before they can ever see the rich and beautiful world that God has made. The elderly are encouraged to get on with the business of dying so that we might take their places. The many forms that violence takes in our world provide stunning reminders of how false have been the illusions about freedom with which we have, for two centuries, been enticed in the West.

Although the brazen promises of the Enlightenment about the possibility of remaking all of life are now dead, the premise on which they were built — freedom from God, freedom from authority, freedom from the past, freedom from evil — simply refuses to die. It is what gives strength to the illusion that life can be remade. And it is this illusion that both feeds and feeds off the idea of progress. But why are these dreams so resistant to the facts? Is it that we are still enamored of the former apostles of this doctrine of progress? That hardly seems likely, for their ideas are a sorry parade of human foolishness. Some people, to be sure, still revere Darwin and his pioneering work, but once the ideas about progress escaped the bounds of biology, they became increasingly mischievous. In politics, twentieth-century fascists looked for a purging out of which the "Pure Man" would arise, while the Marxists and their assorted cousins looked for a utopian reconstruction of the world in which the "New Man" would emerge, riding the wave of state atheism.[4] In psychology, the Freudians' not-so-gentle counsels have sought to loose the deep, repressed drives of crippled bourgeois society in order to bring

---

4. For a discussion of the various totalitarianisms that have dominated the twentieth century, see Paul Johnson, *Modern Times: The World from the Twenties to the Eighties* (New York: Harper & Row, 1983).

freedom and wholeness. In philosophy, some Germans supposed that the Absolute would move through history coming to an evolutionary climax at the high point of all civilizations — perhaps in Germany?[5] In theology, Protestant and Catholic modernists alike envisioned spiritual life emerging in the ideals of human civilization. And in conventional Victorian piety, daily hope was sustained by the thought that every day, in every way, things were getting better and better. Two world wars should have doused the fires of these foolish illusions, but illusions have a way of making short work of reality.

Yet it is interesting that the illusions of progress that went hand in hand with these ideologies have managed to live on despite the fact that the ideologies themselves are now hiding in embarrassment or have already passed onto the junk heap of history. What is it, then, that accounts for the tenacity of the belief? It is not that contemporary people are self-consciously utopian, at least not in obvious ways. No, it is not ideology that seems to fuel this fire but *experience*. More specifically, it is the experience of science. It is the experience of a world made over by technology in which the prospects of conquering disease, discomfort, and distance are large and the expectations of limitless improvement are themselves unlimited. It is this conquest, Christopher Lasch thinks, that has given to science its current aura of immortality and, with that, the immortality of what drives it, the belief in progress.[6]

But progress in manufacturing, with superior articles superseding those of lesser quality or utility, or in science, with better understandings replacing poorer ones, is one thing; progress in the human condition is another. Yet we have demonstrated a capacity to cross over from a faith in the one kind of progress to a faith in another without so much as blinking. It is as if the ability to make better cars and better airplanes and better medicines and better theories imply an ability to

5. The evolutionary outlook has colored nineteenth- and twentieth-century thought a great deal, even among those in whom there appears to have been little consciousness of this fact. An example of this is Albert Schweitzer's paean of praise for the German mind as the pinnacle of human achievement: "When, at some future day, our period of civilization shall lie, closed and completed, before the eyes of later generations, German theology will stand out as a great, a unique phenomenon in the mental and spiritual life of our time. For nowhere save in the German temperament can there be found in the same perfection the living complex of conditions and factors — of philosophical thought, critical acumen, historical insight, and religious feeling — without which no deep theology is possible" (*The Quest of the Historical Jesus: A Critical Study of Its Progress from Reimarus to Wrede*, trans. W. Montgomery [London: Adam & Charles Black, 1911], p. 1).

6. Lasch, *The True and Only Heaven*, p. 48.

make better selves, to transcend not only our own mortality, which would be no small feat, but also our own corruption, which would be an even larger feat. It is, in fact, this assumption of an ability to move from one plateau of achievement to another that has given us a need always to be *post:* we feel compelled to assure ourselves that we are *post*-Puritan, *post*-Christian, and *post*-modern. Our world is *post*-industrial and *post*-business. Our time is *post*-Vietnam, *post*-Watergate, and *post*–Cold War.

The need to be in motion, moving toward the future, to know that we are leaving behind periods of lesser achievement and shaking ourselves free from what is obsolete, is obviously very great. And it is not in itself necessarily wrong. After all, it is the desire for improvement that drives our technology and has given us a shinier, safer, and more abundant world. And it is certainly right that we should want to leave behind the painful and humiliating memories of Vietnam, Watergate, and the Cold War. Some will also think that it is good for the national soul to put to rest the Puritan and Christian worlds as well, in order that the spirit might be unshackled from the dead weight of the past. But it is rather striking that we should now be wanting to put behind us the modernity that has made us what we are. Are we really willing to bite the hand that has fed us so well? More than that, do we really think that as modern people we can extract ourselves from the circumstances of modernity and, in the next stage in the story of our progress, become *post*-modern?

This is the heart of the contemporary intellectual dilemma, the exact nature of which is uncovered by the entirely different ways in which the word *modern* is used. From an intellectual point of view, the modern world began with the Enlightenment, with that project aimed at accounting for the whole of life strictly from within the bounds of natural reason. The modern world cast itself loose from all external authorities and saw in this double action — its rejection of authority and its location of the human interpreter in the center of reality — the ground of all human freedom. That project has now ended. The grand vision ended in modern philosophical bankruptcy as the human interpreter increasingly had nothing to say. Philosophy has slowly constricted its boundaries, to the point that it is now content to work on the small offerings of modern experience, having completely yielded its older belief that there is such a thing as truth and that it can be discovered. Its current agenda is almost entirely pragmatic or, as in Rorty's case, therapeutic. In this sense, then, modernity has died.

It is hard to pin down an exact date on which it was finally conceded that the Enlightenment experiment had miscarried. It could be argued that it was evident already toward the end of the nineteenth century, but certainly by the middle of our century the emptiness of the modern mind could no longer be concealed. But what is significant about this for our purposes is that just as the modern world was dying in its intellectual sense, it was being born in its sociological form. This birth is also difficult to date with precision, but I think it may be useful to locate the transition to what I have called Our Time in the last quarter of the nineteenth century. In this other sense, then, it was at this point that the modern world was being born.

The juxtaposition of these two worlds — of what is modern in an intellectual sense and what is modern in a cultural sense — serves to explain the strange meanderings of contemporary thought. Prior to the emergence of Our Time, intellectuals were enormously powerful in shaping the world. The Enlightenment, which produced political changes of large and sometimes devastating magnitude, was launched by philosophers. This was a time in which ideas counted. In Our Time they do not. What shapes the modern world is not powerful minds but powerful forces, not philosophy but urbanization, capitalism, and technology. As the older quest for truth has collapsed, intellectual life has increasingly become little more than a gloss on the processes of modernization. Intellectuals merely serve as mirrors, reflecting what is taking place in society. They are post-modern in the sense that they are often disillusioned with the emptiness of the old Enlightenment ideals, but they are entirely modern in that they reflect the values of the impersonal processes of modernization. And this is where we encounter the most telling of modern intellectual ambiguities: on the one hand, many intellectuals imagine that they can transcend modernity because they are modern in a sociological sense and believe in progress, but on the other hand, they feel the need to transcend the past because they know that they have to be post-modern in an intellectual sense. They are modern because they have to be post-modern.

It is certainly curious, not to say illuminating, that many of today's expressions of post-modernism are simply continuing what were seen as the anti-modernisms of a century ago. Then, roughly between 1880 and 1920, they were the recoil against modernity, the revolt against an overcivilized world. Solace was sought in the simple life, in quaint mind cures, in the revival of arts and crafts, in the quest for the self and the search for authentic experience. Now these are the means by which we are transcending modernity! Common to both cultural movements, however, is the same disillusionment, the same sense of betrayal.

It is just that now we think that we are going beyond modernity, whereas then we thought that we were standing out of its way.

Toward the end of the nineteenth century, as Our Time began to take shape and form in the psyche, the first widespread symptoms of dis-ease began to be seen. Jackson Lears has traced the progress of this dis-ease, noting how, in the first stage, the external culture began to be crippled. It lost its capacity to transmit either values or meaning, and hence it lost its power to regulate behavior. The emancipated spirits of the late nineteenth century, alive with Enlightenment ideas, imagined that they were actually remaking the world. As the external culture began to give way under this assault, however, they came to discover that the internal world was becoming more and more insubstantial. The anchorage that the internal world of the spirit had found in the supernatural order disappeared in the blaze of enlightened attitudes, and the self, now left completely to itself, cut off from God and from the outside world, began to disappear. Once severed from the larger frameworks of meaning, people became increasingly introspective, and what they gazed upon looked increasingly weightless.

It is this situation that Lears believes best explains some of the strange countermeasures that were adopted, many of which, as a matter of fact, have carried down to this day and become part of the post-modern world. As religion and personal morality both became more problematic, depression became widespread. In the 1880s, it was known as neurasthenia. To deal with this modern plague, self-help therapies of all kinds aimed at the discovery or recovery of the self flooded the market. In the 1990s, of course, they continue unabated. In the 1880s, nervousness had also become epidemic, and there were many remedies on the market to offset this malady, though they could not compare in range and sophistication with what is available for the same problems in the 1990s. In the 1880s, as connections with the past began to slip away, interest in arts and crafts revived, and not a few communities sprang up to preserve ways of life that were fast receding. At about the same time, cults of violence both benign (e.g., the martial arts) and malignant gained popularity. As the society became more fluid and unstable, the need for controls mounted; as these controls grew burdensome, there were some who longed for regeneration of society and saw violence as the way to attain it.[7] This same desire expressed itself at the end of the nineteenth century in more extensive

---

7. See Lears, *No Place for Grace: Antimodernism and the Transformation of American Culture, 1880-1920* (New York: Pantheon Books, 1981), p. 117.

newspaper coverage of violent killings and vivid descriptions of gory accidents (though in comparison to what modern audiences feast upon in the movies today, the accounts were quite mild). And for those who still longed to escape, there was fantasy. In the 1890s, adventure stories filled with heroic exploits not only achieved widespread popularity but came to constitute a staple variety of adult literature, apparently answering a need that in the post-literate world of the 1990s is being met far more commonly by movies and television.

Like these anti-modern sentiments of the nineteenth century, the desire to be post-modern seems to be an expression of our uncertainty about what our intellectual modernity has done to us. And yet we are struggling not just with a sense of uncertainty but with a sense of betrayal. The Enlightenment promises have proved to be empty, and our world, once the stage for our freedom, now looks increasingly hostile and inhospitable to us. We are in the curious position of knowing ourselves to be the children of modernity, the recipients of its blessings and the psychology that goes with them, while at the same time wanting to move beyond the part of it that has betrayed us.[8] It rarely crosses our minds that the ability to emancipate ourselves from what has betrayed us also remains beyond our grasp, another promise that cannot be met. Nevertheless, these strange ambiguities have become powerful ingredients both in the modern mind and in our modern environment.

In architecture, for example, the period of modernism is usually considered to run from the 1930s, with the introduction of the fresh direction in style and design associated with Bauhaus school in Germany, to the end of the 1960s, when it reached its summit of pure perfection in America in the work of Mies van der Rohe, after which some chastening set in and the period of post-modernism began. The breach occurred over the optimism that had driven modernism. Whether in city planning or in domestic design, the modernists had a penchant for utopianism. They thought they could break with the past,

---

8. Thomas Oden has asserted that modernity has died and that its death was everywhere evident even in the Soviet Union. This is a slightly idiosyncratic view of modernity that focuses only on its intellectual dimension and then only on this dimension as it is rooted in the Enlightenment. If modernity is to be viewed only in terms of ideas, this case might be argued with some plausibility, but this is only a partial and insufficient view. Most importantly, it fails to understand the ways in which the social environment shapes consciousness and in turn produces a set of ideas that are matched to the environment. See Oden's *After Modernity . . . What? Agenda for Theology* (Grand Rapids: Zondervan, 1991). Cf. Steven Connor, *Postmodernist Culture: An Introduction to Theories of the Contemporary* (Oxford: Basil Blackwell, 1989).

that human life was an entirely clean sheet upon which they would write. Their creations therefore opened a new chapter in style and design for which there was no obvious precedent. Every problem, it was assumed, had an answer, but the answer came from a source to which no one else had yet had access in quite the same way: modern technology. Armed with this confidence, the modernists set about re-designing life itself.

In the cities, the old and quaint was destroyed to make way for plazas and highways, the indigenous gave way to the homogenized, what was rooted in the past was supplanted by rootless new structures. Many of these bold designs in urban planning failed, however. Some were nothing less than brazen attempts at social engineering. For example, the city of Brazilia was completely planned and largely built before there were any inhabitants to fill it. It was quickly judged to be unlivable, little more than a monument to its planners' arrogance. And Mies van der Rohe's buildings in America are modernist classics — exquisitely sculptural in a cold, metallic way, the glass walls breaking down the distinction between the interior and exterior, the open interiors breaking down the distinctions between the functions of those who worked in them. It was a brave new world that the modernists were opening up, but it left out one important consideration: their buildings were often inhuman. It was because the modernist dream took no account of the human being that it could be oblivious to local culture as well as to the past. This, in fact, was the time when Philip Johnson attempted to launch his International Style, a style that could be used universally, that belonged everywhere in the world because it belonged nowhere in particular, the world cliche culture developing its own architectural voice. It failed. In fact, Robert Campbell has gone so far as to say that architecturally, "this must have been the worst period in the entire history of Western culture, except maybe the grimmest decade of the industrial revolution."[9]

The dream of remaking life was gone by 1970, and the first sign of repentance, modest though it was, was the reappearance of historical flourishes in new buildings. Architects were making their connections with the past again. In the post-modern phase, grand designs no longer sprang full blown from the architect's head, and the rampant individualism of modernism that Ayn Rand liked so well was subdued by more

9. Campbell, "1946/1969: Modern Times," *Architectural Record,* July 1991, p. 168. See also Charles Jencks, *Post-Modernism: The New Classicism in Art and Architecture* (New York: Rizzoli International, 1987).

human considerations connected to local customs, uses, habits, and human needs.[10] Modernism had a definable style because it floated above life; post-modernism has many styles because it reflects the many interests of the past as well as of the present. It is one of the voices of our multiculturalism. While this means that our architecture is no longer driven by hard ideology, it also means that in its eclecticism it is not driven by any sure purpose at all. Perhaps, then, Lears is correct in thinking that in the absence of such a purpose, the visual symbols in our cities can convey no more than modern emptiness and corruption.

The loss of an overarching purpose, which is one of the chief consequences of modernity, has deeply affected most academic fields as well. The old Enlightenment orthodoxy that a rational, objective scholarship is possible has itself fallen prey to what the Enlightenment unleashed. In the absence of assent to a body of universal truth, objectively discovered truths often reflect only the interests and disposition of the scholars concerned. In a climate of relativism, it becomes quite difficult to insist on the universal viability of one's findings. Even in science, Thomas Kuhn demonstrated that what scientists are able to see is very much determined by what they consider to be possible or what they are looking for.[11] In the arts, the revolution in perception has become even more radical. In literature, a whole generation of deconstructionists has emerged within the universities who, despite their calling to be the custodians of the nation's language, now make their living by denying that words have any meanings at all. Words mean only whatever we wish them to mean.[12] And in philosophy, Richard Rorty has asserted that the world of truths that philosophy used to explicate has collapsed and that the only reason to do philosophy now is as personal therapy; if it helps you to think in this sort of way, then you should do so, but the days when your conclusions could be accorded normativity for anyone else are gone.[13]

10. Rand outlines her architectural philosophy in *The Fountainhead* (London: Cassell, 1947). The novel's central character, Howard Roark, designs buildings "not in the tradition of the past, but only in the tradition of Howard Roark."

11. Kuhn, *The Structure of Scientific Revolutions*, 2d ed. (Chicago: Chicago University Press, 1970).

12. See David Lehman, *Signs of the Times: Deconstructionism and the Fall of Paul de Man* (London: Andre Deutsch, 1991); Brian McHale, *Post Modernist Fiction* (London: Routledge, Chapman & Hall, 1987); and Linda Hutcheon, *A Poetics of Postmodernism: History, Theory and Fiction* (New York: Routledge, Chapman & Hall, 1988).

13. See Rorty, *Philosophy and the Mirror of Nature* (Princeton: Princeton University Press, 1979). The same themes are evident in many of Rorty's other works, including *Contingency, Irony, and Solidarity* (Cambridge: Cambridge University Press,

Exactly the same pattern can be seen in theology, too, and it has been taking place at almost exactly the same time. By the end of the 1960s, perhaps signaled initially by the death-of-God theology, it was clear that the Enlightenment project had stalled. It was not that the new thinkers were ready to turn their backs on the Enlightenment; they simply proposed some corrections in it. They, too, began not with divine revelation but with human experience, not with God's interpretation of life but with the interpretation that in our self-asserted freedom we have devised for ourselves. They rejected the idea that there is any center to the meaning that they sought, any normativity to any one proposal. A host of new theologies emerged during the 1970s and 1980s inspired by and growing out of a newly important set of social and political concerns. These arose from what was seen as the oppression that blacks experienced in America, or that the poor experienced in South America, or that women experienced everywhere. It was these experiences that became the organizing centers in these new theologies, none of them making any pretension to having universal truth. They did not believe that there is such a thing. They were, therefore, expressions of our multiculturalism, and the intellectual currency in which they traded was pluralism.

Although there is little agreement as to what it means to be postmodern in theology, precisely because pluralism is at the center of it, the new theologies have typically shared a disaffection with the various forms of fragmentation that modernization has produced. Different as the theologies are, they are in this sense *post*-modern.[14] They are protestations against the rift between ourselves and nature, between ourselves and the divine order, and between individual groups and the human community. They propose to bind up what has been torn apart, in some cases by calling for a return to pantheism or for adopting a view of God's immanence that equates divine activity with the rectification of social wrongs. Such theologies thus reassert the union of nature and human

---

1989) and *Consequences of Pragmatism: Essays, 1972-1980* (Minneapolis: University of Minnesota Press, 1980). Note also Jean-François Lyotard, *The Post-Modern Condition: A Report on Knowledge,* trans. Geoff Bennington and Brian Massumi (Minneapolis: University of Minnesota Press, 1984). For a brief rebuttal of Rorty's earlier work, see Alasdair MacIntyre, "Philosophy and the 'Other' Disciplines, and Their Histories," *Soundings* 55 (Summer 1982): 127-45.

14. On post-modernism in theology see David R. Griffin, *Varieties of Postmodern Theology* (Albany: State University of New York Press, 1988), and Griffin, *Spirituality and Society: Postmodern Visions* (Albany: State University of New York Press, 1988).

nature in a whole that is religious and that gives us the ground for seeking its expression not simply as individuals but in community. In this sense, to be "post-modern" is often to be Eastern in one's spirituality.

Freudian psychology has always made a point of recognizing that there are pairs of opposing drives in the self, and what has given Freudians their distinctive stance is their recognition of the ambivalence that this produces in life. Aggression shows itself as submissiveness, rage as humility, doubt as belief. It is not difficult to see the same kind of ambivalence at work within contemporary culture. Is it not the case that the recoil against modernity in our culture expresses itself as an embrace of modernity, that the eerie sense that the self is disappearing expresses itself as the bright hope that it is being recovered, that anger over life's emptiness expresses itself as joy in its abundance, that fear over life's disintegration expresses itself as confidence in its management, and that the sense that life is beginning to unravel expresses itself as the assurance that it is all progressing?

The fact that we should continue to think of ourselves as *post*-modern rather than as merely anti-modern may therefore be more complicated than one might have guessed at first. But even the Freudians are mistaken: the continuing need to be *post* is still a telling indication of the modern mind. What it tells us, I believe, is that beneath all of the difficulties and disappointments that modernity has brought, there still resides a belief in progress; we continue to think, or perhaps fervently hope, that we are still moving toward a better future. The truth of the matter is that most Americans are impatient with nay-sayers and are disinclined to indulge, or even to attempt to understand, those who think that the basis for such hope might be gone. It is not merely that Americans typically think that such arguments are wrong; more importantly, they think that these arguments are *offensive*. They violate an important tenet of the cultural creed — namely, that there is always hope because things are always improving, despite the fact that under secular auspices there is no truth by which one can judge whether a culture is moving forward or backward.

America loves its optimists. It loves them not only because everyone prefers good news to bad but also because it needs them to affirm this cultural creed. By the same token, it dislikes pessimists. To say that a view is pessimistic is enough to destroy it even before the merits and liabilities of the argument have been aired. The pessimist is going against the cultural grain. More than that, the pessimist is assumed to be violating some kind of deep trust that lingers in the American soul about its own greatness, its destiny. Simply put, the pessimist is un-

American. That being the case, the judgments of the cultural critics who have wondered aloud about the viability of Western culture seem jaundiced and unhelpful, and this regardless of what evidence they advance in support of their judgments. They are taking away hope at the very time when it is most needed.

They may, however, be correct. It may be the case that Christian faith, which has made many easy alliances with modern culture in the past few decades, is also living in a fool's paradise, comforting itself about all of the things that God is doing in society (which is the most commonly heard religious version of this idea of progress) while it is losing its character, if not its soul. It is this theme that I want to engage in the pages that follow. Before I can do so, however, we must return to the narrative with which this chapter began. How did this new civilization, which is the context in which Christian faith must live, arise, and what is America's place in it? How might we describe it? What are its characteristics?

The New Civilization

What lies before the historic divide that occurred at some point during the nineteenth century is a mass of interwoven political, economic, and social events the outworking of which makes up the story of the West. This story continues without interruption, flowing past the divide and on into the present. However, superimposed on the story of the West, and in no way interrupting the flow of its events, is the story of this new civilization. That these two stories are going on at the same time throughout the West, but often following different paths, is what justifies some distinction between these two ages.

The interconnections between these ages are very intricate, but we can at least sketch the outlines of the story, as suggested by Geoffrey Barraclough.[15] The Age of the West in the nineteenth century can more appropriately be characterized as the European Age, for during this era the industrialized nations of Europe cast a long shadow over the earth. In the last quarter of the century, some of these nations were able to convert their industrial power into foreign dominance, dividing

15. In his *Introduction to Contemporary History,* Barraclough makes the argument that the emergence of the modern world has created so large a breach with what lay behind it as to constitute a new period in history. This new period, which he calls *contemporary,* commenced at about the beginning of the twentieth century and roughly matches what I have been referring to as Our Time.

up Africa and parts of East Asia among themselves. Their empires swallowed up a tenth of the world's population and a fifth of its land surface. America, too, felt the attractions of empire building. As a matter of fact, even before the Revolution, George Washington had spoken of the American colonies as a "rising empire" that he hoped would have a large sphere of power; some Americans even envisioned Rome as a kind of antecedent.[16] To be sure, neither Washington nor anyone else at this time could yet speak of America as a nation-state. Still, it should surprise no one that in the next century it, too, followed this old ambition and seized Puerto Rico, Guam, the Philippines, and Hawaii. Even so, its intrusion into the world in the interests of power paled into insignificance in comparison to that of the Europeans.

The era of colonial expansion lasted only for a century or so before its base in Europe began to erode. National rivalries led to two devastating world wars in the twentieth century. These produced the collapse of the political order and the emergence of America to a position of world dominance.[17] Indeed, as early as 1902, W. T. Stead wrote a small book called *The Americanization of the World; or, The Trend of the Twentieth Century.* There was evidence that this prophecy was being fulfilled in 1919, when Woodrow Wilson proposed membership for the United States in the League of Nations. He stated that his country would assume leadership in financial, industrial, and commercial matters. "What Theodore Roosevelt had envisioned some years earlier — the United States playing the dominant role in the balance of world power — was more than ever an indisputable fact," wrote Foster Dulles.[18] After the conclusion of the Second World War, the European colonial landholders were too tired to return to their possessions in Asia or to maintain their possessions in Africa. In the 1950s and 1960s, Africa purged itself of its colonial afflictions. With the wounding of Europe and the dismantling of its far-flung empire, the balance of power shifted unmistakably to America.[19]

16. See R. W. Van Alstyne, *The Rising American Empire* (Oxford: Basil Blackwell, 1960), pp. 1-27.

17. See Hajo Holborn, *The Political Collapse of Europe* (New York: Alfred A. Knopf, 1951).

18. Dulles, *America's Rise to World Power, 1898-1954* (New York: Harper, 1954), p. 128.

19. W. D. Davies has suggested that the effects of this shift in the world's center of gravity, in combination with the growth of knowledge, were also felt in the arena of American theological scholarship. "Time was," he says, "when American biblical scholars were largely dominated by European scholarship. . . . American scholars were then virtually reporters of German academic work. This has

This was not an uncontested development, however. In 1939, Communism was the creed of only one country, the Soviet Union. By the beginning of the 1980s, it had been adopted by a third of the world's peoples. Capitalism, which flourished across nine-tenths of the world in 1939, had been reduced by the 1980s to a minority position that was frequently under attack (along with its partner, democracy) in the United Nations. It is true that the 1990s have brought a completely new picture, given the stunning disintegration of Communism in central Europe and the states that once made up the Soviet Union. But prior to this time, Europe had found itself wedged between two superpowers locked in a rivalry that only served to heighten its sense of insignificance and underscore the passing of its Age.

These events form the backdrop to the breach that has occurred, to the differentiation of these two ages, but the events themselves are not the central story. What is central is not political in nature at all, nor is it limited to the territorial boundaries of the West, although it could not have come about without the achievements of the West. The nature of this new civilization is entirely different. It is rapidly becoming global in its reach, transcending the boundaries of nations, races, religions, and cultures in a completely unprecedented fashion.

The new civilization has arisen almost inadvertently from a series of stunning inventions.[20] They have capitalized on each other and accidentally produced, in their human beneficiaries, new ways of looking at life, new values, new relationships to the society at large, new priorities, new horizons — in short, a new civilization. Beneath this engine of invention has been the Industrial Revolution, the fruit of Western genius, and coming forth from it has been a reorganization of society into cities, centers of commerce and manufacture linked by astonishing lines of information and transport that in turn have become the means of yet more technological invention. What is truly remarkable about this is that such development has followed the same pattern in country after country, with little regard for indigenous habits of mind. It is creating a world civilization that is technological and urban in nature, not national and cultural, and it is pretty much the

---

changed. The explosion [of knowledge] has burst asunder the geographical pattern of the academic scene. . . . A young German scholar may now choose a post in Nashville over one in Göttingen!" This is so, he says, because of the emergence of America to a position of prominence in biblical scholarship ("Reflections on Thirty Years of Biblical Studies," *Scottish Journal of Theology* 39 [1986]: 45).

20. Michael Harrington has explored the theme of inadvertence in *The Accidental Century* (New York: Macmillan, 1965).

same whether one encounters it in London, Tokyo, Hong Kong, Tel Aviv, or Washington. It is dissolving the old order and it is erecting a new one in its place.

This new order is characterized by the rise of global politics, by public outbursts of democracy such as have occurred in China, Russia, the Baltic states, and central Europe in the 1980s and early 1990s (irruptions that are demonstrating once again that capitalism requires democracy and democracy produces capitalism), by giant interlocking economies that cannot be disengaged from one another even if some might wish to separate them, by the generation and transfer of more and more information in less and less time, and by overwhelming technological innovation. This order has given us mass wars, mass knowledge, and mass education. It has produced mass consumption, the most prevalent symbol of which is our new temple to commerce, the shopping mall. It has produced mass organization requiring giant bureaucracies, and it has injected the state into almost every aspect of life. This order has spun off new fields of specialization, and it has sent new knowledge elites into orbit. It has also caused the erosion of ties to country and place and the dissolution of many moral absolutes and much religious belief. Even before the close of the nineteenth century, Barraclough has noted, the forerunners to these new forces "were bringing about fundamental changes at practically every level of living and in practically every quarter of the globe."[21] Today this mighty rolling tide moves on unabated. What we are witnessing is a world drama, the enormity of which may be difficult to take in because we are so close to it. Indeed, we are inescapably a part of it, like small corks bobbing on the ocean's surface, moved by the great swelling forces beneath its surface.

These forces have made a mockery of the idea that Communists are this century's exotic revolutionaries and Westerners its staid conservatives, anxiously preserving their inheritance. In fact, the Communists have struggled mightily to preserve the moral order of their world of unbelief only to be left empty-handed as it has all collapsed about them. Westerners, on the other hand, have surrendered their moral order without so much as a tear. Our Time has stirred to a frenzy the relentless assault on all the old certainties, religious and moral. It has untied our hands. We are now loosed from the old bonds. We spring forth as revolutionaries, prophets in a new millennium of unbelief, sages in a new world that has no horizons, a world that recognizes only one god — Possibility. In the twinkling of an eye, we

21. Barraclough, *An Introduction to Contemporary History*, p. 4.

Westerners, once the custodians of a stable moral order, have become like loosed bats whose silent, unpredictable flight in the new civilization is an omen of something gone dreadfully wrong. It is we who are the revolutionaries; it is the Communists who must now follow us, choking on our dust, fearful of losing sight of us, for they know that we have the surest access to the Promised Land of technology.

Perhaps in time this new age will acquire a name. Perhaps this era will eventually be known as the Pacific Age, in recognition of the shift in power that has occurred and of the site of the major fountains of technological change. For now, however, we know it simply by its processes and results: modernization and modernity, secularization and secularism. It is my contention that of these two sets of couplets, the former are primary and the latter are derivative. Modernity is the consequence of modernization as secularism is the consequence of secularization. These relationships are fundamental to understanding Our Time, so we need to explore them a little further here, especially since so many meanings have been attached to each of these terms.

Modernization and Modernity

Modernization is the process that requires that our society be organized around cities for the purpose of manufacturing and commerce. It is, therefore, a process driven by capitalism and fueled by technological innovation. These forces have reshaped our social landscape and, in turn, have reshaped our inner lives as we have been drawn into the vortex they have created. And it is this vortex that I am calling modernity.

The assumption here is one upon which the sociology of knowledge in particular is predicated — namely, that the external social environment provides the explanation of internal consciousness, that the way we think is a product of the society in which we live.[22] This assumption has not passed without criticism, for it makes a hard and destructive determinism inescapable and it can also produce a harsh cynicism about all knowledge.

We could well think, in this connection, of the optimistic sociological projections that have often been made about the disappearance of all religion in countries that are modernizing. A variety of early regional

22. See, for example, Peter L. Berger and Thomas Luckman, *The Social Construct of Reality: A Treatise in the Sociology of Knowledge* (Garden City, N.Y.: Doubleday, 1966); and Jürgen Habermas, *Knowledge and Human Interests* (Boston: Beacon Press, 1972).

studies showed that modernization is not friendly to religion, and a number of theorists concluded that religion would decline in a country to the extent that it became modernized. But America has proved a stubborn obstacle to the triumph of this theory, for while this country is highly modernized, it also remains highly religious. It was this contradiction of the theory that led Peter Berger to reevaluate the older sociological orthodoxy and to propose that while the social context is significant, there is also a "dialectic" that operates between external context and internal consciousness and allows the traffic to go in both directions. Alasdair MacIntyre has argued in a similar fashion.[23] This is the understanding of modernization that I am drawing on in this discussion. It is the context without which thought, internal psychology, and behavior are inexplicable, and yet they are not simply its products. The social context exercises a shaping influence but not an inescapable determinism.[24] In passing, I might note that theological constructions that avoid the reality of this shaping influence may look nice, but in the end they simply prove to be irrelevant. The context of modernization is unavoidable, discomfiting though it may be. It is, in Berger's words, the "fiery brook" through which the theologian must pass.

What is novel about our situation is not the fact of cities but their size and social dominance.[25] Cities have grown in size because an expanding population has emptied into them. World population has doubled in the past fifty years, and it is projected that by the year 2000 at least another billion and a half people will have joined this crowded earth. Already there are over four hundred cities with populations of over a million people. In 1975, just over 39 percent of the world's people lived in urban areas; in the year 2000, the overall figure is projected to be 79 percent. In the industrialized countries of the West, including America, the figure is projected to be about 95 percent. This

---

23. See MacIntyre, *Secularization and Moral Change* (London: Oxford University Press, 1967).

24. Berger's "dialectic" is an attempt to distinguish the social determination of ideas from their social determinism. He sees a whole series of tensions at work which entail that the world we know is not simply created *in* us but is also created *by* us. He points to tensions between the poles of animality and sociality, nature and society, givenness and possibility, lower and higher, substructure and superstructure, external and internal, facticity and intentionality, self and society. See Os Guinness, "Towards a Reappraisal of Apologetics: Peter L. Berger's Sociology of Knowledge as the Sociological Prolegomena to Christian Apologetics" (Ph.D. diss., Oxford University, 1981), pp. 17-20.

25. See J. John Palen, *The Urban World*, 3d ed. (New York: McGraw-Hill, 1987).

suggests a drastic reshaping of our social environment, a radical departure from what prevailed only a hundred years ago.

In the Third World, cities are not always places of significant industry and commerce; they are much more commonly gathering places for refugees, for the displaced, for exiles, and especially for the young and poor. Today there is not a single Third World city in which the median age of the inhabitants is over twenty. Moreover, 85 percent of the residents of these cities fall below the poverty line, as compared with 18 percent of the residents in cities of the industrialized countries.[26]

In the West, and particularly in America, the cities are not so much homes to the people as they are centers to which they commute for various purposes, principally to work. It is in the cities of the West, constructed as they are to meet the demands of the capitalistic machine, that the values of modernity principally arise. In this context, the term *modernity* refers to the public environment created largely by urbanization, the moral etiquette, style of thought, and relationships of which are shaped by the large, impersonal structures that fill it.

I will explore these values in various ways during the course of this book, but some suggestions as to what is in view are in order here. Perhaps most importantly, at least for Christian faith, this reorganization of society sunders public from private life, creating two spheres in which different values operate; this places a strain on us to be amphibious, to learn to move smoothly from one world to the other each day.[27] The one world is defined by personal relations, and the other by functions within the capitalistic machine. The one is made up of the small insulated islands that are created by home, family, and personal friends, and the other by the interconnected functions of a mammoth system of production and distribution of goods and services in which individuals are important not for who they are or even for the values and beliefs they hold but for what they *do*. In this public world, personal relations may actually become impediments; success in this world may well depend on one's capacity to be impersonal if the efficiency of the business or enterprise requires it.

There are few people who know us in both our worlds — and fewer yet in the circle of those who are important to us. A sense of

26. I am indebted to David Barrett for these figures, which were made available to the plenary speakers at Lausanne II, the international congress on world evangelization that was held in Manila in 1989 and sponsored by the Lausanne Committee for World Evangelization.

27. For more on this, see Arthur Brittan, *The Privatised World* (London: Routledge & Kegan Paul, 1977), pp. 45-76.

anonymity pervades much of our public life, serving as a lubricant to hasten the passage of the new values. These new values arise when work is sundered from character. Gone are the days when we knew the wheelwrights and cobblers who worked for us. The anonymity of our world makes accountability a vague and abstract virtue. The cord has been broken by the distance that has cropped up between the worker and the consumer, a distance imposed by the complexities of modern factory production and the many layers of people who are, in one way or another, involved in the sale and distribution of the product. In the whole process, the worker is disengaged from any sense of responsibility for the quality of the product, any sense of accountability to the person who eventually purchases the product.

The modern workplace not only diminishes accountability but also undercuts the cogency of religious belief and morality. Cities create their own psychological environments by bringing together in close proximity a wide range of worldviews, cultural and ethnic differences, and personal values. The kind of pluralism that is necessary to eliminate antagonisms among the competing views has the effect of reducing the values of each inhabitant to the lowest common denominator. City life requires the kind of friendliness that allows us to cohabit with the mass ethic.[28] It is typically assumed that this sort of friendliness must be divested of moral and religious judgment, since it is difficult for our society to see how judgments about truth and and morals can escape the charge of social bigotry. And so we settle for the kind of friendliness within which all absolutes perish either for lack of interest or because of the demands of the social etiquette.

Once this public life has thus been cut loose from the moorings of the private world, it is inevitably coopted by and hitched up to the machinery of the technological age. Our cognitive ceilings have fallen in on us, leaving only a flat, naturalistic plane along which we view reality and within which the sole ethic is efficiency: what is faster or more productive is good, regardless of its effects on the environment or its cost to people.[29] And this technology powerfully shifts our atten-

28. See Christopher Lasch, *The Culture of Narcissism: American Life in an Age of Diminishing Expectations* (New York: W. W. Norton, 1978), pp. 52-70.

29. In the development of his philosophy of society, Jacques Ellul argues that the fundamental factor in modern social life is rationality. It is rationally ordered, reflecting the uniformity and standardization of its technology. This yields Ellul his key term, *technique*. It is technique that dominates all ethical formulations. See Ellul, *The Technological Society*, trans. John Wilkinson (New York: Alfred A. Knopf, 1964), pp. 3-22.

tion into the future as we are increasingly forced to anticipate and adapt to the oncoming change.[30] This, in turn, produces high levels of anxiety, as we are compelled to focus on the future in anticipation of what is to come, a process that cuts us off from the past almost entirely. It was this effect that Oswald Spengler foresaw, remarkably, at the turn of our century. The "industry of machines," he said, was coming to stand at the center of Western society, and without our being aware of the transformation that is occurring, this mechanistic environment "completely dominates the formulation of ideas and the deduction of so-called laws."[31]

This is the context in which the discussion about the *mass society* first arose, a term whose usefulness has now been overrun by the debate that it provoked. That Our Time is characterized by (and has become a distinct period because of) mass wars, mass consumption, mass education, and mass knowledge is hardly debatable. The question is what all of this means.

There can be little doubt that the effect of modernity is to diminish the importance of what is private in relation to what is public, to sever ties to place, to community, and to family with the result that those who are cut loose are made vulnerable to being reshaped in the image of modernity in a way that was not possible earlier.[32] Those who have contended that modernity makes its recipients passive and empty may perhaps have overstated their case at times; certainly Christopher Lasch's contention that modern culture is inherently narcissistic provoked much indignation.[33] Yet the fact remains that as modernity has

30. Peter L. Berger, *Facing Up to Modernity: Excursions in Society, Politics, and Religion* (New York: Basic Books, 1977), pp. 73-75.

31. Spengler, *The Decline of the West: Form and Actuality*, 2 vols., trans. Charles Francis Atkinson (New York: Alfred A. Knopf, 1929), 2: 469.

32. For an elaboration of this theme, see Jacques Ellul, *Propaganda: The Formation of Men's Attitudes* (New York: Random House, 1973).

33. Peter Homans and L. Shannon Jung offered representative assessments of the thesis that Lasch put forth in *The Culture of Narcissism*, both for and against. Homans declared Lasch to be brilliantly incisive and described his book as "so devastating that it can arouse . . . either a sense of stoic resignation or a frantic desire to rescue society" ("Narcissism Viewed from the Perspective of the History and Psychology of Western Religion," *Journal of Religion* 62 [April 1982]: 186). Jung, on the other hand, dismissed Lasch as irritating and misguided and charged that his book was marred by apocalypticism and pessimism, that it employed confused intellectual categories, and that it projected onto society Lasch's own private forbodings to the extent that "many academic and socially concerned Americans will be irritated" with it ("Beyond Narcissism," *Religion in Life* 49 [Summer 1980]: 211-12).

dissolved the links by which people have been rooted in time and place, it has drawn them into the large impersonal centers of modern culture, only to make those places the centers of loneliness, despite the presence of the many who crowd into them. Mass society is a reality, and because it is unable to fulfill the functions that communities and families once filled, it forces those it embraces to look into themselves for meaning in life.[34]

The centers of modern cultures have nothing to do with geography. In America, for example, they are not identical with Washington, or the places from which power is exercised, although at times they may coincide with these places. Rather, they have to do with a number of large, interlocking systems that form the structure of the society — the economy, for example, and the political world, state and federal government, the universities which manufacture and disseminate knowledge, and the mass media which manufacture and disseminate the images by which we largely understand ourselves. Each of these systems surrounds and envelops us, in the process intruding into our consciousness and carrying its values with it. It is true that those who work within these mega-systems often have little idea that the system of which they are a part really does touch the lives of the citizens, for so many of these structures are impersonal, remote in their workings, and pervaded by a sense of anonymity. Nevertheless, they do impart a sense of what is right and what is wrong, what is important and what is not. Indeed, in a time of growing fragmentation, it is the common experience of these various centers that preserves some level of unity in life by offering a set of common talking points, although this unity is admittedly more a matter of shared experience than of any common agenda or common outlook.

Those who dominate these systems are at the center of power, for the systems in which they work so envelop the citizenry that their operators now have access to the lives of ordinary citizens in a way that is without precedent. Indeed, they now exercise more power than was within the reach of most medieval potentates. In the Middle Ages, presumably, it was possible to live one's life without constantly thinking about the local baron; in America it is impossible to live one's life without a constant awareness of government and its regulations, the vagaries of the economy, the way in which the news is presented, and the way in which global events impinge on local

34. On the question of the mass society, see Edward Shils, *The Constitution of Society* (Chicago: University of Chicago Press, 1982), pp. 93-109.

circumstances.[35] The problem, of course, is that this center is a vortex that draws all of our consciousness into it — and within it there is only emptiness.

This also seems to explain the cultural prominence that managers have acquired in the modern world. They are what stands between human life and chaos, making all of the uncertain possibilities of a life that has few guidelines and markers seem tame and controllable. Indeed, they are the high priests in a rationalizing process. I use the word *rationalizing* here not philosophically (in reference to rationalism) nor psychologically (to suggest an attempt to get around the facts) but sociologically, of the mental counterpart to the technological world. In the technological world, all processes are assumed to be rational in the sense that they are all driven by cause and effect within logically understood systems.[36] It is the experience of this world that leads us to think that the rest of life is like this, too, and it is the manager who gives daily expression to it. The territory under his or her domain is rendered orderly and comprehensible, the flow charts banish any mysteries about how work should be done, and the mechanization of the work is transferred to the relations between the workers. Thus the organization comes to resemble the finely tuned machine that it is meant to reflect. While all of this may be extolled in the interests of greater productivity, it is also the case that it answers the psychological need to reduce the large uncertainties that now encase life to proportions that seem more manageable and less threatening.

I have provided only a spare sketch, but I think it should be sufficient to indicate the way in which I am using the terms *modernization* and *modernity*. Modernization involves the process of social change that has resulted in our urban-centered life. Modernity involves the values that arise from these social changes — values that seem, despite their relativity and anti-religious bias, to offer the only appropriate ways of looking at life amid the technological pyramids that we are building. Modernization and modernity, then, are related as the hand is to the glove, or as the soul is to the body. The former gives life and plausibility to the latter; the latter gives psychological expression to the former.

35. Robert Wuthnow has explored well the theme of the intrusiveness of government in matters of religion. See the statement of this theme in *The Restructuring of American Religion: Society and Faith since World War II* (Princeton: Princeton University Press, 1990), pp. 6-8, 114-17, 319-22.

36. See Peter L. Berger, Brigitte Berger, and Hansfried Kellner, *The Homeless Mind: Modernization and Modern Consciousness* (New York: Random House, 1979), pp. 111-15.

Secularization and Secularism

In identifying modernization as the fundamental force behind the creation of Our Time, I am departing from a broad and angry consensus among the religious that what is most obnoxious about our culture is the growth and persistence of "secular humanism."[37] This perception is not altogether beside the point, but in limiting the causes of irreligion to *ideas* alone, this consensus overlooks the whole social climate, brought about by our new social arrangements, that makes those ideas seem plausible and even inevitable to so many people. It is a social climate that, as we shall see, creates problems for belief that are quite as pernicious and difficult as the problems generated by those who consider themselves to be secular humanists. The very context that makes "secular humanism" formidable is also able to transform religion — even the religion of those who are vociferously opposed to "secular humanism."

It is axiomatic that secularism strips life of the divine, but it is important to see that it does so by relocating the divine in that part of life which is private. Viewing the process from one angle, one can quite validly say that secular humanism is irreligious in its effects; from another angle, it is equally valid to say that it allows for a cohabitation with religion under certain circumstances. Those who have become alarmed by its first aspect, attacking "secular humanism" for its irreligion in the public sphere, may sometimes have done us a disservice by failing to acknowledge its other aspect, its effect in the private sphere, its religiousness. By labeling this foe as they have, these critics have hitched up secularism to humanism in such a way that they do not appear to consider the possibility that secularism might be associated with anything other than humanism. I think it beyond question that there is in fact a worldview that we can appropriately refer to as "secular humanism." But I would argue that there is also something we can appropriately call "secular religiosity" and, indeed, something that could be called "secular evangelicalism." By linking secularism to humanism exclusively, its opponents have established a definitional quarantine that may well blind them to the many other places in which secularism is at work. Specifically, it appears to be blinding them to the way in which secularism is restructuring the Christian ministry — a matter to which I return in a later chapter.

37. For a further elaboration of these issues, see Robert Wuthnow, *The Struggle for America's Soul: Evangelicals, Liberals, and Secularism* (Grand Rapids: William B. Eerdmans, 1989).

In much the same way, the opponents of religion, especially in Europe, have selectively identified certain things as being "really religious." Chief among these has been the church and its belief. Secularism is therefore understood as the process whereby the areas of life over which the church exercises control are returned to the state and a new set of rules is established in place of the old. This is, as David Martin contends, a convenient way of showing that these anti-religious ideologies do now "triumph over such recalcitrant phenomena," for in Europe the church is shrinking.[38] But such a definition tells us little about either secularism or religion, even in Europe. Certainly in the United States, where church and state are constitutionally separated, the definition must be different. In fact, so diverse are the definitions of *secularism* that the functional facility of the word is in some jeopardy.[39]

Secularism is best seen as having two components. What is external and sociological I am calling *secularization;* what is internal and ideological I am calling *secularism.* From the one perspective, what we are describing is the outlook and the values that arise in a society that is no longer taking its bearings from a transcendent order; from another perspective, what we are describing is the track that modernization has taken within the psyche in producing and authenticating those values.

We begin by noting that this is a unique cultural moment. Beneath all of the other major cultures were religious assumptions, whether these came from Hinduism, Islam, or Christianity itself.[40] There are no such religious assumptions beneath our culture, however, and this is the first time any major civilization has attempted to build itself in this way. Our public life finds neither its justification nor its direction from a divine or supernatural order, nor is it dependent, according to Bryan Wilson, on "the maintenance of religious thinking, practices or institutions";[41] it finds its justification, its life, and its direction only from itself. To be sure, assent to such fundamental Christian

38. Martin, *The Religious and the Secular: Studies in Secularization* (New York: Schocken Books, 1969), p. 9.

39. On the range of meanings that attach to the word *secular,* see Martin, *The Religious and the Secular,* pp. 48-57.

40. Both Arnold Toynbee and Christopher Dawson considered the role of religion in other cultures axiomatic. With respect to Dawson's work, see *Religion and World History: A Selection from the Works of Christopher Dawson,* ed. James Oliver and Christina Scott (Garden City, N.Y.: Doubleday-Image, 1975).

41. Wilson, *Religion in Secular Society* (Baltimore: Penguin Books, 1969), p. 258.

beliefs as the existence of God and a moral order, the divinity of Christ, and the inspiration of Scripture remains remarkably high, but these beliefs appear to be stranded on the beaches of private consciousness; certainly they are not appealed to in any debate over the shape of our corporate life. The public square, as Richard Neuhaus has argued, is "naked," stripped of its old values.[42] There is no core of values that is accorded wide assent or commonly invoked in order to regulate the competing interests that jostle one another all the time in a society such as this. Indeed, the assertion that we ought to appeal to such core values is viewed as anti-democratic, as essentially antagonistic to the diversity that is anxiously seeking a public outlet, even though that diversity may threaten the very democracy in whose name it asks for expression.

Neuhaus is also concerned that the new vacuum in the public square may be pushing us ever closer to the dangers of either anarchy or totalitarianism, mindless chaos or mind-chilling control.[43] As a matter of fact, we may have taken the first, small steps into the darkness of this dilemma already. Our drug-infested, crime-ridden inner cities have become miniature workshops in which we can see how the inherent instability of our social order can easily lead to complete disorder. Where those who have no stake in the preservation of order are able to out-muscle those who do, where there is no dynamic operating except that of raw power, then either chaos is not far away or the outer limits of the permissible means of control and law enforcement are being tested. The knife edge between chaos and control is where democracy flourishes, but democracy without a common core of values with which to mediate and moderate the conflicts of competing special interests has yet to be tried. It is this vacuum in our social world, this emptiness, this awesome fragility, this demise of so much that has made Western civilization a truly great civilization that has opened the way for the emergence of pluralism. Among all of the fruits of modernization, it is pluralism, Berger believes, that poses the most significant objection to Christian faith, and so we need briefly to get it in focus.

In society there is no longer any center of values that exerts a centripetal force on our collective life, and in religion the theological center that once held together thought and practice, private and pub-

---

42. See Neuhaus, *The Naked Public Square: Religion and Democracy in America* (Grand Rapids: William B. Eerdmans, 1984).
43. Neuhaus, *The Naked Public Square*, pp. 78-93.

lic, has likewise disappeared. The new emptiness at the heart of both society and religion has been filled by their respective forms of pluralization. What was once a single universe in each case has broken apart into a mass of smaller, independent worlds that are now moving away on their own trajectories. Since this pattern is being repeated in different ways, there are different kinds of pluralization.

In society, these "worlds" are made up of the small units of meaning — "sub-worlds" — in which we exist and through which we pass, perhaps even several times a day.[44] These worlds all have their own values, their own cognitive horizons, their own reasons for and ways of doing things, their own class interests. In many cases, the only things connecting these worlds are the people who shuttle among them. We move from the relationships and values of the family setting to an entirely different set of relationships and values in the workplace, from professional friends to whom we relate in one kind of way to personal friends to whom we relate in another, from service organizations to the larger business and bureaucratic structures in society that we must inhabit at least informationally and psychologically, from the catastrophes and crises beamed into our consciousness each evening by the TV news programs to the soft-peddled amusements and hardcore pornography served up by the entertainment industry.[45] Then we go to church. And lying across these worlds, sometimes identifying with them and sometimes disengaging from them, are the further subcultures associated with age, ethnic background, class interest, and occupation. To move among these multiple worlds smoothly, we have to master the many languages of survival. Not many will be able to surmount this cultural diversity without considerable cognitive dissonance. If society's emptiness produces what Durkheim called *anomie,* the breakdown of social cohesion and then of the meaning of things, then cognitive dissonance produces psychological confusion and anxiety. There was a time when both society and religion were held together by centripetal forces, but now each is being pulled apart by

44. For an exploration of the intersections of these small "sub-worlds" of meaning, see Peter L. Berger, *The Precarious Vision: A Sociologist Looks at Social Fictions and Christian Faith* (Garden City, N.Y.: Doubleday, 1961), pp. 8-101.

45. With the advent of the videocassette recorder and the pervasive availability of pornographic material, ethical resistance is apparently crumbling among evangelicals. A recent survey of clergy, who as a group ranked significantly more conservative than laity in matters of sexual ethics, indicated that 20 percent of the respondents view pornographic matter at least once a month ("The War within Continues," *Leadership* 9 [Winter 1988]: 24).

centrifugal forces, and this is significantly affecting the way in which we see our world.

While it seems to be the case that secularization is the cause and cultural pluralization is the effect, there can be little doubt that, as Berger has argued, each strengthens the other.[46] Our experience of cultural pluralization produces a greater emptiness in the center, and the emptiness in the center in turn demands more pluralization. This constant pressure away from any unifying focus gives powerful impetus to yet another form of pluralization, the breakdown in the unity of our knowledge and the emergence in its place of a mass of specialized fields and disciplines, each with its own assumptions, procedures, and criteria for judgment.

This development has at least been a boon to the publishers of popular magazines. Since 1950, magazines have proliferated at twice the rate of the population's growth. They have served to create nationwide fraternities of people who do not know one another but who nonetheless share in a weekly communion of glossy layouts. Beautiful women, motorbikes, ski slopes, guns, and hundreds of other interests hold the various fraternities together. As entertainment and diversion, this experiment in specialization may not be problematic, but it becomes downright pernicious when we are trying to make sense out of our total world. We shop today in what Bryan Wilson has called a "random supermarket of knowledge."[47] It is the randomness, the lack of connection, the independence of these private worlds of knowing, that fractures reality. If we understand what the physicists are talking about, the sociologists make no sense to us; if we accept Carl Sagan's perspective on the world, we may not be able to enter into Solzhenitsyn's mind. The supermarket in which we shop for knowledge is at once a testimony to our genius in mastering the world and of our capacity for breaking up reality.

The psychological fallout from this constant barrage of changing experiences, changing scenarios, changing worlds, changing worldviews, and changing values — the multilingual commerce of our everyday experience — is dramatic. On the one hand, it greatly accentuates the importance of novelty and spontaneity, as with each new situation, each new opportunity, each new alternative we have

46. Berger contends that secularization produces pluralization, and pluralization increases the secularizing process, but it is pluralization that produces the more serious threat to religion. See Berger, *The Heretical Imperative: Contemporary Possibilities of Religious Affirmation* (Garden City, N.Y.: Doubleday, 1980), p. xi.

47. Wilson, *Religion in Secular Society*, p. 106.

to make a choice.[48] We are, in fact, caught up in a whirlwind of choices that is tearing at the very foundations of our stability. If societies in Eastern Europe under the dominance of Marxist regimes languished for lack of choice, we languish from having too many choices to make. We sometimes define freedom not as the ability to choose but as the opportunity to avoid having to choose. Freedom means being able to "drop out."[49] On the other hand, the relativity and impermanence of everything from values to possessions creates a deep sense of "homelessness," even of lostness, of not belonging, of not having roots in our world, of being unable to find a permanent niche into which we can fit.[50] Amid the peals of freedom, these are the modern thunderclaps of damnation.

The Emperor's Lost Clothes

In the past, Western society was held together by three sinews: tradition, authority, and power. To change the image, these were the garments that covered Western society, and without them it has become indecent. Of these three, tradition might have been the first to go, although it went hand in hand with authority. Tradition is the process whereby one generation inducts its successor into its accumulated wisdom, lore, and values. The family once served as the chief conduit for this transmission, but the family is now collapsing, not merely because of divorce but as a result of affluence and the innovations of a technological age. In a video-saturated culture in which, to play on Auden's lines, "anguish comes by cable, / And the deadly sins can be bought in tins / With instructions on the label," film and television now provide the sorts of values that were once provided by the family. And public education, which used to be another conduit for such value, has also contracted out of this business, pleading that it has an obligation to be value-neutral. So it is that in the new civilization that is emerging, children are lifted away from the older values like anchorless boats on a rising tide.

48. The experience of pluralism creates the need for spontaneity and unpredictability, but the Hegelian mind-set capitalizes on it, as in Jürgen Moltmann's concept of "hope" or his notion of play. See, for example, his *Theology of Play*, trans. Reinhard Ulrich (New York: Harper & Row, 1972).

49. See Erich Fromm, *Escape from Freedom* (New York: Avon Books, 1969).

50. Western individualism further accentuates the sense of loneliness that naturally arises within the context of modernity. See Peter L. Berger, "Western Individuality: Liberation and Loneliness," *Partisan Review* 52 (1985): 323-36.

At the same time, society finds that it can no longer recognize appeals to authority, for any transcendent realm in which these appeals might be lodged has vanished from sight. This is evident in many contexts — in art, literature, philosophy, politics — but a single pattern is common to them all. First, the Christian theism on which Western societies were built was replaced by idealism of one kind or another. This idealism still had a transcendent interest, but it was no longer theistic. Then the idealism collapsed during the nineteenth century. Initially it was replaced by a kind of humanism that was elevated in its ethical and aesthetic interests,[51] but as such it had no durable conceptual base, and so it fell apart. In the political arena it gave way to various totalitarianisms — on the left to Lenin and Marx, and on the right to Hitler and Mussolini. These have now passed, but the moral vacuum they filled for a time remains, not only in politics but in many other aspects of life as well.

The three tendons have thus been reduced. Tradition and authority have been severed; only power remains. It is power alone that must direct our corporate life, power severed from a moral order that might contain and correct it and from the values of the past that might inform it. In a strange testimony to this inner vacuum, the profession of law has risen to such prominence in America that 70 percent of all the lawyers in the world practice here. In the absence of moral obligation and a sense of what is right, disputes are extraordinarily difficult to resolve, and so the set of rules that has emerged under the law must take on duties that were once shouldered by a variety of other institutions — the family, the schools, the church. Now we are left with only the lawyers. It is a terrible thing, Solzhenitsyn said, to live in a society (such as that in the former Soviet Union) where there is no law; it is also a terrible thing to live in a society (such as that in America) where there are only lawyers.

Of course these developments are not solely the result of the impersonal forces of modernization. Our intellectuals have had a hand in it all as well, especially those who have carried along the revolution in thought that the Enlightenment unleashed. The first source of this change in our world created the proud, erect creator who would remake all of life in his or her image; the second source gave to this

---

51. On the older type of humanism, see the description and critique offered by Rosalind Murray in *The Good Pagan's Failure* (New York: Longman, Green, 1939) and more generally Thomas Molnar's *The Pagan Temptation* (Grand Rapids: William B. Eerdmans, 1987).

creator a world in which to live where the illusion seemed to be true. If we were to begin on the one side with Immanuel Kant, we would hear the argument that although we must assume the existence of God if we are to explain ourselves to ourselves as moral beings, yet we cannot know him. Indeed, we do not even know external reality in itself; all we know is our own ideas about external reality, and these ideas do not necessarily correspond with what is there. But from Kant's time to our own day, increasingly the dissolution of religious belief has meant that the source of "authority" could be found only in private, critical self-consciousness, be this at a popular or an academic level. Modern scientific method, therefore, has given a set of rules to the outworkings of critical self-consciousness that produces a substitute set of absolutes, a morality that dictates what will be allowed to pass for legitimate knowledge and what will not.[52] And from the other side, in almost every experience we have of the modern world, from its business enterprises to its television shows, the same conclusion is assumed to be inarguable: the only authority that now remains is that of private experience.

In the nineteenth century in particular, there were numerous attempts to establish a system of morals that did not need to assume the existence of God and his revelation. These experiments were all conducted by a small avant-garde made up of philosophers, novelists, and artists. What has changed is that now the whole of society has become avant-garde. It is the whole of society that is now engaged in this massive experiment to do what no other major civilization has done — to rebuild itself deliberately and self-consciously without religious foundations. And the bottom line of this endeavor is that truth in any absolute sense has gone. Truth, like life, is fractured. Like experience, it is disjointed. Like our perceptions of ourselves, it is uncertain. It takes on different appearances as we move between the small units of meaning that make up our social experience. Like our manners, it must be adapted to each context and it must remain flexible. It is simply a type of etiquette. It has no authority, no sense of rightness, because it can no longer find any anchorage in anything absolute. If it persuades, it does so because our experience has given it its persuasive power — but tomorrow our experience might be different.

52. This theme has been explored incisively by Van Austin Harvey in *The Historian and the Believer: The Morality of Historical Knowledge and Christian Belief* (Philadelphia: Westminster Press, 1981).

I am using the term *secularism*, then, to refer to the values of the modern age, especially where these lead to the restructuring of thought and life to accommodate the absence or irrelevance of God. *Secularization* is the process that creates the public environment in which these values seem natural and inevitable. Secularization, therefore, is almost a synonym for modernization; secularization is that aspect of the modernizing process that produces the values of secularism. Secularization and secularism are related to one another as the glove is to the hand or as the body is to the soul. The former is the public environment created by the modernizing process that produces a conscious counterpart that is its echo and in which the sound of God and of the transcendent order are never heard; the latter is the psychological reflex to our reshaped society.

Not surprisingly, these developments in the modern world have produced what Berger calls a "plausibility crisis" for Christian faith.[53] It is his assumption that Christian belief, like any other kind of belief involving a worldview, needs a set of social relations, a structure of relationships, in which that worldview is seen to "make sense." It is this external network that authenticates the internal belief. The problem facing Christians today is that this network, this structure of relationships, has been profoundly undermined. Outside is a world that ignores what is most important to Christians and that is in fact now organizing itself on the basis of that rejection. Within the larger society, secularism seems natural because its context gives it plausibility; within that same society, Christian faith seems odd, and the context strips it of truthfulness. The bias of our experience in the modern world tilts heavily against a perception that the Christian faith is true and equally heavily toward a perception that secularism is true.

The Boiling of the Frog

It might be argued that this seems like an unusually bleak perspective to offer in the absence of war, at a time when the Western world is

---

53. Modernization threatens all religions with a loss of certainty among their adherents, but in the West this has been the fate of Christianity in particular. This is what Berger calls a "plausibilty crisis." It arises when society is so structured as to make the tenets of faith seem not to be true. In our culture, this development is closely related to the fact that Christians are increasingly seen to be a minority that is being pushed to the periphery by the processes of modernization. Society does not confirm the truthfulness of faith, but it does have the capacity to offer many apparent disconfirmations of it. See Berger, *The Sacred Canopy: Elements of a Sociology of Religion* (Garden City, N.Y.: Doubleday, 1969), pp. 127-53.

awash with plenty, when Communism is retreating on all sides, when the oil is flowing without hindrance from the Middle East. Is it not the case, further, that the Church has throughout its history been surrounded by unbelief? Are the modern forms of unbelief different from those of the past in any way other than their modernity? Unbelief is still unbelief, however it expresses itself. Has not the predicament of the Church implied in this description of the modern world also been exaggerated? Is it not likewise unduly bleak? Indeed, it could even be argued that the West in general and America in particular are moving toward their final ascendancy and that the Church has its best days before it as it shares in this triumph, even as it goes about the necessary business of preaching the gospel.

In the end, only the prophet knows where a nation stands and where the outer boundary that God has placed on its life lies (see Acts 14:15-17; 17:26-28). Nor is it important for anyone else to be able to see this exactly, though in the contemporary world there is much profit to be had from pretending to this knowledge. It is important, however, to see how contemporary cultural developments are shaping the psyche, regardless of how they are going to play out in the nation's future, for this is the only resting place Christian faith has in this generation. Is it the case, then, that today's unbelief is not essentially different from that in the past?

What is new about Our Time is not the presence of modernization or the fact that Christian faith is forced, with or without its consent, to be cognizant of the reshaping of the world. After all, the Protestant Reformation was linked over four centuries ago with the transformation of the medieval world, as one set of social arrangements began to give way to another and the seeds of the modern world were sown. It is open to question whether the link was exactly what Max Weber proposed in *The Protestant Ethic and the Spirit of Capitalism*, but it is hard to deny that what would have been a social revolution without Luther became a religious reformation with him. The cause of Protestant faith soared on the wings of moral and religious discontent in an order already well on the way to dissolution. It was given a voice by technological innovations such as movable type. It traveled along the fissures that were widening in a world in which ideological and political tranquillity could not be sustained. It personalized faith at the very moment when the economic order was becoming individualized through capitalism. In these and many other ways, Protestant faith emerged with the breakdown of the old medieval order and hastened the new social order in a fashion that makes it scarcely credible to contend that the contemporary interplay between Protestant faith and modernity is some kind of novelty. Is it not the case, then, that the argument is greatly overdrawn that we are now entering a new age, an age characterized by larger obstacles of unbelief? The novelty of Our Time, I believe, lies not so much in the fact that it is modern as in three other considerations.

First, modern consciousness is being shaped by a *world* civilization and not merely the homogeneous culture of a particular nation that is in the throes of being modernized. This is not an insignificant difference; in fact, it is what sets us apart from all of those who, prior to this time, have lived within societies in which modernization has been taking place. A civilization that is global in its nature is stripped of all the particularities of any one culture. It belongs to no particular time, place, or people. It is able to become global *because* it is drained of many of those things that ordinarily constitute particular cultures. It is able to belong to everyone because it belongs to no one.

The reasons for the transcultural character of the modern consciousness undoubtedly derive from the fact that capitalism and technology belong to no one in particular, make no bonds in any particular place, and so can flourish in all cultures. This is what the Marxists used to see when they talked about the "alienation of the marketplace," little realizing that the state bureaucracy they spawned would produce its own kind of alienation that would eat away at the vitals of a culture and be just as impersonal as the laws of the marketplace. Indeed, the disdain of this kind of bureaucracy for common people was sharply exposed in the extraordinary reversals recently suffered by the Communist regimes of Europe and the Soviet Union. We have also seen the supranational character of capitalism at work in China. In a remarkable piece of symbolism, on the very night in 1989 when pro-democracy demonstrators were being excoriated by an official spokesman on national television as exponents of "bourgeois liberalism," the broadcast was immediately followed by an advertisement touting Maxwell House coffee to Chinese consumers as "American coffee, for the good life." At the very moment the protests were being so brutally put down, had one looked out on the streets of Shanghai, one would also have seen beyond the government's troops the Marlboro man rounding up strays, and in many other cities in China, even as America and its ideals were being attacked, Coca Cola was being purchased in large quantities.[54]

54. See Fox Butterfield, "American Presence in China Is Small but Far-Reaching," *International Herald Tribune*, 20 July 1989, p. 2.

Modernization has meant a vastly extended control over nature, disease, human mortality, and the circumstances of everyday life; it has also meant that as part of that triumph we must live with "asphalt-culture, uniformity and standardization." What it has brought forth, as Emil Brunner has observed, is "universal cliche-culture, the same films and musical hits from New York to Tokyo, from Cape Town to Stockholm, the same illustrated magazines all over the world, the same menus, the same dance tunes," the demolition of particular cultures before the advance of a universal culture, of quality before quantity.[55] It is precisely because modernity belongs to no one that it can belong to everyone, and this is what makes it empty of many of those things to which people have in the past been committed and which gave them a sense of meaning, often of accomplishment. This emptiness has enabled the world culture to become ubiquitous, but it has also added a new dimension to the experience of being modern.

Second, today's mass media, which are vital conduits for the values arising from modernization, are so intrusive, so pervasive, so enveloping as to render the *experience* of modernity intense to a degree that is without precedent. What began as the physical conquest of our world, the annihilation of its space and time, the control of its forces, and the exploitation of its resources has now become a profoundly *psychological* reality. The benefits of technology bless its beneficiaries but also curse them, because the benefits all come packaged in values that are naturalistic and materialistic. These values fill the air twenty-four hours a day now. They compose the conscious world in which we live. Whatever else it is, Bellah has said, modernization "is always a moral and a religious problem," for it destroys old values and meanings as it creates new ones. In both its destructive and constructive work, the "social forces called into play have been powerful."[56] They have been made unusually intense — indeed, inescapable — in Our Time by the ubiquity and intrusiveness of the mass media.

Third, as a consequence, we are seeing on a social scale that is without precedent the mass experimentation with and adoption of the values of modernity. To be sure, the sharpness of the expression of these values in the academy is blunted before it is widely disseminated and popularly consumed. The transition from depth to breadth, how-

---

55. Brunner, *Christianity and Civilisation*, 2 vols. (New York: Scribner's, 1948-49), 2: 10.

56. Bellah, *Beyond Belief: Essays on Religion in a Post-Traditional World* (New York: Harper & Row, 1970), p. 64.

ever, in no way nullifies the fact that what is being transmitted is modernity. It is the one thing that breaches divisions of wealth and knowledge. The breadth of its presence, then, the depth of its influence, and the extent of its reach in the world all give modernity its marks of uniqueness today. It is this that sets off Our Time from the ages that have belonged to others, even our grandparents, who also ate the delicious fruit from this garden of modernization. And it is this that now poses an unusual threat to the Church.

These three factors are experienced by all in the culture, Christian and non-Christian alike. They have generated enormous power in reshaping the inner psyche of both believers and unbelievers. And precisely because modernization has created an external world in which unbelief seems normal, it has at the same time created a world in which Christian faith is alien. It is the inability to resist this oddness that is now working its havoc on the Christian mind. The Christian mind in the midst of modernity is like the proverbial frog in the pot beneath which a fire has been kindled. Because the water temperature rises slowly, the frog remains unaware of the danger until it is too late. In the same way, the Church often seems to be blithely unaware of the peril that now surrounds it.

It is this threat to Christian faith that forms the backdrop to this study, but by its end I shall seek to argue that though the experience of modernity poses great, though often unseen perils to Christian faith, it also provides a strange ground for hope. It is, perhaps, one of the oddities of God's providence that reformation in the church's life, of which the evangelical world surely stands in need, has often been abetted, if not triggered, by social disorder. Before God rebuilds, he often pulls down and plucks up. Unhealthy habits of mind and injurious patterns of life that might have been in the making for long periods of time are often more easily swept away by social chaos than by a preacher's appeals to conscience. It was so with unhappy regularity throughout the Old Testament, and it seems to have been so throughout the life of the Church. The moments of deep transformation, such as those that occurred at the time of the Reformation, also seem to happen at times of great upheaval in society. I believe that we are now living in such times, and though I see many of the omens that could portend a very troubled future and perhaps the disintegration of Western civilization, this is also a moment when, in God's mercy and providence, the Church could be deeply transformed for good — provided that, unlike the frog, it knows how to jump out of the pot.

These are the profound developments that we will explore in the
pages that follow. We must ask how religion — and especially evangelical religion — is measuring up to Our Time. How has it responded
to the looming vortex in the center of our society, the emptiness left
behind by the disappearance of a common core of values, the disintegration of tradition and authority? And how cognizant is it of pluralization, of how the multiple choices that pluralization forces on us each
day destroy our capacity for truth, not to mention the stability of our
world?

THE CIRCUMSTANCE OF FAITH

CHAPTER III

Things Fall Apart

Turning and turning in the widening gyre
The falcon cannot hear the falconer;
Things fall apart; the center cannot hold;
Mere anarchy is loosed upon the world,
The blood-dimmed tide is loosed, and everywhere
The ceremony of innocence is drowned;
The best lack all conviction, while the worst
Are full of passionate intensity.

William Butler Yeats

THE DISAPPEARANCE OF THEOLOGY from the life of the Church, and the orchestration of that disappearance by some of its leaders, is hard to miss today but, oddly enough, not easy to prove. It is hard to miss in the evangelical world — in the vacuous worship that is so prevalent, for example, in the shift from God to the self as the central focus of faith, in the psychologized preaching that follows this shift, in the erosion of its conviction, in its strident pragmatism, in its inability to think incisively about the culture, in its reveling in the irrational. And it would have made few of these capitulations to modernity had not its capacity for truth diminished. It is not hard to see these things; avoiding them is what is difficult.

It is also difficult to adduce conclusive proof that these deep flaws in contemporary evangelical faith are the result of its having lost its theological soul, that a faith flung out to the periphery is disintegrating because the theological center has not been able to hold. Why is it so difficult? Because the kind of proof that we would find most convincing would require that we be able to show empirically how the intersections between modernized culture, internal psychology, and the structures of belief are all playing out on one another such that theology has become their chief casualty. Social scientists who have tried to explore such questions with the laity have, unfortunately, often found themselves set to a frustrating task. They either ask questions that are so simplistic as to yield superficial answers or they ask more probing and specific questions that tend to provoke doubt and bafflement in those who try to answer.

Moreover, it is important to recognize that there remains a core of mystery within all human motivation; we seldom understand all of the reasons for any of our actions. In this particular case, we are left with our surmises and suspicions about the contemporary restructuring of evangelical faith, but we do not always have the cold, hard proof that we need. Like Supreme Court Justice Potter Stuart, we too know pornography when we see it, but we may not always be able to compile the conclusive, objective proof that will show it up for what it is.

For these reasons, I am advancing my argument cautiously in this book. I am compelled to enter this perplexing terrain, however, because the difficulty I encounter in explaining what has happened weighs far less heavily than does the need to have at least some understanding of it. The stakes are high: the anti-theological mood that now grips the evangelical world is changing its internal configuration, its effectiveness, and its relation to the past. It is severing the link to historical, Protestant orthodoxy. It is emancipating contemporary evangelicals to form casual alliances at will with a multitude of substitutes for this orthodoxy. And the reason for this is that what that orthodoxy had and what contemporary evangelicalism so often lacks is a theology at its center that defines the faith and prescribes the sorts of intellectual and practical relations it should establish in the world.

In this chapter, I want to lay the foundation for exploring these themes. I need to begin by defining the theology that is disappearing and offering some preliminary evidence to substantiate my contention that it is in fact disappearing. The bulk of the evidence will have to come later, and it will be more indirect than direct. In the three chapters that follow, I will be looking at three aspects of a faith that is in process of being shorn of its theology. By working back from the effects, I hope to be able to show that their cause is a lost theological vision at the center, and this in turn will give new cogency to my analysis of the effects. But I hope the preliminary evidence I offer here will be sufficient to provide a working hypothesis that will enable me to develop the parallels between the emergence of Protestant Liberalism earlier this century and the restructuring that is taking place in the evangelical world today.

Theology Disappears

What Is Theology?

What in an earlier age might have been self-evident is no longer so. Today, so many definitions of theology are being offered that one might well wonder how a field experiencing such internal chaos could sustain so many practitioners or that anyone outside the field would take it seriously.[1] "As everyone knows," Ian Ramsey wrote some twenty years ago, "theology is at present in turmoil. . . . Theology seems often to the outsider just so much word-spinning, air-borne discourse which never touches down except disastrously."[2] As he saw it, not only was the Church without theology, but theology was without God. Undoubtedly, some chastening has set in since then among professional theologians, but the chasm between their language and mentality on

---

1. The impact of modernity on the habits of consciousness and on the way in which authority is now conceived has created a crisis for theology. The urgency with which this crisis is felt is probably accurately indicated by the urgency with which the question of theological method is now being discussed. See, for example, Thomas Torrance, *Theological Science* (London: Oxford University Press, 1969); Gerhard Ebeling, *The Study of Theology,* trans. Duane Priebe (Philadelphia: Fortress Press, 1978); Bernard Lonergan, *Method in Theology* (New York: Herder & Herder, 1972); Anders Nygren, *Meaning and Method in Philososphy and Religion: Prolegomena to a Scientific Philosophy of Religion and a Scientific Theology,* trans. Philip Watson (Philadelphia: Fortress Press, 1972); Anton Grabner-Haider, *Theorie der Theologie als Wissenschaft* (München: Kosel-Verlag, 1974); Gordon Kaufman, *An Essay in Theological Method* (Missoula, Mont.: Scholars Press, 1975); Edward Schillebeeckx, *The Understanding of Faith* (New York: Seabury Press, 1974); Wolfhart Pannenberg, *Theology and the Philosophy of Science,* trans. Francis McDonagh (Philadelphia: Westminster Press, 1976); David Tracy, *Blessed Rage for Order: The New Pluralism in Theology* (New York: Seabury Press, 1985); George Lindbeck, *The Nature of Doctrine: Religion and Theology in a Postliberal Age* (Philadelphia: Westminster Press, 1984); and Richard A. Muller, *The Study of Theology: From Biblical Interpretation to Contemporary Formulation* (Grand Rapids: Zondervan, 1991).
2. Ramsey, *Models for Divine Activity* (London: SCM Press, 1973), p. 1.

the one hand and the language and mentality of the Church on the other has, if anything, only widened in the intervening years.

This is, of course, the theme of this book, but I wish to look at it less from the side of the theologians and more from the side of the Church. To this end, I will begin with a definition of theology meant to cover both those with technical interest in its construction and those without such an interest, in hopes of being able to mediate between the several different ways in which we use the word. This is no small undertaking, for, as Edward Farley has noted, these different meanings have become so estranged from one another that they are no longer recognized as references to the same thing.[3] When the word *theology* is used in the Church, it is commonly used simply of someone's private theory about some subject. As the therapeutic culture that modernity has spawned then intrudes into this inner sphere, "theology" tends to lose its doctrinal substance. By contrast, in the academy the word *theology* is sometimes used to described a discipline, similar in kind to history and astronomy, in which the practitioner of learning ought ideally to have no personal involvement. Alternatively, it is also used in the academy as a synonym for Old Testament study, New Testament study, or the study of spirituality, in which case it has lost its status as an independent discipline altogether. Given the different characterizations of theology in Church and academy, it is hard to recognize that it is the same thing at bottom.

It is my contention that *theology* should mean the same thing regardless of whether it is used in the Church or in the academy. There was a time when there was this sort of uniformity of meaning. In the past, the doing of theology encompassed three essential aspects in both the Church and the academy: (1) a confessional element, (2) reflection on this confession, and (3) the cultivation of a set of virtues that are grounded in the first two elements. To be sure, the various theological traditions have not given equal emphasis to these three elements, nor have these elements received equal attention from century to century even within any given tradition. In ages of heresy or schism, for example, the importance of defining what it is that needs to be confessed has often received prominence; in ages of social turmoil or ideological hostility, critical reflection and apologetics have moved to the forefront of Christian attention; and in ages when confessional

3. Farley, "Theology and Practice outside the Clerical Paradigm," in *Practical Theology: The Emerging Field in Theology, Church, and World,* ed. Don S. Browning (San Francisco: Harper & Row, 1983), pp. 22-24.

orthodoxy has not only dominated but, in the process, calcified the church, the cultivation of the virtues, the life of spirituality, has been made more urgent. Nevertheless, despite these shifting emphases, theologians have always seen themselves as having to live and work within the triangle that these three interests form, and what is true of them is also true of the Church as a whole.

Confession, in this understanding, is what the Church believes.[4] It is what crystallizes into doctrine. And, to be more specific, churches with roots in the Protestant Reformation confess the truth that God has given to the Church through the inspired Word of God. There may be disagreements about what the Bible teaches on any one subject, as well as how that teaching should be assembled, but there is unanimous agreement that this authoritative truth lies at the heart of Christian life and practice, for this is what it means to live under the authority of Scripture. It is in this core of confession that the Church's identity is preserved across the ages. This is the watchword by which it is known. Without this knowledge, it is bereft of what defines the Church as the people of God, bereft of the means of belief, worship, sustenance, proclamation, and service. Confession must be at the center of every theology that wants to be seen as *theologia*, the knowledge of God, a knowledge given in and for the people of God.

The second element of theology, reflection, involves the intellectual

---

4. What I am referring to here as a "confessional" element is what Stephen Sykes calls "the public doctrinal inheritance of the Christian tradition," whether this is expressed through the historic creeds and confessions of the church or understood more informally. It is what has been the starting point for all Protestant theology that was conscious of its genesis in the Reformation. Abraham Kuyper, in a typical statement, says that theology has "the revealed knowledge of God as the object of its investigation and raises it to understanding" (*Principles of Sacred Theology*, trans. J. Hendrick DeVries [Grand Rapids: William B. Eerdmans, 1954], p. 299). B. B. Warfield said that theology is concerned with God and his self-disclosure and with "the relations between God and the universe" (*Studies in Theology* [New York: Oxford University Press, 1932], p. 56). James Denney said that theology must begin with God and what he has revealed of himself, but, in the nature of the case, this must involve a particular way of looking at the world. Our doctrine of God, he said, "must contain the ideas and the principles which enable us to look at our life and our world as a whole, and to take them into our religion, instead of leaving them outside" (*Studies in Theology* [Grand Rapids: Baker Book House, 1976], pp. 1-2). In these statements, what I have referred to as the confessional and reflective elements are both endorsed; the third element, the virtues of life, have not always been seen as central to the work of the theologian *as theologian*. This has at times been a significant weakness in Protestant theology, as compared with Catholic, but Puritanism is a reminder that it need not be excluded from the interests of a genuinely Protestant theology.

struggle to understand what it means to be the recipient of God's Word in this present world. It has to proceed down three distinct avenues. First, it must range over the whole of God's disclosure within Scripture, seeking to make the connections between the various parts of Scripture such that God's intent in so revealing his character, acts, and will is made clear. It aims at a comprehensive understanding of what God has given so that his mind will begin to be replicated in the Church's mind. Second, reflection must range over the past, seeking to gather from God's working in the Church the ballast that will steady it in the storms of the present. It is through this kind of reflective work that the spiritual riches of the past are gathered and the present is relativized. The present always needs to be deprived of its pretensions to being the most elevated moment in the story of the human spirit (or, as some charismatics would have it, the most dramatic), for this opens wide the door to pride and folly. Third, reflection must seek to understand the connections between what is confessed and what, in any given society, is taken as normative. This is crucial, for the ideas and assumptions of any age powerfully intrude on the Church's mind. In the West, modernity has determined what is normative. In our particular context, then, we are called to see that the Church does not adapt its thinking to the horizons that modernity prescribes for it but rather that it brings to those horizons the powerful antidote of God's truth. It is not the Word of God but rather modernity that stands in need of being demythologized.

The third element of theology involves the cultivation of those virtues that constitute a wisdom for life, the kind of wisdom in which Christian practice is built on the pillars of confession and surrounded by the scaffolding of reflection. And yet this formulation is too simple, for what I have in mind is a kind of spirituality that is now exceedingly rare — the type of spirituality that is centrally moral in its nature because God is centrally holy in his being, that sees Christian practice not primarily as a matter of technique but as a matter of truth, and that refuses to disjoin practice from thought or thought from practice. Only when this kind of spirituality is present does the sort of wisdom arise by which a person comes to know how to be Christian in any given set of circumstances.

To ask that the Church be thus theological may seem to be asking too much; clearly it is asking too much of the academy. We have come to this pass because for most people these three interests have been disengaged from one another. In the modern period, for example, confession in the sense of a profession about the objective truth of God and his self-disclosure in the space-time world has become most awkward in academia because of its continuing attachment to Enlightenment habits. It is often equally embarrassing in the larger social context because of the way in which modernity has reshaped our sense of what is proper. As a result, confession has either lost weight or disappeared entirely in academic theology. And once confession is lost, reflection is cut loose to find new pastures. Once it has lost its discipline in the Word of God, it finds its subject matter anywhere along a line that runs from Eastern spirituality to radical politics to feminist ideology to environmental concerns. Moreover, class interests then typically intervene and drive a wedge between Church and academy, and the upshot of this is that academic theological reflection, cut loose from both the responsibility of practice and the foundation of confession, is relegated to a small world of the specially interested whose internal conversation is mostly incomprehensible to those who are outside it. Theology, in a historic sense, therefore dies, because all that is left of it is reflection of a philosophical nature.

By a different route, the same thing has happened in the Church, the evangelical wing included. As the nostrums of the therapeutic age supplant confession, and as preaching is psychologized, the meaning of Christian faith becomes privatized. At a single stroke, confession is eviscerated and reflection reduced mainly to thought about one's self. That being the case, the responsibility of seeking to be Christian in the modern world is then transformed into a search for what Farley calls a "technology of practice," for techniques with which to expand the Church and master the self that borrow mainly from business management and psychology. Thus it is that the pastor seeks to embody what modernity admires and to redefine what pastoral ministry now means in light of this culture's two most admired types, the manager and the psychologist. Where this modern "wisdom" comes to supplant confession in defining and disciplining what practice should mean, where reflection has been reduced simply to reflection upon the self, and where the hard work of relating the truth of God's Word to the processes of modern life has been abandoned, there once again theology has died and all that is left of it is an empty shell of what wisdom once used to be. It is this process of reduction — the reduction of the meaning of theology to reflection in the academy and to practice in the evangelical Church — that is the theme of this chapter. Yet before we proceed further, it is important that we understand the novelty of this situation. In eviscerating theology in this way, by substituting for its defining, confessional center a new set of principles (if they can appropriately be called that), evangelicals are moving ever closer to the point at which they will no longer meaningfully be able to speak of themselves as historic Protestants.

That the apostolic churches were confessional and that they confessed the apostolic teaching about the life, death, and resurrection of Christ may be disputed, but only on the most radical redactional reading of the New Testament. And to dispute it further requires of us the extraordinary feat of seeming to know something that is contradicted by all that we have established of the earliest patristic belief. The apostles "delivered" the facts about Christ (1 Cor. 11:23; 15:3), interpreted those facts, and then developed the consequences for Christian life from this. These facts assumed and were articulated within a framework of theism that allowed for the possibility of miracles. In the incarnation and resurrection of Christ, as well as in his ministry on earth, this possibility had become a series of actualities. These acts of God were interpreted and quickly formalized into the gospel message which in the book of Acts (e.g., 13:16-41; 14:15-17; 17:22-31) is adapted to different audiences but contains the same elements in each adapted form. These are, as William Barclay argued with respect to Paul, that history was a preparation for Christ's coming, that God was active in that history (Acts 17:27-28; 13:16-23; 14:17), that in Christ God entered the human situation and now offers forgiveness through Christ's work on the cross (Acts 14:16; 17:30; 13:23), and that despite God's gracious offer the Jews rejected Christ and are now, following his resurrection, subject to God's judgment along with all those who insist on rejecting his Son (Acts 13:27-29, 31, 34-37).[5] All this became part of the "tradition" that was committed to faithful people to transmit to succeeding generations. In this sense, there is undoubtedly a central place given to tradition in the New Testament.[6]

In time, as the New Testament letters were completed and the canon was eventually closed, there seems little doubt that the whole apostolic exposition of the disclosure of God, of his character, acts, and will (especially as these were revealed in Christ), became the substance of what was confessed. To be a believer, then as later, meant believing what the apostles taught. It is in this sense that apostolic succession is

5. Barclay, "A Comparison of Paul's Missionary Preaching and Preaching to the Church," in *Apostolic History and the Gospel*, ed. W. Ward Gasque and Ralph P. Martin (Grand Rapids: William B. Eerdmans, 1970), pp. 165-70.

6. I am referring here not to the supposed line of teaching never committed to writing in which Roman Catholics have always been interested but to the teaching that constituted the very heart of the faith, its very essence. See F. F. Bruce, *Tradition Old and New* (Exeter: Paternoster Press, 1970).

a New Testament truth. Believers succeed the apostles as they accept what the apostles taught. It is a succession not of ecclesiastical power as the Church of Rome teaches but of doctrine.

This is why the apostles not only framed Christian faith in doctrinal terms but called for its preservation and protection in this form. There is no Christian faith in the absence of "sound doctrine" (1 Tim. 1:10; Tit. 1:9), "sound instruction" (1 Tim. 6:3), or the "pattern of sound teaching" (2 Tim. 1:13-14). It is this doctrine, or, more precisely, the truth it contains and expresses, that was "taught" by the apostles and "delivered" to the Church. It is this message that is our only ground for hope (Tit. 1:9) and salvation (1 Cor. 15:2; 1 Pet. 1:23-25). Without it, we have neither the Father nor the Son (2 John 9). Indeed, Paul says that we can grow in Christ only if we stay within this doctrinal framework, for its truth provides the means of our growth (Col. 2:6). It is no wonder that Christians are urged not to depart from the apostolic teaching they received "in the beginning" (John 2:7, 24, 26; 3:11) or from what they had heard (Heb. 2:1), for it is the "faith once for all entrusted to the saints" (Jude 3). Nor should we be amazed to read of Paul's admonition to Timothy that it is only by adhering to this "good teaching" that he will become a "good minister of Jesus Christ" (1 Tim. 4:6). For all of these reasons, the apostles instructed believers to "guard" this faith (2 Tim. 1:13-14; 4:3; cf. Tit. 1:9; Gal. 1:9), defend it (Jude 3), "stand firm" in it, not to "drift" from it, to become "established" in it, and to transmit it intact to succeeding generations.

No one who is familiar with apostolic teaching and practice could imagine that bare, credal orthodoxy alone is being advocated in these passages. It is clear, for example, both from the structure of many of Paul's letters and from many of his specific statements, that he saw belief and practice as inextricably related to each other, the former being the foundation of the latter and the latter being the evidence of the working of the former. This same correlation is forcefully presented in John's first epistle, in which three tests are developed for discerning the presence and authenticity of a biblical spirituality: believing the right doctrine (2:18-27; 4:1-6, 13-21), obedience to right doctrine (2:3-6; 2:28–3:10), and giving expression to right doctrine in a life of love (2:7-11; 3:11-18; 4:7-12). Obedience and love are not substitutes for or alternatives to the doctrine, however; they are the ways — the indispensable ways — in which doctrine is to be worked out in our character, attitudes, relationships, and work. The apostolic exposition of God, his character, his acts, and his will (especially as these were focused in the giving of his incarnate Son) form the foundation without which one cannot have Christian faith.

It is only our familiarity with the New Testament language that hides from us the explosiveness of the apostolic conclusions. Why were they so adamant about the preservation, appropriation, and propagation of this doctrinally framed teaching? The answer is that it is the "truth" (2 Cor. 4:6; Eph. 1:13; Col. 1:5; 2 Tim. 2:15; Tit. 1:14; 1 Pet. 1:22; 2 Pet. 1:12; James 1:8; 3 John 4). It is only by coming to know this "truth" that one comes to know God, for he can be known only through Christ who is the center and object of this teaching (Tit. 2:4; Heb. 10:26; 1 Pet. 1:22; cf. 2 Tim. 3:7).

The apostles asserted that Christ alone is the truth in the midst of a world that was more religiously diverse than any we have known in the West until relatively recently. We today are far closer in religious temper to apostolic times than any period since the Reformation. Indeed, most of the modern period in the West has been quite unlike apostolic times inasmuch as we have been spared interreligious conflict and much of the doubt that invariably accompanies such conflict. It is, therefore, hard to imagine a more specious argument than the one advanced along many fronts today, backed actively by the World Council of Churches and implicitly by the documents of the Second Vatican Council, that the contemporary experience of religious pluralism is the reason that the apostolic formulation of faith can no longer be held! Such assertions make the apostles and often Jesus himself look like innocents who were spared the dreadful dilemmas that, sadly, we have to face with such flinty honesty, in the process divesting ourselves of the very truth that they insisted must be preserved.

Admittedly, the apostolic world was small and ours is not. Theirs, however, was a cauldron of conflicting religious claims within which the Christian movement would have remained tiny but for one fact: the first Christians knew that their faith was absolutely true, that it could brook no rivals, and so they sought no compromises. That was the kind of integrity that God, the Holy Spirit, blessed and used in the ancient world in spreading the knowledge of Christ. We today are not so commonly persuaded or, I dare say, not so commonly blessed. Even among those who seek to guide the Church in its belief, many are of the mind that Christian faith is only relatively true, or they think, against every precept and example that we have in the New Testament, that Christ can be "encountered" in other religions — religions that they view not as rivals but as "interpretations" with which accommodation should be sought. What would have happened over the ages, one wonders, if more of the Church's leaders had been similarly persuaded?

That Christianity is properly confessional, that it is absolutely true, was not doubted by Catholic or Protestant until quite recently. It was a common conviction of its truth that lay behind the fierce debate over what exactly the content of the confession was. Christianity, says Owen Chadwick, was seen as "an unchanging gospel, handed down by pen and mouth from age to age, generation to generation, mother to child, teacher to taught, pulpit to pew . . . that which has been believed in every place, in every century, by all Christian men and women."[7] And he goes on to point out that until the end of the seventeenth century, both Protestants and Catholics believed that there was only one truth that should be confessed. Their argument was not over whether there were multiple truths but simply over what *the* truth was. Bossuet, the greatest Catholic apologist of the time, declared that variation in doctrine, departure from the accepted teaching, was what constituted heresy. There was nothing novel about this. Eusebius in the fourth century also equated innovation with heresy. And this is why the upheaval of the Reformation in the sixteenth century quickly moved from a discussion about biblical theology to a discussion about history. In the following century a series of massive historical studies was published in which the contestants, Catholic and Protestant, sought to show that it was their opponents who had departed from the early doctrinal consensus.[8] The Protestants anchored their case in the patristic period, the teachings of which they largely identified with, arguing that the Reformation was really a contest between patristic and medieval Christianity. Catholics countered that this was a false alternative, for the medieval doctors had simply affirmed what the early fathers had taught. In different ways, for "more than a century after the rupture of the Reformation," Yves Congar notes, "the consensus of the first five centuries was accepted as empirical criteria of authenticity."[9] Both sides accepted the responsibility of defining truly that core of belief without which one would not have Christian faith; neither side countenanced even for a moment the idea that doctrinal confession was an encumbrance that could be discarded.

In retrospect, this "pre-critical" period now looks to many like a time of innocence, if not of intellectual simplicity. Today, in the academy

---

7. Chadwick, *From Bossuet to Newman: The Idea of Doctrinal Development* (Cambridge: Cambridge University Press, 1957), p. 1.

8. A brief discussion of this literature and its significance can be found in my essay "Tradition: A Meeting Place for Catholic and Evangelical Theology?" *Christian Scholar's Review* 5 (1975): 52-57.

9. Congar, *Tradition and Traditions: An Historical and Theological Essay* (New York: Macmillan, 1967), pp. 143-44.

we must struggle with Kant's objections to any epistemology in which God is an object of knowledge, with the huge assault that biblical criticism has mounted on the viability of Scripture as an accessible norm for confession,[10] and with the cultural pluralism that disallows any suggestion that there is only one true religious confession. And in the evangelical Church, with the apparently shriveled sense of truth that lies beneath much of its life and practice, this "pre-critical" world now makes no sense at all, for it defined Christian faith theologically, and that is increasingly alien to the way in which evangelicals now define it. In both the academy and the Church, albeit for slightly different reasons, modernity constitutes a divide across which it is either no longer possible or no longer desirable to reach. It is this new situation that gives a special meaning to the assertion that theology is disappearing.

How Theology Is Disappearing

The disappearance of which I am speaking is not the same as the abduction of a child who is happily playing at home one minute and then is no longer to be found the next. No one has abducted theology in this sense. The disappearance is closer to what happens in homes where the children are ignored and, to all intents and purposes, abandoned. They remain in the home, but they have no place in the family. So it is with theology in the Church. It remains on the edges of evangelical life, but it has been dislodged from its center.

What is happening in the larger secular society with respect to Christian belief helps us to see how this comes about. In an absent-minded way, America still believes quite a lot, and what it believes is still quite traditional.[11] Despite the earlier prophecies that as the culture

10. See H. G. Reventlow, *The Authority of the Bible and the Rise of the Modern World*, trans. John Bowden (Philadelphia: Fortress Press, 1985).

11. See Andrew Greeley, *Unsecular Man: The Persistence of Religion* (New York: Schocken Books, 1972); cf. John Wilson, *Religion in American Society: The Effective Presence* (Englewood Cliffs, N.J.: Prentice-Hall, 1978). The relationship between faith and secular values in America has undoubtedly been worked out in a distinctively American way. Martin Marty has argued that secularism has followed different courses in Europe and Britain when compared with that which it has taken in America because here secularism coexists with religion, whereas in Europe it rejects religion and in Britain it simply ignores it. See Marty, *The Great Schism: Three Paths to the Secular* (New York: Harper & Row, 1969). Will Herberg has presented the same kind of thesis but taken it a step further, arguing that in America, religion is a way of expressing nationhood: announcing that one is Protestant, Catholic, or

became more secularized, religion would vanish, polls now show that substantial belief is still intact. An overwhelming majority, 98 percent, believes in God's existence; 73 percent believe in life after death, 86 percent have full or substantial confidence in the veracity of the Bible because of its inspiration, 74 percent would like a constitutional amendment to allow voluntary prayer in schools, and, with respect to "commitment to Christ," the figure at the high end is 60 percent of men and 72 percent of women among those over the age of fifty.[12]

The question, of course, is what all of this means, for while all of the elements of a traditional Christian faith are apparently surviving modernity, American life is nevertheless being redefined by modernity in such a way that the United States is no longer evidently a Christian country, no matter how loosely the word *Christian* is used. What, then, is the place of this belief in the modern mind? Is it at the center, or is it on the periphery? Does it define who a person is, or must that definition be sought elsewhere? The answers are not hard to see, and they reveal a pattern that is also appearing in the evangelical world as it, too, becomes secularized.

What does it mean, for example, when 91 percent of evangelicals say that their beliefs are "very important" to them,[13] when 93 percent say that they believe in divine judgment, when 96 percent say that they

---

Jew is another way of saying that one is an upright American. However, in order for religion to function this way, it has had to become increasingly vacuous, less defined, so that it can remain acceptable to all. It is this sort of religion that is public in its function, civil in its tone, and undefined in its substance that Robert Bellah has called "civil religion" ("Civil Religion in America," in *Beyond Belief: Essays on Religion in a Post-Traditional World* [New York: Harper & Row, 1970], pp. 168-89). However, as Bryan Wilson comes close to suggesting, it is doubtful that this reality in American life accounts for all of the religion that can be found in the nation. The civil religion thesis arose in part to explain the failure of the prediction that modernization would sweep aside all religion, but it too has failed to provide even a theoretical account of the state of *all* American religion. Robert Wuthnow has taken the analysis of civil religion another step forward and done so with consummate care. He has argued that in the past four decades, two types of civil religion have emerged, one on the political left with interests characteristic of the left and one on the right with interests characteristic of the right. As a rough generalization, mainline denominational activity is seduced by the former, and evangelical church life is seduced by the latter. See Wuthnow, *The Restructuring of American Religion: Society and Faith since World War II* [Princeton: Princeton University Press, 1988]).

12. George Gallup, Jr., and Jim Castelli, *The People's Religion: American Faith in the Nineties* (New York: Macmillan, 1989), p. 64.

13. David Moberg, "The Salience of Religion in Everyday Life: Selected Evidence from Survey Research in Sweden and America," *Sociological Analysis* 43 (Fall 1982): 210.

believe in miracles?[14] It does not necessarily mean all that much. Even in churches that are active and among believers who are religiously observant, it is possible that theology (i.e., a set of beliefs that refers beyond the experiencing subject to the world "out there," natural and supernatural) has become peripheral and remote. Even "those who count themselves as believers, who subscribe to the tenets of a Church, and who attend services regularly," Bryan Wilson has observed, "nevertheless operate in a social space in which their beliefs about the supernatural are rendered in large part irrelevant."[15] Wherever modernity has intruded upon the Church, there the social space even of believers who give assent to the full range of credal elements will be emptied of theology. Even the beliefs of such individuals will have been pushed to the margins of life, the central and integrating role they once had commandeered by other interests.

It is in this sense that it is proper to speak of the disappearance of theology. It is not that the elements of the evangelical credo have vanished; they have not. The fact that they are professed, however, does not necessarily mean that the structure of the historic Protestant faith is still intact. The reason, quite simply, is that while these items of belief are professed, they are increasingly being removed from the center of evangelical life where they defined what that life was, and they are now being relegated to the periphery where their power to define what evangelical life should be is lost. This is not the sort of shift that typical polling will discover, for these items of belief are seldom denied or qualified, but that does not mean that the shift has not occurred. It is evangelical *practice* rather than evangelical profession that reveals the change.

All of this puts rather a different light on what has been hailed as a current renaissance in theological writing. It is indeed the case that in recent years a surprising number of conservative theologies have been written, and more are planned for the future.[16] It would

14. Gallup and Castelli, *The People's Religion*, p. 98.

15. Wilson, *Contemporary Transformations of Religion* (Oxford: Oxford University Press, 1976), p. 6.

16. In April, 1991, Gabriel Fackre delivered his presidential report to the American Theological Society entitled "The State of Systematics: Research and Commentary," in which he documented the swelling tide of new systematics. Among the more conservative of these are the following: Donald Bloesch, *Essentials of Evangelical Theology*, 2 vols. (San Francisco: Harper & Row, 1982); Millard J. Erickson, *Christian Theology* (Grand Rapids: Baker Book House, 1986); Gabriel Fackre, *The Christian Story: A Pastoral Systematics*, 2 vols. (Grand Rapids: William B. Eerdmans, 1985-87); Paul K. Jewett, *God, Creation, and Redemption* (Grand Rapids: William B. Eerdmans, 1991); Gordon Lewis and Bruce Demarest, *Integrative Theology*,

not be unreasonable to conclude from this that the evangelical world is becoming more theological rather than less, that its preoccupation with its center of biblically given truth is increasing rather than diminishing. That conclusion would, however, be quite mistaken, for it overlooks the fact that the constituency for which these books are written is only a very small part of the Church and that the real test is not who buys the books, nor even who reads them, but what effect they have, how they are able to provide for faith a center that is an alternative to what modernity is now pouring into it. As a matter of fact, it is also possible to see this work as corroborating the thesis being offered here. As theology begins to disappear, theologians may have moved to fill the vacuum that has been left behind.

The disappearance of which I am speaking, then, has two sides to it. Theology is disappearing, first, in the sense that it has become dismembered. Moreover, the three constituent elements (confession, reflection, and the cultivation of virtues grounded in confession and reflection), having been separated from one another, are now each attracting different constituencies. Today, there is a large and flourishing establishment of professional scholars dedicated to the refinement and dissemination of biblical knowledge, but reflection on what all of that means in the contemporary world is largely left to others. The most incisive analyses along these lines have, in fact, come from the philosophers, historians, and sociologists — but only rarely do they give any evidence of knowing what the biblical scholars are thinking. And the theorizers of practice, while they tip their hats in the direction of the Bible, quickly look the other way when they get down to the serious business of devising technique for the Church's life. In a historic sense, theology is thus disappearing. Second, it is also disappearing in the sense that while its articles of belief are still professed, they are no longer defining what it means to be an evangelical or how evangelicalism should be practiced. At its center there is now a vacuum into which modernity is pouring, and the result is a faith that, unlike historic orthodoxy, is no longer defining itself theologically.

---

2 vols. (Grand Rapids: Zondervan, 1986-90); Robert Lightner, *Evangelical Theology: A Survey and Review* (Grand Rapids: Baker Book House, 1990); Dale Moody, *Word of Truth: A Summary of Christian Doctrine Based on Biblical Revelation* (Grand Rapids: William B. Eerdmans, 1981); Richard Rice, *The Reign of God: Introduction to Theology from a Seventh Day Adventist Perspective* (Berrien Springs, Mich.: Andrews University Press, 1985); Charles Ryrie, *Basic Theology* (Wheaton, Ill.: Victor Books, 1986); and Geoffrey Wainwright, *Doxology: The Praise of God in Worship, Doctrine and Life — A Systematic Theology* (New York: Oxford University Press, 1980).

That Theology Is Disappearing

It would be quite misleading to suggest that what I have been describing so far is a new phenomenon. It is not. There is an abundant trail of telltale evidence of its occurrence stretching back well into the nineteenth century. Sidney Mead argued, for example, that the passing of the earlier era of Calvinistic spirituality and the subsequent ascendancy of the pietism that accompanied the Second Great Awakening also had the effect of undercutting the place of theology. He contends that the passion for truth was replaced by the passion for souls, and he cites Henry Steele Commager's statement that "during the nineteenth century and well into the twentieth, religion prospered while theology went slowly bankrupt."[17]

This bankruptcy has since spread in a variety of directions. For example, David Roozen has observed that in the old-line denominations, from the 1950s through to the 1980s, religion has consistently prospered at the expense of theology. In the 1950s, what often brought people into the churches was a desire for community, a desire that is quite explicable given the corrosive effects of modernity, but at the same time they began to let go of some of their most important doctrinal beliefs. That trend continued in the 1960s, until, quite suddenly, membership began to disappear along with the beliefs as people began to look for community outside the churches. Unencumbered by Christian theology, some of these people even began to swell the ranks of the cults and Eastern religions.[18]

The same kind of development has taken place in the more obviously evangelical denominations as well, though here in a more sanitized form. Christian beliefs have mostly been retained, but they are not allowed to encumber the search for new forms of spirituality, technique, and community. Among the educated young, however, there has also been an erosion in the cognitive content of the faith. James Davison Hunter's analysis of college and seminary students shows that the more traditional views on the authority of Scripture, the creation and the place of human beings within it, and the uniqueness of Christian salvation are

17. Commager, quoted by Mead in *The Lively Experiment: The Shaping of Christianity in America* (New York: Harper & Row, 1963), p. 55.

18. See David A. Roozen and Jackson W. Carroll, "Recent Trends in Church Membership and Participation: An Introduction," and Dean R. Hoge and David A. Roozen, "Some Sociological Conclusions about Church Trends," in *Understanding Church Growth and Decline, 1950-1978,* ed. Dean R. Hoge and David A. Roozen (New York: Pilgrim Press, 1979), pp. 21-41, 315-33.

all being modified. In this group, he says, there is now "less sharpness, less boldness, and, accordingly, a measure of opaqueness in their theological vision that did not exist in previous generations (at least not to their present extent)." While it would be superficial to say that these groups are becoming more liberal, he believes that there is nevertheless evidence here that the evangelical tradition they represent "is conforming in its own unique way to the cognitive and normative assumptions of modern culture," and this is striking a blow at evangelical self-identity.[19] Furthermore, this inner transformation is opening the door wide to experimentation with new ideas about the self and work and new attitudes toward and involvement in the world.

The same struggles can also be seen in the Southern Baptist Convention, which Nancy T. Ammerman has examined against the same backdrop of modernity. She notes that prior to World War II, 54 percent of Southern Baptists lived on farms or in small towns, but today that figure has fallen to 24 percent, and the migration to the cities appears to have been accompanied by a theological migration. The professionalization that increasingly characterizes our urban world creates its own culture within which profound changes are effected in the morphology of Christian believing. Professionals, those who are better educated, and those who earn more are far more likely to lean toward the left theologically; blue-collar workers, those who are less well educated, and those who earn less are far more likely to lean toward the theological right. Ammerman more specifically associates those whose tastes run toward the left with "the 'new class' of people whose business is knowledge and service. They are the Southern Baptist equivalent of the new evangelicals who embraced the modern world."[20] Those on the right have protested this "disruption of the orthodoxy that had bound Southern Baptists and southern society into a tightly woven cultural web,"[21] but the purity of theology involved in this protest is not above suspicion. It is true that the weapons used in this warfare are credal beliefs. Is it possible, though, that these weapons are being used to fight a cultural war in which the preservation of the old ways and the desire to retain the old power are also important objectives? To the extent that this is true, we can also assume that cultural factors are motivating the warfare on the Funda-

19. Hunter, *Evangelicalism: The Coming Generation* (Chicago: University of Chicago Press, 1987), p. 46.

20. Ammerman, *Baptist Battles: Social Change and Religious Conflict in the Southern Baptist Convention* (New Brunswick, N.J.: Rutgers University Press, 1990), p. 163.

21. Ammerman, *Baptist Battles*, p. 164. Cf. James Garrett and Glenn E. Hinson, *Are Southern Baptists "Evangelicals"?* (Macon: Mercer University Press, 1983).

mentalist side — and also on the opposing side. Something other than theology seems to have found its place in the center of the faith of all the warring factions.

Yet studies like these do not yield as much evidence as one would desire, for they tend to focus on the nature of what is believed rather than its function. It is in the functioning of faith that the most important evidence is to be found for saying that theology is disappearing. Christian practice is quite evidently taking on its own peculiar form in contemporary America. It is being called upon to assume an overriding importance in religious life, to discharge all of the responsibilities that theology in its comprehensiveness once bore. Being practical now substitutes for being theological, for there is little left to theology except practice. Stripped of doctrinal substance and rendered unreflective about and uncritical of the culture, theology now transforms "virtue" into a set of everyday skills for finding success in a world of technology and affluence. Knowing how to be religious now means knowing how to "make it" in a pragmatic world that is decidedly hostile to absolute principles and transcendent meaning and, in consequence, is driven to seek meaning only in self-fulfillment. The fuel for this new practical virtue comes not from the Bible but from the popularized nostrums of psychology, not from the older practices of self-examination and the pursuit of holiness but from the newer concerns for psychological wholeness and happiness in an age of affluence. It should not be hard to see that this new program has nothing in common with the old and that this drastically reduced theological vision has nothing to do with the task that has engaged the church for most of its life.

The new quest for contemporary practicality has transformed the nature of the Christian ministry, the work of the seminaries, and the inner workings in denominational headquarters, and in each case the transformation has sounded the death knell of theology. The Christian ministry has become a profession. In today's seminaries, Edward Farley observed, the "theological student neither studies divinity nor obtains scholarly expertise in theological sciences, but trains for professional activities."[22] In other words, the old divinity has largely died, as has its importance for the Church, and so seminary training increasingly is about inculcating a kind of public demeanor and etiquette, along with know-how in the soul-caring business, to lay paths to successful careers for students. Seminary students are not blind to the fact that the big

22. Farley, *Theologia: The Fragmentation and Unity of Theological Education* (Philadelphia: Fortress Press, 1983), p. 11.

churches and the big salaries often go to those who are untheological or even anti-theological. They know what kind of training they need: they need to become managers who have the status of professionals, not scholars, thinkers, or theologians.

They are coming into a world where, as Bryan Wilson notes, the public's estimation is that the clergy have been replaced by scientists in the work of providing "the intellectual substratum of society" and where the arts and literature have fled their former home in Christian faith.[23] The clergy have been deprived of their old social prestige, and only the acquisition of a sheen of professionalism holds out any hope of redeeming their lost social fortunes. Not surprisingly, in recent years seminaries have found it important to think of themselves as comparable to other professional schools, such as those for law and medicine, and many now offer the Doctor of Ministry degree as a further means of establishing this parity. Unfortunately, the typical seminary does not offer training that can compare with the rigor of these professional schools. The Doctor of Ministry degree is in fact not much of a doctorate; the standards one must meet to receive this degree are frequently well below those required of candidates for the Master of Divinity (a degree that not too long ago was called the Bachelor of Divinity). It is a case of professional elevation not by accomplishment but by linguistic inflation. What used to be the minimum level of knowledge for entry into Christian ministry, gauged by a bachelor's degree, has out of professional necessity and with a wave of the magician's wand now become a doctorate by the addition of what may amount to little more than a set of refresher courses. The tactic appears to have backfired, however. In a recent study measuring social prestige, on a scale from one to one hundred, ministers ranked fifty-second, cheek by jowl with factory foremen and the operators of power stations, far below the medical doctors and lawyers with whom they would like to be confused. In another national poll, only 16 percent of the public expressed confidence in their leadership.

These new concerns, and the new shape that they are giving to the Christian ministry, are well illustrated in *Leadership,* a highly successful journal designed for the clergy that was launched by *Christianity Today* in 1980. What is it that their marketing surveys show clergy most want to know, and how should those matters be treated? Between 1980 and 1988, 80 percent of the journal's material was devoted to the personal crises, perplexities, and challenges encountered by the clergy, and 13 percent of the material was concerned with techniques for managing the church.

23. Wilson, *Religion in Secular Society* (Baltimore: Penguin Books, 1969), p. 96.

Since this is an evangelical publication, it is quite stunning to observe that less than 1 percent of the material made any clear reference to Scripture, still less to any idea that is theological. And despite the fact that the pages of this journal are replete with essays on how to manage every imaginable calamity that our modern world inflicts on people, less than 1 percent of the articles sought in any way to understand that modern world. The articles are single-minded in their devotion to the wisdom that psychology and business management offer and apparently as equally single-minded in their skepticism concerning what Scripture and theology offer for addressing the practical crises of pastoral life. Even when the subjects being discussed were temptation, sexuality, church discipline, church structure, and preaching — subjects about which Scripture has much to say — the authors of the articles in *Leadership* thought that it would be better to look elsewhere for help in their pastoral tasks! Confession has vanished from the pages of this journal, and reflection has never even intruded. What remains of theology, therefore, is only the search for wisdom, and this is now pursued through the professionalization of the pastoral calling. The yearning for wisdom is thus transformed into a yearning to look more like a skilled lawyer, psychologist, or business executive than an ordained minister of the gospel, marching to the beat of the transcendent Drummer.

Robert Bellah has noted that these two types — the psychologist and the manager — model the essential interests of twentieth-century culture. Both types are this-worldly, both are centered on the autonomous individual, both are driven by pragmatic interests, and both are hostile to the old moral order. They are, in fact, the same character in many ways, for both seek to define life by the control they exercise over it, the one with respect to the inner world and the other with respect to the outer world. This is what we admire. And *Leadership* reflects this admiration, attempting to sanctify it with a clerical calling.

Denominational headquarters have not been slow to see that they have a compelling business interest in the shift in clerical outlook as well. Their departments, Charles Kegley asserts, have become like their "counterparts in major industries, increasingly efficient, flashy, and powerful."[24] They have adapted, in other words, to the growing desire to seem more professional. And their bureaucracy sees to it that theology is diminished and rendered harmless by being institutionalized. It is at times put out on public display, but only in the cause of making things

24. Kegley, "God Is Not Dead but Theology Is Dying," *Intellect* 103 (December 1974): 177-81.

efficient, wherever this is possible, or in justifying the waves of popular political interest that reach the pew from time to time. Resources have been steadily withdrawn from the publishing houses that have supported theological publication. Barbara Wheeler observed in a study she conducted that "few denominational officials regard theological publishing as a critical element in their church's mission."[25] Actually, theological publishing is now of much more interest to the large, secular corporations that have gained significant control over the religious book world, producing what she calls the "literary-industrial complex."[26] Their interest is, however, more in profits than in the prophets. And all of these trends are typical, David Martin writes, of religion in the process of being secularized. Religious "passion succumbs to bureaucracy and adjusts itself to politics, power, and authority."[27]

These are, for the most part, only tantalizing evidences of the shifting of the terrain that results from the displacement of theology in the life of the Church; it will be necessary to return to them and develop the shift in more detail later. If what has been glimpsed here is symptomatic of deep changes occurring in evangelicalism, and I believe that it is, then it will not be difficult to see, further, that these changes are replicating the pattern that took root earlier in the Protestant world and produced Liberalism. The two developments are not identical, of course: in the earlier period, Protestantism sought to adapt itself to modernized high culture, whereas today evangelicalism is seeking to adapt itself to modernized low culture. Each emerged with its own characteristic shape, but inasmuch as they share the same modern genes, they have also shared the instinct to abandon theology. It is this point of convergence that needs to be sketched a little further.

A Tale of Two Worlds

The Modernists' World

In the past two centuries in the West, the many new currents of intellectual thought have combined to unnerve theologians mightily,

25. Wheeler, "Theological Publishing: In Need of a Mandate," *Christian Century*, 23 November 1988, p. 1068.

26. Wheeler, "Theological Publishing and Theological Education," *Theological Education* 27 (Autumn 1990): 65-70.

27. Martin, *The Religious and the Secular: Studies in Secularization* (New York: Schocken Books, 1969), p. 23.

for they have called into question the very viability of theology. Troeltsch likened the learned disputes among theologians over what could be confessed in his day to the squabbling of children in a house in which, unknown to them, a fire was raging. The Kantian revolution, he believed, had rocked the world to its very foundations. George Tyrrell, the Roman Catholic Modernist, used the same analogy, saying that the hierarchy was busy papering the attic while the basement was in flames.[28] He also pictured the church as a little alpine village standing in the path of an impending avalanche. Could it, he asked, pick itself up and plant itself elsewhere at the eleventh hour? This same theme was also sounded in Schleiermacher's *On Religion: Speeches to Its Cultured Despisers,* and it is the key to understanding the entire Modernist movement of the nineteenth century, both Catholic and Protestant. Across the board it was conceded that the old faith could no longer be preserved in the old way. A new "synthesis" between modernity and faith would have to be found, Tyrrell said, in which ideas would have to be "pared" off both but from which, he added confidently, nothing essential would be lost.[29] And if this engagement with the modern world did not take place, he warned, Christianity *in toto* would be shrugged off as a useless relic of the past.

Opponents of the Modernists, both Catholic and Protestant, saw in this proposed "synthesis" nothing but the capitulation of those who had lost their nerve. *Pascendi Gregis,* the papal encyclical that beheaded the Catholic Modernists in 1907, even charged that their intent was actually to destroy the Church. J. Gresham Machen, in his book *Christianity and Liberalism,* said much the same thing with respect to the

28. Tyrrell in a letter to Raffalovich dated 1901, Tyrrell-Raffalovich correspondence, Bodleian Library, Oxford University.

29. Tyrrell, "Medievalism and Modernism," *Harvard Theological Review* 1 (July 1908): 308-9. There was, in fact, remarkable uniformity in the understanding of what Modernism entailed, even across the divide that has so often separated Catholics from Protestants. Alfred Loisy's brief definition could have served as the text off which they all worked: "the desire to adapt Catholic faith to the intellectual, moral, and social needs of the present age" (*Simples Réflections sur le Décret du Saint-Office Lamentibili Sane Exitu et sur L'Encyclique Pascendi Dominici Gregis* [Ceffonds: Chez l'Auteur, 1908], p. 15). In recent years there have been many studies of the main proponents of Modernism in Britain and Europe, but two older general studies remain unsurpassed despite their age: Jean Rivière's *Le Modernisme dans L'Eglise: Etude d'Histoire Religieuse Contemporaire* (Paris: Libraire Letouzey et Ane, 1929) and A. R. Vidler's *The Modernist Movement in the Roman Church: Its Origins and Outcome* (Cambridge: Cambridge University Press, 1934). With respect to America, see the sympathetic treatment by William R. Hutchison, *The Modernist Impulse in American Protestantism* (Cambridge: Harvard University Press, 1976).

Protestant Modernists. No doubt both *Pascendi* and Machen were correct in terms of the *results* of Modernism, but they were less accurate in characterizing the *intentions* of the Modernists. Modernists were, in fact, trying to preserve the faith, not destroy it. They saw themselves as the last hope for the salvation of Christian faith before it was finally and ignominiously swept away by modernity.

The turmoil of nineteenth-century intellectual life, then, produced the first major casualty in the theological undertaking, though in the confusion the damage was disguised, and to this day the full consequences have not always been recognized. What happened was that the very notion of doctrine, understood as a body of teaching that prescribes what Christian faith means and to which adherence can accordingly be sought, fell into disrepute. It was, supposedly, discredited by the modern world. And this is the point at which the conventional wisdom today starts. According to Stephen Plattern, for example, the search for theological systems that define what is true needs to be written off as a mere "chasing after moonbeams."[30] According to Frederick W. Dillistone, we need to abandon efforts to develop systematic theology with "the aim of establishing a once-for-all, definitive, orthodox statement of Christian faith."[31] According to Rosemary Radford Ruether, the Enlightenment has made it forever impossible for systematic theologies of the old stripe to stand on their own two feet intellectually.[32] According to José Míguez Bonino, the collapse of theology is little more than a symptom of the collapse of the West and ought not to be the cause of too much hand-wringing.[33] According to Van Harvey, the "chronic ill health" of this once noble discipline should be "alarming to its friends,"[34] but in the end there is little that theologians can do to slow the retreat that modernity has rendered inevitable. It is this weakness, this loss of nerve, that led Peter Berger to scoff that theologians today are so afraid of being pushed into the ditch by modernity that they have decided to fall into it of their own accord.

William Barrett has suggested that Immanuel Kant "is the last great thinker in whom the Western mind is still held together." After Kant, he

30. Plattern, "Discovering the Ether," *Theology* 83 (January 1980): 19.
31. Dillistone, "Systematic Theology Today," *Theology Today* 37 (October 1980): 306.
32. Ruether, "Whatever Happened to Theology?" *Christianity and Crisis* 35 (1975): 109.
33. See José Míguez Bonino, "Whatever Happened to Theology?" *Christianity and Crisis* 35 (1975): 111.
34. See Van A. Harvey, "Whatever Happened to Theology?" *Christianity and Crisis* 35 (1975): 108.

says, "that unity was to fall apart, diverge in a number of directions, become fragmented."[35] Kant seems a weak reed on which to lean so great a weight, however, for his sense of God was vague and the unity of his thought precarious. Heinrich Heine's comparison of Kant and Robespierre is a little disconcerting, but it is the case that the seeds of disunity were already sown in Kant's mind, and their dispersal in his works inaugurated a cognitive Reign of Terror in the academic world.

The collapse of the Western mind after Kant then scattered the human enterprise of understanding to the four winds. The falcon, moving in ever wider circles on the winds of modernity, has lost the voice of the falconer, the whole process greatly accelerated by the growing accumulations of knowledge in all fields that are stored in brains, computers, and libraries, the whole of it now far beyond the reach of even the greatest and most prodigious minds of our time.

The old doctrinal affirmations, the confessions of faith from the period of classical orthodoxy as well as the creeds from the patristic period that sought to summarize biblical truth, are now typically considered naive and completely out of date. They no longer serve as the means for defining what should be confessed, even if they are retained for liturgical purposes. The whole idea of confession, in consequence, has shifted from truth with an external and objective referent to intuition which is internal and subjective. After Kant, furthermore, it is the thinking subject who defines what is to be believed, not some external authority. This shift from external authority to internal authority was sharply focused in the debate that was increasingly joined during the nineteenth century about what the "essence" of Christianity was.[36] I cannot sketch the full scope of this debate here, but it is of interest to note some of its more important moments.

Perhaps the best-known Protestant statement on this matter came at the end of the century in Adolf Harnack's *What Is Christianity?* (though it should also be said that it was one of his less accomplished works). The foundations for this book are actually to be found in his impressive magnum opus, the seven-volume *History of Dogma,* in which he attempted to trace out the rise and fall of the Christian faith. The decline, he argued in this large work, was to be attributed to the baleful habit that emerged very early on of clothing Christian faith in the thought forms of the day,

35. Barrett, *Death of the Soul: From Descartes to the Computer* (Garden City, N.Y.: Doubleday, 1987), p. 52.
36. For an excellent historical analysis of the discussions of Christian "essence," see Stephen Sykes, *The Identity of Christianity: Theologians and the Essence of Christianity from Schleiermacher to Barth* (Philadelphia: Fortress Press, 1984).

especially those that were Hellenistic. This began with the apostles and continued without pause in all the succeeding centuries, the result being that the absolute character of Christian faith was polluted by its union with what was relative. This union produced dogmatic, intellectualizing, external doctrine that passed itself off as authoritative, and Church people were told that they had to assent to it in order to be faithful. This development destroyed the essence of Christian faith.[37] In *What Is Christianity?* Harnack popularized these ideas, searching for the essence of faith not in external doctrine but in internal experience, not in creeds but in religious self-consciousness. Later still, in his last debate with Karl Barth, Harnack stated unambiguously that he could no longer believe in "dogmatic Christianity" and that it should all be replaced by the personal confessions that emerge from our inner spirituality. It was here that one found the unpolluted Christ in his absoluteness. To this Barth predictably retorted that it was here that one found a Christ *relativized* by personal consciousness. In America, Harnack's contention soon passed into Liberal Church life under the catchy slogan "Life, not doctrine."

Soon after Harnack had formulated his theory, a sharp rebuttal was issued by Alfred Loisy, the French Catholic Modernist. There was, in fact, more to this than met the eye, for Loisy had long since lost his faith — a fact that did not emerge until the 1930s, when his memoirs were published — and so his defense of Catholic faith was actually an attempt at secretly undermining it from within. The problem with Harnack, he said, was that a remnant of traditional piety was spoiling his scholarship. Why did the German think that this polluting process began only with the apostles? Was not Jesus himself subject to the same difficulty? In his *L'Evangile et L'Eglise,* Loisy went on to argue that what endures as the essence of faith is not even Jesus' words but his spirit in the Church. What endures is not confession but what is seen to be the *meaning* of that confession in each age. Jesus had predicted the

---

37. What is Christianity? According to Harnack in his famous lectures, "it is not a question of a 'doctrine' being handed down by a uniform repetition and arbitrarily distorted; it is a question of a *life*, again and again kindled afresh, and now burning with a flame of its own. . . . It is true that Christianity has had its classical epoch; nay more, it had a founder who himself was what he taught — to steep ourselves in him is still the chief matter; but to restrict ourselves to him means to take a point of view too low for his significance. Individual religious life was what he wanted to kindle and what he did kindle" (*What Is Christianity?* trans. Thomas Bailey Saunders [London: Williams & Norgate, 1901], p. 11). With respect to the life of this tradition in America, see *Between the Times: The Travail of the Protestant Establishment in America, 1900-1960,* ed. William R. Hutchison (Cambridge: Cambridge University Press, 1989).

kingdom, but, remarkably, the Church had come. His mistake inadvertently produced a success! And Loisy cleverly exploited the idea of doctrinal development, which he linked to Newman, to make all of this sound convincing to Catholic ears. Initially the Catholic hierarchy was surprised and delighted by this defense of orthodoxy, coming as it did from an unexpected quarter; only after Loisy had been embraced did it seem to dawn on certain episcopal minds (mainly among the French) that the means of this defense were so radical that any expression of orthodoxy was now vulnerable to the charge that it was but the passing expression of thought in an age that was itself passing. The essence of Christianity, according to Loisy, could not be located authoritatively in anything Jesus had said, because he had been shown to be something of a blunderer. Enthusiasm for Loisy therefore quickly turned to condemnation — but not before the damage had been done.

To be sure, John Henry Newman would have been appalled to see the use to which his formulation had been put by the Modernists. Nevertheless, Newman's idea did depart significantly from the kind of assurance with which Bossuet had operated — namely, that Catholics in the seventeenth century believed neither more nor less than the apostles had. There plainly had been an addition to the corpus of ideas to which Catholics gave their assent as compared to what the apostles had taught — the role of the pope, the seven sacraments, the hierarchy, the adoration of saints, and the special position accorded Mary. Newman therefore asked what were the circumstances under which these might be seen as legitimate developments from what was seminal but undeveloped in the New Testament,[38] and he then went on to formulate his famous tests for discerning true from false developments in biblical teaching. At the time of the First Vatican Council in 1870, his work was scarcely noticed. Vatican II acknowledged it in a brief summary[39] and instructed Catholic historians that the past was to be examined not as an expression of eternal dogma but as it had actually happened.[40] In the new work that followed, a good example being that on the Council of Trent, the conciliar decrees that had once been considered eternally binding because they were expressions of eternal truth were now presented as "truth" but within the wholly relative

38. Newman, *An Essay on the Development of Doctrine* (Harmondsworth: Penguin, 1974). For a brief acccount of mainly Protestant responses to Newman, see Peter Toon, *The Development of Doctrine in the Church* (Grand Rapids: William B. Eerdmans, 1979).

39. *Dogmatic Constitution on Divine Revelation*, 8.

40. *Decree on Ecumenism*, 10.

circumstances in which the statements were made.[41] Their binding validity was thereby substantially reduced, on the grounds that it was limited by what was known of the issues in question at the time and how they were addressed. The implication was that at another time, the very same issues could produce quite different conciliar decrees! The stockpile of teachings and decrees that once formed a mighty center of affirmation for Catholics has thus begun to melt away.

This relativizing process, which has been handled with the utmost subtlety by scholars, has emerged among the laity in a rather more blatant fashion. During the 1980s, the Vatican, especially under Pope John Paul and Cardinal Ratzinger, has placed great emphasis on the importance of confession and has disciplined some teachers who have appeared to be undercutting Vatican interests. But polls of the Catholic laity indicate that these actions of the pope and his guardians of Catholic doctrine amount to little more than sticking fingers in a dike through which torrents of relativity are now pouring. The American Catholic church is awash with such amazing confessional diversity that its members are frequently indistinguishable from a variety of Protestants and even non-Christians. This stunning diversity in a church that has always been known for its interest in confessional conformity certainly raises the question of whether the Modernists, who were condemned in uncommonly fierce terms in 1907, might not have lost the battle but now, by a strange turn of events, have won the war.[42] Indeed, the decree *Instruction on the*

41. "The decisions of the Council of Trent or of other councils," writes Hans Küng, "cannot be regarded as binding definitions where they concern questions which are being put differently today in the light of completely different problems. . . . No council is granted a fresh revelation; its solutions are tied to the capacities of the theology of its time" (*The Church,* trans. Ray and Rosaleen Ockenden [London: Burns & Oates, 1967], p. 419). It is this view that lies behind the massive reappraisal of this council that has been under way for some twenty years. But this work is predicated on the perception of the church's "historic conditioning," which has ramifications that extend far beyond the work done in the councils. The assumption of historical conditioning has led some to attribute a relativity even to Christ's revelation. The foundations for this view were actually laid before the Second Vatican Council in such works as Gustave Thils's three-volume *Theologie des Realities Terrestres* (Paris: Desclee de Brower, 1946). It is a view that is at considerable variance with what scholasticism has always held, and it is worth recalling that the thought of Thomas Aquinas has been endorsed by over one hundred encyclicals. See Roger Aubert, *La Théologie Catholique au Milieu du XXe Siècle* (Paris: Casterman, 1954).

42. This is the case I have argued with respect to the theology of George Tyrrell in my book *The Prophetic Theology of George Tyrrell,* AAR Studies in Religion, vol. 22 (Chico, Calif.: Scholars Press, 1981).

Ecclesial Vocation of the Theologian, issued in 1990 with the specific intention of silencing Church teachers who disagree with the Church and making that silence a condition of their retaining their roles as Church teachers, sounds remarkably like some of the papal utterances that were sent forth from Rome as Modernism was just gaining momentum at the turn of the century. What has now to be seen is only whether the dissenters will this time succeed in overwhelming the Church or whether, once again, they will be dislodged.

On the Protestant side, it is true that ritual assent continues to be given to the idea that the Bible must, in some fashion, be used confessionally. The problem, however, is that it is used in so many different ways, as David Kelsey has argued, that its role is no longer binding in the same way.[43] Paul Tillich, Karl Barth, and Carl Henry all believed that their theology was "biblical," but the sense in which each did so was quite different, and hence the way in which Scripture functioned to authorize their theologies was quite different. Although the idea of confession has lingered on, clearly what is confessed no longer belongs in or is drawn from the same universe of meaning. Far more commonly, what is confessed has meaning only within a private world of religious consciousness, and this private world all too frequently resonates with the pluralism of the modern world.

What makes the disappearance of confession in academic circles almost inevitable, barring an occasional episode of rebellion such as that mounted by Karl Barth and his allies, is that there is now an insurmountable coalition between the Enlightenment idea that it is the subject who defines reality and the universities that are now structured not only to make this idea normative but also to make its orthodox alternative unacceptable.

In twentieth-century universities, especially in America, the fact that confession is unwanted is communicated in a number of ways. There has been a trend (which peaked in the 1960s) toward replacing departments of theology with departments of religious studies.[44] The new script for study is human experience, not the teaching of the Bible or, for that matter, of the Church. This script encompasses all human experience in all of its religious shades; it is no longer tolerable to

43. Kelsey, *The Uses of Scripture in Recent Theology* (Philadelphia: Fortress Press, 1975).

44. See John F. Wilson, "Introduction: The Background and Present Context of the Study of Religion in Colleges and Universities," in *The Study of Religion in Colleges and Universities,* ed. Paul Ramsay and John F. Wilson (Princeton: Princeton University Press, 1970), pp. 3-22.

restrict academic consideration to what is Christian or Western. The method of study is now scientific, objective, and comparative; the starting point is the assumption that all religions are works of human interpretation and that no one religion has "the truth." And, because the study is conducted under the aegis of the social scientists rather than that of the clergy or theologians, the credibility of the whole undertaking requires that it take place not in the context of the old spirit of belief but rather in the context of the most audacious, irreverent, and skeptical questions, even if the result is to create a maze through which befuddled students will not easily find a way.[45] Unhappily, the demand for pluralistic values, to which unstinting support is given in these departments, itself invariably becomes an unyielding orthodoxy. Faculty in many of these departments will not tolerate those whose views are not pluralistic.

In concert with these changes, the language in which the religious in academia (including theologians) now converse with one another has also changed. The older doctrinal language has been replaced by philosophical language. This, of course, reflects the decline of theology in the universities. Whereas in the nineteenth century the dominant names were those of theologians — Jonathan Edwards, Samuel Hopkins, Nathaniel Emmons, Nathaniel William Taylor, and Charles Hodge — by the turn of the twentieth century, as Bruce Kuklick has suggested, it was the philosophers whose brilliance was especially notable — Charles Pierce, William James, Josiah Royce, Alfred North Whitehead, and John Dewey. At Harvard, Princeton, Chicago, and Columbia, it was the philosophy departments that came to dominate intellectual life, and those interested in theology were increasingly marginalized. These philosophy departments were to the universities what the theology departments had been in the older colleges prior to the Civil War.[46] But there was even more afoot than this, for the great benefit of switching to philosophical language in discussing matters of religion is that it is not confessional. It is owned by no one in particular, and so the same language can be used across religious divides. Discussions about "being" and "existence" are open-ended in a way that discussions about "justification" and "faith" are not. It thus cohered well with the new demands for pluralism. It was the language

45. See Van Austin Harvey, "The Alienated Theologian," *McCormick Quarterly* 23 (May 1970): 234-60.

46. See Bruce Kuklick, *Churchmen and Philosophers: From Jonathan Edwards to John Dewey* (New Haven: Yale University Press, 1985), pp. 191-96.

of adaptation in a context not friendly toward Christian confession. It is not difficult to see here, too, the evidence of a heavy secularizing process at work.[47]

These adaptations in the teaching of religion on our campuses have achieved two main ends. First, they have brought religious studies a measure of academic credibility (or so it is thought), and second, they have brought these departments into working relation with the explosion of new fields, the new lines of inquiry that have opened up in the twentieth-century universities. The relationship between religious studies, even when modified in these ways, and the other disciplines is, however, a very uneasy one.

This uneasiness actually has a long history. Its origin, or at least the first symptoms of the problem, can be seen in the rather strenuous debates that engaged German academics in the eighteenth and nineteenth centuries about the place of theology in the university. In order for this debate to take place, notes Edward Farley, two developments had to have occurred: (1) theology had to separate itself out as a discipline distinct from others, and (2) a consensus had to form concerning how this subject should be thought about, what its method of construction should be, what its "science" was.[48] Once both these things had occurred, then the debate could be joined as to how such a discipline could function in relation to the university's other disciplines.

In Europe, the formation of theology in this twofold sense was attended by the writing of encyclopedias. These works were not mere gatherings of knowledge, essays on an array of topics; rather, they were attempts to set out what kind of knowledge theology was, how it was derived, and how it should function. They were, then, surveys of the field, written for those who were being introduced to it, that made explicit the ways in which the field was to be approached. The writing of these encyclopedias spanned the years from 1760 to the 1880s with alternating outbreaks of intense activity and periods of comparative calm.

At the very moment when the practitioners of theology were thus mapping out their territory, they found themselves engaged in a vigorous debate about whether they should be doing this kind of work in the university. On what grounds could it be considered "scientific"? And if those grounds were not self-evident, should theology be taught

---

47. Cf. Talcott Parsons and Gerald M. Platt, *The American University* (Cambridge: Harvard University Press, 1973), pp. 276-77.

48. Farley, *Theologia*, p. 73.

in the university at all? Kant and Schleiermacher both joined the debate and, as it turned out, on the same side. Kant argued that the grounds for accepting law and medicine in the university were not scientific but utilitarian. The state had a responsibility to make provision for the needs of those in society by establishing faculties for law and medicine. If society's need for lawyers and doctors justified the inclusion of these faculties in the university, then the need for religion justified the inclusion of faculties of theology.[49] Schleiermacher agreed with this justification, although he additionally argued that theology is also a science, since it is concerned with the articulation of the religious life, which is itself empirical.

In America, between about 1870 and 1914, the universities were drastically reorganized, and one of the many results of this was that the European debate about the place of theology on a university campus was replayed here. Prior to this time, American colleges were typically small institutions under denominational control and patterned after the English universities. After they were reorganized on the German model, they began to assert their independence from all external controls, especially those of a religious nature. But while the presence of theology within the German university had been justified on utilitarian grounds, those grounds became extremely dubious in America. Germany had an established state church; in America, this institution was prohibited by the Constitution. How, then, could theology be justified within the university?

The answer has proved difficult to find, but the most favored line of defense has been that on which Schleiermacher stood his ground.[50] If it can be said that theology is empirical in its interests, that it is interested in the analysis of *experience,* then it might find academic acceptance alongside psychology, anthropology, and sociology.

But even this adaptation did not automatically secure acceptance, for these other subjects were themselves under suspicion.[51] No less a figure than William James had to defend his turf. However, his *Principles of Psychology* (1890) did seem to establish the legitimacy of studying

49. See Van Austin Harvey, "On the Intellectual Marginality of American Theology," in *Religion and Twentieth-Century American Intellectual Life,* ed. Michael J. Lacey (New York: Cambridge University Press, 1989), pp. 184-86.

50. See Schleiermacher, *Brief Outline on the Study of Theology,* trans. Terence Tice (Richmond: John Knox Press, 1966).

51. See Murray G. Murphey, "On the Scientific Study of Religion in the United States, 1870-1980," in *Religion and Twentieth-Century American Intellectual Life,* pp. 140-42.

the mind. And, having made this point, he went on to establish the
legitimacy of studying religion in *The Varieties of Religious Experience*
(1902), although this work rendered the confessional element
completely irrelevant. He defined religion as those feelings and acts
that result when a person is oriented to the divine, however the individual wishes to understand that. James argued that there is a reality
other than the mind that intrudes upon the mind, and such intrusions
or felt effects are legitimate subject matter for academic study. In time,
James and his students won acceptance for their sphere of work within
a modern academic setting. Subsequently, working along the same
lines, the sociologists also brought religion into the charmed circle of
academic life. Talcott Parsons's *The Structure of Social Action* was not
only highly acclaimed but also effective in mediating to an American
audience the ideas of such theoreticians as Weber and Durkheim, and
from this there emerged a whole framework for doing social research.
It further enlarged the climate of acceptance for works such as Milton
Yinger's *Religion in the Struggle for Power* (1946) and for the contribution
of such contemporary sociologists as Peter Berger and Robert Bellah.

What is significant about this development is that it carved out a
niche in the American academy for religion provided that it is empirically examined. It established the legitimacy of looking at religion
through the eyes of psychology, anthropology, or sociology. But this
narrows the means of access to religion to the structures of the self,
the tribe, or society, and this necessarily establishes twin biases — a bias
in favor of the sort of classical Liberalism that Schleiermacher argued
for (which seeks the disclosure of God *within* human experience) and
a bias against classical orthodoxy (which builds on revelation the ultimate source of which is *outside* human experience). The university
opens its arms to those theologians who can successfully disguise themselves as psychologists, anthropologists, or sociologists looking for
divine reality within the structures of the self or society, but it is a good
deal less hospitable to those who find it hard, if not impossible, to see
these mediating structures as themselves the vehicles of revelation and
who look instead to Scripture as a confessional source that does not
merely mirror human consciousness but is the means of transcendent
disclosure. Indeed, the university has been so consistently hostile
toward the position that grows out of classical orthodoxy that "theological argumentation has virtually become a forgotten and lost mode
of discourse" among American intellectuals.[52]

52. Harvey, "On the Intellectual Marginality of American Theology," p. 172.

These developments, both European and American, have co-alesced with many other historical developments in society in the modern period both to dislodge theology — especially classical or-thodox theology — from the universities and also to estrange it from the life of the academic guild. Not only has the location of its practice been shifted largely outside the universities (to the seminaries that began to come into being at the beginning of the nineteenth century) but the way in which it proceeds to function has been altered. Where there is a confessional element that is overt and functional, reflection takes a form that is entirely different from that which it commonly takes in the universities, where confession is neither overt nor functional. But it is in the guild that the "official" style of theology is set. It is in the guild that the canons of learned credibility are estab-lished. And insofar as these canons divert reflection from the traditional function of theology, they contribute to its continued breakdown. In the absence of both confession and an overt commitment to devout practice, an already ailing theology is doomed to die.

The Declining Years of Evangelicalism

The disappearance of a confessional element has for quite different reasons also taken place in evangelicalism, and this seeming coinci-dence is producing some rather surprising convergences. In the academy, to be sure, this has been brought about by the tempo of high culture, the demands of intellectual life in the modern world; in evangelicalism, it has been brought about by the tempo of low culture, the way in which popular sentiment is allowed to define what truth is. The common factor, therefore, is not their appearance, nor their class alliances, but rather the trough from which they are both drinking. The trough is modernity, though those in the aca-demic and Liberal world drink from one end and those in the evangelical world drink from the other end. In both cases, however, confession becomes a casualty because modernity is hostile to all truth claims that are absolute and transcendent in nature. What remains is simply reflection in the academy and practice in evangel-icalism.

That this emasculation has taken place among the evangelicals is, on the face of it, most surprising. After all, they have steadfastly resisted until relatively recently every attempt to ease the difficulty implicit in believing in truth in the modern world. They have refused to come to peace with doctrinal change as have Catholics after Newman's time.[53] They staunchly opposed the Modernist effort to surrender doctrine in favor of "life," as if religious consciousness could be a substitute for biblical truth. And it is as doctrinal people that they have defined themselves through much of the twentieth century. But this identity is now rapidly dissipating.

To be sure, reactions to the intrusions of modernization have not been uniform in the evangelical world, thus making generalizations about evangelicals quite precarious. Their responses have been quite varied. At one extreme are those who have recoiled into Anglo-Catholicism in reaction to pietistic subjectivism; at the other are those who have taken their stand on the verities of old-time Fundamentalism as a way of rejecting evangelical softness. But in between these far shores lie the choppy waters that most evangelicals now ply with their boats, and here the winds of modernity blow with disconcerting force, fragmenting what it means to be evangelical. This is because evangelicals have allowed their confessional center to dissipate.

This is a remarkable change when one considers the importance of doctrinal confession to the evangelicals' most numerous immediate forebears, the Fundamentalists. In the 1920s, 1930s, and 1940s Fundamentalists were clearly cognitive aliens within the culture and often used doctrine to define their own cultural boundaries. Doctrine served to seal in believers and seal out unbelievers. As a result, their commitment to the formal and material principles of Protestantism was unyielding. They held to an inspired, authoritative Bible and to the centrality and indispensability of Christ's substitutionary death on the Cross. These beliefs were then hedged about by supporting doctrines the role of which, it would seem, was quite as much to alienate an unbelieving culture as it was to preserve Christian orthodoxy. The miracles of Christ, for example, are a part of the New Testament record, but the way Fundamentalists chose to defend them seemed to be aimed quite as much at posing an affront to a naturalistic age as it was at elucidating the thought of the New Testament. Likewise, the assertion that the Bible should be read "literally" not only signaled the Fundamentalists' intention to take it seriously but also, it would seem, to reject the whole raft of literary theory and critical chicanery that had made a mockery, in learned circles, of biblical inspiration. And when Fundamentalists insisted on the premillennial return of Christ, a view that has a long history but had never before been in vogue prior

53. See James Orr, *The Progress of Dogma* (London: Hodder & Stoughton, 1901); and Toon, *The Development of Doctrine in the Church*.

to the nineteenth century, they were declaring their intention not only to understand biblical prophecy in a certain way but also to reject categorically the Liberals' idea of the growing kingdom of God on earth, a kingdom with interests, it turned out, that coincided exactly with those of the Liberals.

Fundamentalist doctrine on these and related matters was to them as important socially as it was credally. Their doctrine drew a tight perimeter around their counter-community, established a clear border. Rules emerged that warned the unwary as well as the adventurous where enemy territory lay. Those who were headstrong or unwise crossed the border at their own peril and often at a social cost. And within these Fundamentalist counter-communities, mutual therapy was offered against the insidious pressure of creeping doubt that comes, sooner or later, to all cognitive minorities, among whom there inevitably arises the question of why the outside world seems to be doing so well when it knows nothing of true doctrine.[54] Strong, authoritarian preachers emerged whose very demeanor banished doubt on sight. The stronghold of faith was thus made invincible. The excesses and eccentricities of Fundamentalist behavior only underscored the utterly central role that formal doctrine held for them.[55]

When we move from Fundamentalism to evangelicalism, however, we are moving from a counter-community to a community. Fundamentalism was a walled city; evangelicalism is a city. Fundamentalism always had an air of embattlement about it, of being an island in a sea of unremitting hostility. Evangelicalism has reacted against this sense of psychological isolation. It has lowered the barricades. It is open to the world. The great sin in Fundamentalism is to compromise; the great sin in evangelicalism is to be narrow.[56]

The lowering of these barricades coincided, in fact, with a change in the psychological position of evangelicals within the culture, a change that brought them in from the cold and made them part of an accepted, if informal, religious establishment. It is difficult to specify exactly how this internal chemistry worked, but it is beyond dispute *that* it worked.

54. See Peter L. Berger, *A Rumor of Angels: Modern Society and the Rediscovery of the Supernatural* (Garden City, N.Y.: Doubleday-Anchor, 1970), pp. 17-18.
55. See George Marsden, *Fundamentalism and American Culture: The Shaping of Twentieth-Century Evangelicalism, 1870-1925* (New York: Oxford University Press, 1980), pp. 16-18, 102-14, 225-28.
56. See Hunter, *American Evangelicalism: Conservative Religion and the Quandary of Modernity* (New Brunswick, N.J.: Rutgers University Press, 1983), pp. 102-19.

In 1976, America woke up to find itself living in the "Year of the Evangelical." The popular media, which have an acute sense of who has the power and who does not, knew that something had changed. And the change was not simply that President Carter, who was indubitably born again, had made it to the White House. There was, rather, a sinking realization on the part of a profession known for its irreligion that a tradition that had been frequently discounted, except in the hills of Appalachia, had now become virtually ubiquitous. George Gallup, who has been convinced for some time that a religious revival is under way, reported that 34 percent of adults claimed to be born again, and even though considerably less than this seemed to know what that meant, the numbers were still very impressive.

Overnight evangelicals began to be courted, their views given solemn attention. Politicians at election time, like birds anxious to mate, preened themselves before evangelical organizations and constituencies. There was talk — very anxious talk at times — about how far evangelicals might go in trying to change the national agenda, whether they would succeed in "forcing" their morality on everyone else, and whether the alliance with other conservatives would mean the applecart of a two-party political system was going to be completely upset, with the Democrats finding themselves on the underside.

The specter of evangelical faith organizing itself and speaking out after decades in the barren hinterlands of American life took some getting used to, admittedly, but the alarm and anxiety it stirred were not justified. For no sooner had the evangelicals begun to think like the status quo than their theological and moral distinctives began to evaporate like the morning mist. In entering the mainstream of American cultural life, they were brought face to face with the great shaping forces of modern life, and one of the immediate casualties was their sense of truth in both private and public life. Almost immediately, their capacity to think theologically about themselves and their world also disappeared.

The impulses of modernity have generally sundered private from public.[57] The result of this among evangelicals was that their characteristic beliefs were increasingly limited to matters of private experience, increasingly shorn of their distinctive worldview, and increasingly withdrawn from what was external and public. Being evangelical has come to mean simply that one has had a certain kind of religious experience that gives color to the private aspects of daily life but in

---

57. See Hunter, *American Evangelicalism*, pp. 91-94.

which few identifiable theological elements can be discerned or, as it turns out, are necessary. Evangelical faith is pursued as a matter of internal fascination but abandoned as a matter of external and public relevance, except in areas of social relief, where evangelicals have a more exemplary record than any other religious group according to Gallup's polling.

The provision of social relief is a largely neutral activity, however, and it often looks much the same regardless of the disparate theological springs from which it arises. As a matter of fact, it can also serve as a substitute for theology. And so evangelicals have also come to terms psychologically with our society's structural pluralism and its lack of interest in matters of truth. Good works are seldom offensive in the modern world; it is a belief in truth that is troublesome.

In an extraordinary fashion, then, the theological wheel has turned full circle. Evangelicals, no less than the Liberals before them whom they have always berated, have now abandoned doctrine in favor of "life." It is true that they view this life as supernatural in a way that might have discomforted the old Liberals, but their discomfort would only have had to be momentary. For evangelicals today, this life is also an "essence" detached from a cognitive structure, a detachment made necessary by the external modern world in which it no longer has a viable place, and it really does not require a theological view of life. Evangelicals today only have to believe that God can work dramatically within the narrow fissure of internal experience; they have lost interest (or perhaps they can no longer sustain interest) in what the doctrines of creation, common grace, and providence once meant for Christian believers, and even in those doctrines that articulate Christ's death such as justification, redemption, propitiation, and reconciliation. It is enough for them simply to know that Christ somehow died for people.[58] For both Liberals and evangelicals, the search for "essence" has been a tactical retreat. It is not the kind of retreat that the Fundamentalists engineered, preserving their view of the world by separating themselves from the unbelieving world outside. It is a retreat into internal privacy, into a world that need never come to terms with the unbelieving world outside. The evangelical form of separation is as real as was that of the Fundamentalists; it is simply not as effective, and it is much more damaging to the Protestantism of which they are the heirs.

58. See Robert Brow, "Evangelical Megashift," *Christianity Today*, 19 February 1990, pp. 12-14.

The most obvious consequence of this unabashed desertion of the cognitive substance of faith is one that few have pondered, at least out loud. It is the disappearance of conviction. In Our Time, no less than in Yeats's, the best lack all conviction because its ground has vanished. As a matter of fact, in Our Time, the worst are also without passion. And there is a strange irony to how this plays out. One might suppose that the disappearance of conviction would be the stuff of which ecumenical dreams were made, for conviction always plays the spoilsport to dreams of unity. It turns out, however, that here we encounter a small surprise. In the absence of conviction, all belief collapses, even the belief in unity. The energy that is needed to fuel the ecumenical vision evaporates. Nothing now stands in the way of unity, but nothing now impels us toward it either. Nothing impels us at all, so faith must now sweeten its own existence by toying with itself.

The onset of this pall of privatization has worked havoc with the structural cohesion of the evangelical movement. In the 1950s and 1960s, defining evangelical faith was not hard, because evangelicals were anxious to say exactly who they were and what they believed. But in the 1990s, when the movement has become a sprawling empire in which the left hand has no idea that the right hand even exists, definitions of who the evangelicals are frequently reflect the movement's disintegration and, on occasion, the special interest of the authors who offer the definitions.[59]

59. The precise relationships between fundamentalism and the neo-evangelicalism that distinguished itself from Fundamentalism in the 1940s and 1950s and between the neo-evangelicalism of that time and the evangelicalism of today are not nearly as clear as they were once thought to be. While it is true that parts of the neo-evangelical movement grew out of Fundamentalism, parts of it had never been in Fundamentalism and had never withdrawn from the mainline denominations. And the same can be said of evangelicalism today, parts of which have been drawn from sources other than neo-evangelicalism. On this overall development, see the essays by Joel A. Carpenter ("From Fundamentalism to the New Evangelical Coalition"), Leonard I. Sweet ("The 1960s: The Crises of Liberal Christianity and the Public Emergence of Evangelicalism"), and Martin E. Marty ("Fundamentalism as a Social Phenomenon") in *Evangelicalism and Modern America*, ed. George Marsden (Grand Rapids: William B. Eerdmans, 1984), pp. 3-16, 29-45, 56-70. On the widening array of definitions see, for example, Millard Erickson, *The New Evangelical Theology* (Westwood, N.J.: Fleming H. Revell, 1969); Nancy Hardesty, *Women Called to Witness: Evangelical Feminism in the Nineteenth Century* (Nashville: Abingdon, 1984); Donald D. Dayton, *Discovering an Evangelical Heritage* (New York: Harper & Row, 1976); Robert E. Webber, *Evangelicals on the Canterbury Trail: Why Evangelicals Are Attracted to the Liturgical Church* (Waco, Tex.: Word Books, 1985); *The Chicago Declaration*, ed. Ronald Sider (Carol Stream, Ill.: Creation House, 1974); *The Orthodox Evangelicals: Who They Are and What They Are Saying*, ed. Robert Webber and

It has further raised the interesting question of whether there ever was a theological structure that evangelicals commonly held and that held them together in a common world of belief. If there was, it has collapsed, says William Abraham, and his solution is to widen the circle to include traditions and ideas that have not found a welcome in the center in recent decades.[60] Donald Dayton thinks that those who have shown the most concern for theology, including those in the confessional churches as well as those who are generally Reformed, should now be viewed as being peripheral to the evangelical world.[61] He is probably correct in this judgment, but it remains a fact that the work of defining evangelicalism theologically has until quite recently been borne by the kind of people who are now on its periphery. In the 1960s and 1970s, it was such leaders as Carl Henry, E. J. Carnell, Cornelius Van Til, Bernard Ramm, Francis Schaeffer, and Kenneth Kantzer who provided evangelicals with the capital off which they have for the most part been living since, but this capital has now been exhausted. The bank is empty. The growth and prosperity of evangelical institutions during the 1970s and 1980s have brought with them much bureaucracy, and bureaucracy invariably smothers vision, creativity, and even theology. Leadership is now substantially in the hands of the managers, and as a consequence the evangelical capital is not being renewed. The only semblance of cohesion that now remains is simply tactical, never theological. This does not mean that there are no theological agreements among evangelicals around the edges, for there are. What it does mean is that evangelicals are not driven by a theological vision, and those who have risen to positions of leadership most commonly reflect this diminished outlook.

Donald Bloesch (Nashville: Thomas Nelson, 1978); Robert C. Liebman and Robert Wuthnow, *The New Christian Right: Mobilization and Legitimation* (New York: Aldine, 1983); Richard Quebedeaux, *The Young Evangelicals: The Story of the Emergence of a New Generation of Evangelicals* (New York: Harper & Row, 1974); William Abraham, *Recovering the Full Evangelical Tradition* (San Francisco: Harper & Row, 1984); and Donald Dayton, *Discovering an Evangelical Heritage* (New York: Harper & Row, 1976). On the evangelical tradition, see the Leonard I. Sweet's excellent essay "The Evangelical Tradition in America," in *The Evangelical Tradition in America* (Macon: Mercer University Press, 1984), pp. 1-86. For bibliographies, see Richard Pierard, "The Quest for the Historical Evangelicalism: A Bibliographical Excursus," *Fides et Historia*, Spring 1979, pp. 60-72; and the comprehensive study by Judith L. Blumhofer and Joel A. Carpenter, *Twentieth-Century Evangelicalism: A Guide to the Sources* (New York: Garland, 1990).

    60. See Abraham, *The Coming Great Revival*, pp. 27-48.
    61. Dayton, *Discovering an Evangelical Heritage*, p. 20.

As evangelicalism has continued to grow numerically, it has seeped through its older structures and now spills out in all directions, producing a family of hybrids whose theological connections are quite baffling: evangelical Catholics, evangelicals who are Catholic, evangelical liberationalists, evangelical feminists, evangelical ecumenists, ecumenists who are evangelical, young evangelicals, orthodox evangelicals, radical evangelicals, liberal evangelicals, Liberals who are evangelical, and charismatic evangelicals. The word *evangelical*, precisely because it has lost its confessional dimension, has become descriptively anemic. To say that someone is an evangelical says little about what they are likely to believe (although it says more if they are older and less if they are younger). And so the term is forced to compensate for its theological weakness by borrowing meaning from adjectives the very presence of which signals the fragmentation and disintegration of the movement. What is now primary is not what is evangelical but what is adjectivally distinctive, whether Catholic, liberationalist, feminist, ecumenist, young, orthodox, radical, liberal, or charismatic. It is, I believe, the dark prelude to death, when parasites have finally succeeded in bringing down their host. Amid the clamor of all these new models of evangelical faith there is the sound of a death rattle.

The sound of death is hard to hear, however, given the rumble of the large numbers that the evangelical movement has attracted and the chorus of voices being echoed from the cultural pluralism that surrounds it. The pluralism is providing insulation from criticism and reality. It is not hard to see that the disappearance of a center of values in culture is now paralleled by a disappearance of a theological center in evangelicalism. And from both evangelicalism and the larger culture there spin away the miniature worlds of private interest, each with its own trajectory, and each threatening to collide with the other, but each a world unto itself. As theology declines, as the word *evangelical* becomes empty, the adjectives become more important and less yielding, and the means of providing some discipline to their expression become more remote.

Evangelicals who seek to work the theological craft in a way that is recognizably historical and who keep the intellectual company of Athanasius, Augustine, Luther, Calvin, Wesley, Edwards, Hodge, and the like are often quite baffled by all of the other company they seem obliged to keep in contemporary evangelicalism. The new interests and appetites can be brought into relation with historical evangelical or Protestant faith only by a mighty exercise of the imagination and, not infrequently, a tactful aversion of the gaze. Must we swallow these new interests, as we had to swallow vegetables we hated when we were young, in order to preserve our place at the table? There is a yawning chasm between what evangelical faith was in the past and what it frequently is today, between the former spirituality and the contemporary emptiness and accommodation.

The common thread running through this brief survey is the seeming invincibility of modernity and the corresponding inclination to break away from what Christians have traditionally confessed. Modernity allows little room for the preservation of Christian doctrine, and it makes that confession look decidedly suspect. Each of the traditions we have touched upon so far has found its own way of coming to terms with this. For Roman Catholics, it was Newman's theory of doctrinal development; for the Modernists, both Catholic and Protestant, it was the abandonment of the traditional cognitive structures of Christian faith and the relocation of meaning to their inner religious consciousness; for evangelicals, it is a cleavage that has emerged, perhaps unconsciously, between private and public, and the relocation of meaning from the public realm to the private realm, in the process of which it is emptied of theological substance.

There have never been great numbers of theorizers in the world, but that is not to say that people have not lived by knowledge. For much of its life, the Church has struggled to preserve a knowledge common to all — common, that is, to its theologians, clergy, and laity. Its greatest struggles have not been over whether this core of belief should be commonly held but over what should constitute this core. Until the eighteenth century, only a few misguided lights on the misty borderland between orthodoxy and heresy thought to challenge the idea that all Christians should work from the same basis of knowledge. Today, however, that basis has eroded. The single universe of meaning has dissolved, and the single field of discourse that flowed from it has dissipated.

Without a sharp, cogent, differentiating identity, evangelicals, no less than the Liberals before them, are simply absorbed into the conventions of the modern world in which they live. It is no mystery, therefore, why they are failing to out-think their cognitive opponents. The reason is that they are not that different from these opponents, and the motivation to out-think them is no longer compelling. Why is it that with more than a third of the nation's adults in 1990 claiming a born-again experience and many more beyond that claiming allegiance to Christian values, the society moves on oblivious to its religious citizens, reshaping laws and policies as if they were not there? The

answer, in a sense, is that they are not there. They are the people of
the inner life whose relation to the external world is largely a matter
of cognitive disjuncture. Whatever follies the Marxists committed —
and their follies and wickedness have been manifold — they always
had the wisdom to know that if they yielded their worldview, they
yielded their reason for existence. Evangelicals are not quite so wise.

It is this transition from historic Protestantism to modernized
evangelicalism, in which evangelicals who were once cognitive dissi-
dents within the culture are rapidly becoming amicable partners with
it, that is the subject of what now follows. This transition has entailed
banishing theology from its place in the center of evangelical life and
relegating it to the periphery. Behind this banishment is a greatly
diminished sense of truth. Where truth is central in the religious
disposition, theology is always close at hand. As theology has become
dislodged, contemporary evangelicals have become progressively more
remote from their forebears in the faith whose courage and fortitude
produced the rich heritage of historic Protestant orthodoxy. They are,
in fact, now beginning to retread the path that the Protestant Liberals
once trod, and they are doing so, oddly enough, at the very time when
many of the descendants of the Liberals have abandoned this path
because of its spiritual bankruptcy.

For this reason, it might be argued that in the absence of some
notable repentance that would reverse the present direction, evangelicals are now in their declining years. Of course, appearances suggest
quite the contrary: evangelicals seem to be at the zenith of their influence. Influence, however, is not simply a matter of numbers. It is
necessarily bound up with an appropriate relationship with truth and
character, both of which are eroded in every accommodation that is
made to modernity. It is the inextinguishable knowledge of being
owned by the transcendent God that forms character, and his owner-
ship challenges that of every other contender, including that of the
modern world. This is the issue: Who owns evangelicalism? And this
is the subject that we will take up in more detail in the chapters that
follow.

CHAPTER IV

Self-Piety

Amazing grace, how sweet the sound
That saved a stunted self-concept like me,
I once was stressed out, but now am empowered,
Was visually challenged, but now I see.

Doug Marlette

THAT AMERICAN THEOLOGY has characteristics that are distinctively American should not be surprising. We readily see that the Germans and the British, the South Americans and Asians have ways of thinking about Christian faith that seem obviously German, British, South American, and Asian. In America, however, theology is apparently not affected by its context. It is not American in content or tone. It is simply theology! At least, that is what is commonly assumed.

In this and the following chapter I want to look at the unconscious contextualization that goes on in American theology. In this regard I am less interested in how the *culture* has shaped evangelical faith than in how the American *character* has. The focus here, in other words, is more psychological than cultural, though the one is closely related to the other. In this chapter, I will examine how American individualism threatens to undermine the *nature* of theology, and particularly its need for an objective truth, since this is essential to its ability to sustain a public relevance and to our capacity to hold such truth. In Chapter V,

I will examine how American conformity changes the politics of theology and hence its *function*.

It is, of course, no accident that I have identified as the two fundamental aspects of American character its individualism and its conformity. There have been many attempts to define the essence of the American character, not all of them in agreement with one another, but it has been noticeable how often these two aspects appear in these analyses. Whatever else might be said on the subject, these seem to be staple elements in the discussion. Yet it needs to be noted that neither of these traits by itself is unique to America. Individualism is being spread today as far as modernization itself travels, often far from the shores of America, and the psychology of conformity is generated wherever mass societies are formed. It is not individualism and conformity per se that are distinctive to the American character. Rather, as Seymour M. Lipset has noted, the distinction lies in the way they are held together in America. It is the "dynamic interaction" between them, he says, that "has been a constant element in determining American institutions and behavior."[1]

Perhaps it is the case that these seeming opposites have come into such dynamic interaction in the American character because they reflect the experience of having to adjust to the abrupt, seemingly contradictory changes that have so consistently characterized this country. America is an amalgam of opposites, Erik Erikson has observed, a mix of the "migratory and sedentary, individualistic and stylistic, competitive and cooperative, pious and freewheeling, responsible and cynical."[2] In fact, Americans have never sought to moderate these contradictory impulses as have the British. In America, it is not uncivilized to be extreme, as it is in Britain, although that extremism may sometimes have to be internalized. Americans have usually admired those who take things as far as they can be taken. Their inclinations to conformity and individualism do not cancel each other out but are preserved in their opposition to one another. They are allowed to live side by side with each other, without discomfort and, indeed, with much interesting interaction.

Finding the essence of what it means to be American has assumed an importance here that is not paralleled in other nations. There seem to be two main reasons for this. First, the American character takes the

1. Lipset, *The First Nation: The United States in Historical and Comparative Perspective* (New York: Basic Books, 1963), p. 101.
2. Erikson, *Childhood and Society* (New York: W. W. Norton, 1963), p. 286.

place in America that historical memory usually takes in other nations.[3] Behind the French, for example, there is a sense of being Gallic; behind the Norwegians there are the Vikings; behind every Middle Easterner today there is a tribe that has wandered the stony hills around the Mediterranean for centuries; and behind John Stuart Mill, who thought depictions of national character were vulgar, there is a sense of being Anglo-Saxon. Americans, however, have relatively little behind them. Aside from the Indians who were native to America, everyone else is an immigrant or from the stock of immigrants whose heritage lies not so much in the American past but in Europe, Africa, South America, or Asia. If America is not united by ethnicity, language, and religion — which is what unites most other peoples into nations — can it still speak of itself as being a nation? Undoubtedly it can, but what makes it so is a different form of bonding. It is the American character.

Second, the first settlers came upon their "errand into the wilderness" not with an existing sense of nationhood but simply with *ideas*. Americanness was therefore wrought not out of blood but out of a compact — indeed, out of a sense of a divine commission. In time, of course, the commission became a mission, and in yet more time it became a destiny. It is now the obscurity of the manifestation of that

3. See David M. Potter, "The Quest for National Character," in *The Reconstruction of American History*, ed. John Higham (New York: Harper, 1962), pp. 197-220. In identifying the two major aspects of the American character as individualism and conformity, Potter is accepting the main observations of Frederick Jackson Turner and Alexis de Toqueville. Potter is not, however, uncritical of the Turner thesis that the frontier favored the emergence of individualism because of the agrarian context, the absence of such institutions as schools, churches, and government, and the waning influence of civilization. See Turner, *People of Plenty: Economic Abundance and the American Character* (Chicago: University of Chicago Press, 1968), pp. 142-65. On this theme, see also David W. Noble, *Historians against History: The Frontier Thesis and the National Covenant in American Historical Writing since 1830* (Minneapolis: University of Minnesota Press, 1965). The seemingly paradoxical aspect of this character is also explored in William H. Whyte's *The Organization Man* (New York: Simon & Schuster, 1956), the dustjacket of which correctly announces its theme as "The clash between the individualistic beliefs he is expected to follow and the collective life he actually lives." As Erik Erikson has argued, this paradox is rooted in the typical American experience of encountering and having to adjust to opposites. Americans like to be both anchored in the past and afloat on the tide going out into the future, with the result that they tend to be both "migratory and sedentary, individualistic and stylized, competitive and cooperative, pious and freethinking, responsible and freethinking" (*Childhood and Society*, p. 286). For an annotated bibliography on the American character, see *The Character of Americans: A Book of Readings*, rev. ed., ed. Michael McGiffert (Homewood, Ill.: Dorsey Press, 1970), pp. 416-25.

destiny, given the perplexities of the modern world, that nudges the mind to delve back into the character of the nation, to see if perhaps there can be found lodging in some inner place the secret of its being. It is why David Noble thinks that in America the historian has so often also had to serve as its "chief theologian." These, it would seem, are the reasons that the national character has assumed such importance in America.

It is true, of course, that the currents of individualism and of conformity that flow through the American psyche do not exhaust what it means to be American. Perhaps for as long as thirty years now, it has been apparent that ethnicity is also a powerful shaping force. Now in the 1990s, it is seriously challenging the nation's unity and even the supposition that there is such a thing as an American. Proponents of multiculturalism assert that what has passed as national character was nothing more than a Eurocentric, white, male culture that excluded from its center all who were not European, white, and male. America has always been a multiethnic society, though, so this interest in preserving ethnic particularities is not new. And discrimination against minorities is hardly uniquely American; it is known in probably every other country in the world. What is new is that the vision of forging a center strong enough to support this cultural diversity is now being challenged. Only time will tell whether the American character, with its unique blend of individualism and conformity, will be able to hold, whether it will be able to hold within itself these new social impulses with their strident ethnicity.

In this chapter I want to look at one of the most important transformations that has occurred in the modern period. It is that which has turned our individualism into the self movement. When rugged individualism defined the essence of what it meant to be American, Christian faith was choreographed in one way. When the pursuit and satisfaction of the self became the essence of what it meant to be American in the modern world, evangelical faith was choreographed in an entirely different way. Whereas the older kind of individualism sometimes treated theology roughly, the new culture of self dismisses it entirely as irrelevant. That being the case, evangelicalism has increasingly found that the cost of modern relevance has been its own theological evisceration. And, shorn of its theology, evangelicalism has become simply one more expression of the self movement, which also includes many constituencies that do not have the remotest interest in God but with whom evangelicals often make common cause in satisfying the self.

Modern Individuality

The contemporary sense of the individual that Americans have is a complex amalgam. It has been formed by a combination of both ideas and social experience. Because the exact relationship between them is intricate, I need to sketch out my argument rather broadly first before filling in the details about how, in combination, they have produced the modern person whose sense of self is now so fragile and eroded.

With respect to the ideas about the individual, we will begin with the Protestant Reformation and note how its views were mediated on these shores by the Puritans. Subsequently, there emerged a new kind of individuality with a doctrine that was not Christian at all, having arisen, instead, from the Enlightenment. Each source, the Reformation and the Enlightenment, has produced its own kind of individualism. As a rough generalization, we might say that Reformation individualism produces people whose life choices and values have a seriousness and intensity about them that reflect their recognition of an ultimate, divine accountability. It is this sense of a moral universe presided over by God that drives this individualism to eschew all competing authorities, including those of the state, the Church, and, most importantly, the self.

The individualism from the Enlightenment may have superficial similarities to that from the Reformation, but its form of accountability is actually quite different. The eighteenth- and nineteenth-century deists may have believed in an ultimate judgment, but in the twentieth century that sense has faded. The modern children of the Enlightenment have themselves taken God's place. It is to ourselves that we are now accountable. It is because of a sense of self-interest, or self-duty, that we decline to relinquish decisions to others such as the state or the Church — an attitude reflected in the popular assertion that "you have a duty to yourself" to do this or that.

These two streams of thinking have both contributed to the American experience, and at times they have had common interests, differently justified as those might have been. They managed to make common cause in the Revolution, for example. But in other instances they have sharply diverged, as in the current struggle over abortion: Reformation individualism refuses to snuff out the life of an unborn child on the grounds that such an act would be morally reprehensible before God, but Enlightenment individualism suffers few qualms in doing so on the grounds that duty to the self and to personal convenience is the central, overriding consideration.

It is important to realize, however, that human beings are not simply storage facilities for ideas. They are social beings who are in constant communication with their social environment, and this is the other part of the amalgam from which modern individualism has emerged. Indeed, ideas sometimes have an appeal precisely because the social environment makes them seem plausible, makes them seem the "obvious" way to look at life. That being so, it is quite inadequate to look merely at the intellectual sources of modern individualism if we are to understand why modern Americans act as they do.

What, in fact, has happened is that the stream of individualism that flows beneath the surface of American life has had to turn in on itself because of one of the inescapable consequences of modernization — alienation. This is what really differentiates the early individualism of the eighteenth century from its contemporary, secular expression. Today, people increasingly find that they are unable to forge and hold meaningful connections in the outer world, whether in their work, their community, their family, their nation, or their past. Modernity obliges us to turn inward, to relocate the sources of our satisfaction and fulfillment from these connections in the outer world to sources within our selves. Modernity obliges us to psychologize life, to look to the states and vagaries of the self for the reality that was once external. For the most part, evangelicals have failed to see that this shift from the objective to the subjective, this new fascination with the self, is invariably inimical to biblical and historical faith. Robert Nisbet has argued that this self-absorption, which has been passed off by many as the very essence of evangelical faith, is in fact one of the most telling indications of our cultural decay. He quotes Goethe's comment that "ages which are regressive and in process of dissolution are always subjective, whereas the trend in all progressive epochs is objective."[4]

The subjective obsession that also confronts us in religious dress (as is often the case in evangelicalism) sometimes appears in dress that is quite irreligious. Whatever the garb, however, it exhibits the same underlying mentality, the same habits of mind, the same assumption that reality can be accessed only through the self (and by intuition rather than by thought), the same belief that we can attain virtually unlimited personal progress if only we can tap into our own hidden resources. This fascination with the self, made bright with hope by the belief in progress, has proved to be a gold mine for the publishers. In

4. Goethe, quoted by Nisbet in *Twilight of Authority* (New York: Oxford University Press, 1977), p. 139.

the overall religious book market today, 31 percent of all books sold fall into the inspirational and motivational category, and a further 15 percent work these same themes from a New Age angle.

There is, of course, a certain affinity between the Enlightenment vision of the human being at the center of reality, fashioning the world in better and more pleasing ways, and this new modern person who looks for reality only in the self. The modern, self-absorbed individualist is in continuity with the Enlightenment ideal but, in most cases, is not the direct product of the Enlightenment. This person is also the product of the modernization that has been brought about by market economies, technology, urbanization, bureaucracies, and mass communication. The collective effect of these products of modernization — modernity — has coalesced with Enlightenment ideals to produce the new individualist: the Enlightenment posits ultimate authority in the self, and modernity severs the self from any meaningful connections outside itself.[5] Thus, the inward and outward environment become as one; they depend on and reinforce each other.

This confluence of thought and social environment has produced great turbulence and disorder in the modern psyche. It has reshaped the modern understanding of who people are, how they gain access to reality, and how they should govern their behavior. These are themes to which we will return shortly. Before that, though, we need to consider the Protestant Reformation in order to see how its understanding of the individual has been transformed over time to the extent that only a perverted version has survived in contemporary evangelicalism.

The Protestant Reformation

What was revolutionary about the Protestant Reformers was their insistence that God is not savingly known through created nature as

---

5. In *The Closing of the American Mind: How Higher Education Has Failed Democracy and Impoverished the Souls of Today's Student* (New York: Simon & Schuster, 1988), Allan Bloom observes how pervasive relativism is in education and how it undermines the pursuit of knowledge. His observations, though somewhat anecdotal, touched a raw nerve and turned his book into a best-seller. His explanation of this phenomenon, however, is quite improbable. He takes the reader into the back streets of nineteenth-century German philosophy, among thinkers whose names are probably unknown to most students today, to find the answer to this contemporary dilemma. The philosophers he discusses are only remotely connected with contemporary student attitudes. The real answer is much closer at hand. It lies in the cognitive horizons produced by exposure to modernization. Bloom took the path he did because he overlooked the role of social environment.

paganism had proposed, or through human nature as the medieval mystics had thought[6] (and some evangelicals now think), or through the Church and its sacraments as the Roman Catholic Church taught, but directly, by the work of the Holy Spirit and the truth of the biblical Word, the internal and supernatural work of the Spirit creating the spiritual climate in which Scripture might be received. The Reformers rejected all assertions that there are channels of saving grace in nature, human nature, or the Church.[7] They held that there are no intermediaries between God and the sinner save for Christ himself, and they insisted that this unique role could not be usurped without destroying the faith that claimed his name. Christ's role is a sine qua non, they argued, because the judgment of God on the one side and human corruption on the other have produced a double alienation with which he alone can deal. Only through Christ is God's wrath turned aside and human disaffection from God and his rule replaced by a submissive affection.

There are combined in this conception two ideas that it has proved exceedingly difficult to maintain in union: human dignity and human depravity. The Reformers argued for the possibility, based on the image of God and the Spirit's re-creation of that image, of an individual knowledge of God.[8] In this consists our dignity. Modern individualism really arises from this, from the sense that it is the individual who must decide life's ultimate questions and that neither the state nor the Church can legitimately encroach upon this preserve, though each has a God-intended role. At the same time, however, the Reformers professed a belief in human depravity, the corruption of the whole of human nature in all of its parts, which meant not only that no one can know God apart

6. See Steven E. Ozment, *Homo Spiritualis: A Comparative Study of the Anthropology of Johannes Tauler, Jean Gerson and Martin Luther (1509-16) in the Context of Their Theological Thought* (Leiden: E. J. Brill, 1969).

7. The exception to this statement is, of course, Luther's view on baptismal regeneration, but on this he stood alone among the Reformers. See, for example, Philip Edgcumbe Hughes, *Theology of the English Reformers* (Grand Rapids: William B. Eerdmans, 1965), pp. 189-222; and Ronald Wallace, *Calvin's Doctrine of the Word and Sacrament* (Edinburgh: Oliver & Boyd, 1953).

8. Emil Brunner faithfully preserved the Reformers' position on creation and God's revelation through it, while Karl Barth departed from it. See their debate in *Natural Theology: Comprising "Nature and Grace" by Professor Dr. Emil Brunner and the Reply "No!" by Dr. Karl Barth*, trans. Peter Fraenkel (London: Geoffrey Bles, 1946). On Calvin himself, see the competing perspectives offered by T. H. L. Parker in *The Doctrine of the Knowledge of God: A Study in the Theology of John Calvin* (Edinburgh: Oliver & Boyd, 1952) and Edward A. Dowey in *The Knowledge of God in Calvin's Theology* (New York: Columbia University Press, 1952).

from his sovereign work of grace but also that no assertions about the human knowledge of God are beyond criticism. The Reformers were always conscious of the ease with which people slip into ways of thinking or behaving that need to be reformed afresh, and so they were always suspicious of the human enterprise, not least in its religious aspects. They maintained a deep reserve about the self, about the reliability of human reasoning (Luther referred to reason as the devil's whore), about human feelings and perceptions — a reserve that is conspicuous by its absence in evangelical thought and practice today. The Reformers held that human beings should be loved but, because they are sinners, they ought not to be blindly trusted. And they granted that personal experience is powerful because it is intense, but they insisted that we should not allow this power to delude us into thinking that experience is always right. They hammered out an abiding distinction between what is true and what personal experience insists is true in a series of stiff encounters with various Anabaptists.

This radical reshaping of religion by the Protestant Reformers produced the basis for a new social order, although it took some time for this to be worked out. There was at the center of the Reformation gospel a new egalitarianism built upon a foundation not of self-evident natural rights (as in the American Constitution) but rather of common and equal loss — the loss of righteousness and standing before God. It is because no one has any claim on the grace of God, because in sin all stand on the same ground together, that no one can claim to be elevated over anyone else in society on the basis of some hidden, divine order.

The most obvious and tangible outworking the Reformers gave to this belief, interestingly enough, had to do with vocation, with the destruction of the false medieval distinction between the "spiritual" (anything under the Church's control) and the "secular" (anything that was not under the Church's control).[9] Throughout the medieval period, the Church sought to expand, producing some momentous struggles with nations and kings along with some successes in the attempt to spiritualize all of society. By the sixteenth century, though, this experiment was being widely repudiated. New forms of commerce and learning were emerging that did not fit into the old patterns, and the Church was in deep disrepute.

The Reformers' argument was that none of the spheres of responsibility that make up life — being a husband or wife, a father or

---

9. See Gustav Wingren, *Luther on Vocation*, trans. Carl C. Rasmussen (Philadelphia: Muhlenberg Press, 1957).

mother, a craftsman, a citizen in a town, a member of a nation — is intrinsically unspiritual. What makes them so, what makes them "secular," has little to do with what control the Church exercises over them. It has much to do with the manner in which the responsibilities required by that sphere are discharged.

For centuries in Western thought — indeed, from the time of Aristotle onward — it had been assumed that work could be set up on a scale ranging from that which is of supreme value to that which is degrading and irrelevant. The gradations of value on this scale were determined by the relative connection of the work with the mind. Manual work, in which the mind is disengaged from what is done, falls at the low end of this scale; at the other end is work that is purely of the mind, such as the creation of culture. Thus was created a yardstick by which the whole social order could be measured, some workers being accorded great importance and others being relegated to insignificance.[10]

Something rather like this scale has persisted into the modern period. One's relative importance in a capitalistic order is determined by one's facility in producing and accumulating capital. The similarity to the old order is extended by the fact that those with technical and professional skills — certain kinds of thinkers — usually end up on the high end of the scale, while those who can do only manual work usually end up on the low end. This was at the heart of Marx's critique of capitalism: it seemed to him that the managers were living like parasites off the sweat of the masses.

Still, Marx did not propose a different philosophy of work. He merely proposed a different distribution of the profits. His was an argument not about what work *is* but about who should have the money. In this context, Marxism and capitalism (as the latter is actually practiced in secular society) begin to look quite similar. Marxism is, of course, collapsing in most places in the world, but the capitalism to which it has succumbed, while it is much more efficient, is nevertheless just as materialistic. In the one no less than the other, *having* is what defines life, and in neither is poverty ever holy. Secular reformers, Philip Rieff says, are simply asking "for more of everything — more goods, more money, more leisure, in short, more life."[11]

10. See Emil Brunner, *Christianity and Civilization*, 2 vols. (New York: Scribner's, 1848-49), 2: 57-61.

11. Rieff, *The Triumph of the Therapeutic: Uses of Faith after Freud* (New York: Harper & Row, 1966), p. 243. Robert Howard has explored this same theme in *Brave New Workplace: America's Corporate Utopias — How They Create Inequities and Social Conflict in Our Working Lives* (New York: Penguin, 1985).

The Protestant Reformers, however, were concerned less with money than with the nature of work itself. They argued (1) that work is not an end in itself but a means to an end, and (2) that the body cannot be divorced from the spirit, for the spirit comes to expression through the body. At issue for them was not whether we are intellectuals or laborers but whether we undertake our work, whatever it is, in such a way that that our spirituality comes to expression. Even a hangman can do his work as a service to God, said Luther, for God has preserved the state because of the world's fallenness, and he requires justice despite human corruption.

Thus the Reformers resisted the view that only those in clerical ranks were called into the service of God; they insisted that all who were God's through Christ were so called. The sphere in which this calling is exercised is not limited to the Church; it extends to every area in which Christian people work, to the whole range of responsibilities they assume. And the more power that is attached to a calling, they maintained, the greater the responsibility that has to be exercised in its discharge. This rearrangement of ends and means — the refusal to view work as an end in itself rather than the means by which Christian meaning and morality are exhibited — collides resoundingly both with the Marxist and the secular conceptions.

If the genesis of modern individualism lies in the idea of the dignity of the individual, the genesis of modern humanism lies in the failure to acknowledge the companion reality of human depravity. The capacity for ultimate knowledge that we are given by creation is a fearful thing when it is unhitched from the knowledge of sin. This uncoupling gives rise to individuals who are unsuspicious about themselves, who infuse their own ideas with divine authority, who are oblivious to the inherent darkness of human nature. This realization stands behind Reinhold Niebuhr's attacks on political Liberalism, which, he charged, had thrown its lot in with Rousseau, who believed in the inherent goodness of human nature, or with the utilitarians, who made a virtue out of collective selfishness, or with Adam Smith, who saw no danger in the unregulated pursuit of self-interest (an interest that is today more often associated with the conservatives). According to Niebuhr, Liberalism always assumes that the conflict of individual wills will automatically produce social good and that unaided reason can tame the passions of selfish people.[12] But this belief

12. See Niebuhr, *Reflections on the End of an Era* (New York: Scribner's, 1934), p. 113.

that the benevolent goodwill of society will inevitably prevail has been sorely tested — indeed, overthrown — by the succession of appallingly destructive nationalistic conflicts that have scarred the twentieth century. Proponents of this Liberalism appear not to recognize the dark potential of fallen human nature. And, given their reluctance to acknowledge a transcendent authority, they have typically defined immanent authority in only two ways in the modern period — either in terms of the state as in Marxism (or of a nationalism embodied in the state as in Nazism) or in terms of the self as in America.

Of course, much has had to happen in America to allow life to be so radically reshaped. Not least, we have had to witness the collapse of the central core of values in our society, that body of values to which a majority consented and that functioned as a rough guide for how our life should be ordered. As these values have disintegrated, new ways of living have begun to emerge. Accountability, for example, dies when the self is thought to be accountable only to itself, and in its place there has arisen an ethic that resolves everything into a simple proposition: what's right is what feels good. This in turn dictates that the pursuit of affluence as a means to self-fulfillment holds the key to life. One of the subjects who contributed to Robert Bellah's study on modern individualism said, "I've always loved that thing that Mark Twain said about something moral is something you feel good after, . . . and something immoral is something you feel bad after. Which implies that you got to try everything at least once." He added that good results define what is good, and bad results what is bad. Bellah's observation here is that in this schema "utility replaces duty; self-expression unseats authority. 'Being good' becomes 'feeling good.' "[13]

The contribution of the Reformation, therefore, lay in the confession of two theses — (1) that the individual has access to ultimate reality without the interposition of any intermediaries save for the Word written and living, and (2) that this truth must be held in tension with the reality of the corruption of the human being. Note that the companion truth is human corruption, not human creatureliness. Reinhold Niebuhr assumed that the former should be understood in terms of the latter,[14] but the Reformers distinguished sharply between them — as does Scripture. Our access to truth is fractured not by our

13. Robert N. Bellah, Richard Madsen, William M. Sullivan, Ann Swidler, and Steven M. Tipton, *Habits of the Heart: Individualism and Commitment in American Life* (Berkeley and Los Angeles: University of California Press, 1985), pp. 77-78.

14. Reinhold Niebuhr, *The Nature and Destiny of Man*, 2 vols. (New York: Scribner's, 1964), 1: 57-61, 178-85.

smallness, our finitude, or the relativity of our human perspective, not by the limited and fragmented way in which we know things — not, in fact, by any *natural* inability at all. If that were the case, we would be without blame before God, for we could not rightly be expected to know and obey things that we are inherently incapable of knowing and obeying. No, our access to truth is fractured by a *moral* inability. What limits us and what always threatens to pervert what knowledge we do have is not our relativity but our moral corruption.

The Heritage in America

This line of biblical individualism, expressed in relation to God and to the world, was carried to American shores by the Puritans and found embodiment with little change in the society they created. We hear it, for example, in Cotton Mather, who argued that work is designed by God for the good of the community. At the "beginnings of modern liberal individualism," says Robin Lovin, this Puritan theology "sustained an older notion of the self fulfilled in community."[15] The purpose in working, in other words, was neither the self-indulgent accumulation of profits nor even satisfaction in the work itself (though that could well arise) but rather utility to others. And when a community enjoys the meshing of callings, each bearing the values of Christian meaning and morality in the service of others, that community prospers and God is honored. It was this notion of calling that undergirded the way in which communities worked, and in time it served to provide a foundation on which democracy could build.[16]

The Puritan experiment wilted in time, of course, and a new order came to replace it, allowing for more religious diversity (including a rejection of any religion), but the understanding of the individual's place in the world was little modified. It is true that in Benjamin Franklin the explicitly Christian basis for the Puritan's place in the world was replaced by one that was decidedly deistic, but in the Republican phase of the nation's life "the laws of nature," which supposedly also governed human conduct, accomplished results that were often similar to what the Puritans had argued for, at least in terms of the relation between the individual and the community, the place of

15. Lovin, "Equality and Covenant Theology," *Journal of Law and Religion* 2 (1984): 241.
16. See H. Richard Niebuhr, "The Idea of Covenant and American Democracy," *Church History* 23 (1954): 126-33.

conscience, and of work.[17] Indeed, the Puritan sense of self-reliance was later celebrated by Ralph Waldo Emerson. In its outward appearance it still looked quite Puritan in Emerson; the changes took place in its inward character.[18] Nevertheless, this kind of independence became a standard ingredient in the American character. It had fueled the struggle for freedom that led to the Revolution and it has persisted into the modern period.

From early times, Americans have demonstrated an inclination to withdraw from the crowd, to form small private environments of home and friends, to remain fiercely independent of others, to think for themselves, to fashion their own beliefs, to be sure they can provide for and protect themselves, and to owe nothing. It may be that this picture has been painted a little too starkly, for early Americans were not at all prototypes of their modern counterparts. They were individualists in their self-reliance, but they were deeply committed to their communities, and their accomplishments in community were much more remarkable than their accomplishments as individuals.

The openness of the land and the greatness of the opportunity it offered did seem to produce a typically gregarious personality, however; the front porch was an American innovation, after all. It produced citizens who were characteristically independent but who also understood social duty. Their roles as fathers, mothers, clergy, farmers, cobblers, or wheelwrights were always sharply defined, even when those roles overlapped one another, but they were seldom viewed solely as means to the end of material gain, as roles that could be fulfilled in isolation from the larger social good.

In David Riesman's language, this sort of independent citizen was "inner-directed." In the nineteenth century, Tocqueville also took note of this sort of citizen — the person for whom individual character is paramount, the person who devotes himself or herself to tasks or to a career with perseverance, who has clear goals and objectives, who has a clear sense of what life is about, and who probably counts as heroes other individuals who have triumphed over difficulty and adversity because of inner fortitude. This is the person, Riesman says, who would rather be right than be president. Such a person is willing and able to take a lonely stand because his or her strength and direction are

17. See Edmund S. Morgan, "The Puritan Ethic and the American Revolution," *William and Mary Quarterly*, 3d ser., 24 (January 1967): 3-8.
18. See Robert Michaelson, "Changes in the Concept of Calling or Vocation," *New England Quarterly* 26 (1953): 27-43.

internal rather than external. Such a person neither lives by the approval of others nor dies by their disapproval. These characteristics of hard-bitten independence and stoic inner strength were eventually encoded in the uniquely American mythology of the cowboy, which sketched out for millions of young boys what true, virtuous manhood and true, virtuous Americanhood were all about.

In the second half of the nineteenth century, when industrialization was well under way, this person believed in patient accumulation because this person believed in the future. Moderation, sobriety, and self-discipline were prized virtues precisely for this reason. The "deferral of gratification," writes Christopher Lasch, was "not only his principal gratification but the abundant source of profits,"[19] and therein lay a paradox of sorts: the good quite often did well.

Time has shaped this American character in different ways, but it is the most recent chapter in this story that must obviously engage us here. During the 1950s and 1960s, this was a matter that attracted more interest, and its study was accorded more respect than it is today. Then, the direction of the last phase in the changed national character was still sufficiently unclear that it invited serious attention, but now the subject seems to have exhausted itself, or at least it seems to have exhausted our interest in it. The earlier attempts by Margaret Mead, Karen Horney, William Whyte, and David Riesman to depict modern American character have been followed more recently by those of Christopher Lasch, Philip Rieff, Daniel Yankelovich, and Robert Bellah, but these more recent analyses, profound as they are for the most part, have not been as well rewarded by public attention as they deserve. Perhaps it is because what they have attempted to describe is now so commonplace, given the techniques, ubiquity, and effectiveness of television, that the need for understanding the way in which the modern self has been shaped seems to have disappeared entirely. Baseball players are not going to focus their attention on sideline commentary while they are busy playing the game.

The most important change in our national character, the change that accounts for the current absorption in the self both in its religious and nonreligious forms, might be characterized as a shift from an interest in human nature to an interest in personality.[20] From Bacon to Rousseau

19. Lasch, *The Culture of Narcissism: American Life in an Age of Diminishing Expectations* (New York: W. W. Norton, 1978), p. 53.

20. See *A Second Collection: Papers by Bernard J. Lonergan*, ed. William F. J. Ryan and Bernard J. Tyrrell (London: Darton, Longman & Todd, 1974), pp. 69-86.

to Marx there had been an abiding assumption that at bedrock, human nature has certain powers, rationality, and (some have said) goodness that can withstand all outward storms, be they ideological or economic. It was assumed that on this core, this irreducible minimum, the individual could take a stand and launch a counterattack against life. It was further assumed that human nature is an unchanging reality, that we can safely generalize about it, and that if we gain an adequate understanding of it, we will have the key to understanding all human behavior.

But our certainty about this core of human nature has been washed away by the stiff and dangerous currents of modernity. We now have the eerie sensation of the sands shifting under our feet. This is why our culture has now embarked on a "nervous search for the true self," as Bellah puts it, and it is why it is issuing "extravagant conclusions drawn from that search."[21] Human nature seems to have been lost, but human personality can be found, modified, cultivated. It is not on human nature that we now lean but on human personality, and evangelicalism is simply indulging in the religious version of this cultural phenomenon.

The concept of consciousness is different from the older concept of human nature. Consciousness is unique to each individual. Its private impressions, its individuality, its intuitions are set off from what others know and experience. To understand the rules governing human nature is by no means to have gained an understanding of any individual's private consciousness; it is simply to understand human nature. The individual consciousness remains unique. And it is in the individual consciousness that the modern person finds the hidden depths that harbor the meaning to life.

One of the most obvious changes signaling this shift was the way in which human identity came to be discussed after the 1950s. Before this time, identity was discussed in terms of what did not change, in terms of the the thread of continuity that persisted through all of the changing circumstances of a person's life. Identity was a matter of what made a person distinct from other people over time. It was, in other words, what described that person's *nature*. After the 1950s, however, identity came to be associated with *consciousness*, with what was shifting and elusive. By the 1970s, it was increasingly being associated not with the narrative of one's inner life but with the projection of one's public image. Image and inner life were thus disengaged from each other.[22]

---

21. Bellah et al., *Habits of the Heart*, p. 55.
22. See Christopher C. Lasch, *The Minimal Self: Psychic Survival in Troubled Times* (New York: W. W. Norton, 1984).

This being the case, it required great skill to present one's "image." Erving Goffman speaks of modern people as having become performers who stage their own characters and accomplishments. This art often requires freeing oneself from the need to tell the truth and turning instead to "the techniques of management impression."[23] A whole industry has now grown up to teach people how to market themselves by creating effective self-images.

This transition from nature to consciousness has been expressed in many aspects of modern culture, from theology to the way in which life is interpreted in the movies, and so the treatment that follows has to be highly selective. But it is interesting that the theme can be followed out both in popular culture and among the intellectuals.

The drug culture, for example, can be seen as, among other things, an expression of the self movement. When cocaine made a significant entry into American life in the 1920s, it was glamorized as the plaything of the social elite. By the 1970s, when it was common on the streets, and the 1980s, when it became common in executive suites, it had lost its glamour, but it had not changed its nature. The motivation for using drugs, whether on the streets or at the parties of the rich, remained the same: it was believed that the part of the self that is rational could be expanded, altered, transformed, providing heightened access to reality and new states of being. The self, thus manipulated, became the pot of gold at the end of the rainbow.

Martin Buber has traced out the fading sense of God in the modern period, noting (as have many others) that it has been matched by a rising sense of the self.[24] The silence of the transcendent toys with the persistence of our need for it, said Sartre, and it torments us no less today than it ever has. But Sartre chose to resolve the paradox by disregarding the religious need. He spoke of God as "silent," as having the silence of a corpse. Nietzsche thought him to be "dead." Holderlin imagined him "absent." These stark declarations, bare of all subtlety and all doubt, reflect at an intellectual level what is now widely experienced at a cultural level. For while it may seem shocking that Sartre should be so confident a believer in all unbelief, he is not much different from the modern secular person for whom God and the supernatural are absent from the private space in which they live. And

23. Goffman, *The Presentation of Self in Everyday Life* (Garden City, N.Y.: Doubleday, 1959), p. 208.

24. Buber has traced out this collapse of metaphysics and its replacement by psychology in *The Eclipse of God: Studies in the Relation between Religion and Philosophy* (1952; reprint, New York: Harper & Row, 1965).

both, interestingly enough, believe that the self can be manipulated to fill this empty place.[25]

In a secularized age, with its low cognitive ceilings and lost moorings, we have turned in on ourselves. We now seek our access to reality only through the self, having decided that neither God nor his revelation is any longer pertinent. This is to say that when we emptied our world of God and of the absolutes that had directed human life, we did not thereby open up large holes in the architecture of our inner life; rather, we rearranged things to accommodate for these losses. We compensated for all we lost by turning within ourselves. Carl Jung formulated this type of compensation into a law: "For every piece of conscious life that loses its importance and value . . . there arises a compensation in the unconscious."[26]

The ease with which the subjective consciousness can be perverted or, perhaps, diverted is well illustrated for us by Jung. He has recounted how he had to struggle with the fate of his father, a pastor, whose Christian faith collided so painfully with the modern world that he had, several times, to be placed in the lunatic asylum. It was a fate the younger Jung earnestly wished to escape, and in a dream one day he found the way. The solution was to look for God within the self, where sufficient adaptations to the modern world would already have taken place. Once he had found his "subterranean God," he also had found the way, he tells us, to reject the orthodox "Jesus." The outer allegiance was incompatible with the inner devotion.

In this, Jung was no great pioneer, though he gave little indication that he was aware of the many who had trodden this path before him. As a matter of fact, the end of the eighteenth century in Europe saw the first budding of interest in the subjective as a source of inspiration and illumination. Jerome Buckley notes that in England it was really Coleridge who introduced this strange word, *subjective*, to common parlance. In 1840, six years after Coleridge's death, Edward Fitzgerald wrote to Frederick Tennyson in Italy to say that the word had made "considerable progress" and that people now fancied that they understood what it meant.[27] And Wordsworth, after completing the first draft of *The Prelude*, a minutely chronicled saga of his inner life, opined that

25. See William E. Barrett, *Death of the Soul: From Descartes to the Computer* (Garden City, N.Y.: Doubleday, 1987), p. 52.

26. Jung, *Modern Man in Search of a Soul*, trans. W. S. Dell and Cary F. Baynes (New York: Harcourt, Brace, 1933), p. 241.

27. Jerome Hamilton Buckley in *The Turning Key: Autobiography and the Subjective Impulse since 1800* (Cambridge: Harvard University Press, 1984), pp. 2-3.

it was "unprecedented" in literary history that an author should have spoken so much of himself. In America, it was Emerson, Whitman, and James who brought this introspective mood to the great prominence that it enjoyed throughout the nineteenth century.[28] Indeed, Emerson believed that the dissection of consciousness, the struggle to bring to realization what he called "the internalized god," was the distinguishing mark of that century.

On both sides of the Atlantic, literature began to reflect this growing interest in the self. Buckley has found a meager record of only twenty-three British autobiographies before the year 1800, but during the nineteenth century another 175 were published. Journals and diaries also began to flower. It was not simply that these authors felt it was presumptuous to scan the divine and so followed Pope in declaring that "the proper study of mankind is man." Something more radical was afoot. First in Britain and then in America, society found itself no longer able to resist the emancipated and lawless spirits who demanded that they be allowed to divorce themselves from external cultural constraints and write not about the world or universal human nature but rather about themselves, about what they had experienced in their own inner states. It is this line that has come down from Coleridge, through Norman Mailer and the irreverent effusions of Allen Ginsberg and what Robert Phillips calls the "confessional poets" of the 1960s,[29] that has intruded into classrooms across the country in which children are now asked to write on anything they like and simply render their feelings, and that in the 1980s produced a veritable torrent of autobiographical writing. In 1988 alone, Barry Goldwater, Shirley Temple Black, Joan Collins, Kirk Douglas, Michael Jackson — how many have I missed? — all told us about themselves. The public appetite for this material appears not to be diminished by its ultimate banality. And really, we can expect little more from these exercises, given the appallingly limited ability of the self to transcend itself. In *Self-Consciousness,* a book that mimics the form of this autobiographical tradition, John Updike argues that its essential introversion constitutes the most compelling motivation to escape from it. After plumbing the dry well of the self, we have turned to look in myriad ways beyond the

28. That the turn toward subjectivity in American literature occurred through Emerson, Whitman, and James is well documented and argued by Quentin Anderson in *The Imperial Self: An Essay in American Literary and Cultural History* (New York: Alfred A. Knopf, 1971).

29. Phillips, *The Confessional Poets* (Carbondale, Ill.: Southern Illinois University Press, 1973).

"grimly finite facts" of life. A great thirst for transcendence is every-where evident in the West. Some seek it through drugs. Many seek it through the various forms of Eastern mysticism. But beneath all of this searching is the persistent belief that the reason the self has not yielded deep meanings about life is that we simply have not yet learned to penetrate through to its greatest depths.

So when Jung made his discovery, he found something that has in fact become characteristic of the whole modern period. It was for him a discovery so startling that he identified it as the first instance of personal revelation. The truth of the matter, quite obviously, was a little different from that. But what Jung discovered then, evangelicals in droves are apparently discovering now for themselves, with or without the drama of a supposed personal revelation. The difference is that Jung in his clear-eyed way opposed his "subterranean God" to "Jesus," whereas many evangelicals are now naively identifying them. Jesus *is* the "subterranean God"; his contours and attributes are defined by the inner experience of his breathless new followers.

The next step in the unfolding of our individualism is another startling reversal of what we might have expected to happen: the individual loses his or her individuality and is simply absorbed into the mass. Reinhold Niebuhr contended that the self draws its life from its organic relations to family, community, and craft. But modernization destroys these relations, at once both turning people in on themselves and cutting off their sustenance in the external world. Hence, says Niebuhr, "modern civilization creates and destroys the individual."[30]

Modernization has broken up many of the small social units that used to be so important in the raising of children and the shaping of national character, such as the nuclear and extended family, the neigh-borhood, and the larger community. These were the contexts in which children used to learn about life. Today, however, extended families have been scattered by geographical mobility, nuclear families by divorce, and the more functional ethnic and urban neighborhoods by the social and economic forces that make flight to the loose-knit, anony-mous suburbs a temptation. The small social units made up of family and place — units that were once the chief conduits for the transmis-sion of values from one generation to another, in which values were learned in the context of personal relations — are now clogged or broken. The young are cut loose to drift in the sea of impersonal society. How will they learn about life, and what will they learn?

30. Niebuhr, *Reflections on the End of an Era*, p. 104.

It is this situation that is producing what Riesman has called the "other-directed" person, what Horney has called the "neurotic" person, what Lasch has called the "narcissistic" person, what Rieff has called "psychological man," what Buckley has called the "unprecedented self," and what Quentin Anderson has called "the imperial self." This is what Jackson Lears has in mind when he speaks of the modern person as having become "weightless." The language is different, but there is a surprisingly broad consensus regarding the consequences of being modern and the ways in which self-absorption is now playing itself out.

On the whole, contemporary individualism is thoroughly emancipated, declining to draw values from the past (even the previous generation). But, paradoxically, it gives up this emancipation from normative precedents for enslavement to a different sort of external authority — the desire to be like others in the larger culture. This entails more that just peer pressure: we are sensitive not only to the values of close friends and admired acquaintances but also the impersonal voice of fashion, a media consensus, the views of a celluloid idol, the message of a rock star. Having turned inward in a search for meaning, we turn outward in a search for direction, scanning others for the social signals they emit regarding what is in and what is out, what is desirable and what is not. This produces a new kind of conformity. Americans have always been conformist in dress and language; indeed, during the nineteenth century this very sameness carried the revolutionary message that in America all start out on the same footing without distinction. Language and dress did not divide people into classes here. These concerns to be on the same social footing as others are not primarily what drives the "other-directed" person, however. At heart, this person is more interested in attaining the same quality of *inner experience* as others. Outward conformity in dress and language typically follow, not because they are themselves the desired objects but because they convey coded messages that those who wear these clothes or use this slang have arrived at the same inner sanctum of experience.

Typically, the other-directed person thinks little about career, makes few long-term commitments, seems to have no inner core of character, little conscience, and seeks approval and even affection from a surrogate family, "an amorphous and shifting, though contemporary, jury of peers," as Riesman put it.[31] This person is oriented not to inner

31. See David Riesman et al., *The Lonely Crowd: A Study of the Changing American Character,* rev. ed. (New Haven: Yale University Press, 1961), p. 137.

values but to other people. It is in the peer group that acceptance is found and outcasts are named.

The other-directed person understands sex not as an expression of inward commitment to another but as a token of connectedness to others, a sign that he or she is still alive. It is in this sense that Riesman speaks of consumption. He suggests that the other-directed person is a consumer not just of goods but of words, images, and relationships. Relationships within the group become the coin for all of life's transactions as well as the chief test of taste. From one angle, this looks like the most emancipated form of individualism imaginable, but from another it is evident that it actually amounts to a thoroughgoing loss of individualism. As Niebuhr noted long ago, this person lives "by his dependence on the crowd. He feels at home only in the mass. He seeks out crowds which gather at athletic games and public spectacles with almost morbid eagerness. His escape is TV and movies."[32]

The logic of individualism has here run not only to excess but to a kind of squalid decadence. Where once people took pride in their accomplishments and in their character, other-directed individuals think only of how they stand with others. The freedom from all that formerly constrained, such as cultural and family expectations, now "contributes to his insecurity," Lasch argues — an insecurity "which he can overcome only by seeing his 'grandiose self' reflected in the attentions of others, or by attaching himself to those who radiate celebrity, power, and charisma."[33] Where the older type of individualist saw the world as a wilderness to be cleared and shaped in accordance with his or her will, the contemporary narcissist sees it as a mirror in which to preen him or herself; in the television era, the world is no longer hard. As this mood has rippled through the public, it has brought many changes in our public psychology, among them a transformation in the way people view their work. Once people worked to achieve tangible ends, to accomplish things. Now, such accomplishments are of far less significance than one's "image." Once people worked; now they manipulate. Once people sweated; now they seduce. Once people wished to be respected, to have their accomplishments recognized; now they wish to be envied, regardless of whether they are envied for anything they have actually accomplished.

Any social order that is convulsed by change too great or deep to be assimilated finds itself having to deal with all of the afflictions

32. Niebuhr, *Reflections on the End of an Era,* p. 104.
33. Lasch, *The Minimal Self,* p. 10.

that dislocation creates. The word we use to describe this is *alienation*. Although the term first reached us through the mediation of Marxist discourse, I mean something much more profound than it has meant in that context. Alienation has two faces, one individual and the other social. As individuals, Robert Nisbet notes, modern people are "uprooted, alone, without secure status, cut off from community or any system of clear moral purpose. Estrangement is sovereign: estrangement from others, from work, from place, from self."[34] Unhitched from the old certainties, the modern person drifts within a society that is largely experienced as inhospitable. That is why accomplishment in the old order has been replaced by the techniques of survival in the new, and these key not on underlying character but on surface personality, not on achievement but on manipulation. That is why managers and psychologists are so admired: they are controllers. Managers control the external world, and psychologists control the internal world. Both offer results through technique rather than character, and the actions of both implicitly affirm that the chaos of modernity might yet be contained.[35]

The more autonomous this modern person is, the more solitary he or she will be, left without a niche in the world, without any connectedness to the past or, for that matter, to the present. Freedom, unhappily, has dislodged the human spirit; society is remote and inaccessible, "formidable in its heavy structures of organization," says Nisbet, "meaningless from its impersonal complexity."[36] This kind of person, says Jung, stands alone on the precipice of reality, anxiously looking over the edge into a terrifying abyss, somehow unable to draw back from that edge. "The upheaval in our world and the upheaval in our consciousness are one and the same thing."[37] By a strange turn of events, alienation, the bitter fruit of modern individualism, becomes the antithesis of the individualism from which it has arisen, in the end producing, as Rieff says, a "disorganization" in the very personality upon which it counts for survival.

Strangely enough, the modernization that has led to the progressive hollowing out of the self has also led to the production of a surface abundance. The fact that both of these processes have been taking

---

34. Nisbet, *The Sociological Tradition* (New York: Basic Books, 1966), p. 265.
35. This is, of course, an extrapolation of the thesis developed by Jacques Ellul in *The Technological Society*, trans. John Wilkinson (New York: Alfred A. Knopf, 1965).
36. Nisbet, *The Sociological Tradition*, p. 266.
37. Jung, *Modern Man in Search of a Soul*, p. 243.

place simultaneously explains the newest twist in the story. Daniel Yankelovich's research, published in 1981, led him to think that changes taking place in both our culture and our national character were so large as to be the equivalent to the shifting of the continental plates beneath the earth's surface. Of special interest in his analysis was his finding that the nation was overwhelmingly turning to a pursuit of affluence as the means by which to attain self-fulfillment. The pursuit of the self may have ended in bankruptcy, but the pursuit of wealth was meeting with more success. In constant dollars, the average American family income more than doubled during the period from 1953 to 1973, rising from $5,000 to $12,000. The ranks of the middle class swelled as the taste of affluence now became widespread. And apparently a taste of affluence convinced many that to have was to be. Spiritual vacuity and material plenty married one another in a philosophy that became so widespread as to begin to produce a different type of culture. That, at least, was Yankelovich's argument.

This new type of person, Yankelovich believes, actually began emerging on American campuses in the 1960s but was not recognized as such because the search for new values was frequently masked by protest against the Vietnam War. By the early 1970s, however, the search had spread laterally, by moving off the campuses, and vertically, by engaging many of those already well into middle age. Yankelovich estimates, in fact, that 80 percent of Americans are now thus engaged. Their search, he says, is predicated on the belief that the normal routines of life, such as working at a job and raising a family, are not really what life is about. Life begins when these duties are ended and one can turn to genuine self-expression. Life is creativity, a voyage of personal discovery. "At the heart of the self-fulfillment search," says Yankelovich, "is the moral intuition that the very meaning of life resides in its sacred/expressive aspects and that one must fight, if necessary, to make room for them."[38] And in the 1970s, this duty to self, the modern substitute for God, expressed itself in the search for affluence.

As we might expect, the trends that Yankelovich uncovered were not uniform throughout America. He identified strong and weak forms of the search for fulfillment. Among those identified with the strong form, 67 percent spent a great deal of time thinking about self, 56 percent believed that life consists in shaping the self, 58 percent wanted to be well read, 46 percent wanted new experiences, 43 percent con-

38. Yankelovich, "New Rules in American Life: Searching for Fulfillment in a World Turned Upside Down," *Psychology Today*, April 1981, pp. 39-40.

sidered it a good idea to join a self-discovery group, 58 percent said people should be able to live and dress as they desired, and 71 percent wanted more excitement and sensation. But immediately we note some of the contradictions in which this national character became involved. While affluence was seen as a sine qua non for fulfillment, many did not attach great significance to work, which raises the awkward question of how this search is to be financed. In 1970, 34 percent said that work was at the center of their lives; by 1978, this figure had fallen to 13 percent. In 1969, 58 percent reported a belief that hard work always paid off; by 1976, this figure had fallen to 43 percent.[39] In other words, many had come to view prosperity as a right rather than an accomplishment, and it is far from clear who has the obligation to see that that right is honored. Moreover, the attempt to fulfill the self through the self would appear to be an inherently isolating process. Interpersonal relationships inevitably involve conflicts of interest that can be resolved only by compromise and sacrifice. Self-fulfillers place a premium on such relationships, and yet their guiding concern for self-fulfillment, their devotion to self-interest, would seem almost to guarantee that they will not be successful in maintaining them.

I See, Therefore I Am

It is impossible to overlook the importance of television in the shaping of the American character today. It links many of the themes of the analysts we have been considering. In 1948, only 1 percent of the population owned a set; by 1955, this had jumped to 50 percent; by 1985, 99 percent of the nation's households had at least one set, and of these, 93 percent were color. The saturation of our culture with this new technology has had an effect on the development of the modern consciousness as profound and pervasive as that of the printing press in Europe centuries ago. Ours is now the first generation whose daily experience is both shared and interpreted through a single medium to which people in the West (including Japan) are exposed for a considerable portion of their waking hours. In the average American household, the television is on seven hours a day; in Britain, five hours; in Japan, eight hours. Its appeal is attested by the enormous revenues it generates. By some estimates, sales of American programs to Europe totaled $2.7 billion in 1992, a 1,200 percent increase over the figures

39. Yankelovich, *New Rules: Searching for Self-Fulfillment in a World Turned Upside Down* (New York: Random House, 1981), p. 94.

for 1983. Television — and American television in particular — is the voice of our world cliche culture.

I am interested here in the question of how the inner world of the modern person has been shaped by the way that television is used. This is different from the question of how television affects people, although I will grant that this is an important question in its own right. In fact, a good deal of study has been devoted to the effects of television viewing, and although the results are debated, there does seem to be a growing consensus that there is a correlation between television watching and a reduction in one's ability to solve problems, in one's level of imagination, in reading skills, and even in relating to others, not to mention its inculcation of values that are harmful through its depictions of violence, promiscuity, and the desires that advertising seeks to engender. And the disparity between the attitudes of experts and the general public on the question of effects is striking. Psychologists and social scientists argue that watching television creates tension, restlessness, and anxiety; the public finds it to be their most relaxing activity besides actually resting.[40] Experts warn of the detrimental effects of viewing and have produced some highly complex studies on its psychology; the public treats it with complete nonchalance, ranking it as the least demanding activity in which they engage and considering it entirely harmless. They judge that eating demands greater skill than viewing.[41] And they are doing other things during 65.3 percent of the time that the set is on.[42] But regardless of how much attention we are consciously paying to television, it is serving both as a mirror in which modern individuals are looking to find themselves and as the sole partner in conversation that the whole nation has in common, a focal point for the impulses of both conformity and individualism. It is this function of television that is of special interest here.[43]

40. *Television and the Quality of Life: How Viewing Shapes Everyday Experience*, ed. Robert Kubey and Mihaly Csikszentmihalyi (Hillsdale, N.J.: Lawrence Erlbaum Associates, 1990), p. 83.

41. Kubey and Csikszentmihalyi, *Television and the Quality of Life*, p. 81.

42. Kubey and Csikszentmihalyi, *Television and the Quality of Life*, p. 75.

43. I am especially indebted to William J. Donnelly and his book *The Confetti Generation: How the New Communication Technology Is Fragmenting America* (New York: Henry Holt, 1986), in which he has done such a superb job of drawing the connections between Riesman's findings as a social scientist and a convincing evaluation of how television works. In addition to Donnelly's work, I have found the following volumes useful in assessing the role of televison: John Condry, *The Psychology of Television* (Hillsdale, N.J.: Lawrence Erlbaum Associates, 1989); Daniel Czitrom, *Media and the American Mind: From Morse to McLuhan* (Chapel Hill, N.C.:

It was shortly after Riesman's book *The Lonely Crowd* was published that America crossed the line to become a predominantly video culture, in 1955. Television lent itself to the impulses of the other-directed individual that Riesman described. In fact, television presented modern self-absorption as normal and thereby helped to deepen it. It is very possible that without television the other-directed social character would never have become as entrenched as it has.

Other-directed individuals are interested only in what is important to others. This is the shifting field they track with their inner sensors. Television is the perfect tool for them, because it provides an unprecedented record of what is important to society at any given moment, its major events, its latest fashions, its latest beliefs, its latest music, gossip, spats, heroes — every color in the landscape that the cultural chameleon wants to emulate. All of contemporary culture is updated perpetually, instantaneously, and *immediately:* the viewer is always incorporated in the experience being broadcast. Television is, in William Donnelly's phrase, the other-directed individual's "stream of consciousness." To the uprooted, fragile self of the modern individual, television imparts the security of knowing what constitutes an approved life-style, approved fashions, approved tastes, approved thoughts. Indeed, so close is the union between the medium and the modern other-directed character that one wonders whether being American will ever again mean something other than being self-absorbed if television keeps beaming its images into the nation's homes each night.

Once again, however, the very nature of the other-directed personality contains the seeds of its own "disorganization." Television places such a burden of knowledge about others on the fragile self that it is unable to sustain the weight. According to Donnelly, other-directed individuals equate reality with the changing social relationships they feel compelled to reflect within themselves.[44] But television presents so many images, so many shifts and changes without any grounding in time, place, or logic, that it overloads the other-directed viewer. It is

---

University of North Carolina Press, 1982); *Video Culture: A Critical Investigation,* ed. John G. Hanhardt (Layton, Utah: Gibbs M. Smith, 1986); Marshall McLuhan, *Understanding Media: The Extensions of Man* (New York: McGraw-Hill, 1964); *Television: The Critical View,* 3d ed., ed. Horace Newcomb (New York: Oxford University Press, 1982); *Video Icons and Values,* ed. Alan M. Olson, Christopher Parr, and Debra Parr (Albany: State University of New York Press, 1990); and Elayne Rapping, *The Looking Glass World of Nonfiction TV* (Boston: South End Press, 1987).
    44. Donnelly, *The Confetti Generation,* pp. 56-57.

one thing to emulate a father or mother in the context of the home, with its dependable routines and stable beliefs. It is an entirely different matter to try to emulate fashions and fads that change overnight and that have no charm beyond the claim to be new or scandalous. And so, for a generation that has turned for guidance to television rather than family, church, and place, the failure of the medium to offer any simple or consistent reading of the diverse external world has slowly led to the realization that the inner-directed journey is ultimately unfulfilling, that the self is really an illusion.

As the world became more complex in the 1950s and 1960s and vocational choices multiplied, other-directed individuals found that their own self-awareness was becoming unbearable. The certitudes that had once been relayed by family and rooted in place were now gone, replaced by the impersonal images that flickered across their television screens for an average of a little over 3 seconds each (by 1991, the time that an image remained on the screen had fallen on average to 2.9 seconds).[45] Between the images there were few links, at least of a rational kind, for television is a dramatic medium the angles, images, and sequences of which are strategically chosen for their effect on the viewer. In place of the older certitudes came deep anxiety — anxiety that was in part expressed in the mass rebellions of the young in the 1960s and 1970s.

But at the same time that television was playing out its role as a mass medium, exerting a sort of universal peer pressure on viewers regarding what sorts of clothes they should wear, what sorts of music they should listen to, what sorts of ideas they should entertain, what sorts of people they should scorn, and what sorts of things they might legitimately hope for, it was also lending itself to private interpretation. There has, in fact, been a learned debate about whether television viewers are active or simply passive as the images shift before their waiting eyes. Are these images simply received, as a cup might receive the water that is poured into it, or do viewers have to work to receive them as they have to make an effort to feed themselves? But this question, though related to what I have called private interpretation, is also a little different.

Television images are fragmentary. They have what Donnelly has called a "low intensity of definition." They are not linked organically with one another; what links do exist are formed in the viewer's feelings and imagination. For this reason, Jeremy Murray-Brown speaks of

45. Kubey and Csikszentmihalyi, *Television and the Quality of Life*, pp. 25-26.

television as "a medium whose very nature repudiates the path of intellectual knowledge," because it uses drama rather than argument to deliver essentially "emotional information," and the value of its product is measured less by its truthfulness than by its emotional impact.[46] Nevertheless, the makers of television also allow for different messages to be received by the viewer because they allow the viewer to complete what is shown to them in different ways. Television is thus quite different from such things as instruction manuals and geology textbooks. The authors of such volumes write with the intent of communicating specific information and in the hope that all who read it will derive the same information in the same way. These sorts of books are high in definitional content, in contrast to which television is low. It requires little effort to process television's images but quite a lot of effort to complete them. It is by this sleight of hand, in fact, that it gains significant access to the viewer's inner consciousness.

Television has thus entered the inner sanctum of our lives, touching us at points that are most acutely sensitive, inviting us to compare ourselves with the world that it presents, and inviting us to make of that world what we will. We can, in fact complete it differently for our own needs and purposes. The reality of this private kind of translation has been shown again and again. The soap opera *Dynasty,* for example, was popular in the gay community in the 1980s. On the face of it, this seems quite strange, for Joan Collins, who played the lead character, Alexis, was not only catty and scheming but also exuded ripened sexuality, and in considerable quantity. As one featured in *Playboy,* she hardly seems the stuff of which gay fantasies might be made. But as it turns out, there was in this series a sexual ambiguity that the broader public hardly caught at all. For while Alexis's sexual charms were rather obvious, she also dressed in masculine ways, with pronounced shoulder pads and severe lines. It was in this conjunction of masculinity and femininity that gays found the ambiguity in which they felt at home. The rest of America did not see it this way at all.

The same kind of thing also happened with an earlier series, *Prisoner,* when it was shown in Australia. The episodes were built around the theme of how some strong women in prison were able to outwit the oppressive, inhuman system in which they were forced to live. This program became extremely popular with Australian schoolchildren not so much because it was a good story but because they saw in it a reflection of their own private world. They identified themselves

---

46. Jeremy Murray-Brown, "Video Ergo Sum," in *Video Icons and Values,* p. 23.

with the prisoners, their schools with the prison, and their teachers with the wardens![47] They saw themselves as incarcerated, separated from friends, deprived of rights, forced to do work they despised, subject to petty rules and the threat of gangs — exactly as the prisoners were. Indeed, so great was the effect of this series that complaints multiplied that it was teaching children insubordination. For some reason, however, this series had a rather different effect in America when it was first shown. Television allows room for different messages to be taken from it.[48]

My argument here is not that television brainwashes people so much as that it serves as a vehicle for identifying what one needs to know in order to get along in our culture. At one and the same time, it creates both the sort of other-directed person who seeks only to be like everyone else and a modified inner-directed individual who is completely emancipated from the past, the external world, and any sense of community. In its pictures, viewers see themselves as unique, but in their uniqueness they want only to be like everyone else, to drive the same cars, to wear the same clothes, to drink the same beer. And so it is that in this context both conformity and individualism have played themselves out. What Riesman, Lasch, and Yankelovich described at an intellectual level, the makers of television realize visually before the whole nation each day.

The Naked Public Square

The term *culture* has developed an enormous range of meanings over the years as it has moved away from its original imported sense and been used in a variety of different contexts. When it was first introduced to Europe by Kant, and to America by Lister B. Ward, its meaning was close to the Latin *cultura*, which conveyed the idea of the cultivation of soil in preparation for seeding. A "cultured" person was one who was conversant with and valued what was best in art, literature, and music. By cultivating these interests, it was assumed, good values would begin to sprout in the soul. A cultured person hoped to become a better person because of this cultivation.

47. See Robert Hodge and David Tripp, *Children and Television: A Semiotic Approach* (Stanford: Stanford University Press, 1986), pp. 184-87.
48. For a comparison of how the television series *Dallas* was viewed in Germany with how it was viewed in America, see Herta Herzog Massing, "Decoding 'Dallas': Comparing American and German Viewers," in *Television in Society*, ed. Arthur Asa Berger (New Brunswick, N.J.: Transaction Books, 1986), pp. 95-103.

More recently, however, *culture* has been used less personally and more socially, at first in distinction to civilization but now often as an equivalent to it. That is how I am using the word here, to signify the set of values, the network of beliefs that are institutionalized in a people's collective life and that govern their behavior. Culture, then, is the outward discipline in which inherited meanings and morality, beliefs and ways of behaving are preserved.[49] It is that collectively assumed scheme of understanding that defines both what is normal and what meanings we should attach to public behavior. It is what reveals eccentrics for their eccentricity, rebels for their rebellion, no-gooders for not doing good. It is what tells us what owning a Cadillac means, what significance being gay has, how we can measure someone whom we learn is a doctor, an engineer, a street artist, or homeless. It is what gives us our inner coordinates, the markers beside the trail that, from infancy onward, slowly leads us to civilized life. Culture never manages to mow down the verdant undergrowth of human lawlessness, of course; it simply forces it out of sight. It sublimates what is dark and wanton, or, if it cannot manage to do that, it exacts penalties for unwanted public displays.

This is not to say that culture is simply a set of "dos" and "don'ts," however. It is also, as Rieff says, "what directs the self outward toward the communal purposes in which alone the self can be realized and satisfied."[50] As Western culture has withered away and been replaced by Our Time, it has lost its power to regulate belief and behavior. Indeed, we are losing those connections beyond and outside of the self without which the human spirit cannot be satisfied. In the Middle Ages, the artist took the eye of the beholder out into the world to see the Church, its Savior, its truth; today, the artist usually takes the eye of the beholder into the self of the artist. In art, as in life, the search for the self is simply incompatible with the pursuit of communal and political good. Or perhaps the matter should be put even more pointedly: the external discipline of the culture is now denied in the name of the emancipated self. The retreat into a psychologized under-standing of ourselves and our world is the very means that is used to paralyze the outside world in its traditional functions of regulating

49. You will note that I have not extended this definition to encompass "popular culture." Popular culture is important as an index to the mass mind, but it is not what I am principally concerned about here. The basis for my definition is found in T. S. Eliot's *Christianity and Culture: The Idea of a Christian Society and Notes Towards the Definition of Culture* (New York: Harcourt, Brace, 1968).

50. Rieff, *The Triumph of the Therapeutic*, p. 4.

behavior. Whenever a culture loses its ability to require what is normative, it is dying. Are we then surprised to learn from a survey of high school students in 1990 that while three quarters saw their careers as very important, less than a quarter said they would be willing to expend any effort to make their communities better places, only a small minority would be willing to serve in the armed forces even if the country were under threat or attack, the overwhelming majority was grossly ignorant of political affairs, and most of those who are eligible to vote have declined to do so?

The quest for the self is now undoing both private and public life, and this undoing is evident even in our schools, one of the purposes of which has always been to induct children into this external culture. Our schools now decline to educate students regarding matters of right and wrong, preferring instead to preserve and explore human relations. As Gerald Grant has observed, a teacher is less likely to insist that cheating is wrong than to ask why a cheater cheats. Moral questions thus disappear into psychological speculation, and, in the process, consideration of one's responsibility to others gives way to concern for one's responsibility to oneself. Returning to the example of the cheater, the assumption seems to be that the problem can be resolved if the individual is detached from responsibility to the community — but that is precisely the opposite of what the moral wisdom of the West has known to be true for centuries.[51] What has happened, of course, is that all the external demands have collapsed, leaving only the self, and then, in a surprising and painful turn of events, the self has proceeded to disintegrate. Perhaps, writes Richard Weaver, "the most painful experience of modern consciousness is the loss of center; yet, this is the inevitable result of centuries of insistence that society yield its form."[52]

The moral hedges that surrounded our collective life have been trampled down. That is the paramount truth. What once was sublimated is now, in all of its raw and often violent nature, spewed forth in the name of liberty or self-expression. What once had to be private is now paraded publicly for the gallery of voyeurs. The virtues of the old privacy, such as reticence and modesty, are looked upon today as maladies. What was once unseemly is now commonplace. What was

51. See Grant, *The World We Created at Hamilton High* (Cambridge: Harvard University Press, 1988), p. 185.
52. Weaver, *Ideas Have Consequences* (Chicago: Chicago University Press, 1948), p. 35.

once instinct is now truth. What was once feeling is now belief. Then the best were always people of conviction; now they seldom are. Then self-control was virtue; now it is bondage. We are getting to know one another in ways we could not before, says Rieff, and what we are seeing is not pleasant. The concealment of self that was once of the essence of civility has now become a social and psychological problem to be resolved through release. In short, whereas once we were directed by a culture that had originally learned its habits from the Christian faith, we are now being directed by a culture that has learned its habits from the psychologists — and evangelicals in large numbers have come to assume that this is actually what faith is all about.

Western culture once valued the higher achievements of human nature — reasoned discourse, the good use of language, fair and impartial law, the importance of our collective memory, tradition, the core of moral axioms to which collective consent was given, those aesthetic achievements in the arts that represented the high-water marks of the human spirit. These are now all in retreat. Reasoned discourse has largely disappeared; in a nation of plummeting literacy, language has been reduced to the lowest common denominator, to the vulgar catch phrases of the youth culture;[53] the core of values has disintegrated; the arts are degraded; the law is politicized;[54] politics is trivialized. In place of high culture, we have what is low. Unruly instinctual drives replace thought; the darker side of human nature destroys the nobler, leaving a trail of pornography, violence, and indifference. Perhaps this is the triumph of the id over the superego, as the Freudians say; certainly it is the passing of the old order and the ascendancy of a new order that celebrates the collapse of the barriers that once held back the darker reaches of the human spirit. In a strangely perverse fashion, many now maintain that it is precisely in giving expression to those darker reaches that we will find release from our guilt, anxiety, and alienation.

What is now in place is not exactly an alternative system of belief. What is in place is no system of belief at all. It is more like a vacuum into the quiet emptiness of which the self is reaching for meaning — and finding only itself. But this is to put the matter more passively than is warranted. Vacuums may be empty, but they are highly destructive. The "systematic hunting down of all settled conviction," writes Rieff, "represents the anti-cultural predicate upon which mod-

---

53. See Nisbet, *Twilight of Authority*, pp. 125-31.
54. For an extended development of this assertion, see Robert H. Bork, *The Tempting of America: The Political Seduction of the Law* (New York: Free Press, 1989).

ern personality is being organized."[55] Its essence is not right doctrine, values, and behavior; its essence is the freedom to have no doctrines, no values, to be free to follow the stream of instinct that flows from the self wherever it may lead, a point that the evangelical apologists for this approach advocate quite unabashedly and unselfconsciously.

We are therefore accomplishing in our culture what only such dystopian writers as Aldous Huxley and George Orwell ever imagined. We are replacing the categories of good and evil with the pale absolutes that arise from the media world — entertainment and boredom. It is not by struggle, still less by grace, that we have eliminated the corruption from human nature of which the Reformers were so aware. We have done it simply by a fresh definition. Evil is boredom, and that is remedied with far greater ease than sin. It is remedied not by Christ but by a cable hookup.

Rieff's "psychological man" has no interest in ultimate concerns, in searching out meaning that is outside of the self and that cannot be experienced; the doctrinal imagination has long since atrophied. It is in the self that meaning is uncovered. Meaning *is* the self, the uncovering of the self, the stroking of the self, the attendance to its needs. Outside of this small inland retreat, there is only the inhospitable terrain of modernity, in which the search for meaning is so complex, so exhausting, so nerve-shattering, that only fools attempt it.

The first signs of the demise in Western culture became evident in the nineteenth century, and at least a few viewed them with great alarm. Their voices were seldom heeded because they sounded so apocalyptic, so extremist. Today we view these same developments, now much more clearly because they loom so much larger, with passionless detachment, much like a zoologist might view the pieces of a small animal that has been dismembered. The difference lies in the fact that nineteenth-century observers thought the human spirit would not survive, unscathed and undamaged, from the developments that seemed to be shaping up; today, we think it can. We see ourselves as small ships that have been obliged to take to the high seas because a plague is ravaging the land in whose ports we were moored. We have little apprehension about the voyage itself; indeed, we are exhilarated by it. It is exciting. It is a new experience. It is our "sacred" duty to undertake it. One by one, each in our own psychological barks, we cast loose in innocence. But it is a troubled innocence.

The American way of life may be the envy of the world, its gadgets

55. Rieff, *The Triumph of the Therapeutic*, p. 13.

and accoutrements sought after and emulated, but the American version of happiness, it turns out, is quite lethal. America is a violent and disturbed country. Its teenagers have the highest suicide rate in the world (in 1991, more teenage boys died from gunshot wounds than from all natural causes combined); it leads the world in the consumption of drugs, legal and illegal, in addictions of various kinds, in divorce, in the incidence of depressive illness, and in the marketing of a vast range of therapies to counteract these problems — all of which points to a vast underlying unhappiness.[56] It is this that continues to feed and to substantiate a need for the continuing psychologizing of life. The psychologists who embody and service this need are frequently the exegetes of American anti-religion — but they are also the last and only hope for happiness in America.

The Revised (Evangelical) Version

The Symptoms

Gordon Wright and Arthur Mejia have said that if "the dominant type of the twentieth century is really what Rieff calls 'psychological man,' the consequences for western society are quite incalculable."[57] The consequence for the evangelical Church are quite incalculable, too, though I will make some attempt to calculate them. Such a calculation is by no means easy to make, however, for despite the boldness with which pollsters reduce the complexities of psychological reality to easily digested statistics, the fact remains that motivations of all kinds are extraordinarily complex, but this is especially the case with religious motivation. We can catch glimpses of the iceberg of psychologized life throughout evangelicalism; it remains difficult to determine how much of it lies hidden below the water line. What we can see, though, is visible from many different angles.

It is not difficult to see, for example, that in popular evangelical journals as well as in much sermonic fare, the older ideas that happiness is properly a by-product of moral behavior rather than the object of pursuit itself and that the self is found only when it is lost are no longer much in favor. The connections between morality and happi-

---

56. See Arnold A. Rogow, *The Dying of the Light: A Searching Look at America Today* (New York: G. P. Putnam, 1975), p. 236.
57. Rieff, *The Triumph of the Therapeutic*, p. xi.

ness have become quite tenuous, it would seem, because personality is generally assumed to have little to do with human nature. Certainly in America, but sometimes it would seem also in American evangelicalism, it is not good character that we value as much as good feelings. To the extent to which this is true of evangelicalism, it is a remarkable development. Is not the self movement evidence of our collective unhappiness and insecurity? It is only the hungry, after all, who are always thinking of food; those who are not deprived occupy themselves with other thoughts. It is only the unhappy who are constantly preoccupied with happiness, only those crippled by a sense of their own insubstantial self who expend their lives in its pursuit. Why, then, are many turning to these symbols of our cultural failure and fear for the materials with which to redefine evangelical faith?

The answer, it would seem, is that this adaptation of evangelical faith has been highly successful, and its costs are apparently not self-evident. As it happens, the reshaping of the American character has coincided exactly with the reshaping of evangelical faith that has been going on for more than a century, speeded up by the revivals that coursed through the land from one end of the nineteenth century to the other and that shifted the theological axis from a predominantly Calvinistic orientation to a typically Arminian orientation. If Americans now envy the inner experience of others, evangelicals have their own inner experience to offer — indeed, to market — so what may be justified on religious grounds is rewarded not for its religious faithfulness but for its cultural appeal.

The attraction of evangelical faith, then, has been very intimately tied up with this reshaping of the American character. Evangelicals have always insisted that Christ is a person who can and should be known personally; he is not simply an item on a creed to which assent should be given. But from this point they have drawn conclusions that become increasingly injurious. They have proceeded to seek assurance of faith not in terms of the objective truthfulness of the biblical teaching but in terms of the efficacy of its subjective experience. Testimonies have become indispensable items in the evangelistic fare. Testifying to having experienced Christ personally is peculiarly seductive in the modern context, because it opens up to view an *inner experience* that responds to the hunger of the "other-directed" individual but often sacrifices its objective truth value in doing so. The question it poses to the outsider is not whether Christ is objectively real but simply whether the experience is appealing, whether it seems to have worked, whether having it will bring one inside the group and give one connections to others.

In any genuine knowledge of God, there is an experience of his grace and power, informed by the written Scriptures, mediated by the Holy Spirit, and based upon the work of Christ on the Cross. What is not so clear from the New Testament is that this experience should itself become the *source* of our knowledge of God or that it should be used to commend that knowledge to others. To be sure, there was plenty of witnessing that went on in the early Church, but it is anything but clear that this should be understood as the use of personal autobiography to persuade others that they should commit themselves to Christ.[58] New Testament witness was witness to the objective truth of Christian faith, truth that had been experienced; our witness today is witness to our own faith, and in affirming its validity we may become less interested in its truthfulness that in the fact that it seems to work. Evangelical hymnody today is changing direction to reflect this experience-centered focus.[59]

This adaptation has enabled evangelicalism to orient itself to our consumer culture and the habits of mind that go with it. The televangelists, whether deliberately or simply intuitively, have exploited this to their considerable advantage. Their type of ministry, in which serious thought has been supplanted by slickly packaged experience, is easy on the mind. Sustaining orthodoxy and framing Christian belief in doctrinal terms requires habits of reflection and judgment that are simply out of place in our culture and increasingly are disappearing from evangelicalism as well.[60] Bryan Wilson charges that these virtues have been replaced in these ministries by assumptions that are far more at home in the modern world. Today we "demand instant access to authentic reality," he says, and these ministries do indeed offer instant and painless access, the authenticity of which is "guaranteed by subjective feeling, reinforced by group-engendered emotions"; the televangelists capitalize on the widespread perception that "reality is to be felt rather than cognitively realized."[61] Feeling is rapid, but learning is

58. See Allison A. Trites's comprehensive study *The New Testament Concept of Witness* (London: Cambridge University Press, 1977). The essence of his argument can also be found in his briefer *New Testament Witness in Today's World* (Valley Forge, Pa.: Judson Press, 1983).

59. See Bill Hopkinson, "Changes in the Emphasis of Evangelical Belief, 1970-80: Evidence from New Hymnody," *Churchman* 95 (1981): 123-38.

60. For documentation of the perversion of doctrine among some evangelicals, see Walter Martin's essay "You Shall Be as Gods" and Rod Rosenbladt's "Who Do Televangelists Say That I Am?" in *The Agony of Deceit,* ed. Michael Horton (Chicago: Moody Press, 1990), pp. 89-106, 107-22.

61. Wilson, *Contemporary Transformations of Religion* (Oxford: Oxford University Press, 1976), pp. 86-87.

slow. Credit cards allow us to have without having to wait; the message of the televangelists has been that we can likewise have divine results without having to wait — indeed, without even having to think.

There can be no question that this type of consumer religion opens itself up to accommodating the bizarre. In every other aspect of the commercial world the bizarre proves salable because it either fascinates or amuses us. Ours is a generation that craves amusement. Phoenix First Assembly might serve as an illustration of how one church among many has incorporated this aspect into its appeal. Situated on seventy-two sunny acres in Phoenix, Arizona, the church has the look of a country club. It currently boasts an attendance of around ten thousand each Sunday, up from only two hundred in 1979. It is a megachurch, an expanding church. A reporter who visited it described the minister's plans to build a replica of Jerusalem nearby, "with camels and everything," as well as an amphitheater with "prayer gardens and caves." It is a church of drama. The preacher punctuates his sermons with eye-catching and heart-stopping antics such as his personal flight to heaven on invisible wires, and his use of a chain saw to topple a tree in order to give punch to a point, and his incorporation of "a rented elephant, kangaroo and zebra" in a Christmas service.[62] Other churches have gone to similar lengths, featuring skydivers dropping in during a sermon, bodybuilders breaking boards at the pulpit, and prayer groups outfitting themselves in combat fatigues.

Aside from the commercial appeal, however, the growth in this type of evangelical faith in America is in part also to be explained by the powerful undercurrents of self-absorption that course through the modern psyche. Many charismatics have made the experience of God rather than the truth of God foundational. The self therefore becomes pivotal. This, in turn, links with the deep subterranean sense of progress that is inescapable in America, as the proponents of this movement tout it as the most recent cresting of the Spirit. Here is the cutting edge of progress in what God is now doing. This by itself is a validation of all that takes place within this movement and within its churches. In America, it has always been hard to quarrel with success; it is even more futile when there are those who are convinced that the success has been divinely produced. Yet, if one understands modernity, it is not difficult to imagine that much of what is vaunted as the Spirit's work may have causes that are rather more natural. Nor is it difficult

62. Robert Johnson, "Preaching a Gospel of Acquisition: A Showy Sect Prospers," *Wall Street Journal*, 11 December 1990, p. A9.

to understand that where a religion is busy accommodating itself to culture there will be a period of success before the disillusionment sets in. In the end, those who promote the sort of Christianity that accommodates the culture always have to answer the question as to what they are offering in Christ that cannot be had from purely secular sources.

In another age, Robert Schuller's ministry, for example, might well have been viewed not as Christian ministry at all, but as comedy. Would it not be possible to view him as providing a biting parody of American self-absorption? Sin, he says with a cherubic smile, is not what shatters our relationship to God; the true culprit is the jaundiced eye that we have turned on ourselves. The problem is that we do not esteem ourselves enough. In the Crystal Cathedral, therefore, let the word *sin* be banished, whether in song, Scripture, or prayer. There is never any confession there. Then again, Christ was not drawing a profound moral compass in the Sermon on the Mount; he was just giving us a set of "be (happy) attitudes." The word was, don't worry, be happy. And God is not so mean as to judge; he is actually very amiable and benign. Comedy this devastating would be too risky for most to attempt. But Schuller is no comic. He earnestly wants us to believe all of this, and many do. When he makes these pronouncements, he attracts a large and devoted Christian following. What is the appeal?

The answer, it would seem, is that Schuller is adroitly, if unconsciously, riding the stream of modernity. By Yankelovich's estimate, 80 percent of the nation is now engaged in the search for new rules premised on the search for and discovery of the self. Schuller is offering in easily digestible bites the therapeutic model of life through which the healing of the bruised self is found. He is by no means alone in this; he is simply the most shameless.

In 1983, James Hunter published the results of his analysis of the eight most prolific evangelical presses. He found that 87.8 percent of the titles published dealt with subjects related to the self, its discovery and nurture and the resolution of its problems and tensions. The remaining 12.2 percent of the titles published had to carry the rest of the cargo.[63]

---

63. Hunter classified the evangelical literature that reflected the interests of the self movement into three groups. First, there were books on self-actualization, such as Josephson's *God's Key to Health and Happiness,* LaHaye's *Transformed Temperaments,* Osborne's *The Art of Understanding Yourself,* Bustanby's *You Can Change Your Personality,* and Ahlem's *Do I Have to Be Me?* Second, there was a category of books dealing with emotional and psychological problems such as guilt, depression, tension, and anxiety. Included here were Adolph's *Release from Tension,* Narramore's *This Way to Happiness,* Caldwell's *You Can Prevent a Nervous Breakdown,* Eggum's

To be sure, these figures can yield only tentative conclusions. We might draw firmer conclusions if we knew how many copies of each title were sold. And of course it would be better yet if we could somehow determine how many of the purchased books were actually read. And it would be best of all if we could know why the books were purchased and what effects they had on the readers. Nevertheless, Hunter's finding is quite in line with Yankelovich's estimate, and it does support the conclusion that a turn has occurred within evangelicalism characterized by "an incessant preoccupation with the hitherto 'undiscovered' complexities of one's individual subjectivity."[64] Moreover, this would seem to be not merely a passing fad but, rather, evidence of a deep transformation. In a study of the coming evangelical generation published in 1987, Hunter found "an accentuation of subjectivity and the virtual veneration of the self, exhibited in deliberate efforts to achieve self-understanding, self-improvement, and self-fulfillment."[65] A survey of evangelical college students revealed that 62 percent believed that realizing one's potential as a human being is as important as looking out for the interests of others, and 87 percent said that they were working hard at self-improvement.

Indeed, *The Serendipity Bible for Groups* (the second largest selling Bible version in 1989) owns this as the foundation of the whole enterprise. Speaking of the theological assumptions beneath the entire series of studies, Lyman Coleman begins with the affirmation that "you are created in the image of God and endowed with unlimited potential"[66] and indicates that the main point of studying the Bible is to elicit this potential. He tells us that only five to ten percent of our human potential is actually used; the rest lies buried beneath "a pile of fears, failures, painful childhood memories, broken dreams, mistakes and guilt feelings."[67] It is in the encounter group in which the Bible is used as an instrument to explore inner feelings that this potential can be

---

Feeling Good about Feeling Bad, and Brandt's *I Want Happiness, Now!* Third, there was a category of what he called hedonistic books such as Schuller's *Self-Love* and *You Can Become the Person You Want to Be,* Larson's *Dare to Live Now,* and Grimes's *How to Become Your Own Best Self.* See Hunter, *American Evangelicalism: Conservative Religion and the Quandary of Modernity* (New Brunswick, N.J.: Rutgers University Press, 1983), pp. 94-98.

64. Hunter, *American Evangelicalism,* p. 92.
65. Hunter, *Evangelicalism: The Coming Generation* (Chicago: University of Chicago Press, 1987), p. 65.
66. Coleman, *Encyclopedia of Serendipity* (N.p.: Serendipity House, 1976), p. 23.
67. Coleman, *Destiny: Discovering Your Call* (Waco, Tex.: Creative Resources, 1975), p. 4.

found and the stream of negativity stopped. Discovering our own "unlimited potential" is what Christianity is all about.

Descartes argued "I think, therefore I am," and people after Freud translated that into the modern vernacular by saying, "I *feel*, therefore I am a self";[68] modern evangelicals of the relational type seem to have added their own quirk to it by saying that "I feel *religiously*, therefore I am a self." The search for the religious self then becomes a search for religious good feelings. But the problem with making good feelings the end for which one is searching is, as Henry Fairlie argues, that it is possible to feel good about oneself, even religiously, "in states of total vacuity, euphoria, intoxication, and self-indulgence, and it is even possible when we are doing wrong and know what we are doing."[69]

This kind of self-fascination is by no means an excrescence of an otherwise robust sector of religious life. It is at the very center of evangelicalism. For further evidence that this is so, we can turn again to *Leadership* magazine, a journal dedicated to providing resources for evangelical pastors. As we noted earlier, an analysis of its contents during the 1980s shows that this highly successful journal appeared to believe that the most fruitful sources from which to draw for Christian ministry were popularized versions of psychology and business management; indeed, these are the only sources from which it has drawn. Of all the essays that appeared between 1980 and 1988, less than 1 percent made even a remote reference to Scripture or any theological idea, despite the fact that a number of the topics dealt with are themselves treated in the Bible. As the journal turns away from the Bible to what it apparently assumes are more fruitful sources of knowledge, it is redefining Christian ministry and the pastor who accepts its point of view. In the study, the evangelical pastor is now the C.E.O.; in the pulpit, the pastor is a psychologist whose task it is to engineer good relations and warm feelings.

The Results

As it turns out, the Church has walked this path before, during the earlier part of this century when Liberalism was in the ascendancy. In

---

68. See Rollo May, "The Birth and the Collapse of the Western Idea of Self," *The World and I* 4 (August 1989): 524. In this same vein, one notes, for example, that Keith Miller and Bruce Larson's *The Edge of Adventure: An Experiment in Faith* (Waco, Tex.: Word Books, 1974), for which there is an accompanying study guide, are completely autobiographical.

69. Fairlie, *The Seven Deadly Sins Today* (Notre Dame, Ind.: University of Notre Dame Press, 1979), p. 40.

that context, however, the program was intentional; now it is uninten-
tional. Then the pursuit of the self was a deliberate part of the theological agenda; now it is a by-product of contemporary culture. It
nevertheless remains the case that what theological modernism failed
to accomplish, modernization is now bringing to fruition.

Harry Emerson Fosdick, for example, was a leading American
proponent not only of Liberalism but also of a theory of the self that he
pioneered in *Christianity and Progress, As I See Religion,* and *On Being a Real
Person.* His theology of the person was built on the ideas of the immanence of God in human personality and the perfectibility of human
nature. He spoke enthusiastically of the unlimited inner potential that
only had to be found and cultivated. In fact, Fosdick was tapping into a
habit of mind that expressed nineteenth-century American confidence
and had come to the surface previously in many different ways. Fosdick
simply made this propensity explicitly theological, and his work has been
accorded the tribute of imitation. From Fosdick the ideas traveled to
Norman Vincent Peale and then to Robert Schuller, and now they have
become commonplace throughout much of the evangelical world. Bruce
Larson was right to speak of the basis of his so-called relational theology
as a "liberal" view of human nature; that is precisely what it is.[70]

The parallels between Fosdick's search for the "real person" and
the evangelical search for psychological wholeness are not, of course,
exact. As a matter of fact, the earlier Liberalism was a far more serious
enterprise theologically than evangelicalism typically is today. The
failure of Liberalism, however, does provide a salutary reminder of the
fatal weaknesses that run through these therapeutic models of salvation
and that, in turn, undercut our capacity to do serious theology. Three
of these fault lines are particularly dangerous.

First, the psychologizing of life cuts the nerve of evangelical
identity because the common assumption beneath the self movement
is the perfectibility of human nature, and this assumption is anathema
to the Christian gospel.[71] It is no accident that its theoreticians (e.g.,

70. See Larson, *The Relational Revolution: An Invitation to Discover an Exciting
Future for Our Life Together* (Waco, Tex.: Word Books, 1976), p. 105.

71. See John Passmore, *The Perfectibility of Man* (New York: Scribner's, 1971),
p. 49. For good general critiques on the role and function of psychology in faith,
see Paul C. Vitz, *Psychology as Religion: The Cult of Self Worship* (Grand Rapids:
William B. Eerdmans, 1977); William Kirk Kilpatrick, *Psychological Seduction: The
Failure of Modern Psychology* (New York: Thomas Nelson, 1983); David G. Benner,
Psychotherapy and the Spiritual Quest (Grand Rapids: Baker Book House, 1990); and
Thomas Szasz, *The Myth of Psychotherapy* (Garden City, N.Y.: Doubleday-Anchor,
1979).

Abraham Maslow, Carl Rogers, Eric Fromm, and Rollo May) are all humanists. It is precisely this sort of assumption that neither evangelical theology nor evangelical piety should be making. The biblical gospel asserts the very reverse — namely, that the self is twisted, that it is maladjusted in its relationship to both God and others, that it is full of deceit and rationalizations, that it is lawless, that it is in rebellion, and indeed that one must die to self in order to live.[72] It is this that is at the heart of the biblical gospel, this that is at the center of Christian character. There is abundant evidence that people become strong by suppressing what is unworthy within them, not by expressing it. This kind of suppression should not be confused with Freud's ideas about repression. Repression is an irrational and unconscious mechanism; suppression is a conscious and rational act undertaken out of moral concern and a sense of being owned by Christ. It is perhaps paradoxical that self-denial should build character and that self-fascination, more than anything else, should undercut it. In any event, without this bedrock of Christian character, Christian theology becomes a shaky enterprise, often lacking the sure-footed resolve and strength it needs to unmask the worldliness of the culture and to proclaim the truth of God's revelation.

I am not speaking here of the loss of a few moral precepts. In this modern age, the absence of moral fiber attests to an erosion of what constitutes the person, and that is an even more profound deficit. The psychologizing of life is, I believe, a reflexive response to the emptiness, the vacuity, of the self. It is the mechanism that replaces inner substance with the sheath of experience, the means by which the

72. The Christian self movement, insofar as it seeks biblical warrant, has turned to the second great commandment, to "love your neighbor as yourself" (Matt. 22:39). Self-love, it is argued, is here being held up as something that is not only possible but expected and desired. John Stott, however, has rightly countered that this is incorrect for three reasons. First, self-love is not a virtue commended but a reality of human life that is recognized: we should at least try to love others as much as we love ourselves. Second, agape love always entails sacrifice and service, and what sense does it make to speak of sacrificing ourselves to ourselves? Third, self-love is, from a biblical point of view, synonymous with pride, and as such it is roundly condemned (e.g., in 2 Tim. 3:2, 4). See Stott, "Must I Really Love Myself?" *Christianity Today*, 5 May 1978, pp. 34-35. Stott later expanded this initial critique in *The Cross of Christ* (Leicester: Inter-Varsity Press, 1986), pp. 274-94, 327-37. Here he relates the issues of self-love to the nature of Christ's work on the Cross and the nature of God as sufferer. For an incisive study of the psychological aspects of this issue, see David G. Myers, *The Inflated Self: Human Illusions and the Biblical Call to Hope* (New York: Seabury Press, 1981). See also Henry Fairlie's excellent analysis of pride in *The Seven Deadly Sins Today*, pp. 37-58.

core of selfhood disappears into a collage of shifting images. The individual thus becomes a part of, if not an illustration of, the new world that we are busy making, a world consisting of nothing but images — television images, self-images, political images, ad images. "Psychological man" is of recent vintage as a cultural type, but the erosion of the self has been long in the making. Toward the end of the nineteenth century, Europeans were already charting the loss of inner terrain, but somehow in America all of this seemed unreal, the preoccupation of effete European intellectuals. But there is no question now that the cultural process has overtaken us, its corrosive force dissolving not only the bonds of society but also the seams that once held our inner worlds together.

A new species is now adrift in the world and washing up all along the shores of evangelical life. It is a species eager to exchange enduring qualities for a spate of exciting new experiences, a species that thinks in terms of images rather than truths, that has no place from which to view the world but shifts from peephole to peephole in an attempt to catch the passing sights, a voyeur rather than a thinker, guided by a compass of circumstance rather than belief.

This is a new species, certainly as a religious phenomenon, but the means of its creation is not new. Beneath this "psychological man" is an evisceration of the self, an emptying out of being. In 1925, T. S. Eliot, with the searing words of the prophet, spoke of this erosion of the inner substance that left behind only empty, whimpering shells:

> We are the hollow men
> We are the stuffed men
> Leaning together
> Headpiece filled with straw. Alas!
> Our dried voices, when
> We whisper together
> Are quiet and meaningless
> As wind in dry grass
> Or rats' feet over broken glass
> In our dry cellar.[73]

Our cellars, too, are dry and are empty, despite our most exalted efforts to replace what we have lost with the plastic and chrome artifacts of the modern world. But the experience of abundance not only fails

73. Eliot, "The Hollow Men," in *The Complete Poems and Plays* (New York: Harcourt, Brace, 1952), p. 56.

to prop up our inner reality but actually serves to pervert our moral compass. Asceticism, or self-denial in any form, has become the new immorality; self-indulgence is the new gospel. It is this psychology, the embers of which are constantly blown into fresh spurts of flame by the advertisers who would have us abandon all our old cultural inhibitions, that has long been at the root of our decaying culture. But never mind that, we are told. The Holy Spirit is freshly baptizing this psychological and cultural decay in the so-called "health and wealth gospel" so widely promulgated (or at least tacitly allowed) among Pentecostals, a "gospel" that offers mighty abundance for the asking and defines human wholeness in terms of having everything one desires. And the same Holy Spirit, in less brassy ways, spills out through the rest of the evangelical world, offering happiness to those who get in touch with themselves. The Old Testament prophets, who were not innocent of human depravity, might well hear in all of this a depth of folly and self-deception that even they would find quite novel.

To the extent that the currents of modernity are washing away our internal reality, producing "Shape without form, shade without colour, / Paralyzed force, gesture without motion" — to that extent, the capacity to think theologically is being emptied out, too. There is a profound correlation between the functioning of a substantial moral self and the ability to sustain a substantial theology that has moral force. The latter needs the former; the collapse of the former leads to the disappearance of the latter.

Second, the psychologizing of life undermines the desire and capacity to think, without which theology is obviously impossible. The psychologizing process identifies access to reality with subjective experience rather than objective thought. Alasdair McIntyre contends that the presumption in favor of feeling over thought predominates in academia as well, to the point that the value of argument has simply disappeared. Questions of moment are now settled by how people feel about them. There are, in fact, only two ways in which they can be resolved: either by the rousing of emotion or by the exercise of external power. The prospects of settling questions by reasoned deliberation and debate have greatly dimmed, because, in the end, the collapse of the belief in truth and the habit of listening to the self have united to destroy what academic life once demanded.[74]

The consequence of these developments in the evangelical

---

74. See McIntyre, *After Virtue: A Study in Moral Theory* (Notre Dame, Ind.: University of Notre Dame Press, 1981).

Church is that attention has been focused within rather than without. Evangelicals choose what is spontaneous over what is static, "becoming" over "being," what is exciting over what is true. And when the shroud of the Holy Spirit is spread over the whole enterprise, when it is asserted and believed that the Spirit is responsible for introducing many of the changes that are actually the products of modernized culture, then the art of discrimination is also unceremoniously surrendered. How, then, can theology be done?

Nisbet has argued that there are striking parallels between the end of the Roman Empire and what seem to be the closing days of our own. In both, a "spreading wave of unreason" has given witness not to new and hidden depths within the self that we think we have discovered but simply to a "failure of nerve." Today as then, he says, we experience irruptions of the occult, outbreaks of the antirational, the triumph of belief in blind fortune, the reign of chance, and the "generalized retreat into the subjective recesses of consciousness."[75] As a result, we have made the salvation of the ego paramount and have subjugated the whole of life to this end. But this strategy of personal survival is inimical to serious thought, simply because serious thought has no part in this strategy for personal survival.

At first glance, this may not seem to be so large a loss. After all, the cognitive side of Christian faith has largely become the property of those in the academic guild (if not by outright claim, at least by practical default), contributing to a parting of the ways in the evangelical world. Those who wish to explore the cognitive demands of faith may do so, even to the extent of viewing it as philosophy, and those who wish to explore its psychological meaning may do so, even to the extent of viewing Christian faith as tool of self-discovery. And this amicable parting accords well with the values that this culture now considers primary, such as the importance of allowing for diversity, of allowing for multiple ways of thinking about and expressing the full range of modern experience, of granting equal weight to each opinion and according equal validity to each search for personal authenticity. Indeed, the fact that this parting of the ways has been so amicable, so uncontested, is taken as a sign of maturity. Finally evangelicals have emancipated themselves from the dreadful Fundamentalist scourge of dividing at the drop of a hat.

This happy outcome is not without its costs, however. The sort of Christian faith that is conceived in the womb of the self is quite

75. Nisbet, *Twilight of Authority*, p. 9.

different from the historic Christian faith. It is a smaller thing, shrunken in its ability to understand the world and to stand up in it. The self is a canvas too narrow, too cramped, to contain the largeness of Christian truth. Where the self circumscribes the significance of Christian faith, good and evil are reduced to a sense of well-being or its absence, God's place in the world is reduced to the domain of private consciousness, his external acts of redemption are trimmed to fit the experience of personal salvation, his providence in the world diminishes to whatever is necessary to ensure one's having a good day, his Word becomes intuition, and conviction fades into evanescent opinion. Theology becomes therapy, and all the telltale symptoms of the therapeutic model of faith begin to surface. The biblical interest in righteousness is replaced by a search for happiness, holiness by wholeness, truth by feeling, ethics by feeling good about one's self. The world shrinks to the range of personal circumstances; the community of faith shrinks to a circle of personal friends. The past recedes. The Church recedes. The world recedes. All that remains is the self.

What remains is, in fact, a paltry thing. But what is being destroyed is not paltry and insignificant at all. Simply put, the psychologizing of faith is destroying the Christian mind. It is destroying Christian habits of thought because it is destroying the capacity to think about life in a Christian fashion. It is as if the topsoil were being washed away, leaving the land barren and incapable of being cultivated. It can no longer sustain the bountiful harvest of being able to discern between good and evil, to think about all of life in terms of God and his purposes, to construct a way of being that accords with his Word, and to contest the norms of cultural plausibility. All of this is lost. And when people are no longer compelled by God's truth, they can be compelled by anything, the more so if it has the sheen of excitement or the lure of the novel or the illicit about it. The heretics of old, one suspects, would be sick with envy if they knew of the easy pickings that can now be had in the Church.

When the Christian mind erodes, the possibility of doing theology erodes with it. The Church is, as I have argued, the primary auditor of theology. It is for the Church that theology is written. But in the absence of its fundamental audience, theology languishes as surely as an orchestra would in the absence of music lovers or a novelist would in the absence of a reading public.

Biblical faith is not just about ideas and doctrines; that needs to be said. In our contemporary climate, however, this is taken as license to imagine that it is not about objective truth at all, that it extends only to what is privately and subjectively appealing. If there is no truth, however, then there is no theology; we are left with only the creation of symbols of reality that interpret inner experience.

But biblical faith *is* about truth. God has described himself and his works to us in the language of the Bible, and it is quite presumptuous for us to say that we have found a better way to hear him (through our own experience) and a better way to find reality (by constructing it within the self). The Old Testament prophets made this same protest against the paganism of their day, with its assumption that truth is purely subjective and that one discovers it through intuition rather than through the understanding. In place of such empty superstitions, the prophets provided compelling analyses of their world that assumed the objectivity of the moral order and the sovereign presence of God in creation and history. Their boldness of thought will be ours only when we renounce the failure of nerve evidenced by our retreat into the self and take up their conviction about the objectivity of truth.

Third, the psychologizing of life vitiates the theological agenda because it severs interest in the outside world. The self movement has arisen with a generation of men and women who have been denied a significant role in society. To be sure, society rewards social utility. It needs its doctors, scientists, engineers, lawyers, and managers, and it rewards them commensurately. At the same time, it condemns all to search for their significance in the private sphere rather than the public sphere, for the structures that depend on the scientists, engineers, and managers have become too large, remote, and impersonal to satisfy too many personal needs. It is only in our *private* life, with all its internal rages, fears, hopes, and longings, that we are left to find whatever meaning we can. This situation is so intolerable, Alasdair MacIntyre argues, that we attempt to relieve it through an "overpersonalization of that life,"[76] by blowing up into exaggerated proportions the importance of the vagaries of the inner life. Today, says Buckley, we have to grasp individual worth by magnifying "subjective consciousness," because the larger external world has been shut off from us as a place of meaning. The interior life is now everything, and social life is nothing.[77]

Indeed, if Rieff is correct, we are now pursuing the self at the price of culture; the satisfaction of the self is the immediate cause of

76. MacIntyre, *Against the Self-Images of the Age: Essays on Ideology and Philosophy* (New York: Schocken Books, 1971), p. 35.
77. Buckley, *The Turning Key*, p. 11.

the paralysis of culture. And Rieff has also argued that culture is not merely a set of moral restraints but the outlet for the human spirit; it is the collective organization of human interests, vocations, the expression of mutual dependencies in which we find our meaning. The self is fulfilled only by overturning these cultural controls and denying community responsibilities. And the same is true now of the evangelical world as well. Those who wish for the remission of doctrinal controls now far outnumber those who argue for their preservation, just as in the larger society. Furthermore, evangelical faith has diminished, for many of its followers, to the point that it is now just one more way of being, one more way of experiencing, that offers little beyond the self and asks for less. It no longer has the materials at hand — the convictions about the objectivity of truth — with which to build a public theology, a theology that encompasses all of life.

To be sure, evangelicals have notched up considerable successes in the realm of social activity and are more likely to be involved in various forms of social ministry than any other religious group. Only time will tell whether this accomplishment can be sustained alongside the burgeoning appetite for self-fulfillment, however. Self-fulfillment is a solitary pursuit, after all. The inclination to be socially involved may simply be a response to a need to be active or a sense of pity that may be commendable without being substantial enough to serve as a basis for theology. The real reason that a capitulation to the self movement will put an end to theology among evangelicals is that self-seekers simply have no compelling motivation to sustain any interest in community life. It is no accident that *Leadership,* which devoted essay upon essay to discussing the sorrows and woes that the modern world spills into the Church — sexual abuse, drugs, loneliness, adultery, pornography — devoted considerably less than 1 percent of its essays to attempting in any way to understand that world. There is no cultural analysis in its pages. It is simply interested in how life's sorrows can be *managed.*

And so it is that the first fruit of the Reformation gospel, a sense of individual responsibility before God in matters of faith and work, has become the very means by which that faith is eviscerated, work has been rendered meaningless, and the theology by which God's activity in the world was understood has been made redundant. The powerful vision of a humanity corrupted by sin being released to stand before God in all his glory and converse with him, gripped by the magnificent certainty of his truth, is now dying. It is being edged out by the small and tawdry interest of the self in itself, the self standing in the inner counsels of its own piety, the one hand bargaining with the other. That is how our individualism has betrayed us. Evangelicalism may use a different kind of language than the secular culture uses to describe this movement, but it is the same movement nonetheless. That, however, is only half the story; it is a reflection on only half the American character. It is to the other half that we now need to turn, to the rise of Everyperson.

CHAPTER V

The Rise of Everyperson

He who first shortened the labor of Copyists by device of Movable Types was disbanding hired Armies, and cashiering most Kings and Senates, and creating a whole new democratic world: he had invented the Art of printing.

Thomas Carlyle

Anyone wishing to save humanity today must first of all save the word.

Jacques Ellul

As people become more involved, they know less and less.

Marshall McLuhan

AMERICANS THINK OF THEMSELVES as individualists, and they are, but they are also conformists. Neither characteristic, of course, is unique to Americans. Indeed, under the circumstances of modernization, both individualism and conformity find new forms of expression in many countries other than America. It is, however, in the interaction of these traits that something distinctively American emerges. We considered individualism in the previous chapter, and now it is time to turn to the theme of conformity as it has been expressed in evangelical faith.

I base my contention that Americans are conformists on more than just visible evidence, although such evidence does provide some compelling support for the case. The genius of America's enormously virile economic system has been its capacity to standardize its products and services, and the result is a society in which there is much sameness. From coast to coast, one sees the same autos, the same clothes, the same refrigerators, the same urban skylines, the same urban blight, the same television fare, the same airlines, and the same fast food outlets. Everything looks pretty much the same. But does this kind of standardization necessarily imply conformity? It need not, but as it happens, this outward conformity is a matter not merely of economics but also of psychology. This common economic life, this mass market, is the final flowering of the revolutionary changes that were set in motion in 1776. It is important that we note this, because the same cultural forces that have shaped the American character have also shaped the American church. The same psychological undertow that churns beneath American society also churns beneath American theology.

In what follows, I will first offer a brief sketch of the characteristics and psychology of an archetypal representative of contemporary mass culture — Everyperson. Of particular interest in this connection is the manner in which knowledge is redefined and its function in society changes where Everyperson rises to dominance. This process has been amplified by the advent of television, although the exact way in which this medium facilitates the reinterpretation of knowledge may not always be clear.

Having established this background, I will proceed to show how evangelical faith changes when it is constructed in the psyche of Everyperson. It is my contention that this transformation is profoundly radical — more radical in the evangelical Church than in the society at large — and that in turn the whole role of leadership is also changed, because the democratic impulses loosed by the Revolution immediately relocated the control and definition of what that faith should be from a trained ecclesiastical elite to an untrained populace. This shift may have produced some gains, but it also resulted in some losses. For one thing, there has been a tendency to associate theology with elitist interests, and a subsequent drive to rid the evangelical faith of them both. Popular evangelical faith has developed a bias against theology (not to mention against the intellect), and what is more, it has elevated the bias to the level of a virtue, defending it as vigorously as democracy.[1]

---

1. At issue here is the way in which the democratic mind-set has reordered Christian faith, the obverse of what theologically liberal churchmen envisioned

In the presence of this bias, the leader is reduced to serving as a cautious pollster.

Who Is Everyperson?

The cultural character that I have called Everyperson is not simply the ordinary or average person, although, as Ann Douglas notes, the "exaltation of the average" is "the trademark of mass culture,"[2] and mass culture is where Everyperson is to be found. But Everyperson stands for more than simply those who straddle the central percentages in opinion polls, though this character does find special comfort in being in the middle. Rather, I have in mind the person who is the product of the American experience of democracy, the person for whom democracy is not simply a political system but an entire world-view and for whom, therefore, culture and truth belong to the *people*. This is to say that Everyperson believes that culture and truth are properly governed by and used for the people and, further, that the custodians of culture and truth must exercise their custodial responsibilities within the jaws of popular consensus. They can lead only to the extent that they appeal to the people, and hence they must find the legitimation of their leadership in public opinion.

Immediately it becomes apparent that there is something paradoxical about this character, for in America, the love of freedom, from which individualism arises, is as fierce as the love of equality, from which conformity arises. To love both freedom and equality, and to love both with an equal devotion, is so much a part of being American that if one were to wonder aloud, as Europeans often did

---

earlier in this century — namely, that democracy in the political realm had a religious character. Their vision developed into "a variety of the 'religion of democracy' that was a prophetic faith in the spiritual oneness of Christianity and democracy, based on the democratic theology of Christianity and concerned primarily with the survival of Christianity in troubled modern democracies" (Jan C. Dawson, "The Religion of Democracy in Early Twentieth-Century America," *Journal of Church and State* 27 [Winter 1985]: 47). At the same time, Stow Persons has observed that political theorists have displayed a singular disinclination to consider popular opinion when formulating their theories. See "Public Opinion: A Democratic Dilemma," in *American Character and Culture in a Changing World: Some Twentieth-Century Perspectives,* ed. John A. Hague (Westport, Conn.: Greenwood Press, 1979), pp. 172-83.

2. Ann Douglas, *The Feminization of American Culture* (New York: Alfred A. Knopf, 1977), p. 4.

last century,[3] whether these loves were compatible with one another, one would surely invite a few sideways glances. Europeans, however, were baffled by this double insistence; they argued that differences must arise wherever freedom reigns, because people are all differently gifted. Freedom must produce significant inequalities, they argued, enabling some to acquire great fortunes while leaving others impoverished, for example, and enabling some to become educated while others remain illiterate. They did not immediately understand that Americans were realizing equality in a manner that managed to reconcile what seem to be contradictory interests.

In other societies, David Potter notes, liberty has been understood as the freedom to be different from others, and equality has been understood as a right to be like others; given such understandings, it was inevitable that liberty and equality should part company and head off in opposite directions. Not so in America. In America, liberty has come to mean "freedom to grasp opportunity," and equality has come to mean freedom to grasp opportunity in the same way that others are able to grasp it, to "have universal opportunity to move through a scale which traversed many levels," at one end of which might be a log cabin and at the other end of which might be the White House.[4] Concepts that were considered contradictory in Europe became synonymous in America. It is in this union of seeming opposites that the other union of seeming opposites — individualism and conformity — is nurtured. Since Americans believe in both freedom and equality, they find nothing strange in wanting to be both individualists and conformists.

But what exactly does equality mean in this context? Certainly neither Tocqueville nor the Puritans before him believed in equality of possessions; nowhere, Tocqueville said, is "stronger scorn expressed for the theory of permanent equality of property" than in America, and though "the love of money has a greater grip on men's hearts" here than in any other country, it nevertheless "circulates with in-

---

3. In the eighteenth and nineteenth centuries, "American" and "European" were often used as contrasting and contradictory ways of looking at life, though in the twentieth century the sense of contrast has diminished. See Daniel J. Boorstin, *America and the Image of Europe: Reflections on American Thought* (New York: World Publishing, 1968), pp. 19-39. See also Max Berger, *The British Traveller in America, 1836-1860* (New York: Columbia University Press, 1943); Robert W. Smuts, *European Impressions of the American Worker* (New York: King's Crown Press, 1953); and Frances Trollope, *Domestic Manners of the Americans* (London: Whittaker, Treacher, 1832).

4. Potter, *People of Plenty: Economic Abundance and the American Character* (Chicago: University of Chicago Press, 1968), pp. 91-92.

credible rapidity," no two successive generations enjoying its blessings.[5] Was it, then, equality of opportunity? Certainly that belief has sustained Americans across the years — the belief that here as in no other land, those of insignificant birth can rise to positions of great prominence and power, those suckled in poverty can attain great riches. The accidents of birth, whether physical or social, have traditionally not been viewed as impediments to advancement. This myth has probably served to stifle more simmering discontent than anything else in the country's two centuries of independence, but however precious and powerful it remains for Americans, most of them have moments when they suspect that it is a lie, especially those who now constitute our underclass, those who have trouble enough finding a job, much less success. In an increasingly complex and technological age, opportunity does not beckon to all in the same way, and not all can respond in the same way. Equal effort is not equally rewarded. There are, to be sure, Cinderella stories. Henry Kissinger, born in Germany, rose to become perhaps as influential a Secretary of State as any in the twentieth century with the possible exception of John Foster Dulles. One would not have to look far, however, to find other European immigrants who managed to rise no further than the welfare rolls. No, at the heart of this belief was not equality of possessions or attainments or talents but rather equality of worth.

The root of this belief, in fact, went back to the Puritans and behind them to the Protestant Reformers, but in the American experiment it took on its own particular expression. Being equal, Potter asserts, has meant starting out on the same footing in the conquest of America.[6] It has meant that no one should have a head start because of family blood. America would never have been conquered if talent and enterprise could not have been rewarded. It is true that this state of affairs made it possible for some to amass fortunes while others did not, but such inequities were always tolerated. America soon developed its own aristocracy, as Tocqueville noted, but it was based on wealth — an aristocracy on whom America has never frowned and has in fact always indulged. In 1990, 10 percent of the population held 36 percent of the nation's income, and the wealthiest 1 percent in the country returned only 27 percent of their income in taxes, down from 39 percent in 1966. Elsewhere in the world,

5. Tocqueville, *Democracy in America*, book 1, ed. J. P. Morgan, trans. George Lawrence (Garden City, N.Y.: Doubleday, 1969), p. 54.

6. Potter, "The Quest for National Character," in *The Reconstruction of American History*, ed. John Higham (New York: Harper, 1962), pp. 214-15.

this might very well have been all the tinder that was needed for a revolution. But not in America.

In America, it is the aristocracy based on blood that has always been resented, not the aristocracy of wealth. America would not tolerate the idea that because of family lines some should start life elevated over or ahead of others. It was one thing if some could succeed and others could not; it was something entirely different if only some could attempt the undertaking simply because of who they were, and others could not. Differences in talent and accomplishment were acceptable; differences in privilege were not. It was in this that America's distinctiveness lay. "We have no princes for whom we toil, starve, and bleed," exulted Hector St. John de Crèvecoeur, the Frenchman who settled in New Jersey in 1765 before becoming the French proconsul in New York. We are, he concluded, "the most perfect society now existing in the world."[7]

What started out as a political system has now broadened out into a worldview that encompasses the workplace, dress, cuisine, patterns of consumption, and, of course, religion. In our time, the wealthy, the middle class, and the poor have "come closer to living alike, dressing alike, eating the same food, enjoying the same entertainments, sharing the same advantages than at any time since the Civil War," said Henry Steele Commager, and he went on to add that while the disparity in wealth has grown, the comforts and security that wealth commands are accessible to more than ever before.[8] We live "in the same kind of houses, doing the same kind of work, using the same machinery, reading the same newspapers," he said; we all use "the same soap, eat the same breakfast food, laugh at the same radio jokes, admire the same movie stars, and digest the same magazine articles."[9] And he might also have said that we are all developing the same kind of religiosity. Our democracy, driven by its highly successful capitalistic engine, has proved to be one of the most effective devices ever conceived for inducting people into a common experience — the experience many now instinctively think of as being American, of having equal access to the good life, of having the same things, the same ideas, the same experiences. Democracy, Boorstin asserts, "made society into a mirror where

7. Crèvecoeur, *Letters from an American Farmer* (New York: E. P. Dutton, 1962), pp. 40-41.

8. Commager, *The American Mind: An Interpretation of American Thought and Character since the 1880s* (New Haven: Yale University Press, 1950), p. 408.

9. Commager, *The American Mind*, p. 422.

people saw the way things were, and made that the measure of the way things ought to be."[10]

Moreover, what William Whyte observed some time ago has only intensified: increasing numbers have vowed not simply to work in organizations but to *belong* to them.[11] The bureaucracy that presides over the plenty in which we bask also absorbs our souls into its own life, regimenting behavior and ordering our expectations in such a way that they conform with one another and with the organization. We are, indeed, now truly equal. The charm of America originally was its difference, its uniqueness, but Boorstin argues that in its fulfillment, the uniqueness of America has evolved into a capacity to erase uniqueness.[12] There is one aspect of this psychological equality that is especially important for our purposes, however — the way in which knowledge, like everything else in America, has become democratized.

The Middling Standard

The revolutions of nineteenth-century Europe were aimed at dispossessing aristocracies of their power and land, but the Revolution in America was different. There was not much of an entrenched aristocracy here, and in any event land was in plentiful supply. Once matters of power and self-determination were settled, the revolutionary impulses moved in a direction that was quite novel. Knowledge, which had once been the preserve of the well-to-do, was increasingly and deliberately opened to the masses. And theological knowledge, once the preserve of theologians and the clerical well-to-do, was democratized along with the rest of it. Across the board, people aspired to knowledge that they judged to be useful, both in the schools and in the Church.

It was this assurance of common access that provided the bedrock for the sovereignty of the people expressed in the country's democratic institutions, but it also produced a leveling effect in society that touched the Christian faith almost immediately and has continued to affect it to this day. In America, Tocqueville observed, "primary education is within reach of all; higher education is hardly available at all." The

10. Daniel J. Boorstin, *The Americans*, vol. 2: *The Democratic Experience* (New York: Random House, 1973), pp. 449-50.

11. See Whyte, *The Organization Man* (New York: Simon & Schuster, 1956).

12. Boorstin, *The Americans*, p. 307.

result was that in no other country in the world, he said, are there "so few ignorant and so few learned individuals."[13] Here, he said, there is no class that brings with it a hereditary love of learning; rather, a "middling standard" prevails for all. Some have to be raised to it, others have to reduce themselves to it. And the consequence, he said, is that "one finds a vast multitude of people with roughly the same ideas about religion, history, science, political economy, legislation, and government."[14] Moreover, it is not only the case that Americans share the same ideas but that the shared ideas all have the same *quality*. Despite the fact that in the twentieth century proportionately more people have received college and university degrees, their notion of equality has not changed much. The situation Tocqueville described still prevails, because the driving force here is not educational but social and psychological. Some have to be raised to meet that middling standard, but those who attempt to exceed it are usually resented. Today, a display of intellect will draw the same sort of reaction that an appeal to blood lines would have drawn in the midst of the Revolution. It reeks of aristocratic pretension. It is simply un-American.

Early on, Americans distinguished themselves from Europeans by trying to merge the streams of aristocratic and folk culture, streams that elsewhere frequently flow in different beds. They remain divided in Britain even today, for example. The "thinking class" has its own vocabulary, newspapers, art, dress, sports, clubs, and television programming (BBC 3). The children of this class have always had easy access to Oxford and Cambridge, although in this century the talented children of the "working class" have been allowed some access to the privilege and the rewards that this brings. The working class likewise has had its own vocabulary, newspapers, arts, dress, sports, and pubs. These two cultures, aristocratic and folk, have remained quite distinct from one another. The lines are rarely crossed from either side, even in education. Proportionately, only one fifth as many people are able to go to college or university in Britain as are able to in America.

From the very beginning in America, the ideal was that learning should be accessible to all, though the genesis of that belief was curious. America was founded not by wild and bloody revolutionaries in the streets but by a group of intellectuals, men of extraordinary ability and erudition who stood many prevailing English cultural assumptions on their heads. In another time, intellectuals such as these might have

13. Tocqueville, *Democracy in America*, book 1, p. 55.
14. Tocqueville, *Democracy in America*, book 1, p. 55.

been marooned in the universities, reduced to dispatching their judgments about how to prosecute the grievances with England only to the learned journals. In this case, however, the most learned and proficient were in the center of the fray. They were in the place where popular prejudices are often most secure from serious analysis, and it was here that they brought to bear the prowess and accomplishments of high, literate culture. Moreover, from this position of power they addressed a nation that was probably more literate than any other at the time. Indeed, between 1790 and 1810, newspapers grew in number from 90 to 370.[15] By the early part of the nineteenth century, the country was flooded with books, pamphlets, and magazines, many of them the vehicles of new ideas, political and otherwise. America was ripe for an experiment in which knowledge would be seen to be the preserve not only of the high bred but also of the people.

Literacy rates are not always easy to ascertain, to be sure, and it is also the case that the ability to read does not necessarily carry with it the capacity to think, a point for which Bloom made a spirited case in *The Closing of the American Mind*. But it is nevertheless worth noting that the ability to read was advanced in America far beyond that in England. If the ability to sign one's name can be taken as an indication of at least some degree of literacy, then it would appear that in mid-seventeenth-century England, somewhere between 30 and 40 percent of the men were literate. This varied by region and even more noticeably by class. With respect to the latter, about 95 percent of the clergy and gentry were literate, about 65 percent of the yeomen, and about 25 percent of the husbandmen and laborers.[16] By the mid-nineteenth century, these figures had improved. By then, just over 60 percent of the men and 36 percent of the women were literate.[17]

In the Puritan settlements in America, the education of children was required immediately, in sharp contrast to the situation in England, where schooling was voluntary, frequently out of reach for those lower down the social scale, and of decidedly uneven quality where it was provided. Kenneth Lockridge notes that Puritan religion "was the

---

15. Nathan O. Hatch, *The Democratization of American Christianity* (New Haven: Yale University Press, 1989), p. 25.

16. David Cressy, "The Environment for Literacy: Accomplishment and Context in Seventeenth-Century England and New England," in *Literacy in Historical Perspective*, ed. Daniel P. Resnick (Washington: Library of Congress, 1983), p. 38.

17. Thomas W. Laqueur, "Toward a Cultural Ecology of Literacy in England, 1600-1850," in *Literacy in Historical Perspective*, p. 45.

major force in teaching men and often women to read,"[18] and the results were spectacular. Although the literacy rate for men in New England remained steady at about 60 percent between 1650 and 1700, after this time it climbed, reaching 80 percent by mid-century. The figures were lower in Virginia, but there can be no doubt that one immediate effect of Puritan faith was a literate society. Neil Postman notes, in this connection, that Thomas Paine's *Common Sense,* which is not a popular book by contemporary standards, nevertheless sold 100,000 copies in the first two months of its life and probably close to 400,000 copies overall.[19] Relative to the population, the equivalent today would be for an author to sell 8 million in the first two months and 32 million overall. Noah Webster's *American Spelling Book* sold 24 million copies between 1783 and 1843. And the *Personal Memoirs of General U. S. Grant,* penned as he was dying and published in 1885, netted the author's widow $200,000 in royalties in the first six months and the publisher $600,000 in the first year.[20] The first edition of 150,000 sold out in three weeks. Before a second edition could be rushed through the groaning binderies, orders for the book had surpassed 300,000. America early became a print society and provided its young with the requisite skills of literacy. Indeed, in the mid-nineteenth century in New England, the literacy rate was around 95 percent, and the schools that produced this remarkable achievement were considered models of educational virtue by those in other countries.

It is no surprise to find, therefore, that in the early days Harvard and Yale had among their students many sons of the soil, which was never the case at either Oxford or Cambridge. In America, the marks of aristocratic culture and distinction disappeared, and those who may have belonged in a lower class in England and had cultural interests commensurate with that class were here absorbed into a common current of thinking and learning. This "middling standard" in learning bred its own "middling standard" in culture, which attempted to hold together what in Europe was (and remains) divided.

This situation has changed drastically in society today, however. America is regressing in its capacity to read, and, unlike the Puritans,

18. Kenneth Lockridge, "Literacy in Early America, 1650-1800," in *Literacy and Social Development in the West,* ed. Harvey J. Graff (New York: Cambridge University Press, 1979), p. 183.

19. Neil Postman, *Amusing Ourselves to Death: Public Discourse in the Age of Show Business* (New York: Penguin Books, 1985), pp. 34-35.

20. John Tebbel, *A History of Book Publishing in the United States,* 3 vols. (New York: R. R. Bowker, 1975), 2: 524-26.

today's evangelicals are happily participating in the religious aspect of this decline, sometimes even hastening it. Today's level of literacy is close to what first pertained when the settlers arrived — a level they viewed as unacceptable and sought to change immediately. When G. K. Chesterton visited America in the 1930s, he observed that New York's Times Square would be a magnificent spectacle if one did not have to read the signs. Using that criterion today, one might be tempted to say that its magnificence must be increasing, since the numbers of those who cannot read the signs have risen significantly.

Beyond this, populist tastes have now assumed the dominant place in American culture, because television has been able to purvey them so effectively and, in the process, to push other kinds of taste and ability to the cultural periphery. Politics and religion (especially evangelical religion) are only two of the most obvious locations where popular culture, which increasingly cares little for the printed word and the kind of discourse that goes with it, has now achieved a marked dominance.

Although the gap between the literacy rates of men and women has now closed, it remains the case that only about two thirds of adult Americans can read, and the problem is no longer concentrated among the rural poor. In Boston, for example, 40 percent of the adult population is illiterate. Among American adults generally, 16 percent of whites, 44 percent of blacks, and 56 percent of Hispanics are functionally illiterate. In the world, the United States now ranks forty-ninth among 158 nations in literacy.[21] This decline is rather strikingly symbolized in a new Bible translation being prepared for adults, *The Everyday Bible: Clearly Translated for Life.* Actually, it is not new. It started out as a children's Bible, translated at a fourth-grade level, and it is simply being reissued with minor modifications as an adult's Bible.

To be sure, there has been debate over the exact connection between this sinking level of literacy and the advent of television and other social factors, but it seems safe enough to say that television

---

21. See Jonathan Kozol, *Illiterate America* (Garden City, N.Y.: Doubleday-Anchor, 1985), pp. 4-5. Cf. E. D. Hirsch, *Cultural Literacy: What Every American Needs to Know* (Boston: Houghton Mifflin, 1987), pp. 4-5. A recent study suggests that the erosion of literacy seems to be paralleled by an erosion of knowledge in the universities. In American colleges and universities, 78 percent of the undergraduate degrees do not require a course in Western civilization, 38 percent do not require a history course, 77 percent do not require a foreign language, 41 percent do not require mathematics, and 33 percent do not require any courses in the natural or physical sciences (see Lynne V. Cheney, *Fifty Hours: A Core Curriculum for College Students* [Washington: National Endowment for the Humanities, 1989], pp. 7-8).

competes with the printed page and has done much to erode habits essential to the print culture. The result is that it has given a new and potentially revolutionary turn to the establishment of society's "middling standard."

Les Liaisons Dangereuses

Ours is the first generation whose experience of the world is both interpreted by and channeled through the same medium. As a matter of fact, television may give to this nation of immigrants what it presently lacks by way of a mother tongue. Or, more correctly, it may provide a substitute for a mother tongue. Language is what typically carries all of the markers that define national consciousness, but according to Jeremy Murray-Brown, in America it is television that is "providing a sense of common identity to the diverse groups that make up this pluralistic society."[22] While the various television viewers may be conversing among themselves in Spanish, Vietnamese, Polish, or Italian, their sense of participation in American life is largely being elicited not by language but by the video images. Thus it is that at moments of high crisis, such as the Challenger space shuttle disaster or the allied war against Iraq, Americans are glued to their sets. They want the latest information, but they also want to share in a national experience. And indeed, the fact that so many are watching the same images at the same time may seem to be the last vestige of solidarity that remains in a vastly diverse and fragmenting society. This is illusion, however; this is not solidarity but simply a multiplication of individual experience stripped of all relational connections. Sixty million people may watch the same images, but each does so individually, not in communion with others.

This is not to say that television fails to nurture a very powerful psychological egalitarianism, however. Television is beamed to all without discrimination. It is open to all, accessible to all. There is no class, no ethnic minority, no level of illiteracy that bars any from holding communion with this magical screen. In the experience of watching it, every type of person has found a single point of unity. "By the mere act of watching television," says William J. Donnelly, "a het-

22. Murray-Brown, "Video Ergo Sum," in *Video Icons and Values*, ed. Alan M. Olson, Christopher Parr, and Debra Parr (Albany: State University of New York, 1990), p. 20.

erogeneous society engages in a purely homogeneous activity."[23] Paul Hirsch concurs, saying that the most potent effect of television on society has been its "provision of a centrally produced, standardized, and homogeneous culture."[24] And I would add that it is a standardized, homogeneous culture in which many of the abilities and achievements of the older, more literate culture simply wither and die.

It would of course be foolish to imagine that this is the outcome of some sinister social experimentation, though Marxists have had their suspicions along these lines. The truth is less ugly but not less troubling. It is that American television is driven by commercial interests, by the need to appeal to the largest possible mass audience. Programmers have traditionally worked to determine what sort of material will appeal to the largest possible percentage of a diverse viewing public — to men and women, the young, the middle-aged, and the old, to people from different ethnic backgrounds and with different class ties, and so on. The most commercially successful programs are those that, as John Fiske puts it, "homogenize this variety."[25] The result is a product — and that is the correct word — that appeals broadly by thinning its substance, by ensuring that all can find connections with it, by demanding little of the viewer, and by offending as few people as possible. The resulting banality and emptiness are then concealed beneath a dramatic veneer that the medium has virtually perfected.

Were that the extent of television's sins, its critics on both the Right and the Left could not do much more than bewail the decline of America's cultural taste. But more is at issue here than just taste. In order to become commercially successful, programs must not only be easy on the mind but must in fact create an alternative reality. Television is first and foremost an entertainment machine, a fount of distraction that enables millions of Americans to "enter a different world that is more pleasant and less difficult in almost every way" than the one in which they actually live.[26] It creates a world of optimism and good cheer relatively free of unhappy endings, because unhappy endings are bad business. It creates a world in which ordinary people

23. Donnelly, *The Confetti Generation: How the New Communication Technology Is Fragmenting America* (New York: Henry Holt, 1986), p. 51.

24. Hirsch, "The Role of Television and Popular Culture in Contemporary Society," in *Television: The Critical View*, 3d ed., ed. Horace Newcomb (Oxford: Oxford University Press, 1982), p. 280.

25. Fiske, *Television Culture* (London: Methuen, 1987), p. 37.

26. Ben Stein, "Fantasy and Culture on Television," in *Television in Society*, ed. Arthur Asa Berger (New Brunswick, N.J.: Transaction Books, 1986), p. 215.

have big ideas and only small frustrations, a world filled with wacky escapades rather than irredeemably boring routine and hopelessness. How many leading characters in television series have to cope with chronic, draining problems — months of unemployment, say, or failing parents, or an unglamorous illness like rheumatoid arthritis or multiple sclerosis? Television entertainments tend to avoid problems that can't be solved by the end of the hour; in some ways they turn their backs on messy reality altogether, weaving a fiction of happy automatons with gleaming teeth, well-kept homes, shiny new cars, and hair that is never mussed for long. Even the villains in these shows are a good deal more attractive than the sorts of villains that turn up in real life. Television rarely attempts to portray the internal disintegration that addictions to power, sex, money, and violence produce. In television's fantasy world, gangsters are sophisticated and intelligent, and prostitutes are glamorous and healthy, untouched by the violence, manipulation, and fear that plagues the real world's mean streets. On the whole, commercial television makes no pretense of having a social conscience. Its perspective on life is not moral. It is not even real.[27]

On the surface this may seem innocent enough. What is the harm in a mere entertainment, a diversion from the harsh realities that surround us? Need we deprive ourselves of this device, this electronic analgesic that can relieve for brief moments the pain of life's burdens and disappointments? Many studies have suggested that the medium is not as innocent as it may seem. They typically focus on either the direct or indirect effects of watching television. Among its indirect effects they point to the fact that watching television precludes our engaging in other activities, such as reading, conversing, and the like. With respect to its direct effects, some have sought to show that in one way or another television inclines viewers to adopt its values and emulate the sorts of behavior it presents, such as using violence to gain desired ends, being sexually promiscuous, and mistreating minorities and those who are weak.[28] What may be quite as important as all of these, however, is the restructuring of human consciousness that the medium effects.[29]

27. See Boorstin, *The Americans*, pp. 392-97; see also Boorstin, *The Image; or, What Happened to the American Dream* (New York: Atheneum, 1962), pp. 7-44.

28. Erving Goffman, for example, has argued that the way in which sex roles and gender symbolism appear in advertising actually presents a visual anthropology. See *Gender Advertisements* (New York: Harper & Row, 1979).

29. Walter J. Ong persuasively pursues this theme in *Interfaces of the Word: Studies in the Evolution of Consciousness and Culture* (Ithaca, N.Y.: Cornell University Press, 1977).

Television serves up a stream of fleeting images that, as I suggested earlier, are arranged more to produce a dramatic effect than to convey consistent ideas in a logical manner. It is of the very essence of television that it is impermanent. Viewers are meant to *experience* the programming, not to think about it. How often do we stop to reflect on an image the way we stop to reflect on a passage in a book? There is nothing leisurely about the pace of commercial television. A show's producers have just so much time to grab their audience, and so overwhelmingly they are inclined to appeal to the viewer's feelings rather than his or her intellect. Feelings are easily aroused; thought, less so. Moreover, there is a sense in which the sort of programming that appeals to feelings is more egalitarian: everyone has feelings; not everyone has the ability to think and analyze. And the economic realities of commercial television drive it to appeal to the lowest common denominator. The networks can make a lot more cash from advertising shown during a romantic miniseries or a potboiler movie of the week than during a documentary on migrant workers. But one effect of aiming at the lowest common denominator is that television tends to affirm the side of the American character that likes being the same as everyone else. There are some areas in which new technologies are making it possible for the television industry to produce programming specially designed for smaller target audiences (e.g., the Lifetime channel aimed principally at women, the Arts & Entertainment channel aimed principally at upscale urban viewers, Nickelodeon aimed principally at children, and now even an all-cartoon channel and an all–science fiction channel), but on the whole, television remains the quintessential mass medium.

It is open to debate whether the invention of the printing press was by itself responsible for ending feudal society in Europe, but there is no doubt that where a print culture has flourished, so, too, has individualism.[30] It is easy to see why. In the Middle Ages, people learned within a network of personal relations. In these largely preliterate societies, as in traditional societies outside of Europe even today, knowledge about life was transmitted by rehearsal, for there were no written documents that were widely accessible. The tribe or clan would relive its past together, reaffirm its meaning, reappropriate the old wisdom, and in some cases reaffirm faith in the old gods. This was done collectively through a variety of forms, such as dance, religious

---

30. See Walter J. Ong, *The Presence of the Word: Some Prolegomena for Cultural and Religious History* (New Haven: Yale University Press, 1967), p. 54.

ritual, and stylized narrative. With the arrival of the printing press, it became possible and feasible to transmit all of the old wisdom through books rather than in the old ways. The book, as a result, rendered the community redundant.

Under the aegis of television, however, a strange reversal begins to take place, and though this new situation is not exactly identical to what pertained with the introduction of the printing press, the parallels are close enough to warrant attention. With our electronic wizardry, we are able to relay whatever meaning is to be found within the modern world by a means other than the printed page and in a way that replaces the printed page. We are creating a new tribe based not on relational but electronic connections. We are creating a new tribal democracy that has the character of the tribe while retaining the form of a democracy.[31] It is a tribe in which self-understanding comes less from the word and more from sight and sound, less from thought and more from experience. It is an electronic tribe whose dance, ritual, and wisdom now come in living color, disgorged into the living room in phantom images.

Television is a populist medium that not only circumvents all elites, cultural, intellectual, and social, but also renders the print culture increasingly irrelevant. In the West to this point, print has preserved society's past and values; for better or for worse, values today are being most effectively transmitted within the video culture. The cultural mantle has passed from the users of words to the makers of images.

Analysts continue to debate the exact connection between this transition and the growing illiteracy throughout the West (it is less pronounced in Europe than in the United States), but it does seem clear that a different set of mental habits is now following in the wake of this transition. The video culture has its own set of criteria for determining meaning, and they are very different from what pertained in the older print culture.[32] What this video culture does is to produce an astounding plethora of sights, sounds, impressions, and information

31. This is the thesis of Marshall McLuhan in *The Gutenberg Galaxy: The Making of Typographic Man* (Toronto: University of Toronto Press, 1962). Although McLuhan's many critics have been able to show that some of the claims he has made are implausible and some of his perspectives, which are not informed by a social understanding of television's effects but by literary taste, cannot be substantiated, they have not yet dislodged his central insights. For some of the early and quite typical exchanges, see *McLuhan — Hot and Cool: A Critical Symposium with a Rebuttal by McLuhan,* ed. Gerald Emmanuel Stearn (New York: Dial Press, 1967).

32. See Leonore Langsdorf, "The Emperor Has Only Clothes: Toward a Hermeneutic of the Video Text," in *Video Icons and Values,* p. 46.

that simply forces the viewer into operating with the kind of eclecticism that can accommodate all that is offered. Questions about what is right and what is true tend to recede, for what viewers believe or what they value tend to be settled by the need of the moment. It is the satisfaction of the self that becomes paramount, because viewers are typically cast in the role of consumers. They look for satisfaction in front of the television set in much the same way they do in the supermarket. In this context, as Donnelly has suggested, "when all ideas are equal, when all religions, life-styles, and perceptions are equally valid, equally in-different, and equally undifferentiated," they can be given value only "by the choice of the specific individual."[33] The determination of what constitutes truth has increasingly little connection with the ways in which this determination was made in the print culture.

Brief though this sketch has been, it has pointed to two enduring characteristics of the workings of democracy, at least in America: (1) the emphasis on private decision, on making up one's mind for oneself and, in so doing, taking one's destiny in one's own hands; and (2) the considerable importance of the public in which one's views find their validation. It is between these two poles of individualism and confor-mity, rooted as they are in freedom and equality, that Americans have lived out their lives.

In the modern period, however, an important transformation has occurred on both sides of this paradox. On the one side, as we saw in the last chapter, individualism has been translated into the language of the therapeutic society. Thus it is that making up one's mind for oneself has come to mean following one's inner impulses (which may be more intuitive than reasoned), and taking one's destiny into one's own hands has come to mean finding one's inner potential in the process of self-fulfillment. On the other side, the public in which we seek validation for our private impulses no longer bears much resem-blance to the family, community, or religious tradition that used to serve this purpose. Now it is an impersonal society, as mirrored in the mass media, that typically confirms private choices and assures the individual that he or she is really not that different from others. And the mirror of the mass media, inasmuch as it reflects the habits of the video culture, inevitably supersedes the older ways of thinking as-sociated with the print culture. It is thus that a postliterate conscious-ness both validates modern individualism and, however subtly, coerces those choices and judgments into new paths.

33. Donnelly, *The Confetti Generation*, p. 182.

Postcards from the Edge

The sweeping changes in the ecclesiastical topography that followed the Revolution have been examined from many angles, but Nathan Hatch has argued persuasively that the new theological mood that accompanied them was actually less their cause than their result and that the process of democratization was central to this transformation. It was, in fact, as much a conquest of class as it was a conquest of theology. In the decades following the Revolution, Christians of all kinds yoked "strenuous demands for revivals, in the name of George Whitefield, with calls for the expansion of popular sovereignty, in the name of the Revolution,"[34] and the result was the transformation of their churches in organization, belief, and practice. "As religious disunity was followed by religious multiplicity," writes Richard Hofstadter, "Americans uprooted church establishments and embraced religious liberty."[35]

These populist religious movements — including those of the Methodists, the Baptists, the Mormons, and even the Universalists — shared significant characteristics with populist political movements.[36] In both the religious and political movements, there emerged leaders who were able to appeal to the masses, to recruit followers and bind them together with common ideals and effective means of communication, and to encourage the sort of participation by commoners that is essential to democracy.[37] These movements offered environments in which ordinary, often untrained people were encouraged to act on their own impulses, unhampered by the doctrines of the past, whether Christian or political, and they also offered bonds that provided a defense against contrary viewpoints.

In this lies both the strength and vulnerability of modern evangelicalism. Its strength has always been its identification with people. As

34. Hatch, *The Democratization of American Christianity*, p. 7. Hatch's view has been challenged on some particulars by Jon Butler. Specifically, Butler argues that the revivals actually enlarged the role of the *clergy* rather than that of the laity. This, however, was true only in selective areas and was mostly not true of the Methodists and especially not true of the Baptists. See Butler, *Awash in a Sea of Faith: The Christianization of the American People, 1550-1865* (Cambridge: Harvard University Press, 1990).

35. Hofstadter, *Anti-Intellectualism in American Life* (New York: Vintage Books, 1963), p. 81.

36. On political populism, see Christopher Lasch, *The True and Only Heaven: Progress and Its Critics* (New York: W. W. Norton, 1990), pp. 168-225.

37. Hatch, *The Democratization of American Christianity*, p. 58.

Hatch notes, while others in America were giving their attention to building impressive religious institutions, and while many of the graduates of Harvard, Yale, and Princeton in the early part of the nineteenth century continued to reflect in their ministries the older world of privilege, deference, and learning, the Baptists, Methodists, and Disciples of Christ were out on the highways and byways winning the soul of America. They profoundly affected the nation. There was, however, a cost to be paid in the upheavals that accompanied these ministries.

This ambitious drive produced some savage anti-clericalism, for example, not so much because of the undercurrents of anti-intellectualism as because the insurgent leaders were "intent on destroying the monopoly of classically educated and university trained clergymen."[38] Their sermons were therefore typically colloquial, "employing daring pulpit storytelling, no-holds-barred appeals, overt humor, strident attacks, graphic application, and intimate personal experience."[39] Knut Hamsun, the Norwegian Nobel prize winner, noted this when he visited America in the 1880s, observing that the typical sermon did "not contain theology but morality. . . . They do not develop the mind, though they are entertaining."[40] The point of it all was to engage the audience. Charles Finney despised sermons that were formally delivered on the ground that they put content ahead of communication, and although both Finney and Dwight L. Moody had their own theologies, they both vigorously opposed "the formal study of divinity."[41] Leonard Sweet has argued that Jacksonian politics embodied "not so much a defense of the rising common man as a defense of the ability of the common man to rise" despite the stratification in society; correspondingly, he has argued that the new-measures revivalism of Finney and others expressed "less a faith in the worth and dignity of the common man than a demand that the common man become worthy and dignified."[42] In practice, however, the worth and dignity of the common person were championed in expressions of faith in this person's ability to take matters into his or her own hands.

38. Hatch, *The Democratization of American Christianity*, p. 162.
39. Hatch, *The Democratization of American Christianity*, p. 57.
40. Hamsun, *The Cultural Life of Modern America*, ed. and trans. Barbara Gordon Morgridge (Cambridge: Harvard University Press, 1969), p. 121.
41. Nathan O. Hatch, "Evangelicalism as a Democratic Movement," in *Evangelicals and Modern America*, ed. George Marsden (Grand Rapids: William B. Eerdmans, 1984), p. 74.
42. Leonard I. Sweet, "View of Man Inherent in the New Measures Revivalism," *Church History* 45 (June 1976): 221.

As this psychology took root in the mass movements of Christian faith at the beginning of the nineteenth century, certain predictable characteristics began to emerge. First, in all of these movements, the distinction between clergy and laity was erased and with it the deference toward learned opinion. Leadership was redefined on the basis of new democratic assumptions, which "sent external religious authority into headlong retreat and elicited from below powerful visions of faith that seemed more authentic and self evident."[43] In place of the old respect for learning, which the clergy had embodied, was a new confidence in personal intuitions of the unlearned, untrained person about what was right and true. Second, the ability to judge doctrine, even to formulate it, was therefore assumed to be part of a common rather than a privileged inheritance, something that inherently belonged to the people. It was not a matter for which great learning was necessary but for which common instincts were sufficient. Third, these movements were driven by the hope that this emancipation from the past might introduce a new order of social and religious relations — perhaps the millennium itself.

To those who spoke the new language of freedom, those churches that had been numerically superior at the time of the Revolution — the Anglicans, Presbyterians, and Congregationalists — now looked decidedly suspect. Their clergy had the appearance of a privileged class still interested in amplifying its privileges, their creeds bore the stink of the corruptions of the past still being made official, and their sermons contained the language of an aristocracy still not adjusted to the people. With the Revolution came deep yearnings among ordinary Christians for churches emancipated from the past, freed from vested privilege, for leaders who would be like the people and who would preach in the vernacular, for worship that expressed the sentiments of the masses rather than the interests of the empowered elite. Calvinistic orthodoxy, which looked to be unhappily anchored in the older world of hierarchy and privilege and hence appeared to be decidedly undemocratic, was put to flight before Arminianism. The church-centered faith that had been favored before the Revolution retreated before itinerant revivalism, reasoned faith retreated before exuberant testimony, and theological confession retreated before the axioms of experience. When "the commoner rose to power," says Hatch, "people of ideas found their authority circumscribed."[44] Never again, he adds, would America produce people

43. Hatch, *The Democratization of American Christianity*, p. 34.
44. Hatch, *The Democratization of American Christianity*, p. 162.

of the caliber of Adams, Jefferson, and Madison in the realm of politics, or of Jonathan Edwards in the realm of theology.

By 1855, those who had been first were last, and those who had been last were first. The largest Protestant denominations were now the Methodists, the Baptists, and (a distant third) the Presbyterians. In fact, the Methodists and Baptists together constituted 70 percent of the Protestant population — a predominance that has largely persisted to the present day. In this broad-scale triumph of Arminianism over Calvinism, says William McLoughlin, we see "the theological side of the political shift toward democracy."[45]

What this meant — and what it continues to mean — is that at the psychological center of much evangelical faith are two ideas that are also at the heart of the practice of democracy: (1) the audience is sovereign, and (2) ideas find legitimacy and value only within the marketplace.[46] Ideas have no intrinsic or self-evident value; it is the people's *right* to give ideas their legitimacy. One implication of this belief is that the work of doing theology ought not to be left to an intellectual elite who may think that they are gifted for and called to do such work and may consider the discovery of truth to be an end in itself. Rather, it should be taken on by those who can persuade the masses of the usefulness of the ideas. And there probably is no clearer illustration of how these assumptions have changed the nature of evangelical faith in the recent past than the transformation that has occurred in the pages of *Christianity Today*.

Christianity Today was born in 1956 at almost exactly the moment when Americans entered the Age of Television; 1955 was the year when 50 percent of Americans owned television sets, and by 1960 the overwhelming majority had purchased their passports to the new Promised Land of video experience. The early years of *Christianity Today,* perhaps out of financial exigency, showed no recognition of the new Age that had dawned, but as black and white sets increasingly gave way to color, so too did *Christianity Today*. The cheap, pulpy paper on which it had begun its life gave way to bright, colorful coated stock in the 1970s.

It was not only television that apparently made its mark on the magazine but consumerism as well. Between 1950 and 1973, the average annual income in America, measured in constant dollars, more

45. McLoughlin, "Pietism and the American Character," in *The American Experience: Approaches to the Study of the United States,* ed. S. Hennig Cohen (Boston: Houghton Mifflin, 1968), p. 44.

46. See Hatch, "Evangelicalism as a Democratic Movement," pp. 73-76.

than doubled from $5,000 to $12,000. Since then, family income has on average remained stationary in real dollars. But this earlier advance greatly swelled the ranks of the middle class and greatly fueled the fires of consumerism. The connection between these two things does not lie simply in the fact that the middle class has more money to spend. Rather, the middle-class person has an *attitude* toward consumption that is different from that of the poor. The poor have no faith in the future and no hope that they will be able to control the circumstances of their lives in the future. They spend as they have. The middle class believes in the stability of life and in the measure of control that can be exercised through predictable income and acquisition. Middle-class purchasing is therefore both more deliberate and more premeditated. The middle-class person believes that investments of time in a job and money in the stock market will pay off. This person looks for the sort of stability that will, as Elliot Liebow says, "permit the consumption of the investment at a time, place and manner of his own choosing and to his greater satisfaction."[47] And, over time, *Christianity Today* began to cater to this mind-set.

When *Christianity Today* began, advertising was minimal, modest, and circumspect, taking up a mere 3 to 7 percent of the space in the editions of 1959. Three decades later, in the editions of 1989, advertising filled anywhere from 30 to 48 percent of the space.[48] Along with the expected fare of books and educational institutions were added advertisements for jobs, media professionals, fund-raising businesses, Sunday School peanut butter, Pioneer Clubs grape jelly, and a handy mini-catalog for Christmas shoppers. In this latter advertising insert, one could find a large selection of thoughtful gifts, including a gold-embossed ring that had been made, the reader was told, "to unite the body of Christ." The line between commerce and religion, it seems, was becoming just a bit thin. All of this, however, was but the setting for the most drastic transformation.

47. Liebow, *Tally's Corner: A Study of Street Corner Negro Men* (Boston: Brown, Little, 1967), p. 65.

48. I have analyzed the whole of *Christianity Today*, from its inception to the present, with the intention of showing exactly where the transitions in subject matter occurred. Although the conclusions from this broader study are not included here, it did confirm that the two years selected for comparison here, 1959 and 1989, were not unrepresentative or unusual years. I chose 1959 as the first year simply because this seemed to be the first year in which it might be said that the magazine had taken root and, further, that it had had sufficient time to solidify its direction. I chose 1989 as the comparison year simply because it came three decades later, which seemed like a useful period to measure.

At the beginning of *Christianity Today*'s fourth year, its editor at the time, Carl F. H. Henry, described the publication as a journal of "international, interdenominational scholarship" with "the largest circulation in the world to the Protestant ministry and lay leadership."[49] Its mix of articles was simple and consistent. In 1959, 20 percent of the magazine was given to covering religious news, 15 percent to reviewing books of serious scholarship, and 36 percent to expounding the content of the Bible and the meaning of biblical doctrine for the modern world. Three decades later, having responded to the suggestions of sophisticated marketing surveys, the editors had changed the content drastically. The news coverage was doubled from 20 to 40 percent, the book section was cut from 15 to 9 percent (and what was chosen for review was sometimes lacking in serious content), and the biblical and doctrinal content was reduced from 36 to 8 percent. In place of the former commitment to biblically derived truth was a whole new interest in success stories about churches and ministries, as well as personal testimonies. These were not featured at all in 1959, but in 1989 they accounted for 19 percent of the content. Thus, whereas the magazine had formerly looked outward, offering biblically informed and incisive critiques of church and society, it now looked inward, and its analyses of church and society read more like journalistic dispatches from the cheering section.

In 1959, there was a regular section entitled "A Layman and His Faith." Themes explored that year included the nature of biblical revelation, the nature of God, the person and work of Christ, the nature of the gospel and Christian salvation, human nature, and sin. By 1989, this column had been replaced by a variety of features that, if they had been published under a single heading, might have been called "Laypeople Look at Themselves." Here were the success stories of Christian ministry as well as all the staple themes of the self movement — the pains of growing up, the pains of growing up as a Fundamentalist kid, the pains of a mid-life crisis, the problems of marriage, the problems when marriages break up, struggling with homosexuality, struggling with less money than we would like, struggling with a diet. In these three decades, the laity had apparently moved from a doctrinally framed faith the central concern of which was truth to a therapeutically constructed faith the central concern of which was psychological survival. Christian truth went from being an end in itself to

49. Henry, "The Mission of a Magazine," *Christianity Today*, 12 October 1959, p. 20.

being merely the means to personal healing. Thus was biblical truth eclipsed by the self and holiness by wholeness.

This shift is evident in many other changes in the publication as well. Consider, for example, the respective treatments of Easter in these two years, 1959 and 1989. In 1959, there were no fewer than six articles on this theme, all with substantial biblical, theological content, and there was, additionally, an editorial.[50] These essays developed the doctrine of justification, Christ's substitution on the Cross, and the way in which the theology of the Cross interprets and is tied into its events. There was a critique of the way in which some theologians were attempting to dissolve the historicity of Christ's resurrection by the literary device of myth and an apologetic for the empty tomb and its meaning. The final essay was an exposition of the meaning of the resurrection in the lives of some New Testament figures. In 1989, there were five articles. One was an excellent exposition of the significance of the resurrection for biblical faith; the other four were reflections on personal experience, each inexplicably linked to one of the days between Maundy Thursday and Easter Sunday.[51] The most that can be said of these devotionals is that something in the account in the Gospels must have started the mental ball rolling, but the reflections themselves did not always make it easy to judge what that might have been. What we really learned from these reflections was something about their authors and very little about biblical faith.

By 1989, then, the transition had been completed. *Christianity Today* now looked like a poor cousin to *Time* magazine, basically a news magazine that was simply a little more pious and a little less interesting than the genuine article. And, like *Time*, it has repackaged its content for the video age, using abbreviated stories and lots of color graphics to encourage a leisurely, recreational reading of the magazine. This is not a particularly happy development in the pages of a magazine covering the secular fabric of society, but it a cause for considerably

50. Appearing in the March 16 issue were the following: James I. Packer, "God's Justification of Sinners," pp. 3-6; William Fitch, "The Glory of the Cross," pp. 7-9; Merrill C. Tenney, "The Essence of the Gospel," pp. 9-12; and Carl F. H. Henry, "The Resurrection and Modern Life," pp. 20-27. Appearing in the March 30 issue were the following: Philip Edgcumbe Hughes, "Myth in Modern Theology," pp. 7-9; Wilbur M. Smith, "The Witness of the Empty Tomb," pp. 9-12; and Erling C. Olsen, "Relevancy of the Resurrection," pp. 12-14.

51. All of the following appeared in the March 17 issue: Walter Wangerin, "Maundy Thursday," pp. 19-21; Virginia Stem Owens, "Good Friday," pp. 21-23; Eugene H. Peterson, "Holy Saturday," pp. 23-25; Philip Yancey, "Easter Sunday," pp. 25-27; and Michael Green, "Why the Resurrection Matters," pp. 28-32.

graver concern when the Christian faith is used as a matter for our distraction and entertainment.

With the ascension to power of the pollster at *Christianity Today* to the role of ethicist and visionary, theologian and practitioner, prescribing what could be believed and what should be practiced, spiritual atrophy was not far away. By 1989, gone was the vision in which the magazine was born, gone was its moral and intellectual fiber, and gone was its ability to call the evangelical constituency to greater Christian faithfulness. Reflecting the nostrums of the therapeutic society had been transformed from a vice into a virtue, and popularity had been transformed from something incidental to Christian truth to something central to it.

Innocent Radicals

This triumph of the audience, which in contemporary evangelicalism has often also been a triumph of modernity, has been effected far more radically among evangelicals than in the nation as a whole. The reason, it would seem, is that the nation is encumbered by a set of immovable institutions sanctioned by the Constitution, whereas evangelical faith has almost entirely liberated itself from the inconveniences and constraints that institutions might impose upon it. If the evangelical world has its theology, it is neither codified nor dignified as is the nation's law. It is often haphazard, often no deeper than popular slogans, and often serves only to define the outer parameters of faith rather than to explore and confess what that faith means. Furthermore, it is open to revision on a whim or by a strong leader. And if evangelicals have their churchly structures, they are not permanent as are the structures of the nation's government. They can be set up, taken down, moved around, or dispensed with at will. The result is that, for better or for worse, democratic assumptions in religious mass movements suffer few of the frustrations that they do in the nation at large. This comparison, however, needs a little more elaboration.

In eighteenth-century America, democracy offered a means of revolting not merely against England but more generally against all who were in power — against the landed gentry, the socially privileged. "Democratic ideals," Richard Hofstadter has noted wryly, "are most likely to take root among discontented and oppressed classes, rising middle classes, or perhaps some sections of an old alienated, and partially disinherited aristocracy, but they do not appeal to a privileged class that is still amplifying its privileges."[52] If democracy appealed to some, it was a frightening prospect to others. Indeed, even some of those most emancipated by Enlightenment ideals viewed it as a scourge to be avoided at all costs. They feared that in the heart of popular sentiment there were seeds of violence that might sweep from power not only those who occupied the places of privilege but all decency and order in the society as well, to the great detriment of all.

The genius of the American experiment really lay in the fact that despite this deeply seated antipathy to popular sentiment, it was decided that the government should, in fact, be responsive to it. George Washington deliberately turned his back on those who hankered after military dictatorship even as he turned from those who still saw in the English monarchy a source of social stability. Instead, he and the other leaders embarked on a course of action that had at its very center a strange and striking paradox: the government would rest upon the people in whom they had no confidence. It would be built upon those whose sentiments could not be trusted.[53] It was this paradox that produced the system of checks and balances in government the novelty of which spawned deep apprehension and soaring hope and sometimes both by turns in the same people. The novelty of the system did not lie in the fact that checks and balances had been devised to limit power in, and disperse it from, the center. After all, many of the crowned heads in England and Europe had had to resist those who were intent upon discreetly dismantling royal power, and some, as during the Tudor and Stuart periods in England, had had to negotiate compromises that limited their power. Rather, the novelty of the American arrangement lay in the fact that the negotiations took place in a democratic rather than an aristocratic setting. And it was by no means clear that the experiment would succeed, at least not at the beginning. For the privileged, however, it did seem as if some minimal safeguards had been found against the wild excesses to which the untutored masses might happily capitulate with little provocation, and for the masses it seemed that some minimal safeguards had been found against the excesses to which aristocratic rule often ran.

With the passage of the years, the two sides of this paradox have been given their due in a relatively benign manner, and the fearful social contradictions involved in this experiment in democracy have

52. Hofstadter, *The American Political Tradition* (New York: Vintage Books, 1957), p. 5.
53. Hofstadter, *The American Political Tradition*, p. 7.

been tamed. Each, as a matter of a fact, now has to be content with finding fulfillment within the unrelieved confusion that a modern democracy has come to entail. It is a situation from which small comforts can, nevertheless, be drawn. American democracy is now so cumbersome, so muscle-bound in its organization, so restricted by inertia that not even the most malevolent, scheming dictators nor the most rampantly destructive crowds could make the slightest dent in it. It gives freedom, but the asking price is our willingness to live with perpetual governmental confusion and unending bureaucratic inefficiency. And it promises relief from neither.

We have thus come to terms with the paradox, but it has been no easy accomplishment. The early years, when America ceased to be a colony and became a nation, were fraught with such alarming danger, punctuated by such perpetual agitation, spiced by so much pungent debate that it was by no means certain that both sides of the paradox would receive their just due. It is certainly the case that in the first few decades of the nation's life, those who sought to govern sometimes gave evidence of being less than enthusiastic about giving weight to the views of the governed; those who were being governed were frequently restive under and even irreverent about those who governed. The working accord that was finally struck was, however, somewhat different from that which the same process of democratization produced in most evangelical churches.

In these churches, the uncommon person, the person of ideas, has been completely displaced by the common person, and whereas in the larger society popular opinion must reckon with the dreadful inertia of government as well as legal precedent and procedure, in the churches it does not. There are no constraints against mass opinion. Indeed, here the people of power are those who can mobilize mass opinion, and such opinion is mobilized on the simple assumption that the people know best. Sometimes this has preserved the practice of evangelical faith from the perversions of high culture, but as often as not it has also exposed evangelical faith to the corruptions of popular culture.

There They Go, and I Am Their Leader

Central to the American experiment have been the two seemingly contradictory values of freedom and equality; central to the American character are their immediate by-products, individualism and conformity; and central to the character of American evangelical faith are the ways in which these by-products shape its theology. The former impulse affects its *nature;* the latter affects its *function.* It is with the latter, with the way theology now functions given the undercurrents of conformity, that we are here concerned.

The psychological undertow of conformity, which may be evidenced as a desire to be the same as everyone else but more commonly as a desire to have the same *quality* of experience or the same *quality* of ideas as everyone else, is what determines how leadership will now be permitted to work. More precisely, it sets the limits on what kind of theological idea can take root in the evangelical Church, who can plant it, and when they will be allowed to do so. It is redefining what theological leadership can mean and, by virtue of that fact, what theological leadership *should* mean if it is to function in the Church. That is to say, it is redefining Christian theology.

In a democracy, every person's vote has the same weight, regardless of how well or badly informed it is. And in a democratized faith, such as we see in the evangelical world, every person's intuitions are likewise granted equal value. To think otherwise, it is argued, would be to fall into the elitist trap of imagining that some have a larger access to truth and hence deserve a larger religious privilege than others. It was this sort of presumption, predicated on class assumptions, that in the past added passion to the Revolution. And in the evangelical world, it is the counter-revolution that is now firmly entrenched. Common access to truth is understood to mean common *possession* of truth. If everyone's intuitions about God and life stand on the same plane, it is assumed that they are all equally valid, equally true, and equally useful. At the very least, it has become awkward to suggest that the intuitions someone has found to be valid, true, and useful might be nothing of the kind. After all, one does not question the propriety of extending the vote to all, and it seems quite as arrogant and offensive to question extending a presumption of common insight to all. Furthermore, just as politicians hold office only by consent of the sovereign electorate, so Church leaders should fulfill their responsibilities within the limits of popularly held ideas. When the religious audience is thus sovereign, its leadership is appropriately refined. The best pollster now makes the best leader, for all ideas must find their sanction, even their legitimacy, in the audience, and who knows the audience better than a pollster?

To be sure, this is not a flattering way of describing those leaders who have succumbed to popular evangelical sentiment. It is more flattering to talk instead of "servant leadership." That has the ring of piety about it. But it is a false piety, for it plays on an understanding of servanthood that is antithetical to the biblical understanding. Contemporary servant leaders are typically individuals without any ideas of their own, people whose convictions shift with the popular opinion to which they assiduously attune themselves, people who bow to the wishes of "the body" from whom their direction and standing derive. They lead by holding aloft moist fingers to sense the changes in the wind. In all this they show themselves to be different indeed from the One who embodied what servanthood was intended to be and who never once tailored his teaching to what he judged the popular reception of it would be — unless he was an exceedingly poor judge of what the crowds and religious leaders had in mind as they heard him. And to suppose that he derived the legitimacy to teach from the implied permission of those who heard him is to misunderstand both the Gospels and Christ himself. It is a supposition that also leads to the misunderstanding of Christian faith and why God provides the teachers that it and the Church needs.

The fundamental requirement of the Christian leader is not a knowledge of where the stream of popular opinion is flowing but a knowledge of where the stream of God's truth lies. There can be no leadership without a vision of both what the Church has become and what, under God, it should be. Only a genuine leader has such vision. Those who do not, those who are the servants merely of popular opinion, seldom amount to more than the blind leaders of the blind that Jesus castigated. How so? It is because, in the modern context at least, popular opinion frequently carries within itself the corruptions of popular culture. And simply because it is so broadly endorsed, popular opinion conveys a sort of legitimacy to this corruption. The preference of our video culture for intuition over reason and feeling over truth have been transferred to the realm of faith. Faith that appeals to reason — even reason exercised through biblical exposition — is doomed to failure; faith that appeals to feelings, on the other hand, seems for that reason to be assured of success. So it is that democratized faith, faith driven by the urge to conform, settles into its niche in the world. And that is precisely what, in biblical terms, it has settled into: *the world.* For worldliness is that system of values which in any culture has the fallen sinner at its center, which takes no account of God or his Word, and which therefore views sin as normal and righteousness as abnormal.

I should make something clear here: I am *not* arguing that Christian faith should be held captive to the interests only of high culture, that it should be only for elites, that its worship and ways of thought should be those with which only the most educated are comfortable. My point is that Christian faith should not be captive to anyone. It should not be defined by the interests of low culture any more than those of high. It should not be driven by the felt needs of the masses any more than by the prejudices of elites. It should not be perverted by the political warfare of race, class, or gender. Christian faith should be defined and driven only by truth as this has been biblically given. More than that, it is Christian truth that should be taking captive culture both high and low, the elites and the masses, the special interests of the rich and poor, men and women, racial minorities and majorities. Christian faith is not a tool for reaching some desired goal, be it psychological, sexual, economic, or racial. Christian faith is itself the goal, and the strife among these components in the human story should be serving as the means by which people come to it.

Genuine leadership in the Church, therefore, is not a matter of finding out what everyone wants and already knows and articulating it; genuine leadership is a matter of teaching and explaining what has not been so well grasped, where the demands of God's truth and the habits of the culture pull in opposite directions. Genuine leadership is a matter of finding ways of reaching greater Christian faithfulness and offering greater Christian service. And the one flows from the other. There is no such thing as Christian service that is unfaithful to God and his truth. And God's truth is simply not the same thing as the aggregate of Christian intuitions in the Church. If that were the case, the prophets in the Old Testament and the apostles in the New could have left the business of leading to those who did not care about the nature of these intuitions. But they *did* care about the nature of these intuitions, many of which were profoundly wrong. And their caring, their faithfulness, was often very costly.

Without this costly caring, there is no leadership. Without leadership, there is no articulated vision. And in the absence of public vision, it is easy to equate the norms of culture with the truths of God. Without real leaders, God's people are led by the pollsters — which is to say, they lead themselves. And if this means, as it often does in the modern world, that theology becomes either so diminished in importance or so eviscerated in nature as to lose its ability to impart the vision of God that alone can sustain his people in the cauldron of modernity, then Christian faith is also lost.

The powerful undertow of conformity goes a long way toward explaining the dearth of leaders in the evangelical world, for it does not allow anyone to be different without paying a heavy price. Genuine leaders often have to be different. They often have to articulate the truth of God's Word among those who do not fully understand its demands and implications. To clarify what people do not understand and mobilize them behind the implementation of what they do understand is what leadership is all about. The evangelical world does not have an overabundance of those who can undertake such a responsibility and withstand the pressures to conform to what is widely held, no matter how incorrectly. In the evangelical world, there are many organizers and many managers but only a very few leaders. There are only a few because there can be no leadership without a vision, and the ability to see is now in very scarce supply.

And seeing is what theology is all about. It is about seeing the truth of God, seeing the gaping chasm that lies between that truth and the nostrums of modernized society, seeing how to practice that truth in this world. The assumption that this is an elitist preoccupation is as mistaken as the assumption that Christianity is an elitist faith. All are summoned to believe, though some are able to grasp the implications of that belief for the modern world more profoundly than others. And all are summoned to understand the rudiments of theology, though some may be able to go on to plumb its profundities. Without theology, however, there is no faith, no believing, no Christian hope. And the Church's loss of preoccupation with theology goes a long way toward explaining its current weakness: it has inadvertently exchanged the sensibilities of modern culture for the truth of Christ.

How, then, are those most immediately engaged in the task of leadership in the Church going about their business? It is to the modern redefinition of the meaning of pastoral calling that we must turn next.

CHAPTER VI

The New Disablers

> *It is the first and great work of ministers of Christ to acquaint men with that God made them, and is their happiness: to open to them the treasures of His goodness, and to tell them of the glory that is in His presence, which all His chosen people shall enjoy. . . . Having shewed them the right end, our next work is to acquaint them with the right means of attaining it.*
>
> Richard Baxter

Two MODELS OF PASTORAL MINISTRY have been vying for the Protestant mind in the twentieth century, especially in its evangelical expression. Each arises from its own culture. In the one case, it is the culture of theological truth, and in the other case that of modern professionalization. Each has its own distinctive way of thinking about the ministry — its nature, objectives, and methods — and each has its own distinctive way of thinking about the place of theology in all of this.

In the one model, theology is foundational, and in the other it is only peripheral. In the one, theological truth explains why there is a ministry at all, what it is about, and why the Church without it will shrivel and die. In the other, this reasoning is marginalized so that what shapes, explains, and drives the work of ministry arises from the needs of a modern profession. And it is my contention that the presence of this latter model in the Church goes a long way toward explaining

218

the growing enfeeblement of the Church inwardly despite its outward growth. This model is ascending, even as the other is declining, and with its ascendancy the attacks upon theology grow more strident and the appetite for it diminishes.

It is often argued that this transformation is long overdue, that it has come about because theology has become moribund and irrelevant, that what succeeds in this postliterate society is not what theology has to offer. The Church, in setting out along this new path, is simply making its peace with reality. It is always the case, of course, that charges like this do have at least some small justification. Theology may be moribund and irrelevant, but it would appear that this is more an excuse than a reason for engaging in this new style of ministry. Indeed, in this chapter I am proposing a quite different reason — namely, that the new direction should be understood mainly as a psychological reaction to the growing irrelevance of ministers in society.

This is not a problem of particularly recent vintage, of course. The pastoral ministry has been culturally adrift for a long time. It has been dislodged from the network of what is meaningful and valuable in society. This has created a sense of uneasiness that has settled over the work of ministers like a thick fog. Richard Niebuhr spoke to this point some three decades ago when he described the "prevailing mistiness" that had engulfed the ministry and suggested that it had become a "perplexed profession."[1] In the time since then, the mists seem not to have lifted appreciably, nor have the perplexities eased, the reason being that the ways in which modernization is intruding on the shaping and practice of the ministry are not always being perceived with great clarity.

There can be no doubt that the discomfort and ambiguity that ministers experience are just two of the many consequences of the growing secularization of the modern world. Ministers must ply their trade in a sea of unbelief, and the institutions that modernization creates offer no plausibility for the work they do. There is little in the experience of the modern person that suggests that pastoral work, at least as it has been traditionally defined, makes sense. Bankers and lawyers work within structures that have meaning in the modern context: our world is very much about commerce and litigation. Banks and courts have procedures and offer services that are perceived as

---

1. See H. Richard Niebuhr's discussion of the changing shape of ministry in *The Purpose of the Church and Its Ministry* (New York: Harper & Row, 1965), pp. 48-94.

necessary in the modern world. But what ministers are engaged in has no institutional recognition in the public square because there are not many who recognize its relevance in that context. They and their work are increasingly being pushed to the margins of society, and the bonds between them and what is considered meaningful are increasingly strained, if not broken.

The ways in which the Christian ministry was viewed changed dramatically about halfway through the nineteenth century. The high social standing that ministers once enjoyed began to pass, and the sure purpose with which they did their work began to fade. To take one measure, in novelistic treatments, clergy were increasingly portrayed as strained, unhappy figures, if not outright scoundrels.

To be sure, ministers were not held in universally high esteem prior to 1850; there was a small but pugnacious literature in which they were systematically debunked.[2] One common enough theme in this sort of literature was clergy who exploited their opportunities to despoil innocent women, but this was not a common public perception. By the 1850s, however, matters were changing. From about this time onward, ministers were increasingly portrayed in fiction as either irrelevant or worthy of derision. Figures from Nathaniel Hawthorne's Arthur Dimmesdale to Sinclair Lewis's Elmer Gantry to Peter DeVries's Andrew Mackerel are all symbols of the fallen esteem in which the clergy have come to be held, be they Calvinist or Arminian, evangelical or liberal.

One stumbles upon the most important change connected with the way in which clergy are viewed almost incidentally, however, in the unfavorable comparisons that are frequently made in novels between clergy and physicians. Much of modern fiction seems to assume that

2. For a discussion of this literature, see David S. Reynolds, *Faith in Fiction: The Emergence of Religious Literature in America* (Cambridge: Harvard University Press, 1981), pp. 169-96. Reynolds's work is chronologically arranged and encompasses more than just works featuring ministers. On this narrower theme, see Horton Davies, *A Mirror of the Ministry in Modern Novels* (New York: Oxford University Press, 1959); Grier Nichol, "The Image of the Protestant Minister in the Christian Social Novel," *Church History* 38 (September 1968): 319-34; and Gilbert P. Voight, "The Protestant Minister in American Fiction," *The Lutheran Quarterly* 11 (February 1959): 3-13. Two dissertations presenting useful discussions are Ernest Eugene Bennett's "The Image of the Christian Clergyman in Modern Fiction and Drama" (Ph.D. diss., Vanderbilt University, 1970) and Emerson Clayton Shuck's "Clergymen in Representational American Fiction, 1830-1930" (Ph.D. diss., University of Wisconsin, 1943). Although somewhat dated, there is still useful bibliographical data in Nelson R. Burr's *Critical Bibliography of Religion in America* (Princeton: Princeton University Press, 1961), pp. 851-908.

those proficient in the curing of the body are also more adept at curing the soul than are clergy.[3] Of those novels that have significant roles for clergy, over half also include physicians, and though in some of these novels they work together, more commonly the minister comes off looking weak and incompetent next to his or her medical counterpart.[4] John Updike's work provides a good illustration of this. While relatively few clergy show up in his novels, the Episcopal priests in *Roger's Version* and *Rabbit, Run* offer some pointed commentary. The trendy but pathetic Jack Eccles in *Rabbit, Run* is left, like so many of Updike's characters, to flutter feebly and helplessly around the bright light of sex. His interest in the kids' religious questions is at best only tepid, but he is aroused by their discussions of sexual intimacy. By contrast, Updike treats the medical profession with some awe. The help that is not to be had from the Reverend Jack Eccles for life's dilemmas and pains can be found in the office of the local doctor.[5]

There can be little doubt that it is the realization of their sinking fortunes that has inclined the clergy to give their concentrated attention to the problem of how to present themselves instead as serious professionals in the modern world. This, in fact, is the theme of this chapter. My argument is that this attempt has resulted in a drastic transformation in the role of the clergy, that it has left behind the older model of a theologically based and sustained understanding of the ministry, and that the results are unhappy. More than that, clergy have assumed for their new model of pastoral life a surrogate theology that arises not from theological truth at all but from the demands of the profession of which they are now a part. So I shall go on to argue that one can make a virtual correlation between the degree to which the clergy are professionalized and the degree to which they will have forfeited, or deliberately abandoned, their fundamental task of being brokers of truth. And at the root of this transformation is a naivete about culture, for it has not been discerned that the translation of the clerical calling into the language of professionalization involves an immersion in the *culture* of professionalization. Professionalization is an awkward, inept language of translation for pastoral calling. How professionals work in the modern world is quite different in many

3. For a succinct overview of this shift in perceptions, see John T. McNeill, *A History of the Cure of Souls* (New York: Harper & Row, 1972).
4. See Bennett, "The Image of the Christian Clergyman in Modern Fiction and Drama," p. 49.
5. See Wesley A. Kort, *Shriven Selves: Religious Problems in Recent American Fiction* (Philadelphia: Fortress Press, 1972), pp. 15-16.

respects from the way in which pastors should be working. Those who
use its techniques, who live by its values and norms, frequently end
up disabling the Church.

In order to explore this thesis, we will first examine the nature
of professionalization. Second, we will consider why and how the clergy
became professionalized. Third, we will explore the consequences of
this transformation in the formulation and teaching of the knowledge
of God.[6]

The New Mandarins

When Louis Brandeis addressed the students at Brown in 1912, he
noted the beginnings of what has become a modern phenomenon. It
is that occupations quickly aspire to becoming professions. At that time,
he argued, the traditional three — theology, law, and medicine — had
just been joined by business. Engineering, forestry, and "scientific
agriculture" were on the brink, and not far behind them were manufacturing, merchandising, transportation, and finance. And so the
process has continued. Today, our soldiers, athletes, and beauticians
all claim to be professionals.

His addition of business to the older troika of professions was
especially interesting, because it had always been assumed that what
distinguished a profession from a mere occupation was the presence
of an altruistic motive, and business is not easily seen as running on
the high-octane fuel of disinterest. How, then, would Brandeis define
a profession? He gave three characteristics: (1) it is an occupation

6. Because I have argued that the Church is the primary auditor of theology,
it follows that the work of the pastor and that of the theologian will closely parallel
one another. I have developed several brief essays outlining how I believe the latter
should work and one in which I have described preaching in this theological
context: "The Nature and Function of Theology," in *The Use of the Bible in Theology:
Evangelical Options*, ed. Robert K. Johnston (Atlanta: John Knox Press, 1983), pp.
175-99; "An American Evangelical Theology: The Painful Transition from *Theoria*
to *Praxis*," in *Evangelicalism and Modern America*, ed. George Marsden (Grand Rapids:
William B. Eerdmans, 1984), pp. 83-93; "Word and World: Biblical Authority and
the Quandary of Modernity," in *Evangelical Affirmations*, ed. Kenneth S. Kantzer
and Carl F. H. Henry (Grand Rapids: Zondervan, 1990), pp. 153-76; "The Theologian's Craft," in *Doing Theology in Today's World: Essays in Honor of Kenneth S. Kantzer*,
ed. John Woodbridge and Thomas McComiskey (Grand Rapids: Zondervan, 1991);
and "The Theology of Preaching," in *God's Living Word: Essays on Preaching*, ed.
Theodore Stylianopolous (Brookline, Mass.: Holy Cross Orthodox Press, 1983), pp.
57-70.

requiring training that "is intellectual in nature," (2) it is an occupation pursued "largely for others," and (3) it is an occupation in which success is not measured by "the amount of financial return."[7]

That Brandeis should seriously have envisioned professionals as sufficiently altruistic that they could be expected to elevate the moral tone of society now strikes us as faintly amusing. The proliferation of rapacious and ethically indifferent lawyers, larcenous medical practitioners, and high-finance extortioners on Wall Street would seem to indicate that being a professional has come to mean something a little less exalted ethically than what he hoped was the case. And if it is true that beauticians and athletes are also to be considered professionals, then the requisite training that "is intellectual in nature" would seem to have undergone some rather interesting changes as well. In truth, of course, Brandeis's definition, which was for a long time held to be standard, is no longer applicable. So what does it mean to be a professional today?

It is difficult to come to a clear definition of what constitutes a profession for three main reasons.[8] First, the term *professional* has developed a technical and a colloquial meaning, and the line between the two is fuzzy enough that it can be difficult to determine the sense in which some occupations are referred to as professions. In common parlance, the term may mean nothing more than "skilled." One might observe, for example, that a plumber did a tricky piece of repair work "very professionally" and mean simply that he or she joined the pipes

7. Brandeis, *Business: A Profession* (Boston: Small Maynard, 1914), p. 2.

8. For preliminary discussions of the difficulty in defining what in general constitutes a profession, see Morris L. Cogan, "The Problem of Defining a Profession," *Annals of the American Academy of Political and Social Science* 297 (January 1955): 105-11; and Cogan, "Toward a Definition of Profession," *Harvard Educational Review* 23 (Winter 1953): 33-50. For a discussion of this issue with respect to the clergy, see Everett C. Hughes, "Are the Clergy a Profession?" in *Theological Education as Professional Education* (Dayton: American Association of Theological Schools, 1969), pp. 149-55. Foundational to Hughes's essay is "Professions," *Daedalus* 92 (1963): 655-68. Sociological analyses have been especially useful in defining the nature of a profession. See, for example, Talcott Parsons, "Professions," *International Encyclopedia of the Social Sciences*, vol. 12, ed. David L. Sills (New York: Macmillan, 1969), pp. 536-47; Amitai Etzioni, *Modern Organization* (Englewood Cliffs, N.J.: Prentice-Hall, 1964); Etzioni, *The Semi-Professions and their Organization* (New York: Free Press, 1969); and Everett C. Hughes, *Education for the Professions of Medicine, Law, Theology, and Social Welfare: A Report Prepared for the Carnegie Commission on Higher Education* (New York: McGraw-Hill, 1973). On theological education in this matrix, see James M. Gustafson, "Theological Education as Professional Education," *Theological Education* 5 (Spring 1969): 243-67.

cleanly and successfully. But clearly, not every individual who does a job skillfully is thereby rendered a professional.

Second, the altruism that once distinguished the professions has disappeared, and so it is no longer possible to think of them as standing apart from the capitalistic enterprise. They are not alternatives to capitalism but the bones and arteries, the voice and feet through which it lives.[9] The professions today are the most amply rewarded occupations, and professionals dominate the capitalistic enterprise. Without them, capitalism as we know it would be impossible. Professionals are, in fact, the new mandarins.

Third, the question of class has intruded on the definition of what constitutes a professional, making distinctions yet harder to draw. Many Americans equate membership in the middle class with professional status. And whereas it is still a matter of debate among sociologists and others who exactly it is that constitutes the middle class, something like 80 percent of the American public believe they belong to it. They think of the middle class in terms of three characteristics that have little connection with the pre-Revolutionary class structure: those who are middle class have acquired a professional skill, they enjoy the social prestige that goes with having that skill, and they expect to enjoy a life-style commensurate with that skill and that prestige. Despite that widespread belief, however, not every occupation in which the middle class engages is in strict terms a profession.

Clearly there is a good deal of variation in our understanding of what constitutes a professional. For our purposes here, I will draw on the characteristics that are common to most of them in defining a professional as an individual who has received training and education to develop an ability, usually intellectual in nature, that can be exploited in the interests of both acquisition and aspiration.[10] Professionalization therefore carries with it both the idea of fees charged and the idea of a career pursued. And the degree of specialization that professionals have typically grants them a monopoly over the work for which they charge fees. In order to sustain this monopoly, most professionals join others in the same profession to maintain organizations that control who can do the work and how it should be done.

9. See Talcott Parsons, *Essays in Sociological Theory* (New York: Free Press, 1954), pp. 34-35.
10. See Burton J. Bledstein, *The Culture of Professionalism: The Middle Class and the Development of Higher Education in America* (New York: W. W. Norton, 1976), p. 4.

Probably the most important element in this definition is that of specialization.[11] As the complexity of society has grown, it has become increasingly unwise to depend on the older system of trial and error to produce workers for the marketplace. Employers increasingly seek out and depend on people who have been trained to perform tasks in specific areas — tasks that no one can adequately perform without receiving the specific and rigorous training.[12] This specialization, coupled with the kind of community that results from bonding among professionals in the same vocation, is what produces the organization's culture. By this I mean the values, interests, and way of looking at life that are common to those in a profession. It is my contention (1) that this culture is now defining how skill and proficiency should be understood in the ministry and (2) that this definition is not always consistent with how the pastoral ministry would, if it were true to itself, define them.

It was in the final quarter of the nineteenth century that most of the professions with which we are most familiar became organized. It was then that the lawyers, librarians, chemists, veterinarians, and a host of others formed national organizations, and it was also during this period that the many specialties in medicine formed their own organizations and associations. This large organizing effort, it so happened, coincided with the decline of public esteem in which the clergy were held. Establishing the exact correlation between the two developments is not easy, but the long history of an established Church ministry in New England does provide some interesting data for looking at the nature of this relationship.

Interest in the ministry had been sagging relative to interest in the other occupations for some time prior to the period of large-scale professionalization in the late nineteenth century, which would seem to suggest that the two developments are not connected at all. We have already taken note of Ebenezer Porter's estimate that between 1620 and 1720, about one in two graduates from Harvard and Yale entered the ministry; between 1720 and 1770 the number of graduates from these and other colleges had fallen to one in three; between 1770 and 1800, it was one in five; and between 1800 and 1810, it was one in six. His estimate does appear to be a little pessimistic, but other sources serve to confirm the fact that a perceptible downward trend continued

11. On specialization, see Parsons, *Essays in Sociological Theory*, pp. 41-42.
12. See William J. McLoughlin, *Patterns of Professional Education* (New York: G. P. Putnam, 1960), p. 1.

throughout the nineteenth century.[13] Among thirty-seven colleges and universities that were surveyed later, the ministry fell as a professional choice from 30 percent in 1820 to 25 percent in 1840 and to 20 percent in 1860. Church leaders continued to lament this situation.[14] The same pattern was confirmed still later, in 1899, when a survey was made of the existence of schools dedicated to professional training in such areas as theology, law, medicine, dentistry, pharmacy, and veterinary science. In the first quarter of the nineteenth century, schools for theological training constituted 51 percent of the total, but by the final quarter of the century that figure had fallen to 16 percent.

These statistics are misleading, however, for three reasons. First, America was becoming an increasingly complex society, especially during the nineteenth century as it became industrialized, and it needed an increasingly diverse workforce. It was hardly to be expected that half of the colleges' graduates would continue to go into the ministry. Second, the decline that Porter lamented was especially troubling to the older denominations that had favored a learned ministry, such as the Presbyterians and Congregationalists, but it seldom troubled the newer denominations that were coming into prominence, such as the Methodists and Baptists, many of whose clergy were not university trained. The decline in the percentages of college graduates entering the ministry therefore is more of a measure of the decline of the older denominations than it is an accurate measure of the whole Christian picture. Third, the emergence of new occupations offered alternatives to those who might have gravitated toward the ministry solely for the social prestige and reasonably comfortable living it had traditionally offered. Revivalists who assaulted the established ministry in the nineteenth century were not without some justification. When it was seen as a means to social prominence, to which young men aspired at an early age, it did collect those whose suitability for the calling appears to have been quite minimal.

And yet, while it may be difficult to establish an exact correlation between the rise of the professions and the decline in the public perception of the ministry, it would be unwise to ignore the apparent coincidence altogether. In fact, I believe that the subtleties and complexities in this nexus of the rise of the professions and the fall of the ministry hold significant clues about why the ministry in the twentieth century has taken the shape that it has.

13. Donald M. Scott, *From Office to Profession: The New England Ministry, 1750-1850* (Philadelphia: University of Pennsylvania Press, 1978), p. 60.

14. Bledstein, *The Culture of Professionalism*, p. 198.

The New Knowledge

The Ministry and the Market

When Knut Hamsun visited America in 1888, he recorded his amazement at the disparity between the training provided for medical doctors and that provided for ministers. While theological studies took three years, medical studies took at most one and sometimes no more than a few months. The contrast, as he put it, was "one year to learn how to save people for life on earth, three years to learn how to give advance warning of — eternal death"![15] He was not alone in lamenting the poverty of the medical training that was available. In 1910, Abraham Flexner published *Medical Education in the United States and Canada*, in which he excoriated the universities for the shabbiness and unevenness of the training they offered. At the time, medical education seldom involved any hands-on training in hospitals or laboratories or even any dissection work, the students were typically released to practice without having passed any examinations, and the fees were all pocketed by the instructors, many of whom were quite ignorant. But the medical community managed to put its house in order in a relatively short period of time and today can claim to have trained the most highly proficient specialists in the world.[16] Their success in this endeavor has been duplicated in many other professions as well.

Even though the theological community started from a substantially more solid base, it moved far more slowly toward formalizing its education to produce skilled practitioners. In 1924, Robert Kelly wrote a book quite similar to Flexner's, entitled *Theological Education in America*. The sorry story it told seemed not entirely believable, and so William Adams Brown and Mark A. May undertook a more ambitious survey, the results of which appeared in 1934 in the four-volume work *The Education of American Ministers*. It was this study that moved the Association of Theological Schools (A.T.S.) to begin regulating seminary education.[17]

15. Hamsun, *The Cultural Life of Modern America*, ed. and trans. Barbara Gordon Morgridge (Cambridge: Harvard University Press, 1969), p. 120.

16. For an account of this see Ronald L. Numbers, "The Rise and Fall of the American Medical Profession," in *The Professions in American History*, ed. Nathan O. Hatch (Notre Dame, Ind.: University of Notre Dame Press, 1988), pp. 51-72.

17. The Association of Theological Schools had, in fact, been founded some time before the publication of the 1934 study. Harvard President A. Lawrence Lowell had invited representatives of Protestant seminaries to attend a conference

It is interesting to note that at about the same time this large study was being done, A. M. Carr-Saunders and P. A. Wilson were writing the definitive history of the professions.[18] Although Carr-Saunders and Wilson introduced the reader to the rich and diverse field of the modern professions, from masseurs to mine managers, they declined to recognize the ministry. This venerable profession was viewed as being so remote from the structures of the modern world as not to warrant any mention at all in the new configuration of the professions. Such judgments have persisted, and the churches and seminaries have decided that the situation must be reversed. The means they have chosen to turn things around is the professionalization of the clergy. But in today's world, they have no choice but to work out this process within contours prescribed by modernization. Two features of the modern process of professionalization are especially important in this context: impermanence and marketability.

By the middle of the nineteenth century, when novelists were beginning to cast ministers in awkward or embarrassing roles, the clergy had already been experiencing social damage for a long time. The most remarkable thing about pastoral life in the eighteenth century was the extent to which pastors and their communities were bonded together. For example, of the 221 who graduated from Yale College between the years of 1745 and 1775 and went into the ministry, 71 percent remained in the church to which they were first called until their deaths. Only 4 percent held four or more pastorates.[19] By contrast, today the average pastoral stint is as low as two years in some areas and denominations and seldom more than three years. Lying between the eighteenth century and our own is a cluster of steadily declining graph lines indicating shorter and shorter tenures, growing pastoral impermanence, and increasingly shallow bonds between pastors and their churches.

It did take some time for churches in Puritan New England to establish a steady pattern in the relation between pastors and churches,

---

to consider theological education in the aftermath of the First World War. The fifty-three delegates who attended contributed to the formation of A.T.S. But the 1934 study served to heighten a sense that more vigorous procedures for guaranteeing uniform standards in educational quality were needed.

18. A. M. Carr-Saunders and P. A. Wilson, *The Professions* (Oxford: Clarendon Press, 1933).

19. Donald M. Scott, *Pastors and Providence: Changing Ministerial Styles in Nineteenth-Century America* (Evanston, Ill.: Seabury-Weston Theological Seminary, 1975), p. 4.

but this was largely achieved by 1670. Among Presbyterians and Congregationalists in New Hampshire, for example, the average pastoral tenure in a church at this time was twenty years, and the figure did not fall below this level until the beginning of the nineteenth century. A serious decline seems to have begun in 1808. By 1810, the figure had fallen to fifteen years; by 1830, to five years; and by 1860, to less than four years.[20]

To be sure, a number of factors in the life of the nation affected the length of pastoral tenures over the years. Disestablishment of the churches was obviously important in this regard. The eighteenth-century Great Awakening dislodged a few from their comfortable livings. So, too, did theological controversy, especially in the nineteenth century, some of it stirred by the Second Great Awakening and some of it by other factors. And, from time to time, lean economic times or changing patterns of prosperity affected the viability of some churches. But the overall steadiness of the decline during the nineteenth century is remarkable. The pattern remained essentially unchanged despite many variables that came into play. It was about the same regardless of the amount of education the pastors received. It was about the same for churches that changed denominations as for those that did not. It was about the same in churches that eventually became extinct as in those that did not. There is every indication that these figures indicate a profound and deep change that was long in the making. It cut so wide a swath, and did so with such consistency, that its causes can only superficially be attributed to the churches themselves; in fact, the explanation for the change must lie in external social realities.

It was typical in the eighteenth century for a church and its minister to enter into a compact that was sometimes legal in character but always morally binding and generally understood to last for the duration of the minister's life. It was possible for a minister to move from one church to another, but only with the consent of both the original church and the surrounding churches (in the case of Congregationalists) or those in the presbytery (in the case of Presbyterians). By the middle of the nineteenth century, this pattern had collapsed. The terms of the contract had been reduced from life to five years at the most and sometimes to as little as one year, and from this time forward partings between churches and their pastors became commonplace and almost expected. The links between pastors and churches

20. Daniel H. Calhoun, *Professional Lives in America: Structure and Aspiration, 1750-1850* (Cambridge: Harvard University Press, 1965), pp. 116-57.

became as thin and tenuous as the links between audiences and the circuit riders or wandering evangelists who visited them. The final and most exaggerated expression of this sort of disconnected ministry is today's television pastor, who "serves" a flock whom he or she never sees, and who remains ignorant of their troubles, distant and detached.

At the beginning of the nineteenth century, the minister was still often seen as holding an office that had large social importance and not simply as providing spiritual services for a fee. Permanence was important for the minister and his church because, as we noted with respect to the town of Wenham, the church was at the center of the social order. The premature departure of a minister was likely to cause a great disruption in a town's life. There is compelling evidence to suggest that many churches during this period clung to their ministers, sometimes despite appallingly inept preaching, apparently preferring to suffer spiritual impoverishment than to suffer the social upheaval that would follow the loss of a minister. And it was not at all uncommon for a church to hire an assistant to prop up an aging or irascible minister so that continuity would be preserved, rather than resorting to the more obvious expedient of dismissing the disagreeable or elderly gentleman. Given the closeness of these ties, it is not surprising that the rhetoric associated with calling a minister was similar to that of a marriage ceremony; the forms spoke of the church and the minister being "united" to one another.

It was in this role, then, that the New England minister in particular acted as the focus of the town's life, dispensed its moral teaching, organized much of its life, and became an integral part of many of its families. Having a minister functioning in this role transformed a mere community into a town, and it gave the minister a public role to play in the exercise of his ministry.

As we have already noted, however, the churches began to experience waves and outbursts of democratic protest at the beginning of nineteenth century. "As religious disunity was followed by religious multiplicity," Hofstadter writes, "Americans uprooted church establishments and embraced religious liberty."[21] As it happened, this change coincided with the weakening of the ties between churches and their clergy. At the same time other professionals, such as lawyers and doctors, were beginning to gain significant control over their respective fields, ministers were being dislodged from theirs, edged out of the center of the towns and cities in which they had long exercised con-

21. Hofstadter, *Anti-Intellectualism in American Life* (New York: Vintage Books, 1963), p. 81.

siderable social influence. Once dislodged, they were reduced to the uncertain fate of seeking clienteles in the free-for-all created by American denominationalism and democracy. They had only their wits to live by as the skills over which they had once exercised a monopoly were increasingly claimed by laity who, unlearned as they might have been, claimed the right to exercise their own ministerial gifts as the final blessing of democracy in action.[22] It is this situation that holds the key to understanding something else that is characteristically modern: the idea of a career and, not least, a career in the Church.

The notion that one's occupation might serve as the means to provide a career was quite foreign at the beginning of the nineteenth century but quite common by its end. Having a career came to mean making progress, moving from preparatory stages of accomplishment up the ladder to larger honor and responsibilities. The occupation in which one was engaged was no longer an end in itself but the means to an end — specifically, the elevation or enrichment of the worker. This represented a great change in the way that work was conceived. In the older order, Burton Bledstein notes, "competence, knowledge, and preparation were less important in evaluating the skills of a professional than were dedication to the community, sincerity, trust, permanence, honorable reputation, and righteous behavior."[23] The older order viewed a profession not as the means of a career in the modern sense, as a platform from which to ascend to larger visibility or gain, but rather as the means by which one might do public good.

These changes also echoed rather ominously through the ministry. For if it is the case that careers can be had in the Church, then it is inevitable that ministers will be judged by the height to which they ascend on the ladder of achievement, and they in turn will judge the Church on the extent to which it facilitates this ascent. It is a little difficult to see how such calculations can be reconciled with the biblical notion of service, the call to serve the Church without thought of what one might receive in return. Furthermore, careers are determined by market conditions. After the Civil War, American colleges were slowly transformed into the universities that we know today, and part of that transformation involved

22. For an excellent discussion of some of these changes, see two essays by Sidney E. Mead: "The Rise of the Evangelical Conception of Ministry in America, 1607-1850," in *The Ministry in Historical Perspective*, ed. H. Richard Niebuhr and Daniel Day Williams (New York: Harper, 1956), pp. 207-49; and "Denominationalism: The Shape of Protestantism in America," *Church History* 33 (December 1954): 291-320.

23. Bledstein, *The Culture of Professionalism*, p. 172.

thinking of education less as immersion in knowledge for its own sake and more as preparation for a career opportunity created by the market. When these habits were imported into the seminaries, an anti-theological temper soon followed. Here, too, the focus shifted from knowledge for its own sake to knowledge that was practical and useful. The implication was that knowledge is marketable. The consequence was a burst of interest in matters of practical application and a corresponding loss of interest in the field of classical theological study.

It has to be said, however, that this change did reflect the changing position of the minister, which was forcing a redefinition of his or her work. It is now their lot to wander from church to church, seldom finding a secure or long-lasting position, and so they have been obliged to define their ministry in terms of its marketability. The market has come to dominate the way in which they exercise their ministry, often taking precedence over the matter of internal calling and over personal spirituality. Whereas ministers once focused on such staple interests as brokering God's truth, caring for the sick and ailing, and building up Christian character and understanding, they now have to extend their energies to a whole new line of responsibilities, which in some cases eclipse the older and more foundational responsibilities.

The major 1934 study by Brown and May identified five clerical roles. The minister was to be a teacher, preacher, worship leader, pastor, and administrator.[24] In 1980, when David Schuller produced his large analysis of what pertained in forty-seven of America's denominations, the list of roles had swelled to nine. In addition to the older functions, in 1980 the minister was expected to have an open and affirming style, know how to foster friendship in the church, be aware of denominational activities, be able to lead the church's participation in political discussion of matters of moment, and provide a witness against the world's injustice.[25] In other words, to the spiritual calling of serving God's people have been added sociological demands: the management of conflict, the ability to manage relations between professional and client, and the ability to apply Christian ideas in a changing world in such a way that congregations are at least able to believe that they have thought significant thoughts about their society.

By 1986, the list of ministerial roles had expanded still further,

---

24. William Adams Brown and Mark A. May, *The Education of American Ministers*, 4 vols. (New York: Institute of Social and Religious Research, 1934), 1: 21.

25. David S. Schuller, Merton P. Strommen, and Milo L. Brekke, *Ministry in America* (San Francisco: Harper & Row, 1980), pp. 25-26.

according to a major new study, to fourteen. And it is interesting to note that the new expectations were reported in evangelical as well as nonevangelical churches. Evangelical churches gave their top priority to planning ability, facility in leading worship, and sensitivity to the congregation. This was followed, in order, by spiritual development of the congregation and pastoral counseling for those in need, visiting the sick, and support of the church's stewardship program. These were followed by three equally ranked activities: providing administrative leadership, involving the laity in the church's programs, and supporting the church's mission in the world. Holding issues of social justice before the congregation was listed last as a pastoral priority.[26]

In this new clerical order, technical and managerial competence in the church have plainly come to dominate the definition of pastoral service. It is true that matters of spirituality loom large in the churches, but it is not at all clear that churches expect the pastor to do anything more than to be a good friend. The older role of the pastor as broker of truth has been eclipsed by the newer managerial functions.

This transition parallels what has happened in all of the professions. It is evident in the shift in emphasis that Bledstein noted from the old-world insistence that what defined a professional was a long-lasting dedication to the community and the virtues of sincerity, trust, and honorable reputation to the modern insistence that professionalization is shaped solely by a marketable competence in a particular field. It is evident in the shift from the old image of a soldier as an individual embodying heroism and glory to the new image of the soldier as a detached but competent technician of destruction. It is evident in the changing job requirements for public high school administrators, who were once selected because they embodied certain educational values but are now more commonly chosen for "competence in interpersonal skills, fairness in enforcing rules, and strength to withstand conflict." In a context of aggrieved and competing interest groups, the modern school administrator will inevitably be tempted to avoid taking a stand for anything in particular and instead to "fall back into the role of passive agent of process."[27]

And so it is in the Church. Modern clergy are inclined to let professional functions determine the shape of their ministerial service.

26. *Church Planning Inventory: Comparative Tabulations — Seventy-two Congregations* (Hartford, Conn.: Hartford Seminary Center for Social and Religious Research, 1986), p. 6.

27. Kevin Ryan and George F. McLean, *Character Development in Schools and Beyond* (New York: Praeger, 1978), pp. 124-25.

And since clergy often have to perform their professional functions in a context of those aggrieved and even competing in the Church, they, too, are inevitably tempted to adopt "the role of passive agent of process." In this way, professional demeanor weighs more heavily than does theological ability. According to the Schuller study, the most desired clerical quality is an "open, affirming" style and that which is the most abhorred is a style marked by "legalism" in matters of truth and ethics, a style that excludes the participation of others or is domineering. The open and affirming minister relates warmly to others, affirming them even in stressful situations, carrying out his or her responsibilities with cool competence, facilitating the sharing of views and experiences, being vulnerable, being suggestible, being willing to be led even as he or she leads. What Jackson Carroll observed earlier has not changed appreciably: the minister's authority and professional status rides not on his or her character, ability to expound the Word of God, or theological skill in relating that Word to the contemporary world but on interpersonal skills, administrative talents, and ability to organize the community.[28]

But why has professional status become so important in ministerial ranks? The answer is not hard to find. In general, the esteem in which we are held by our contemporaries has little to do with the intrinsic value of the work we do. The research that has been done on social stratification all seems to indicate that standing in society is determined by the values functioning in that society. In America, importance is conferred by professional standing.[29] By the end of the 1960s and the early 1970s, ministerial standing in society was plainly in need of serious professional upgrading, indisputable evidence for which was provided, as Glenn T. Miller notes, by the fact that ministers were suffering serious status anxieties.[30] The power that inward calling

28. Carroll, "Seminaries and Seminarians: A Study of the Professional Socialization of Protestant Clergymen" (Ph.D. diss., Princeton Theological Seminary, 1970), p. 306.

29. Joseph H. Fichter, *Religion as an Occupation: A Study in the Sociology of Professions* (Notre Dame, Ind.: University of Notre Dame Press, 1961), 115. See also Albert J. Reiss, Cecil C. North, Paul K. Hatt, and Otis D. Duncan, *Occupation and Social Status* (New York: Free Press, 1961); and *Occupational Prestige in Comparative Perspective*, ed. D. J. Treiman (San Diego: Academic Press, 1977).

30. Miller, "Professionals and Pedagogues: A Survey of Theological Education," in *Altered Landscapes: Christianity in America, 1935-1985*, ed. David W. Lotz (Grand Rapids: William B. Eerdmans, 1989), p. 200. To date, this essay is probably the most useful compact summary to have been produced on the shape of modern theological education in America, and I am indebted to it at a number of points in this discussion.

had once exerted on private consciousness, the sense of "standing" before God, of doing his work by making known his truth, apparently was not enough.

The realization that the ministry was culturally adrift proved both alarming and disconcerting, and the response that was made across the board, under the careful direction of the Association of Theological Schools, was to upgrade degree nomenclature. What had been the B.D. became the M.Div. in the early 1970s, and, for those seeking upward mobility, the D.Min. was shortly thereafter added to the arsenal of social tools. For those middle-class congregations that wanted to be served by a professional and those ministers who wanted their service validated by a doctorate, a remedy was now at hand. Thus was the D.Min. born; in two decades, over ten thousand of these degrees have been issued.[31]

It was, of course, the old market mechanism at work. In the 1970s, many seminaries were hard-pressed financially, and the D.Min. was a lucrative new product to sell.[32] At the same time, many ministers were

---

31. There was a lengthy and complex discussion about a professional degree like the D.Min. long before it was actually born. The A.T.S. had proposed such a degree in 1942, but the response from the seminaries was not positive. In 1950, the attempt was made again, but of the hundred seminaries in the A.T.S., only seven said that they would offer it if it were inaugurated. No action was taken. In the 1960s, however, the hand of the A.T.S. was forced when the Divinity School at the University of Chicago, the School of Theology at Claremont, and San Francisco Theological Seminary launched their own degrees before receiving A.T.S. approval. In the period between 1966 and 1968, the Committee on Standards for a Professional Doctorate presented its standards for the degree to the A.T.S. Unfortunately, the higher standards for which they argued (notably, that two languages other than English should be required and that candidates for the degree should be able to integrate the classical disciplines into their ministry practice) were consistently voted down. The period between 1970 and 1978 was one of trial for this increasingly popular degree. At the end of this period, a task force appointed by the president of A.T.S., Dr. David Hubbard, reported back on the considerable misgivings that many had about the degree. Among the reported concerns were the following: many did not believe a doctorate should be given for what basically amounted to continuing education, there was a lack of academic excellence among the students, quality control tended to be deficient in the degree programs, many of the faculty in the classical disciplines were unwilling to participate in the programs because they were suspicious of the merits of the degree, and many of the participating institutions appeared to have chosen to offer the degree more for financial reasons than for academic reasons. This brief history is drawn from Robert George Duffett's "History and Development of the Doctor of Ministry Degree at the Minnesota Consortium of Theological Schools, 1957-1985" (Ph.D. diss., Graduate College of the University of Iowa, 1986), pp. 108-94.

32. The judgment expressed here is a minority view. A far more positive view is characteristic of those who are active participants in offering the degree,

hard-pressed psychologically as they sensed the decline of their profession, their growing marginalization in society, and the corresponding loss of power and influence that that entailed. And so the shotgun marriage was consummated.

The direction that this degree has taken since its inception has not been very reassuring, however, and, given its genesis, it would be surprising if it had been. The quality of D.Min. degrees undoubtedly varies a lot, but there are a substantial number whose academic or intellectual demands are not great. What in many other professions are simply summer courses for updating, refresher courses mandated for continuing certification in the profession but with no significance for any degree, became the royal route that many ministers traveled toward a doctorate. Good students are able to capitalize on their opportunities, of course, even when the instruction is mediocre, and undoubtedly some of our newly minted clerical doctors have done so. But what draws ministers to these minimalist degrees, and why do seminaries offer them? It strains one's credulity a little to think that it is only a love of learning that has produced this happy match. After all, among those who have graduated with the degree, 78 percent expressed the view that they now expected to be more respected in the community, and 73 percent expected to be paid more. The upshot of it all, in fact, is that some seminaries that might have suffered an ignominious demise survived because of the D.Min. degree, and ministers who might have floundered in their careers have now gotten ahead. At least they are seen to have gotten ahead, and that, in a world where image counts as much as reality, is what actually counts.

The pastoral ministry is thus being professionalized. It is being anchored firmly in the middle class, and the attitudes of those who are themselves professionals or who constantly deal with them are increasingly defining who the minister is. Once again, it is the old market mechanism at work — ministers defining themselves as a product for which there is a market. And so they feel they must present themselves as having a desired competence, and that competence, as it turns out,

---

including some faculty and school administrators, and the beneficiaries of the degree, including candidates and recipients. However, a significant number of faculty still have deep reservations about the degree because of its lack of clear definition and because of their unease over the economic motives that drive it. See Jackson W. Carroll and Barbara Wheeler, "Study of Doctor of Ministry Programs," report conducted under the auspices of Auburn Theological Seminary and Hartford Seminary's Center for Social and Religious Research, 1987, Appendix: Graduates, p. 3.

is largely managerial. They must be able to manage the unruly and painful forces within the human psyche as well as the turbulent and equally unruly forces in the organization of the Church.

But in all this maneuvering, they are losing precisely what makes this professional, this technician of church life, different from any other manager of a human enterprise. Virtually everything that the minister does has a secular counterpart. Preaching finds its echoes in secular teaching and counseling. Evangelism finds its echoes in sales. Pastoral counseling finds its echoes in the efforts of the case worker. Church ritual finds its echoes in the formal procedures of the court and legislature. And the administration of Church programs finds its echoes in the management of countless secular organizations.[33] So what is it that distinguishes ministers from their secular counterparts?

The answer, of course, is that ministerial function should be defined by ministerial being, that what a minister does should grow out of that minister's calling, out of the fabric of truth of which that minister is an exponent. Ministerial being should be defined, if the New Testament is to be allowed any say in the matter, by worthy character, a passion for truth, and the kind of wise love that yokes together this character and this passion in the service of others.[34] But professionalization has worked to undo this relationship, for the market in which ministers must function is shaping who they must be in a way that makes connections to this world of truth uneasy and often unnecessary. Office disappears in profession, believing in doing, thought in "personality." And so, once again, the wheel has come full circle. The image of the pastor that dominated Protestant Liberalism has returned to dominate Protestant evangelicalism.

In 1912, Washington Gladden published *The Christian Pastor and the Working Church*, in which he argued that the older idea of the pastor as the broker of truth should give way to the newer idea of the pastor as the friend of all. This was the genesis of pastoral psychology and the clinical movement, and further, it was the first stirring of an anti-theological breeze that soon grew to gale force. In the interests of serving "life, not doctrine," the Liberals sought to remake Christian faith. It is no small irony that the evangelical faith that so stiffly resisted this modernism has now been substantially overcome by moderniza-

33. See Barbara Nachman, "Crosscurrents in the Occupational Evolution of Religious Careers," in *Evolving Religious Careers*, ed. Bartlett E. Willis (Washington: Center for Applied Research in the Apostolate, 1970), p. 11.

34. See, for example, Derek J. Tidball, *Skillful Shepherds* (Grand Rapids: Zondervan, 1986), pp. 55-146.

tion, that what the one could not succeed in doing the other has achieved with little effort or notice. But this is only one angle on the matter; we need now to turn from ministerial nature to ministerial nurture for another angle.

The Ministry and the Guild

The education that ministers receive has been affected by two large transformations, one that took place at the beginning of the nineteenth century and the other that took place at the end. At the beginning, the first seminaries came into being, producing at least two obvious but by no means insignificant changes. First, by centralizing the training that pastors received, the seminaries were able to provide ministers with an education that was more encompassing and well-rounded than that received by those who studied as apprentices under individual ministers. Even so, seminary education remained liable to a certain parochialism, since the seminaries typically developed into independent institutions outside the context of the college. More importantly, however, the creation of these independent seminaries also led, almost by accident, to the understanding that theology was something with which the clergy alone should be engaged. After all, it was only those who were headed for ordained ministry who, until very recently, ever went to seminary. It was almost inevitable, then, that theology would come to be seen as part of that specialization which defined ministers as professionals in contradistinction to the laity.

The transformation that took place at the other end of the nineteenth century — actually between about 1870 and 1914 — warrants more attention, however. The first, the creation of the seminaries, clearly fueled the professionalization of the clergy, in the process taking its toll on the ability and willingness of the laity to think about matters theological. The second — the transformation of the older colleges into the modern universities — is more significant because it has so deeply affected the kind of education that is now provided for ministers. It has also deeply affected views of what clerical knowledge is and how it should work in a modern profession.

As America has changed, the older agricultural-religious society giving way to modern urban-secularized society, the nature of higher education has had to change, too. The most important aspect of this transformation, however, is often missed. It is usually assumed that the most significant change has been the marginalization of religion in institutions of higher education, a change paralleling what has happened in the larger society. I certainly would not minimize the importance of this change, but it is actually only one part of a much larger picture. As Christian faith has been eclipsed, the unitary view of the world that it offered has also been eclipsed — and this is decisive. And it is quite evident that this is what has happened when we compare how institutions of higher learning functioned prior to the Civil War with how they function today. Then, colleges really tried to be universities; today, our universities have become multiversities.

The antebellum colleges, largely founded and governed as Christian institutions, were not without their critics, for they were not without their flaws. At their worst, they sacrificed the development of character to that of intellect, competence to Christian orthodoxy, and the faculty to the needs of the curriculum. Teaching, which was typically done by rote memorization, dictation, and recitation, was no doubt dull, though Richard Hofstadter exaggerates when he says that it was "neither gratifying nor particularly useful to go to college" then.[35] And their worldview was also a bit leaky.[36] Nevertheless, both here and in Britain,[37] education was predicated on the belief that the world could be understood whole, that fields of learning could all find their place under the single umbrella of discovering God's truth in God's world. And it was for this reason that these colleges could be said "to have had a soul in the sense of a central animating principle."[38]

But first in Britain and then in America, this worldview was overcome by the extraordinary intellectual and social changes that engulfed the Western world. American higher education adjusted by transforming colleges into universities fashioned on the German model. By the time the change was complete, around World War I, generalists had been replaced by specialists, John Henry Newman's "eternal truths" had been replaced by discoveries that were typically understood naturalistically, and moral philosophy had been replaced by science as the capstone of the college experience. Newman's "uni-

35. Hofstadter, "The Revolution in Higher Education," in *Paths of American Thought,* ed. Arthur M. Schlesinger and Morton White (Boston: Houghton Mifflin, 1963), p. 272.

36. See George M. Marsden, "The Collapse of American Evangelical Education," in *Faith and Rationality: Reason and Belief in God,* ed. Alvin Plantinga and Nicholas Wolterstorff (Notre Dame, Ind.: University of Notre Dame Press, 1983), pp. 219-64.

37. John Henry Newman drew up the intellectual plans for Dublin University and included them in *The Idea of a University* (New York: Longmans, 1947).

38. Clark Kerr, *The Uses of the University* (Cambridge: Harvard University Press, 1963), p. 1.

versal man," who was also the ideal of the older American colleges, was gone forever. It was no longer possible to cross and then synthesize multiple fields of knowledge, since that knowledge began to grow exponentially. The difference between the older college and the newer university was the difference, in Clark Kerr's words, between "a village with its priests" and a "city of infinite variety."[39] In the latter there is both less community and less confinement; there are more possibilities for excitement and for getting lost.

The twentieth century has seen an astonishing growth in the knowledge industry. The universities have had to add new professional schools and new departments and to increase the number of faculty dramatically. Since the beginning of this century, the overall population in the United States has grown about threefold, from 75 million to 260 million, but the number of college and university teachers has grown fiftyfold, from 10,000 in 1900 to 500,000 today. It is growth demanded by both the market for education and the need for more research. When Brandeis addressed the students at Brown in 1912, business was the most lucrative and probably the most influential profession in the nation, but now that importance has been transferred to the beneficiaries of the new specialization in knowledge — medical doctors, lawyers, accountants, managers, and technicians of various kinds. This has led some to think that we now live in a "post-business" society.[40] And all of this is fueled by substantial investments and an endless outpouring of learned journals (there are about 100,000 in print at any given time). Worldwide, about one thousand books appear each day, the

39. Kerr, *The Uses of the University*, p. 41.

40. See Peter F. Drucker, *The New Realities: In Government and Politics, in Economics and Business, in Society and Worldview* (New York: Harper & Row, 1984), pp. 173-86. This cultural transition helps explain some of the enormous strains in evangelical seminaries resulting from conflicts among three different mind-sets present in them. First, there is the mind-set of the trustees, who are inclined to make seminaries conform more to the model of the antebellum college than that of the modern university; they are also often representative of the older middle class and, significantly, of the older business establishment. Second, in many seminaries, the faculty represent the interests, habits, and values of the "new class" (those occupied with the production and distribution of symbolic knowledge as opposed to goods and services — a class made up of the academy, the media, and the like), which has risen to dominance in our society in the postwar period. Third, there is the populist mind-set of the larger evangelical world that is hostile to the academic guild and not always fully comprehending of the older business establishment. The confluence of these three mind-sets, the basic interests of which are quite often irreconcilable, has resulted in many seminaries becoming extremely fragile.

largest percentage of which by far are of Western origin. One suspects that this accelerated pace in publishing is not driven entirely by the love of learning; capitalism is not a stranger in the groves of academe. And the rapid obsolescence of books, as new "products" jostle the old off the shelves, only sharpens Samuel Johnson's jibe that the library provides the most striking evidence of the vanity of human hopes. It is now estimated that the production, dissemination, and consumption of knowledge in the United States accounts for about a third of its Gross Domestic Product.

This multiplication of knowledge has both increased the number of fields and departments that are needed for its management and redefined the internal structure of the university. Departments, whose boundaries are clearly marked and defended, typically face outward from the university. They orient themselves not to the common enterprise of learning in the university but to interests shared with similar departments in other universities and with the professions they have spawned in society. The effect of specialization, not infrequently, is to diminish the capacity of graduates to think about their world in an interconnected way. Instead, it makes them into technicians of narrow scope, collectors of knowledge in different fields. Different fields have to be traversed in the interest of a liberal arts education, but they do not have to be synthesized. This breakdown in what it means to learn and the politics generated by this breakdown are two of the irritants responsible for producing a budding literature of discontent with the whole system.[41]

41. Some of these attacks are narrowly focused, and a number of the more recent volumes have been sharply critical. See, for example, Roger Kimball, *Tenured Radicals: How Politics Has Corrupted Our Higher Education* (New York: Harper & Row, 1990); David E. Purpel, *The Moral and Spiritual Crisis in Education: A Curriculum for Justice and Compassion in Education* (Westport, Conn.: Bergin & Garvey, 1988); Page Smith, *Killing the Spirit: Higher Education in America* (New York: Viking Press, 1990); Bruce Wilshire, *The Moral Collapse of the University: Professionalism, Purity and Alienation* (Albany: State University of New York Press, 1990). For a less critical assessment, see David Riesman, *On Higher Education: The Academic Enterprise in an Era of Student Consumerism* (San Francisco: Jossey-Bass, 1980). It is interesting to note that although some of the charges are new, such as Page Smith's contention that most research now being turned out is worthless, some of the underlying contentions are not new. Nels Ferré has argued, for example, that "the crisis of the university is the crisis of the world; no university can escape being adversely affected by unstable cultural patterns and unpredictable political conditions. The crisis of the world, on the other hand, is in large measure attributable to the crisis in higher education" (*Christian Faith and Higher Education* [New York: Harper, 1954], p. 233). Christopher Dawson made the same argument from the Roman Catholic side in

The connection between these developments and the kind of education to which pastors are exposed is made through their teachers and the literature they are obliged to read as seminary students. Increasingly, evangelical seminary professors are being trained in the universities,[42] and there is little question that they have brought into the seminaries much of the culture of professionalization. As in the university, so in the seminary, the specialists of various kinds who make their offerings in the programs typically face outward rather than inward. Their primary associations are with those in the same field, first in the seminary and then outside it. The professional associations provide the linking agencies for their ongoing conversation far more commonly than the enterprise on campus in which they are involved. The central core here, too, is gone. The small world of each specialist's group spins off into its own orbit, often refusing to contribute to a commonly owned and disciplined understanding of what the education is all about, and most commonly these groups gain their independence by assaulting theology. It is, after all, theology that has traditionally defined the core around which the other subjects have spun.

This outcome is well illustrated in a 1970 collection entitled *What Theologians Do*. The editor of the volume, F. G. Healey, is decidedly wrong when he promises the reader that the twelve essays it contains provide "a view of Christian theology as a whole."[43] The essayists are all very distinguished scholars, but unfortunately only one of the twelve is a theologian. What the book actually catalogues is the insurrection of the constituent disciplines of theology against theology itself. The chosen essayists take the reader through the fields of Old Testament study, intertestamental literature, New Testament study, Church history, worship, ethics, the scientific study of other religions, and a number of other fields. All of this is of great interest to theologians, but it can hardly be claimed that, having read the book, a reader will be too much wiser about what theologians do.

The Crisis of Western Education (New York: Sheed & Ward, 1961). The most current assessment is Ernest L. Boyer's *Scholarship Reconsidered: Priorities of the Professoriate* (Princeton: Carnegie Foundation for the Advancement of Teaching, 1990). His argument is predicated on the assertion that the professoriate has passed through a difficult period and new measurements of what constitutes scholarship are now needed.

42. See Mark A. Noll, *Between Faith and Criticism: Evangelicals, Scholarship, and the Bible in America* (San Francisco: Harper & Row, 1982), pp. 126, 205-7.

43. Healey, *What Theologians Do* (Grand Rapids: William B. Eerdmans, 1970), p. 7.

The most striking fact about the seminary education of the past fifty years is that as it has oriented itself to professional goals, theology, as Glenn Miller notes, has been "orphaned." Indeed, a history of these years could well be written with very little reference to theological issues at all or to the role that theologians have played in or out of their seminaries.[44] And the issue here is not simply territorial control. It is not simply the fact that the amount of theology required within seminary curricula has steadily diminished. The issue is that theology once pervaded everything that was taught, but now it no longer does; theology was once was considered essential to the doing of ministry, but now it no longer is; seminaries were once determined by that theology, but now they no longer are. Now, the great preponderance of faculty, even in evangelical seminaries, think little of theology, work little with it, and shrug off its importance in their own field. Some even campaign actively against it. And now the number of students headed for the pastoral ministry who imagine that they can exercise their calling without reference to what was once considered essential and indispensable is growing.

It is important to see, however, that something much more has been afoot in all of this than simply the intrusion into the seminary of modern specialization and the associated curse of the fragmentation of knowledge. None of this would have had a fraction of the effect that it has had if it had not coalesced with the drive to professionalize the ministry. But since the 1970s, professionalization has been the expressed intention of the A.T.S., and the seminaries under its jurisdiction have had to comply in order to retain their accreditation.

Although the stated aim of this shift in direction is to produce greater pastoral proficiency, the means adopted has allowed the needs of the profession to define the course of training that is offered. And this means that the determination of what is to be studied is no longer grounded in theology, as has been the case over most of the Church's life, but in the vocation to which the student is headed.[45] The unifying center, therefore, is no longer theological truth but whatever it is that the student needs in order to become a religious professional. Whereas the unity once lay in the theology that was taught, it now lies in the needs in the Church that the minister will have to manage. There is not, therefore, a conceptual link between what is studied in theology and what will be

---

44. See Miller, "Professionals and Pedagogues," p. 203.
45. See Edward Farley, *Theologia: The Fragmentation and Unity of Theological Education* (Philadelphia: Fortress Press, 1983), p. 129.

practiced in the Church, but simply a pragmatic rationale that asks only what specific help theological knowledge can offer for the needs that arise. When the tasks of the ministry provide the criteria for what should be studied, then the alienation of theology becomes almost inevitable, because what those tasks call for can be provided without any justification from theology. Modern church life and theology are therefore in competition for the soul of the seminary.[46]

I am not suggesting here that theology is unconnected to modern church life or that theologians are somehow opposed to practical training for seminarians. That is simply untrue. The point I am trying to make is that traditional priorities have been upended. The rationale for offering seminary courses is often simply that they will contribute to the practice of a professionalized ministry. It is their practical value that justifies their presence, not their contribution to understanding the world, the Church, human life, or the character of God and his works within a theological framework. Today's students are given an arsenal of specialists' tools and left to find a unifying principle, some means for orchestrating their use, in the practice of ministry itself; the seminaries have essentially abandoned attempts to present the theologically formulated knowledge of God as a unifying principle for the use of these tools. Professionalization has thus alienated theology from education within the seminary and, in consequence, dispatched into the churches individuals who may be bright with the sheen of professionalization but are frequently devoid of any theological interest or ability.

Thus there have converged from two directions forces of enormous influence in the remaking of the pastoral soul. From the one side come the powerful undercurrents connected with survival. Survival is now seen to be inextricably linked with gathering the accoutrements of professional standing. What this entails is not a greater attachment to the details of practical application of theological truth in today's world but rather a greater application to discovering the marks of being professional — a course that frequently requires an emancipation from theology.[47]

And from the other side comes the fragmenting of knowledge within the seminary curriculum. Subjects and fields develop their own literatures, working assumptions, vocabularies, technical terms, criteria for what is true and false, and canons of what literature and what views should be common knowledge among those working in the subjects.

46. See Farley, *Theologia*, p. 127.
47. See Farley, *Theologia*, p. 11.

The result of this is a profound increase in knowledge but often an equally profound loss in understanding what it all means, how it is all interconnected, how knowledge in one field should inform that in another. This is the bane of every seminarian's existence. The dissociated fields — biblical studies, theology, church history, homiletics, ethics, pastoral psychology, missiology — become a rain of hard pellets relentlessly bombarding those who are on the pilgrimage to graduation. Students are left more or less defenseless as they run this gantlet, supplied with little help in their efforts to determine how to relate the fields one to another. In the end, the only warrant for their having to endure the onslaught is that somehow and someday it will all come together in a church.

Toward a New Order of Sacred Fools

I want now to draw the various threads of this discussion together. It will not be easy, because the threads are numerous and often seemingly unrelated. This is what has hobbled so many of the attempts to think afresh about the ministry, about what needs to be done to prepare for it, and about its role in the Church.

I began this chapter with the assertion that in the twentieth century, American clergy have adopted professionalization as a means to reverse their sagging social fortunes and to prepare the sort of Church leadership that will be most effective in the modern world. I further asserted that this new development, which has been formalized in all the seminaries over which the A.T.S. has jurisdiction, has had some unhappy results. Most important among these is the inculcation of habits of thought that are unfriendly toward theology, a development that has rendered ministers less willing and able to mediate theological truth to the Church. To the extent that this is occurring, a vital link in the doing of theology has been snapped, for it is the Church that should be the primary auditor for theology. I would now like to bring these general assertions into sharper focus by considering three related topics.

The Minister in Search of a Niche

It is one of the anomalies of the ministry today that, on the one hand, theology has accidentally been coopted by the clergy and, on the other, that the training they typically receive disengages theology from the life of the Church. Theology therefore finds a resting place neither in the Church (since it tends to be viewed as a clerical preserve) nor in the clerical soul (since clergy must serve in the Church). Clerical training is on the whole biased against theology, but so too is the Church's life. Among other things, the Church has been hesitant to trespass on professional clerical turf, and it is uncertain what theology has to contribute to making it a thriving enterprise. Theology thus stands hopelessly marooned in a nether world that no one wants to enter.

It is not hard to see why clergy should have embarked on their movement toward professionalization. After all, that is how other professionals acquired their standing in society. It was by gaining control over their specialized fields that medical doctors, lawyers, architects, accountants, and engineers secured their own space and social standing for themselves. Professionalization, however, is itself a culture, and the values by which it operates are not always friendly to pastoral calling and character. For the most part, American clergy have not understood this. They grabbed at professionalization like a drowning man might grab at a life jacket, but having thus been saved, they must now live by its limitations and dictates.

Other professionals have been able to define and control their social space because they can claim a monopoly over the work that they do. Within a narrow domain, they exercise sovereignty (as evidenced by the fact that they can maintain their fees at a high level). Control over one's work, over who can perform it, is essential to survival in the capitalistic enterprise. It is what Ivan Illich vehemently denounces as the setting up of cartels. The professions, he complains, "are more deeply entrenched than a Byzantine bureaucracy, more international than a world church, more stable than a labor union, endowed with wider competencies than any shaman, and equipped with a tighter hold over those they claim as victims than any mafia."[48]

When the habits of professionalization are transferred to the Church, they immediately begin to accentuate *differences* between the pastor and the congregation, in the same way they accentuate the differences between doctors and their patients, lawyers and their clients. The difference arises from the fact that one possesses technical knowledge that the other does not. When this model is transferred to the Church, however, it produces at least two adverse consequences.

First, the assumption that a professionalized clergy tends to make — namely, that they have a monopoly over the work in which they

48. Illich et al., *Disabling Professions* (New York: Marion Boyars, 1978), p. 15.

have specialized — sits very uneasy on the evangelical soul. The sense of disquiet may be explained in a number of ways. For some it seems like a violation of the priesthood of all believers; for some it seems like a violation of congregational polity; and for some it just seems undemocratic. The problem for the clergy here is that they occupy a different sort of position than other professionals. The clients of doctors, lawyers, and the like are largely ignorant of the field of knowledge in which they seek help, but in matters of faith, the "client" typically claims considerable knowledge. Indeed, a recent advertisement in *Christianity Today* that invited its readers to "join a church with 200 ministers — and no laymen" may be much closer to the evangelical heartbeat than are the ministers who view themselves as specialists.

The concern of the laity in this regard is not without its justification. While it is true that the teacher of the Bible has a special authority in the Church, this authority derives not from the professionalized status of the teacher but from the Word that is being taught, not from the minister's office but from the truth that it is his or her duty to expound. This was one of the basic affirmations of the Protestant Reformation, and it would be strange to expect that evangelicals who rejected the magisterium of the Catholic Church should now be pleased to accept the magisterium of a modern clerical profession.

Furthermore, if a minister wants both to claim a monopoly over some part of the work and to respect the assumption of the congregation that it knows something about its own faith, he or she will almost certainly have to become a specialist in matters that are frankly peripheral to the life of faith — such matters as church administration, denominational politics, psychological counseling, and the like. According to Edward Farley, this clearly amounts to "a nontheological approach to church leadership because it permits a set of negotiations or unstated expectations between minister and congregation to determine the leader's nature, task, and responsibilities."[49] It is thus that we have allowed the theology to be drained from the ministry even as we nevertheless continue to expect it to function in the nurturing of the knowledge of God in the Church. We laugh at those who think theology is important, and then are shocked to find in our midst the superficial and unbelieving. We allow our pastors to be rendered sterile through their yearning for professionalization and then bid them to be fruitful in their work.[50]

49. Farley, *Theologia*, p. 176.
50. Cf. C. S. Lewis, *The Abolition of Man* (New York: Macmillan, 1947), p. 35.

Pastors once believed that they were called to think about life, to think in ways that were centered in and disciplined by the truth of God's Word, although, as Tocqueville observed, there has always been a tendency latent in the American soul to think of religion in terms of its utility rather than its truth.[51] Modernity has now exaggerated this tendency to the extent that the older ways of understanding the pastor's responsibilities are disappearing, along with the older ideas about training pastors for their work. As the technological world has encroached upon the pastorate, management by technique has come to replace management by truth. The almost total absence of biblical and theological grounding for the material presented in *Leadership* magazine that we have already noted is the rule now, not the exception. It is not understanding that this material seeks but a way to manage the church's problems. It is not truth that is wanted but technique.

And so the professionalized pastor has often reduced the uncontrollable world of God's truth by procedure, using committees to diminish the Church and psychological techniques to diminish the soul. Rough truth gives way to smooth practice, the transcendent gives way to the procedural, the jerks and moments of discovery when God's world illumines our own give way to moments in which our world brings his into tame submission. As the world of Christian truth breaks down, the hands of the professionals reach up to seize and overcome what is not rightfully theirs. And what is the result?

The result, according to Stanley Hauerwas and William Willimon, is practical atheism, regardless of whether it is the Liberals or the Fundamentalists who are busy at it. It is an atheism that reduces the Church to nothing more than the services it offers or the good feelings the minister can generate. In other words, where professionalization is at work, there the ministry will typically be deprived of its transcendence and reduced to little more than a helping profession. The kind of sentimentality it offers, they declare, "has become the most detrimental corruption of the church and ministry" today. "Without God, without the one whose death on the cross challenges all our good feelings, who stands beyond and over against our human anxieties, all

51. This does not mean, of course, that Tocqueville believed that religion was unimportant in America. Quite the contrary: he believed it was far more significant for Americans than it was for many Europeans, and one of the reasons cited for this was the separation of Church and state in America in contrast to their reliance on one another in Europe. See Tocqueville, *Democracy in America*, book 1, ed. J. P. Morgan, trans. George Lawrence (Garden City, N.Y.: Doubleday, 1969), pp. 294-301.

we have left is sentiment, a saccharine residue of theism in demise."[52] It is the kind of sentimentality that wants to listen without judging, that has opinions but little interest in truth, that is sympathetic but has no passion for that which is right. It is under this guise of piety — indeed, of professionalization — that pastoral unbelief lives out its life.

The Minister as Impermanent

Impermanence, we noted earlier, has become one of the defining characteristics of the twentieth century. It is a thread that is impossible to remove from the fabric of modern life. It runs through our relationships to place, through vocation, through the manufactured goods we use, through our families. One of the most deeply ingrained features of modern experience is the belief that nothing lasts, so most people find it quite natural that churches and their ministers should constantly be seeking different partners. And, given the fact that in any given year an average of about 20 percent of adults will move (more in urban areas, less in rural areas), even pastors who remain anchored in one place cannot sustain a relationship with a congregation.

The combination of professionalization and this impermanence has encouraged pastors to suppose that it is proper for them to seek careers. When they cannot form lasting relationships in a particular community, they are tempted to look inward for the measure of fruitfulness rather than outward. They will be tempted to seek first a career rather than to make an enduring contribution to the people in a particular place. But how can the biblical teaching on service be reconciled with the psychological appetites for greater visibility and power that careers generate? Perhaps, instead of seeking a career, the modern minister would find it easier to model the virtues of humility and self-sacrifice by seeking to be a fool.

The sort of fool I have in mind here is not the fool of modern parlance, the sort of fool one does not suffer gladly, but rather an archetypal character from the Middle Ages. Medieval society had a pyramidal class structure, with layer upon layer from the base to the apex. It was important for people to know exactly where they were situated in the hierarchy, whom they took orders from and whom they gave orders to, for violations of the etiquette could have serious consequences. The higher one was in the system, the more rarefied and

---

52. Hauerwas and Willimon, "Ministry as More Than a Helping Profession," *Christian Century*, 15 March 1989, p. 282.

parochial was the air that one breathed, for one received advice and reproof only from those of similar or superior standing. There was one exception to the constraints of this system, however: the jester was emancipated from its bonds and granted immunity from punishment for violating its strictures.[53] Viewed as belonging to no class, jesters in effect stood on a par with everyone. So long as they cloaked their advice in humor, jesters were able to say things to kings and princes that might have been fatal for anyone else to say. Happy was the king who had a good fool. And happy are those churches whose ministers are likewise emancipated from the bonds of class interest and social expectation, freed to expose the follies of modernity in the light of God's truth.

The source of this freedom for today's ministers is located at the very heart of their vocation. The source lies not in their professional status or their current location along the trajectory of a career. It lies in the fact that they serve the living God, who is no respecter of persons, in the fact that they are the servants of his Word and Son, before whom all will be judged. It is this understanding that gives ministers the freedom to remain in one location however long it takes to make theological truth a central and effective part of their ministry, regardless of whether their careers pass them by in the meantime. But, assuming that our ministers do allow themselves to stay in one place long enough, how successful will they be in refocusing their ministries on theological truth?

The Minister as Theologian

There are, happily, many ministers who have broken the professional mold, although they have done so only against great odds, and, as a consequence, they have often had to work on the fringes of evangelical life. In order to break the mold, most have to turn on its head the kind of training they received in seminary. They have to resist the inclination to look to the life of the Church as the center that defines what they should do and turn instead to the knowledge of God to unify

---

53. See Ralf Dahrendorf, "The Intellectual and Society: The Social Function of the Fool in the Twentieth Century," in *On Intellectuals: Case Studies*, ed. Philip Rieff (Garden City, N.Y.: Doubleday, 1970), pp. 53-56. Dahrendorf characterizes the intellectual as this sort of fool, an individual emancipated from class interest, but his thesis seems far less plausible today in light of the "new class" theory, which suggests that intellectuals in modern society do indeed have considerable class interests. See also the seminal work by Florian Znaniecki in *The Social Role of the Man of Knowledge* (New York: Harper & Row, 1968).

their activities in the Church. They must somehow span the gap between the Church and things theological, a gap created when the clergy coopted theology and removed it from the soul of the Church. They have to be able to see through our modernity with such clarity that they can discern where and how its pluralism and secularism work. Those who manage to do so go on to preach with passion the truth of God's Word, reflecting on that truth and seeking out the points at which it intersects with modern life. There they uncover a wisdom that will not be coopted by the self movement, a wisdom centered instead in the objectivity of God's truth and in the transcendent God to whom it points. It is by no means easy for ministers to avoid the shoals that lie before them. Take, for example, the matter of preaching.

Many factors affect the way that preaching is done in any given age, and it would probably be impossible to establish an indisputable cause-and-effect relationship between the presence of the habits of professionalization and the way in which preaching excellence is judged today. Still, it is at least reasonable to assume that contemporary judgments about what constitutes excellence in preaching will give us some indication of the view of ministry that is held by those making the judgments.

It is, therefore, a matter of no small interest to discover how two important preaching journals view this matter. The analysis that was undertaken sought to classify published sermons into four categories: (1) those in which both the content of the sermon and its organization were determined by the biblical passage under consideration, (2) those in which the content was explicitly biblical but the preacher took the liberty of imposing his or her own organization upon it, (3) those in which neither the content nor the organization arose from the biblical passage but what was said was at least identifiable as being Christian, and (4) those in which neither the content nor the organization arose from a biblical passage and in which the content was not discernibly or obviously Christian.

The sermons of evangelicals published in these journals fell into the following categories: 24.5 percent in the first, 22.5 percent in the second, 39 percent in the third, and 14 percent in the fourth.[54] That

---

54. This analysis was done on two hundred sermons, half from *Pulpit Digest* and the other half from *Preaching*. They covered the time span from January-February 1981 to March-April 1991 in the former case and July-August 1985 to JanuaryFebruary 1991 in the latter. The figures given in the text are averages of the figures from both journals. I am grateful to James Singleton, who extended his own doctoral research to include this work and who, therefore, provided the foundation for my own judgments.

means that of these model sermons, less than half are explicitly biblical, and a significant number are not discernibly Christian at all. They could have been given by a secular psychologist in a setting like the Rotary Club.

Even more significant than these findings was a discovery relating to the orientation of the sermons. Only 19.5 percent were grounded in or related in any way to the nature, character, and will of God. At issue here is not whether the sermons were *about* God; there are many other legitimate subjects about which a preacher might wish to discourse on a Sunday morning. Rather, at issue is whether the reality, character, and acts of God provided an explicit foundation for what the preacher said about the life of faith, or whether the life of faith was presented as making some kind of internal sense without reference to the character, will, and acts of God. At issue, in short, was the prevailing *Geist* in today's pulpit. Is it anthropocentric or is it theocentric? The overwhelming proportion of the sermons analyzed — more than 80 percent — were anthropocentric. It is as if God has become an awkward appendage to the practice of evangelical faith, at least as measured by the pulpit. Indeed, it would seem from these sermons that God and the supernatural order are related only with difficulty to the life of faith; in any event, he does not seem to be at its center. Contemporary sermons are reserving the center for the issues that engage us in the course of life, or, more specifically, for the self. It is around this surrogate center that God and his world are made to spin.

It would, of course, be foolish to imagine that great preaching could be commonplace, for greatness is, by definition, always in short supply. Indeed, this has always been one of the anomalies of Protestantism. It places vast importance on the preaching of the Word, but it has not always produced individuals who can preach that Word effectively. A generation ago, Charles Brown addressed the pastoral world on this very subject. "When we think of the weak, inefficient [i.e., ineffective] preaching that is being perpetrated on a patient, trusting public," he sighed, "we marvel that the Christian religion has stood up under it without being annihilated." He went on to offer the judgment that "if our faith had not been divine in its origin and essence it would have collapsed long ago."[55] Yet despite this perennial discontent, it is hard not to think that in our own time we are seeing a decline

55. Brown, "The Training of a Minister," in *Education for Christian Service* (New Haven: Yale University Press, 1922), p. 9.

in serious, biblical preaching, the kind that arises out of a depth of theological character in the preacher and that has the effect in the hearer of replicating itself in such a way that there is a deep sense of standing in the presence and truth of God. If preaching, like the ministry, is now defined by the needs of the Church rather than the fabric of truth in the Bible, should this be a surprising discovery? And how is the Church to rise above its own small interests to be captured by the large vision of the greatness of God, of his truth, of his grace, and of his purposes if the pulpit is little more than a sounding board from which the Church hears itself? And if it is thus held captive by its own self, how will it be able to see beyond itself and nourish what Richard Weaver calls its "metaphysical dream of the world"?

If the figures cited above do bear any significant relation to what the people in the pew are thinking and hearing, then we have the makings of a kind of faith that is only tenuously related to the Word of God, that is not much nurtured by it, that is not much anchored in the character and greatness of God, and that is almost completely unaware of the culture that surrounds it, for in virtually none of the sermons analyzed was there any attempt made to take account of the modernity into which the Word was preached. This is professionalization at both its best and worst. It is at its best in the sense that it best reveals the true colors of the culture of professionalization in which the meaning of the pastorate is now being sought; it is at its worst in the sense that the cost to Christian truth is now quite obvious.

The ability of ministers to do theology, to be able to expound the Word of God and bring its truth into vital relation with the modern world in such a way that moral character is formed and Christian wisdom results, is more important for Protestants than for Catholics. The Catholic priest, in church at least, is largely a liturgical functionary for whom the magisterium provides the teaching and the sacraments the mystery. The Protestant minister, by contrast, must teach, must bring the congregation into the presence of God through his truth and by his Spirit, and, in that process, must find those depths of divine relationship for which sacramental mystery is but a pale substitute. It is by this same Word that meaning is to be given, and to the extent to which ministers are failing in this work, they are failing the Church and even disabling it. They are leaving it vulnerable to all of the seductions of modernity precisely because they have not provided the alternative, which is a view of life centered in God and his truth. Without this, the Church is left empty of meaning.

And meaning, after all, is what religion is about. If there is a lesson to be learned from the demise of Liberalism, Leonard Sweet has argued, it is at this point. The constant minimalizing of what faith meant, the reductions and modifications aimed at meeting the demands of the age, the slick shifting and moving to catch the prevailing cultural winds took away the ability of Liberalism to speak to the most basic aspects of meaning. Soon, "a good church was not a believing church, but a working church, a church of constant to-ing and fro-ing, with lots of task forces and especially lots of committees." The Church became a place to get things done, and its fidelity came to be measured by the activities it arranged. But these activities had less and less to do with the love of God and more and more to do with the love of neighbor until in the end the one was subsumed under the other. And then this love for neighbor itself underwent further transformation so that faith came to mean little more than seeking justice in the world, and while that is a characteristically Christian concern, it is not distinctively Christian.[56] The path that this earlier Liberalism followed is now, perhaps entirely unconsciously, being replicated in evangelicalism, especially where the culture of professionalization is stripping it of a functioning, transcendent reference point in the Word of God.

An earlier Langdon Gilkey asked how Jesus Christ can, in fact, be Lord of his Church. His answer, rich with Reformation overtones, was that both those who stand in the pulpit and those who listen are alike "servants of the Word." This Word, he said, now languishes because the Church has lost "the category of truth." Furthermore, "if the congregation is to hear and obey the Word in its midst, the denominational church must lose its fear of and scorn for theology, and its resistance to the teaching of doctrine in the church." Unless this happens, Christianity will remain simply a cultural convenience that will be discarded every time its teaching threatens our way of life. It will be powerless to yield the meaning that we need, powerless to preserve us in the way of God as we seek.[57]

It should now be clear that there are two quite different models of ministry at work in the evangelical Church today, and theology is located quite differently in each. In the model of the Church that has its roots in the Reformation and in the Puritanism that followed,

56. See Leonard I. Sweet, "The Modernization of Protestant Religion in America," in *Altered Landscapes*, pp. 33-34.

57. Gilkey, *How the Church Can Minister to the World without Losing Itself* (New York: Harper & Row, 1964), pp. 85, 96.

theology is essential and central;[58] in its modern-day evangelical descendants, however, theology is often only instrumental and peripheral.[59] In the one, theology provides the culture in which ministry is
understood and practiced; in the other, this culture is provided by
professionalization.

The difference between the two models is not that theology is
present in one but not the other. Theology is professed and believed
in both. But in the one, theology is the reason for ministry, the basis
for ministry; it provides the criteria by which success in ministry is
measured. In the other, theology does none of these things; here the
ministry provides its own rationale, its own criteria, its own techniques.
The second model does not reject theology; it simply displaces it so
that it no longer gives the profession of ministry its heart and fire.

This shift from the older theological model for ministry in the
Church to the newer professionalized model has produced an entirely
different understanding of the relationship between theory and practice. In the older model, *theology* was synonymous with the knowledge
of God, the inward disposition that this knowledge produced, the
wisdom for life that it generated, the inclination to serve God and his
truth in the world, and action in the world was always implied in what
was known. It was not another kind of knowledge with a set of separate
rules and operating procedures. To know God was to be owned by
him in Christ, to be his servant, to have found the center into which
all of life — not merely its cognitive aspects — should flow. It was to
have found the center from which all practice, including that of the
ministry, should flow.

In the new model, however, theology and practice have disen-

58. The loss of this older Protestant tradition is now being explored by
James E. Bradley under an A.T.S. grant. I am grateful to him for allowing me to
see two of his unpublished chapters. A brief summary of his work to date is to be
found in Fuller Theological Seminary's *Theology, News and Notes*, October 1988, pp.
18-26.

59. Peter Wagner has provided a good illustration of the ambiguous role
theology now plays in the evangelical world. In discussing the paradigm of church
growth to which he is committed, Wagner first of all affirms that he does believe
in theology, but then he immediately qualifies the affirmation. The church growth
movement, he says, "is deeply rooted in theological traditions, but it does not study
theology for theology's sake." What, then, is the place of theology? It is, he tells us,
simply a "tool." It is necessary for the church's health, but when all is said and
done it is nothing more than a tool. See his essay, "Church Growth Research: The
Paradigm and Its Applications," in *Understanding Church Growth and Decline, 1950-
1978*, ed. Dean R. Hoge and David A. Roozen (New York: Pilgrim Press, 1979),
pp. 270-87.

gaged from one another, and the center around which Christian thought turns has shifted from God to the Church. The new model restricts theology to the academy, ensuring that it touches only the edges of Church life. The life of the Church provides a surrogate "truth" for Christian thought in this model. This life provides the justification for all theological learning. The skills and techniques requisite for the management of the Church determine what theology should be studied, not the importance of the truth itself.

What this means in practice is that the minister, like a small boat cast loose upon the high seas, has become vulnerable to a multitude of perils. Within the Church, strong winds are blowing from a range of religious consumers who look to the churches and ministers to meet their needs — and who quickly look elsewhere if they feel those needs are not being met. Basically, these consumers are looking for the sort of thing the self movement is offering; they just want it in evangelical dress. A genuinely biblical and God-centered ministry is almost certain to collide head-on with the self-absorption and anthropocentric focus that are now normative in so many evangelical churches. The collisions take place in the soul of the minister and at the expense of his or her career.

The attempt to steer around these shoals, using professionalization as the rudder, has not only complicated the exercise of a genuinely biblical ministry but has failed in other ways as well. In 1966, according to a Harris poll, 41 percent of the public expressed great confidence in the leadership of the clergy. This figure dropped steadily to just 16 percent by 1989 — the lowest rating given for the leaders of any of the major institutions, including medicine, the military, government, and the press. The attempt by ministers to reach professional parity with lawyers and physicians has not impressed the public, and it has not been successful in its original objectives in the Church either.

That the strategy has miscarried is a matter of some poignancy, for so many of those who have sought the refuge of professionalization have, nevertheless, virtue in many other ways. They are the ones who have so often forfeited the access to affluence that the culture desires. They have relegated themselves to the edges of what the culture considers important. And they have shown themselves to be content do their essentially private work — addressing the moments of pain, bereavement, depression, and confusion that visit their flocks — without much public recognition or even awareness of the deeply perplexing circumstances in which they are called upon to serve as Christ's ministers. Their virtue is known to God and few others. Yet the very willingness of ministers to be countercultural in these ways leads me to think that if they could be persuaded that the translation of their calling into a profession is, in fact, the result of enculturation, then it would not be difficult for them simply to extend their own practiced countercultural character and, in the process, begin recovering the basis for a serious renewal of Christian faith. For if the self-orientation in the Church has reordered the *nature* of theology, and the rise of the religious consumer has reordered its *function*, then no amount of management or psychology is going to resolve the issues. It is not management that the Church needs but reformation, and reformation does not compel the professionalized. Is it not yet clear that if the Church does indeed stand in need of reformation, then a rethinking of the training for and the practice of the ministry should be a part of that change? And would not many ministers welcome being emancipated to change? I believe that they would, that they find themselves as much captive to expectations with which they have little sympathy as the Church does. And so the diminished status of the ministry may, paradoxically, provide a path to its recovery. There is a better way, a way more conducive to thinking biblical thoughts and establishing biblical priorities in the Church than what is now entrenched throughout much of the evangelical world.

CHAPTER VII

The Habits of God

The realism of the Bible consists in its close attention to the facts of history. . . . These are the facts of God.

G. Ernest Wright

IT IS HARD TO MISS the fact that much of the Bible is written in narrative form, but the importance of this form now seems to be lost on many of us. Narrative theologians have tried to correct this deficiency, but for the most part they have succeeded only in bolstering the thought that we should pay more attention to stories, to how they work as literature and how they affect the mind. Narrative theology has not helped us much in understanding why God chose to reveal himself through the story of Israel's life, a story that reached its climax in the life, death, and resurrection of Christ.[1]

In the 1980s, proponents of the various forms of narrative theology contended that what the Bible does is develop its own story of

---

1. For a good, though brief overview of narrative theology, see Gabriel Fackre, "Narrative Theology: An Overview," *Interpretation* 37 (October 1983): 340-52. In any account of narrative theology, it would be a mistake to overlook the importance of the Yale theologians. In particular, see Brevard Childs, "The Canonical Approach and the 'New Yale Theology,'" in *The New Testament as Canon: An Introduction* (Philadelphia: Fortress Press, 1984), pp. 541-46; Hans W. Frei, *The Eclipse of Biblical Narrative: A Study in Eighteenth and Nineteenth Century Hermeneutics* (New Haven: Yale University Press, 1974); and George A. Lindbeck, "The Bible as Realistic Narrative," *Journal of Ecumenical Studies* 17 (1980): 81-85.

God, a story with a beginning and an end, a story told by a set of narrators who chose which details to use or omit. Many also contended that the historical details recorded in the Bible are not necessarily accurate, that they are for the most part incidental to the story, which retains its power and meaning regardless of the accuracy of the details. According to Hans Frei, the biblical story is "history-like" but not necessarily historical. This explains why different narrative theologians have moved down different paths, some choosing to tell God's story through the biblical materials, others the stories of the communities of faith, and some even their own stories.

The importance of the story form in the Bible does not lie in the story form itself, however. Its importance lies in the fact that as a narrative of God's acts in the external world, it has yielded truth that is as objective as the events to which it is wedded. It was this that was distinctive in the biblical period, and it is this that is decisive for ours.

It is not possible to explore all of the angles of the biblical narrative in this context, of course. We have to turn our attention to those aspects of the narrative that bear most directly on the question of the current displacement of theology. Specifically, we must look at the biblical conviction about truth, its nature, its authority, and its function. There are those who would question whether the understanding of truth held by the biblical authors can be at the heart of the way in which we think about ourselves and our world today,[2] but I believe we can at least show that their conviction about truth was at the center of the way in which *they* saw *their* world.

The prophets of the Old Testament and the apostles of the New in fact take the modern breath away, for they had a certainty about the existence, character, and purposes of God — a certainty about his truth — that seems to have faded in the bright light of the modern world. They were convinced that God's revelation, of which they were the vehicles and custodians, was true. True in an absolute sense. It was not merely true *to them;* it was not merely true *in their time;* it was not

---

2. The most persistent attack on the cognitive aspect of truth has been based upon the work of linguistic philosophers such as Wittgenstein, Heidegger, and Chomsky, who argue that linguistic propositions cannot be used to describe reality, which is better grasped intuitively in the self. For Hans Küng's use of such arguments, see *Infallible? An Inquiry,* trans. Edward Quinn (Garden City, N.Y.: Doubleday, 1971), pp. 157-75. But Donald Mackinnon has asserted that without a cognitively known transcendent referent, worship is reduced to nothing more than a private emotion and theology to autobiography (see *Explorations in Theology* [London: SCM Press, 1979], pp. 70-89). Carl F. H. Henry has mounted this century's most substantial defense of the necessity of cognitive content of truth in *God, Revelation and Authority,* 6 vols. (Waco, Tex.: Word Books, 1976-83).

true *approximately*. What God had given was true universally, absolutely, and enduringly.

Today that sounds jarring and improbable. It is therefore often argued, at least in the academic world, that we are now so distant from the biblical cultures, not only in time but, more importantly, in terms of mental habits, that it is no longer possible for us to take our cognitive bearings from the biblical Word. They could think in terms of truth because their world was so small; we can no longer do so because our world is so big. They were blessed with an uncomplicated parochialism; we have been cursed with citizenship in the global village. This argument has taken many forms in the modern period, but beneath most of them lie three assumptions.

First, it is often assumed, albeit obliquely, that the human spirit has progressed in such a way that what is culturally older is of less value. It is true that this brassy evolutionary argument is not received with the same unqualified confidence that it was in the nineteenth century, but it has not died. Then, the argument owed much of its life to the academy, to Darwin and the philosophers who followed him, and to the biblical scholars who echoed their line of thought;[3] today, it is our modern world, the capitalism and technology of which force the mind into the future and for which the word *obsolete* has a funereal feel about it, that fuels the search for intellectual innovation and spreads a dread of the past as if it were a plague.[4] This is our secular "salvation history," erected quite deliberately as an alternative to the biblical model by the children of the Enlightenment, which promises a this-worldly deliverance. It posits salvation in abundance. Its "Word" is secular reason, and its eschatology, its hope, is that as the human spirit progresses, it will emerge from the darkness of its own misdeeds and perhaps even triumph over the misfortunes that life turns up with such disconcerting regularity.[5] The chief appeal of this ambiguous hope seems to lie in the fact that there is no alternative. Only individuals with an unusually flinty inner makeup

3. On the background to this development, see Richard Hofstadter, *Social Darwinism in American Thought* (New York: George Braziller, 1959), and Thomas Steven Molnar, *Utopia: The Perennial Heresy* (New York: Sheed & Ward, 1967). For the development within biblical studies, see Stephen Neill, *The Interpretation of the New Testament, 1861-1961* (London: Oxford University Press, 1964).

4. Modernization, says Peter Berger, "everywhere . . . means a powerful shift in attention from past and present to the future," and he adds that "the temporality within which this future is conceived is of a very peculiar kind — it is precise, measurable and, at least in principle, subject to human control" (*Facing Up to Modernity: Excursions in Society, Politics, and Religion* [New York: Basic Books, 1977], p. 73).

5. See Langdon Gilkey, *Society and the Sacred: Toward a Theology of Culture in Decline* (New York: Crossroad, 1981), pp. 3-12.

can live without hope of any kind, so it is perhaps not surprising that many should settle for what hope they can find, even so paltry a hope as that manufactured from a questionable assumption about progress.

Second, it is commonly assumed that no one today can slip back into an ancient worldview and make it their own, that worldviews are not like garments that can be put on or taken off at will.[6] Worldviews are wed to the psychology of a particular age and imparted with its experiences. Our worldview is modern, and it no longer allows us to think in terms of the supernatural or absolute truth as the biblical authors could. This case was argued from the biblical side by the Bultmann school, whose arguments have now become passé, but the issue has by no means subsided.

Third, in theology it is often argued that we face an unprecedented degree of religious pluralism today, that we are bombarded by such a multiplicity of ultimate claims that we are no longer able to indulge the sort of intellectual simplicity that characterized the biblical writers. They could believe in absolute truth, in the uniqueness of biblical faith; we cannot. It is a simple matter of honesty that we no longer pretend that we can.[7]

These are not small matters. They deserve far more consideration than I can offer here. But, on the first point, it should at least be noted that those who can sustain a faith in progress in the human spirit of this magnitude in the midst of the most brutal and destructive century in history are capable of a credulity that far exceeds the belief required for thinking that God has given a truth that is final and enduring.

Second, a cogent argument can be made that the experience of this relativistic and highly pluralistic world does not impose itself on us as if we were mute objects simply waiting to receive its impress. We have to interpret it.[8] It does not follow that those who live in such a world *must*

6. See Rudolf Bultmann, *Kerygma and Myth: A Theological Debate*, trans. Reginald H. Fuller (London: S.P.C.K., 1954), pp. 3-5.

7. See Paul F. Knitter, *No Other Name? A Critical Survey of Christian Attitudes toward the World Religions* (Maryknoll, N.Y.: Orbis Books, 1989); and *The Myth of Christian Uniqueness: Toward a Pluralistic Theology of Religions*, ed. John Hick and Paul F. Knitter (Maryknoll, N.Y.: Orbis Books, 1987).

8. Peter Berger's thesis in *The Heretical Imperative* assumes the modern bifurcation between what is private and what is public and relegates the origination of religion to what is private. Its truth value is then to be ascertained by the plausibility structure of modern scientific inquiry. His "heresy" is the acknowledgment that religion is generically the same and thus contemporary expressions form a pluralistic mosaic. What Berger is unable to answer, however, is how personal autobiography can or should be imperative to anyone else. Berger is quite correct to see that there is an interpretive element; his problem is that he has no external, objective norm other than what appears plausible by which to judge interpreted religious experience.

It is not possible even to outline an epistemology here, though what I have see everything as relative. For all the arguments that have been made about the way in which the organization of our external world, with its rationalization and pluralization, necessarily imposes itself upon the organization of our internal world, it has never been conclusively shown that we have lost all freedom in thinking about the nature of reality. If ideas were in fact determined, then it would be an exercise in futility to attempt to discern the true from the false, as futile as to attempt to decide whether or not the sun should be allowed to rise each day. What would be the point of writing a book, engaging in argument, seeking to persuade others of the validity of a viewpoint, if all ideas were already determined? The very attempt to persuade others that ideas are determined is itself a tacit concession that they are not.

Third, it is of course true that religious pluralism is something of a novelty for us in the West. For the first time in many centuries, we are emerging from a protective cocoon created first by the conquests of the Islamic armies that began in the sixth century and that squeezed Christian faith into Europe, containing it there, and then by the massive Christianizing of Europe under Catholic and then Protestant auspices that subsequently kept the other religions out. As a result, until relatively recently the knowledge of other religions was seldom first-hand or intense. This has now all changed. In America today, there are no fewer than 1,200 organized religious bodies, ranging from Presbyterians of one kind or another to Satanists; and Moslems now outnumber Methodists.[9] Until quite recently, America has been very remote, in this respect, from the world inhabited by the biblical authors.

Beyond this, we are now experiencing religion that is quite pagan in its nature, and this, too, is novel. It is surely one of the many anomalies of Our Time that while our secularized culture rejects the notion of any divine presence in the world, any divine referent upon whom we can

---

in mind does follow some of Michael Polanyi's work. He has argued that even in science, the objectivity of the findings depends in some measure on the subjectivity of the interpreter. See Polanyi, *Personal Knowledge: Towards a Post-Critical Philosophy* (Chicago: University of Chicago Press, 1974), and *Knowing and Being*, ed. Marjorie Greene (Chicago: University of Chicago Press, 1969). Although somewhat less radical, Thomas Kuhn has argued that it is this factor alone that explains how scientific breakthroughs occur; see *The Structure of Scientific Revolutions*, 2d ed. (Chicago: University of Chicago Press, 1970). Just as there is an interpretive element in science, there is an objective element in biblical faith, and the interpretive element cannot substitute for or swing loose from the objective element.

9. This figure is derived from Gordon J. Melton, *A Directory of the Religious Bodies in the United States* (New York: Garland, 1977). See also his more recent *Bibliographical Dictionary of American Cult and Sect Leaders* (New York: Garland, 1986).

take our bearings, any ultimate source of knowledge, it is at the same time oozing with the supernatural. Secular society strips us of the possibility of having the truth of God, but it seems powerless to resist the astonishing plethora of religions that all are seeking their own market niche. The world, so recently emptied of the divine, is now awash with supernatural intrusions, with strange voices and mystical experiences of every conceivable kind, in everything from the more exotic varieties of the New Age movement to a revived interest in the horoscope columns in daily newspapers and widespread belief in such things as extrasensory perception and UFOs. That these developments are occurring simultaneously is eloquent testimony to the fact that the human spirit resists being neutered. If modernization has robbed our culture of the divine, it has in doing so also sown the seeds of longing for some inner sense of the supernatural and perhaps also for dramatic intrusions of the divine in healings or even the sort of primeval, supernatural savagery that has come to expression in some cults.

But while religious pluralism may be a novel experience for us, it is putting us in touch with the world that surrounded the biblical authors probably more directly than any other. The pluralism and the paganism of Our Time were the common experience of the prophets and apostles. In Mesopotamia, there were thousands of gods and goddesses, many of which were known to the Israelites — indeed, sometimes known too well. In Christ's time, there were hundreds of sects of one kind or another along the Mediterranean rim. Moreover, there was the official Roman religion that blended politics and religion through a deification of the Caesars, in due course becoming a formidable enemy to Christian faith. And there was Greek philosophy as well, much of it also functioning as a set of competing religions. Pluralism was the stuff of everyday life in biblical times.

Nothing, therefore, could be more remarkable than to hear the contention, even from those within the Church, that the existence of religious pluralism today makes belief in the uniqueness of Christianity quite impossible.[10] Had this been the necessary consequence of en-

---

10. The World Council of Churches, for example, issued excerpts from an ecumenical consultation held in Baar in 1990 that essentially abandoned Christian uniqueness. "Because we have seen and experienced goodness, truth, and holiness among followers of other paths and ways than that of Jesus Christ, we are forced to confront with total seriousness the question raised in the [WCC] Guidelines on Dialogue (1979) concerning the universal creative and redemptive activity of God towards all humankind and the particular redemptive activity of God in the history of Israel and in the person and work of Jesus Christ (para. 23). We find ourselves

countering a multitude of other religions, Moses, Isaiah, Jesus, and Paul would have given up biblical faith long before it became fashionable in Our Time to do so.

The transition, then, from the way in which the biblical authors thought about their world, with all of its religious pluralism, to how we should think about ours, with all of its competing religious claims, is shorter, less complex, and easier than it has been in centuries. Indeed, it involves no transition at all, despite our modernity, for religiously our world looks remarkably like theirs.

In order to think biblically about our world, we have to put ourselves in the minds of Jeremiah, Isaiah, Paul, and Peter and accept for ourselves the norms and habits by which they functioned. And their starting place was this category of truth. Truth to them was not privatized. It was not synonymous with personal insight, with private intuition. It was not sought in the self at all, as a matter of fact, but in history — the history that God wrote and interpreted — and it was therefore objective, public, and authoritative. Here lay the great divide between the pagans and the prophets: the pagans thought of truth in terms of private intuition, and the prophets did not. The same divide today separates moderns, for whom truth is a matter of private insight, from biblical Christianity, for which it cannot be.

The distinctiveness of Israel's way of thinking about God and his truth is probably lost on the modern Church, because most people are unaware of how this way of thinking contrasted with the ways in which pagan religion thought about the gods. I wish, therefore, to take a brief detour through the surrounding cultures before returning to Israel, because I think that our own religious proximity to these times makes it all the more important now to understand where Israel was so different.

The Pagan Mind

By the third millennium B.C., animism in the Near Eastern nations had given way to an elaborate polytheism that was also pantheistic. The

recognizing a need to move beyond a theology which confines salvation to the explicit personal commitment of Christ." The statement goes on to say that God works through Christ redemptively in all of history and through the other religions. (See the World Council of Churches' "Ecumenical Press Service," 90.09.22.) For an alternative view of the relation between Christianity and paganism in the post-biblical period, see Thomas Steven Molnar, *The Pagan Temptation* (Grand Rapids: William B. Eerdmans, 1987).

pagan mind did not distinguish between what was natural and what was supernatural; rather, it identified the one with the other, viewing the supernatural as coming to expression through the natural. The gods had divided the natural sphere among themselves and were revealed in its workings. The supernatural was therefore known by *experience* rather than by detached thought.

The pagan gods numbered in the thousands, but they were typically ordered hierarchically. In Mesopotamia, for example, Anu, the god of the sky, reigned at the apex with his chief executive, Enlil, the god of the storm. There was Euki, the god of the waters; Sin, the moon god; and Shamash, the sun god. Beneath them were whole ranks of gods and goddesses arranged in a kind of managerial structure, an ancient bureaucracy, each with specific areas of responsibility.[11] Enbilulu, for example, was the "canal inspector" who managed the Tigris and Euphrates, ensuring that they flowed freely and yielded up a harvest of fish.[12] The Hittites placed the sun god of Heaven and the sun goddess at the head of the divine structure and ranked beneath them numerous weather gods.[13]

Prior to the first millennium, these schemes of belief underwent some changes, and they varied in their details from tribe to tribe and place to place, but in time the overall picture became quite standard. It was, for the most part, an ordered relationship to the natural world, although conflicts sometimes broke out between the gods and goddesses over territorial prerogatives, and these deities were also capable of malignant actions against human beings for no other reason than that they felt malignant. The clouds could bring gentle rains to nourish crops or hail to destroy them; the sun could warm the soil or bake it dry; the earth could nurture life or bring it to ruin in the terror of an earthquake. Discerning why one experienced nature in one form rather than another was therefore a matter of no small importance. But how should one make this discernment?

To the pagan mind, many of the distinctions that used to be of the essence of Western thought and which, in fact, sprang originally from the Bible, were simply not operative. First, as we have noted, the pagan failed to make a distinction between the natural and the supernatural.

11. For a full discussion, see Thorkild Jacobsen, *The Treasures of Darkness: A History of Mesopotamian Religion* (New Haven: Yale University Press, 1976).

12. Mircea Eliade, *From Primitives to Zen: A Thematic Sourcebook in the History of Religions* (London: Collins, 1967), p. 21.

13. O. R. Gurney, *Some Aspects of Hittite Religion* (New York: Oxford University Press, 1977), p. 4.

To the pagan mind, nature was alive with divine presences, linked to them in rhythms that were cosmic and supernatural. The seasons of sowing and harvesting, the rhythms of spring, summer, fall, and winter, of the dying and regeneration of nature — all these were as much supernatural as natural. Mountains and rivers, deserts and farmlands all had their heavenly counterparts. In Mesopotamia, the Tigris River reflected the star Anunit; in Babylon, the city of Nineveh was the reflection of a divine prototype, the constellation of Ursa Major. All things terrestrial were the shadows of things celestial. By the same token, things terrestrial were alive with the powers of celestial beings. All the powers of nature — thunderstorm, lightning, drought, famine, earthquake — were personified, and the people saw themselves as inescapably a part of the pulsating rhythms of the cosmos. And if one were in contact with the gods and goddesses through these rhythms, then every act, as Mircea Eliade notes, whether "hunting, fishing, agriculture; games, conflict, sexuality — in some way participates in the sacred."[14] By the same token, since every act had divine significance, every act had the potential for alienating the gods, who might retaliate in some way.

Second, these ancient cultures failed to distinguish between objective and subjective reality (and, as part of that, between appearance and reality) — a distinction that is increasingly lost for modern Americans, too, as we shall see. They did not distinguish between perceptions of the world — its shape, color, and texture — and the world itself. The two were one. Their perception *was* the world; appearance *was* reality. Nor did they think that dreams had less reality than their senses. They believed the world was inhabited by divine presences, and they viewed dreams as a special means of access to this reality, a sort of experience that was quite as "real" as what their senses told them about the nature of things. They believed that they could hear the voices of the gods in their dreams in a way that they could not by viewing the natural world. This was as true for the Babylonians as it was for the Egyptians and the Greeks.

The power of these divinities was always experienced as immanent, however, and it was more sensed than known. Intuition and imagination, not to mention dreams, were considered far more potent as vehicles of knowledge than reason. These peoples "could reason logically, but they did not often care to do it. For the detachment which a purely intellectual attitude implies is hardly compatible with their most significant experi-

---

14. Eliade, *Cosmos and History: The Myth of the Eternal Return* (New York: Harper & Row, 1954), p. 28.

ence of reality."[15] When calamity struck, therefore, one's best ally was not understanding first of all but intuition and then, if circumstances warranted it, the men of magic who could discern which god was venting its divine displeasure and how it might be appeased.

Third, they did not distinguish between the living and the dead. The dead were thought to inhabit the same world as the living, to be as much a part of it as the living, to be present in it in the same way. This belief, too, is returning: a 1984 survey found that 27 percent of Americans claim to have spoken to the dead. The living and the dead, the natural and the supernatural were all part of a single reality. If the dead could communicate with the living, the living could affect the gods, and what was visible could be moved and changed by what was invisible.

Although this sketch is sparse and general, it is sufficient to establish six important points about the pagan mind, each of which has at least its echoes in the modern mind:

1. Insofar as they were known, the gods were known through *nature*. Pagans began with the experiences of nature and from this generated countless myths about the activities of the gods that explained why life had turned out the way it had or why it had yielded the experiences that it had.

2. Pagans proceeded from the basis of their *experience* to understand the supernatural. Apart from nature there was no other revelation, and apart from experience there was no other means of knowing the intent of the gods. The pagan mind did not search for truth so much as it looked for the meaning of experience.[16]

3. The supernatural realm was neither stable nor predictable. The gods inflicted calamity on the earth either because of the surfacing of some dark intent within themselves or because of the outbreak of rivalries and territorial disputes. It was the uncertainty over these intentions that produced the system of appeasement represented by pagan religious rites. These rites and sacrifices were a form of systematized, organized bribery designed to relieve the gods' anger or forestall further venting of their displeasure on the earth. Making sacrifices basically amounted to paying protection money. Assurance about the efficacy of these actions, however, was never guaranteed; only experience and hindsight could tell whether they had had the desired effect.

4. The pagan divinities were sexual, and this meant that their

15. Henri Frankfort, A. H. Frankfort, John A. Wilson, and Thorkild Jacobsen, *Before Philosophy* (Harmondsworth, U.K.: Penguin, 1967), p. 19.
16. Frankfort et al., *Before Philosophy*, p. 14.

religion had sexual overtones as well. Cult prostitution and an intense interest in fertility and reproduction (evident in child sacrifice and other rites) were common.[17] Sexual rites were accorded considerable celestial significance and were viewed as a means of identifying with nature's rhythms and placating the gods when disharmony broke out.

5. It is obvious that the pagan mind had no moral categories superseding the relativities of daily life. Pagans made no appeal to moral absolutes. They determined what was right experimentally. They understood the art of living to consist in bringing oneself into harmony with the rhythms of nature and the ways of the gods. The same sort of thing has been true of all pantheistic religions: the supreme norm is always the status quo, whatever that might be and however it might change, because nature, in all of its workings, is viewed as a reflection of the workings of a higher being or order of beings. Pagan religion sought to bring society into harmony not with moral absolutes but with the rhythms of life.

6. History had no real value for the pagans; their lives were centered in the experience of the moment. They sought in a variety of ways to cut their ties to the past and to focus instead on the future. They sought out predictable cycles of regeneration in emulation of the rhythms of nature, the annual passage through the seasons from autumnal death to springtime rebirth. And they found history especially irrelevant in their efforts to know the gods; here, too, experience was everything, for the activity of the gods in the past offered no reliable indications of how they might act in the future.

In contrast to this outlook, these habits of mind, what made the faith of Israel unique? It was not just that it was faith in Yahweh — and Yahweh alone — important though that obviously was. It was how Yahweh made himself known and how, in consequence, his people thought about the world. The saving revelation of God, unlike the intimations of the gods, came not in nature with its storms, misfortunes, and rejuvenations; it came not in human nature with its whisperings and intuitions; it came in *history*.[18] It came in a history

17. Eliade, *From Primitives to Zen*, p. 21.

18. In the depiction of the religious differences between Israel and its neighbors, I am especially indebted to G. Ernest Wright, *The Old Testament against Its Environment* (London: SCM Press, 1960). A huge amount of new material has come to light in the last thirty years, especially from the archaeologists, but Wright's main points remain intact. Though somewhat dated, there is also useful material in Norman H. Snaith's *The Distinctive Ideas of the Old Testament* (London: Epworth Press, 1950).

that was external, objective, known to Israel and its neighbors. Paul treated this history not simply as an interesting case study of how God works in the world but as the only message about God's working that we have (Acts 13:16-48). And later, when he stood before Agrippa and testified to his faith, he pointed to the culmination to these divine acts in the resurrection of Christ — a matter, he said, of which the king could not be ignorant, "because it was not done in a corner" (Acts 26:26). The resurrection of Christ had nothing to do with the religious imagination, nothing to do with parables of existence and symbols of inner experience; it had everything to do with an act of God that was public, external, and objective. And herein lies the crucial difference between the pagan and the biblical minds. For the latter, as G. Ernest Wright argued in an earlier attempt to resuscitate the importance of the biblical narrative, it is "the objectivity of God's historical acts which are the focus of attention"; for the former it is "the subjectivity of inner, emotional, diffuse and mystical experience."[19]

In consequence, because this history was Israel's alone, the biblical authors of both the Old and New Testaments did not believe that God was to be found in other faiths. In the Bible we find none of the tortured analyses of other religions that so engage many of the churchly today, still less the easy bonhomie with which those of other religions are welcomed as fellow travelers, and even less the common assumption that God is found within private experience that each individual must interpret for him or herself. And we miss the point entirely if we suppose that the reason for this is that the Hebrews of the Old Testament lacked the analytical skills to do these interfaith analyses,[20] because these skills had not yet been developed by the

19. Wright, *God Who Acts: Biblical Theology as Recital* (London: SCM Press, 1952), p. 55. Despite making some substantial gains, the biblical theology movement lacked staying power. For a few years, it did manage to raise concern about the disappearance of the Bible in the Church and countered this trend with an insistence on the importance of careful study of the Bible. But its Achilles' heel was its failure to see that the acts of God were not mute but interpreted acts: God who acted in history also acted in the prophets to express the meaning of his acts. This is to say that the definition of a divine act propounded by the biblical theology movement was too narrow. On the central concern of the movement, see James D. Smart, *The Strange Silence of the Bible in the Church: A Study in Hermeneutics* (Philadelphia: Westminster Press, 1970); on the demise of the movement, see Brevard S. Childs, *Biblical Theology in Crisis* (Philadelphia: Westminster Press, 1970); on the definition of what is historical, see Maurice Wiles, *Explorations in Theology* (London: SCM Press, 1979), pp. 53-65.

20. Wright, *The Old Testament Environment*, p. 22.

Greeks.[21] Even the authors of the New Testament, who presumably might have known better, since they came after the Greeks, nevertheless showed the same disinclination to think in this way. No, the answer is much simpler than that: the biblical authors wrote from the conviction of the uniqueness of biblical faith — a uniqueness that was not a matter of perception but of fact, not simply of their inner experience but of the objective facts of their history. The locus of its revelation was not in the human imagination but in history. It was this that protected the uniqueness of their faith, because it secured the objectivity of the revelation upon which that faith rested.

Pagan cultures encountered their gods and goddesses in nature. The gods were to nature what the soul is to the body: they animated it and gave it its awesomeness. The Hebrews encountered their God in history. Yahweh disclosed himself in actions that were prophetically interpreted and that marked the Israelites as a people covenantally distinguished as his own. They did not expect encounters with God in nature, as did the pagans. In fact, it may be the case that in the "nature" psalms, such as Psalm 8, we can hear a voice mocking the Egyptians and Mesopotamians for their confusion of the supernatural and natural. For the psalmist, nature reflects the greatness of God but it neither discloses his saving intentions nor mediates his direct presence. Yahweh's designs were defined by his acts in history as prophetically interpreted, not his acts in nature or his immanental presence in human nature.

The Biblical Mind

Within the limited scope of this chapter, it is not possible to develop a complete account of what a theology of the two testaments, built around this history, would look like, nor is it necessary to do so. What I have in view as singularly important if we are to begin the recovery of theology in the Church — its sine qua non — is not a particular belief. Nor is it initially any particular method for displaying these biblical materials around certain themes. It is something far more basic than that. It is our capacity to wrench ourselves free from the subjective preoccupation of our modernized culture (the same sort of liberation

21. The distinction between Hebrew and Greek ways of thought has been exaggerated. See James Barr, *The Semantics of Biblical Language* (London: Oxford University Press, 1961), pp. 9-20.

that converted pagans had to find in the early centuries of Christian life) and to occupy ourselves instead with the objective interests of the biblical. Without such a transformation, particular ways of thinking, or the methods by which they proceed, either fall to the ground and die for want of some receptive soil or they are reduced to being little more than illustrations of our own inner life. I intend, therefore, to sketch out in only the briefest, most elementary way what it is that we have in Scripture — and this only with an eye to seeing what kind of mental habits need to be cultivated if we are to enter into it and make its truth our own.

It goes without saying that the Bible has a narrative with a beginning and an end, a narrative that unfolds within history, the meaning of which God himself supplies.[22] Yet even a description so sparse and basic as this features a number of important elements: (1) the biblical narrative works itself out in *history;* (2) the meaning of the narrative resides in its events and yet must be supplied by *God;* and (3) the meaning of the biblical narrative cannot be fully known until it is completed, which is to say that *eschatology* is indispensable to its meaning. Each of these points has been vigorously disputed, and beneath each lies a nest of controverted issues and problems.[23] It is not possible for me to follow the many lines of discussion they have provoked; I simply want to trace the implications of each out a bit.

---

22. "Biblical theology," writes G. Ernest Wright, "is first and foremost a theology of recital, in which Biblical man confesses his faith by reciting the formative events of his history as the redemptive handiwork of God. The realism of the Bible consists in its close attention to the facts of history and of tradition because these facts are the facts of God" (*God Who Acts,* p. 38). In recent years this assertion has made its reappearance in narrative theology. Unfortunately, the emphasis has increasingly shifted from the narrative to the narrator, from the events of the story to the inner life of the storyteller, so that God's story and our own become increasingly blurred. Because stories can be evocative, there is probably validity to the criticism that narrative theology has its appeal in the current situation because it is able to carry on its business without having to confront the cognitive ambiguity that is now often associated with Christian truth. For accounts of the movement, see Lonnie D. Kliever, *The Shattered Spectrum: A Survey of Contemporary Theology* (Atlanta: John Knox Press, 1981), pp. 153-84.

23. The basic issues in debate are well reviewed in two volumes by Gerhard F. Hasel, *Old Testament Theology: Basic Issues* (Grand Rapids: William B. Eerdmans, 1975) and *New Testament Theology: Basic Issues* (Grand Rapids: William B. Eerdmans, 1977). On the narrower question of the relation between the Testaments, see D. L. Baker, *Two Testaments: One Bible* (Downers Grove, Ill.: InterVarsity Press, 1976). These discussions might helpfully be read in the much wider frame that is offered by Robert Morgan and John Barton in *Biblical Interpretation* (New York: Oxford University Press, 1989).

Unlike Israel's pagan neighbors, the biblical authors did not view history as terrifying, and unlike modernized Americans, they did not view it as worthless. To the contrary, they viewed it as the very arena of redemption. Their identity as a people rested on three great events in their past that revealed the intent of God for them: the call of Abraham, the deliverance from Egypt, and the establishment of the Davidic kingdom.[24] These events also provided the framework within which Paul made his justification for believing that Christ was God's final, culminating act in redemptive history (Acts 13:16-48).

It is clear that these events were viewed in this way throughout the Testaments. With reference to the first of them, we can begin by noting, for example, that God identifies himself as the God of "Abraham" or "the God of Abraham, the God of Isaac, and the God of Jacob" (Gen. 26:24; Exod. 3:6, 15-16; 4:5), thus linking the disclosure of his character and purposes to the history that was inaugurated with the patriarchs. Nor was this linkage a matter of merely passing importance; it was a matter of enduring truth. In his debate with the Sadducees, Jesus pointed to this relationship as evidence of the reality of resurrection. Resurrection was presupposed by the fact that God spoke of himself as still being the God of Abraham, Isaac, and Jacob (Matt. 22:32; Mark 12:26; Luke 20:37).

God's act of delivering his people at the Exodus was another event lodged forever in Jewish consciousness that exhibited the nature of God's saving purpose in the world. Repeatedly, after this time, the Hebrews are described as those who came up "out of Egypt" (Exod. 3:11; 13:9, 16; Num. 11:20; 22:11; 32:11; Deut. 16:6; Josh. 2:10; 5:6; Judg. 2:1; 1 Sam. 15:6; 1 Chron. 17:21; Hos. 11:1; cf. Matt. 2:15), and it was God's intent in confronting Pharaoh prior to the Exodus to reveal to him his purposes and power (Exod. 7:17; 8:16; 9:14). Only in their darkest moments did those who had been delivered forget to whom they belonged, sometimes even ascribing their freedom to the work of the pagan gods (Exod. 32:4; cf. Judg. 2:1-5; 6:8-10; 10:10-16;

24. See Francis Foulkes, *The Acts of God: A Study of the Basis of Typology in the Old Testament* (London: Tyndale Press, 1958), p. 14. Although brief, Foulkes's study is seminal in its treatment; I am indebted to his work and have summarized his argument in the pages that follow. It is the work of Gerhard von Rad in particular that has revived typological interpretation. See his summary essay, "Typological Interpretation of the Old Testament," in *Essays in Old Testament Interpretation*, ed. Claus Westermann (London: SCM Press, 1963), pp. 17-39. The major difficulty with von Rad's approach is his assumption that the acts of God were not presented in the context of a theology of their own and that this theology has had to be exposed in the Hexateuch by a rearrangement of its materials.

Ps. 78:11; Neh. 9:17). Indeed, it would be impossible to understand the later prophetic ministries of Isaiah, Jeremiah, Hosea, Amos, and Micah had the Exodus not occurred, because each saw it as the moment when the nation was born and the time when it had to assume the moral and spiritual responsibilities of being a delivered people. Each of their ministries might be summed up as calling the people of God to be Exodus people. We have here, then, not only the calling into being of Israel as God's people but also the disclosure of God's character and power in the very warp and woof of history. The Exodus was no religious symbol, no product of the religious imagination, and God's deliverance of his people was objectively wrought and not at all dependent for its realization on internal discernment.

It goes without saying that each of the acts of God, while being indisputably historical, also had to have its meaning divinely revealed. No doubt, from an Egyptian point of view, the Exodus, to take one example, was an awesome display of power — power that was not simply natural but also supernatural. The waters through which the Israelites passed had religious significance to the Egyptians, as did the frogs that had plagued the land, and hence the release of the Israelites had no small religious significance. Their God had asserted himself against the gods of the Egyptians. The Egyptians could not know, however, what meaning God attached to this most important of Old Testament events, nor how its significance would be played out prophetically in the life of his people, nor how it prefigured an even greater deliverance to come, nor how it was an exhibition of his greatness, grace, and mercy. That was something only God himself could reveal, and he revealed it over time to the prophets and then later to some of the New Testament authors. What lodged in Israel's mind was both the historical event and its meaning, which had been divinely given. And so when we come to the Psalms, for example, the Exodus inspires praise (Pss. 66; 106; 135), offers comfort in distress (77), teaches about the need for trust (78), gives encouragement to prayer (80), warns about disobedience (81), inspires thanksgiving (105; 136), and is the ground for awe (114). No Egyptian who witnessed the emancipation of the Jews would have stumbled upon such meanings naturally, no matter how sagacious that person was. The saving purposes of God are entirely hidden from all human scrutiny until he chooses to make them known as he did in this event through the Scripture.[25]

25. The pagans believed that their gods could act upon history and afflict people's lives directly, as Bertil Albrektson argues in *History and the Gods: An Essay*

It was Barth's desire to protect this truth, especially from the mischief that Liberal biblical scholarship had visited upon it, that led him to disengage God's saving history from the warp and woof of the events in which it was given. This did indeed secure these events from the intrusion of Liberal scholarship, but at some considerable cost, for in the end this robs truth of its objective grounding by removing the defining connections with the history in which it was given. More recently, Wolfhart Pannenberg has attempted to correct this imbalance by asserting the opposite extreme. He contends that God's revelation in history is "open to anyone with eyes to see" and that it can be read with the same "natural knowledge" with which all history is read.[26] He is right enough in asserting that the events of God's salvation history are indeed as discernible as any other events, but he is wrong in asserting that their meaning relative to the unfolding of God's purposes is evident in the events themselves. On that point, Barth was correct: the meaning must be given by God himself.

So it was that the Israelites were called to remember the stream of divine activity by which God called, shaped, owned, and protected his people. Each generation, "your children and to their children after them," was to be taught what God had done (Deut. 4:9; cf. Deut. 3:24; 1 Sam. 12:7; Ps. 103:7; 105:27; 145:4, 6, 12). Each generation was to be taught the meaning of the feasts, the memorials, and the law which drew out the moral significance of God's redemptive work. They were repeatedly counseled to know this history (e.g., Deut. 5:15; 7:18; 15:3; 25:17-19), because it was in this history that they would learn about the God who called them (Ps. 9:11; 66:5; 74:12; 77:11-12; 86:10; 96:3; 103:6; 105:1; 106:2). It was this history out of which the first creeds were distilled (Deut. 6:20-24; 26:5-9; Josh. 24:2-13), and it was never,

<hr>

on the Idea of Historical Events as Divine Manifestation in the Ancient Near East and in Israel (Lund: C. W. K. Gleerup, 1967), pp. 16-41. But there were significant differences between the actions of these gods and the actions of Yahweh. First, the interventions of these gods were always unpredictable, whereas those of Yahweh were always fundamentally redemptive. Second, though the pagan gods could act upon history, they remained a part of the cosmic system of nature; Yahweh remained outside of it. Third, the gods could be searched out in nature, but Yahweh could not be found by human industry; indeed, it was he who found his people. All of this clearly undercuts James Barr's argument that one of the points of similarity between pagan religions and biblical religion is the centering of revelation in history and through the acts of the divine. See Barr, Explorations in Theology IV: The Scope and Authority of the Bible (London, SCM Press, 1979), 14-24.

26. Pannenberg, in Revelation as History, ed. Wolfhart Pannenberg, trans. David Granskou and Edward Quinn (London: Sheed & Ward, 1969), p. 135.

therefore, simply a bare rendering of the facts. It was a rendering of their *meaning,* and it was in the conjunction of event and meaning that Israel's theology was forged, a theology that was to be laid to heart.

The Exodus was followed in time by the establishment of the monarchy. This was not a novel idea even within Israel, for shortly after the establishment in Palestine, Gideon was asked to rule over the tribes because of the threat posed by the Midianites (Judg. 8:22), and later, under threat from the Ammonites, Jephthah asked for such a position if he were to assume responsibility for defense. Indeed, the book of Judges ends by offering as an explanation for the persistent social chaos the fact that "in those days Israel had no king; everyone did as he saw fit" (Judg. 21:25). The Hebrews were to learn from bitter experience that kings provided no panaceas. And yet, when they viewed David as God taught them to view him (2 Sam. 15:1-37), they saw a king who came close to the ideal, despite his evident and serious sins. His dynasty, based on the covenant into which he had entered (Ps. 132:11-18), lasted as long as the southern kingdom and provided the historical framework through which God extended his rule beyond Israel's borders — in the end, into the far reaches of the world through Christ, who was seen as sitting upon David's throne. It was thus that the history upon which God's people built their understanding, the meaning of which was given to them by God himself, was projected into the future. Even yet, the full meaning of this history lies beyond the present moment.

Jesus began his ministry by announcing the arrival of this kingdom of God (Mark 1:15), yet it is clear that his understanding opens a new chapter in the history of this idea. Language about God's kingdom is scarce in the Apocrypha, in rabbinic literature, and even in the Dead Sea scrolls, but Jesus used the language in his discourses frequently. And in his teaching it takes on fresh meaning. No longer does it signify a geographical identity; rather, it signifies God's rule. The transition was made from place to people, and with that transition a new missionary mandate was given to the new people of God.

This is why, in Gospel references to the establishment of the kingdom, the initiative is always seen to lie with God: this is no ordinary political realm to be carved out by guile or force of arms. The kingdom is God's to give away. It is *his,* and in his gift of it, his majesty, grace, and glory are manifested (Luke 12:31; 23:51; Matt. 6:10). It is ours not to create but simply to accept by faith and with gratitude (Matt. 21:43; Luke 12:32). God builds it; we can never destroy it (Matt. 25:34; Luke 10:11). We can seek it, ask for it, and enter it, but it is his to give, for he has made it.

By the time we reach the Gospels, the reign of God narrows from its broader reaches in the Old Testament, where it is typically described as extending to the whole of creation. In the Gospels, God's kingdom has two foci — salvation and judgment. And the fact that it is Jesus who inaugurates it, thus doing the work that only God can do (God alone saves and judges), is an implicit argument for his divinity that should not be underestimated. It is by God alone that we can be saved from sin, death, and the devil; it is by God alone that we are judged. And the Gospels indicate that Christ undertakes both of these activities by way of establishing his kingdom. He saves and he judges. The first theme, salvation, is more commonly associated with his incarnation, and the second theme, judgment, with his return. It is thus that the promise to David is finally realized, thus that his greater Son comes to sit upon his throne forever. And so, as the gospel of his grace is spread, we immediately find Luke reporting that Cretans and Arabs spoke of "the wonders of God" (Acts 2:11).

In the Old Testament, Israel, by the acts and Word of God, was wrenched free of the pagan habit of thinking of life as endless cyclical repetition rather than movement toward a specific destination. Israel was taught to understand itself as having been caught up in the redemptive and revelational purposes of God, purposes that kept bursting through the seams of its collective national life in unexpected and sometimes unmanageable ways. While, from one angle, God regularized the life of his people, from another he regularly disconcerted them, for a number of his promises could be fulfilled only in a context larger than that of the nation to which he made them. Israel was always called to expand its perspective, to look beyond itself and its present to a future in which Christ would mount David's throne and enact a new Exodus, this time from sin and judgment. The New Testament epistles amply work out the ways in which Christ brought to its final realization the promises made long ago to Abraham.

The Jews had traditionally divided time into two ages — the age before the coming of Messiah, in which sin and death reigned, and the age that would follow his coming, when these scourges would cease. The early Christians were led to see that something far more complex was afoot, and it is one of the genuine gains of New Testament scholarship in the twentieth century that we have built this into the way we understand the apostolic mind at work.[27] Especially in the letters of Paul, but

---

27. See Oscar Cullmann, "The Connection of Primal Events and End Events with the New Testament Redemption History," in *The Old Testament and Christian Faith*, ed. Bernhard W. Anderson (New York: Harper & Row, 1963), pp. 115-23. Cullmann

evident throughout the other epistles as well, there appears the understanding that these two ages are running concurrently with each other,
the "age to come" now inaugurated and penetrating this "present age."
The domain of the Messiah, Christ's kingdom, is thus not an earthly
realm, for the beginning of his rule has already begun, but its completion
is yet to come. Only with its completion, at the return of Christ, will the
biblical promises made to God's people be fully realized. The culmination of Israel's life in the Old Testament is not an *earthly* future, therefore,
but an eternal future — something that is already suggested by the later
prophets, who saw the coming of a new Exodus from bondage not to the
Egyptians but to sin, death, and the devil.

We have, then, a salvation history, an interpreted narrative of God's
acts and redemptive purposes that is as unique as the God in whom it is
centered. It was unique in the ancient world, as we have seen, and it is
unique in ours. It begins with three main events — the call of Abraham,
the deliverance from Egypt, and the establishment of David's throne.
These events form the most important parts of the public framework
within which God and his work are understood in the Old Testament; in
the New Testament, the incarnation, death, resurrection, and return of
Christ bring each of these events to final fruition. It is in Christ that we
become Abraham's children, in Christ that we become God's children,
in Christ that we become God's subjects. It is because of Christ that
Abraham's children become as numerous as the stars above and these
children are finally able to enter the Promised Land, which is now
cleansed forever of all sin, suffering, and tears, and in which God's rule
is so established that it will never again be contested.

The resurrection of Christ, in which this redemptive history from
the Old Testament is completed and declared, also challenged every
other ancient religious worldview. For, as Pannenberg notes, after the
resurrection, the prevailing Greek habit of looking for "religion-in-
general" was directly challenged by the particularity of the truth claims
about Christ.[28] The early Christians did not preach their *experience* of

---

also developed this theme in *Christ and Time: The Primitive Christian Conception of Time
and History,* trans. Floyd V. Filson (Philadelphia: Westminster Press, 1950). The
general picture was, however, anticipated by Geerhardus Vos in *Pauline Eschatology*
(Grand Rapids: Baker Book House, 1979), pp. 1-41.

28. Pannenberg, "Focal Essay: The Revelation of God in Jesus of Nazareth,"
in *New Frontiers in Theology,* vol. 3: *Theology as History,* ed. James M. Robinson and
John B. Cobb (New York: Harper & Row, 1967), pp. 106-7. See his longer treatment
of the resurrection in *Jesus: God and Man,* trans. Lewis L. Wilkins and Duane A.
Priebe (Philadelphia: Westminster Press, 1968), pp. 88-114.

Christ; that would have been to promote a form of religion like any
other form of religion. Rather, they preached the Christ of that experience. They preached not what was internally interesting but what
was externally true. God had raised him from the dead, and this was
a matter of history, not simply of internal perception. The bells that
rang in celebration of God's conquest over sin, death, and the devil
also summoned every competing religious view into judgment. This
event invalidated every pretension to absoluteness in the ancient world
— as it does in the modern world.

The fact that God's truth was transmitted through events external
to the individual meant that it was objective, and the fact that it was
objective meant, further, that his truth was *public*.[29] It was truth for the
open market, truth for the nation, truth for other nations. The content
of this truth could not be privatized, reduced within private consciousness. Those who were trained by biblical revelation could not follow the
path of the pagans, who established faith on their experience of nature
and their intuitions regarding human nature. Their faith was grounded
solely in the objective and public nature of God's Word. They stood alone
among these ancient cultures, their faith distinctive and unique.

Furthermore, inasmuch as the meaning of God's redemptive acts
was not discovered by human insight and sagacity but was rather given
by God himself, that revelation was authoritative. The Church through
the ages has always assumed and respected the authority of Scripture. It
was never questioned until the modern period, and it has only become
a problem because some have suggested that God did not interpret —
perhaps could not interpret — the meaning of his acts or that the record
of the acts themselves is awry. Both of these assertions, however, are
typically made not on historical grounds but on philosophical grounds.
It is not the narrative of God's acts that makes it hard for us to believe in
the authority of their meaning; it is the modern world.

29. Only a source of truth that is both objective and transcendent can have
a relevance that is public in the sense that its assertions and claims have meaning
across the whole spectrum of life. It is this goal that David Tracy has pursued,
perhaps more tenaciously than any other contemporary theologian, but his project
is fatally flawed by his belief that his criteria for truth and falsehood can be found
within communities of discourse in society. In this post-modern context, where
meaning has contracted into the self, criteria for discerning truth from falsehood
become almost as numerous as the discerners. See Tracy, "Theology as Public
Discourse," *Christian Century*, 13 March 1975, pp. 280-84; and "The Role of Theology in Public Life," *Word and World* 4 (Summer 1984): 230-39. His fullest statement
is to be found in *The Analogical Imagination: Christian Theology and the Culture of
Pluralism* (New York: Crossroad, 1985).

The Modern Mind

It is the biblical world of meaning, its way of interpreting life, into which we are invited to enter, to make its world our own. We stand at its door, like Bunyan's Pilgrim before the Cross, the bundle of our self-understanding and of our self-interpreted world upon our back. This bundle, as with that of our sin, must be abandoned. If we are to enter this new world of meaning, we will have to do so hermeneutically naked, our modern horizons and tastes, our modern fascination with ourselves wrenched from us and abandoned on entry.[30] For we come to *take* from this new world, not to give. We come to take meaning; we come to give up the narrative of our own life with its parables of self-constructed meaning in order to find the truth that God has given in his own narrative.

And here, strangely enough, lies the watershed both of the ancient and the modern worlds. Where is the locus of God's truth to be found? To the pagan who heard the voice of the gods within, who listened to the whisperings of intuition, and to the modern who similarly listens within for the voice of self, the answer is the same. For the Israelite it was different. The Bible is not a remarkable illustration of what we have already heard within ourselves; it is a remarkable discovery of what we have not and cannot hear within ourselves. Thus, our inward sense of God and our intuitions about meaning are irrelevant in any effort to differentiate biblical truth from pagan belief. It is how we apply ourselves to learn what God has disclosed of himself in a realm outside ourselves that is important. And unless we steadfastly maintain this distinction in the face of the modern pressures to destroy it, we will soon find that we are using the Bible merely to corroborate the validity of what we have already found within our own religious consciousness — which is another way of saying that we are putting ourselves in place of the Bible. It is another way of reasserting the old paganism. When that happens, theology is irredeemably reduced to autobiography, and preaching degenerates into mere storytelling.

In many ways, then, we are witness to a convergence of the premodern and the modern worlds, as improbable as that might seem. On the surface, it may seem that the modern world with its speed and technology, its conquest over space and time, its abundance and convenience, grows daily more remote from the world of Elijah, Jeremiah,

---

30. See Vern Sheridan Poythress, "God's Lordship in Interpretation," *Westminster Theological Journal* 50 (Spring 1988): 27-64.

Jesus, and Paul. But in a deeper sense, as Western civilization passes into the late evening of its life and as the Christian values it has borne across the centuries fade into the shadows, alternative ways of thinking are emerging that parallel much of what occurred in the pre-modern world.

The bottom line for our modernized world is that there is no truth; the bottom line for Christian consciousness is precisely the opposite. The Christian predisposition to believe in the kind of truth that is objective and public and that reflects ultimate reality cuts across the grain of what modernity considers plausible.

A Christian mind sees truth as objective. It seeks to understand reality as it is in itself, not as it seems to the subject. The modern mind, no less than the pagan, finds this distinction at least difficult and probably impossible — because modernity admits of no exits, no escape from the darkness imposed by its diminished horizons of knowledge. That is not to say that there actually is no exit. Indeed, the exit is there to be found; it is simply difficult to do so in the dark. The Christian mind has sought and found a way to understand life in the light of revelation; the modern mind rejects that light and turns instead to private experience for illumination. The Christian mind accepts God's pronouncements concerning the meaning of life as the only true measure in that regard; the modern mind rejects such revelation as the figment of a religious imagination.

Today, reality is so privatized and relativized that truth is often understood only in terms of what it means to each person. A pragmatic culture will see *truth* as whatever works for any given person. Such a culture will interpret the statement that Christianity is true to mean simply that Christianity is one way of life that has worked for someone, but that would not be to say that any other way of life might not work just as well for someone else.

If Elijah on Mount Carmel, or any of the prophets in their encounters with other gods and religions, or Jesus in the Gospels, or Paul at the Areopagus functioned with a concept of truth as relativized as this, we would have a very different Bible indeed! The reason that they believed in truth in a way that we frequently do not had nothing to do with their parochialism and our relative sophistication but with their understanding of its objectivity and our loss of that understanding. They believed that the truth about God had been given in a history that was external to the interpreter and could not be changed; we believe that such truth is frequently given only in the self, if it is given at all, and that its content does change. We believe that it varies from person to person, time to time, and culture to culture just as consciousness varies from person to person, time to time, and culture to culture. The pagan religions, over against which that of Israel was established, denied the distinction between what was objective and what was subjective, and so, too, does the modernized mind. The prophets had to point again and again to the history in which God had disclosed himself as the antidote to the pagan habit of looking for divine meaning in nature and the intimations of human nature. The prophetic interpretation of the meaning of God was an interpretation not of their experience but of the nation's *history*. They were interpreting the external acts of God in a history that was objective, by a Word that was divinely given and was not a result of their own sagacity or personal insight. And we need that same objectivity if we are to find again a fully active Christian mind today. It is this history, which can neither be changed nor obliterated, that anchors God's truth in a realm that is always outside our own private perceptions. It is this that strikes down the habit of thinking that truth is simply what is true *to us*. It contradicts all that is fundamental to the modernized mind.

The contraction of reality into the self, whether in its Liberal or evangelical versions, introduces nothing more or less than the reordering of reality by our modernized world, and the first casualty of this reordering, with respect to the mind, is the belief that truth is something that should be found outside of our own subjective consciousness. It is simply incontrovertible that the disappearance of a belief in truth of this order destroys both the soil in which any theology must grow and the criterion by which it must be judged. Without this criterion, "theology" becomes autobiography, and, no matter how revealing it is of the person who "shares" it, it can have no public significance.

It is precisely because Christian faith presents itself as objectively true that it has always exalted teaching. If there is a religion in the world that "exalts the teaching office," James Orr said, "it is safe to say that it is the religion of Jesus Christ." He went on to note that the doctrinal element, the substance of what could be taught, was conspicuous by its absence in paganism, whereas, by contrast, one of the distinguishing characteristics of the New Testament is the fact that it is "full of doctrine." The New Testament "comes to men with definite, positive teaching; it claims to be the truth; it bases religion on knowledge. . . . A religion based on mere feeling is the vaguest, most unreliable, most unstable of all things. A strong, stable, religious life can be built on no other ground than that of intelligent conviction."[31]

31. Orr, *The Christian View of God and His World as Centering in the Incarnation* (New York: Scribner's, 1897), p. 20.

Intelligent conviction requires for its underpinning and, indeed, its explanation, a truth that is objectively true. Unless truth is objective, it cannot be declared to others, cannot be taught to others, cannot be required of others. Wherever biblical religion has been recovered, the recovery of the teaching office is never far behind. Nor is the kind of biblical preaching the life and force of which is the truth of Scripture. And wherever this preaching takes root, there the desire to know and practice God's truth begins to blossom. And this is the soil, the only soil, in which theology can grow.

CHAPTER VIII

The Reform of Evangelicalism

Let us act with humility, cast ourselves at one another's feet, join hands with each other, and help one another. For here we battle not against pope or emperor, but against the devil, and do you imagine that he is asleep?

Martin Luther

And Thou, O most merciful Father, we beseech Thee for Thy mercy's sake, continue Thy grace and favour toward us: let the sun of Thy gospel never go down out of our hearts; let Thy truth abide, and be established among us forever. . . . Apparel us thoroughly in Christ, that he may live in us, and so Thy name may be glorified in the sight of all the world. Amen.

John Jewel

THERE IS A CURIOUS TALE, now almost forgotten, about a garden in Chelsea, London. This garden was originally laid out in the seventeenth century, and it was here that cotton seed was later grown that was sent to Georgia, then a debtor's colony. That was in 1732. In 1793, Georgia also produced the cotton gin, a device that in a matter of years made cotton growing an enormously successful enterprise throughout much of the American South.

During the Civil War, however, the South was blockaded, with devastating consequences for England, for in the years since that seed had first been sent to Georgia, about one fifth of the English had come to depend on the importation of American cotton for their livelihood. The consequences of the Northern blockade were so serious that important politicians began to urge British intervention in the War on the side of the Confederate army. That never happened, of course, but it was not because the stakes were low. By sending this cotton to America, England almost brought about its own undoing. By losing control over it and becoming so dependent upon it, England became a victim of its original provision.

This curious little tale is not unlike the one that can be told about the modern world, for this world is now putting in jeopardy the faith that, in so many ways, lies at its foundations. The twin sources of the modern world — capitalism and technology — both arose in immediate connection with Reformation faith. Capitalism has mightily reshaped our world, encouraging and facilitating the redistribution of the population from rural areas to the cities and, at the same time, fanning the need for freedom. And the assumptions of Reformation faith provided the sort of platform on which science could build — belief in the objectivity of the world and the regularity of its working. The first came from the Christian doctrine of creation and the second from the doctrine of providence. Further, Reformation faith, with its doctrines of calling and common grace, gave to this work an importance it had lacked under Catholicism. Science began to flourish, and in due time the technology with which we are now so familiar emerged and became the lifeblood of modernization. Moreover, this whole enterprise was accorded legitimacy by the theistic framework in which it was undertaken, even by the likes of Jefferson, whose beliefs in the nature and works of God were somewhat unorthodox.

In our day, this framework has been eaten away by secularism, and the fruits of this enterprise that in time grew from the Reformation period — capitalism, urbanization, technology, the mass media — have become surrogates for God by providing a total context in which life is lived and from which God himself is typically excluded. Thus it is that Christian faith now finds itself marginalized in the world it indirectly helped to bring forth. Furthermore, in its evangelical expression, this faith has now become perilously dependent on the modern world in which its faith no longer has a comfortable place.

This strange reversal of fortune is putting an entirely new twist on the ways in which we must now think about belief and unbelief. In fact, this new angle has provided the conceptual framework for this book. I know I have more assumed than explained this framework in these pages; my intent has simply been to supply some analysis and critique of the modern world and to suggest some of the ways in which its values and habits have intruded on the evangelical world. It is my plan to devote a second volume to further explanation of the conceptual framework and to the development of some constructive responses to the situation I have described in this book. In this concluding chapter, I would like to anticipate briefly some of the terrain I hope to cover in the next volume.

Whatever else might be said about Paul Tillich's theology, he was undoubtedly correct in thinking that every person has objects and interests that are for them matters of "ultimate concern." They are the focus of our need to transcend ourselves and they are the means of doing so. They are surrogates for God. And the modern world has become, for so many, a matter of ultimacy. All moderns are, in this sense, believers. Their world gives them their values and horizons, their life and sustenance, and they look for nothing outside of or beyond what modernity provides. They live by it, and in the end they die by it. This book, by contrast, has been written from the perspective of an unrepentant unbeliever. That is to say, I do not believe in much that is present because I believe too much in what is now thought not to be present. I disbelieve in the modern world because I believe in God, in his truth, and in his Christ.

The question, then, is not whether people believe or not. The only question to be settled is *what* they believe in. Those who are secular believe exclusively in modernity. I do not believe in modernity at all. Most evangelicals, however, are mild, closet believers, and to the extent that this is true, their internal life will tend to tilt away from belief in God and his truth and toward modernity. This, of course, portends certain disaster unless it is the case, as most evangelicals seem to assume, that modern culture is neutral in its values and so does not pose the threat of alienating people from God.

In the preceding chapters I have tried to document the evangelical bias toward modernity; in the book that follows I will turn to the means by which this drift toward modernity might be reversed. Here I would like to sketch some outlines of that argument briefly. I will proceed (1) by exploring a little further what belief and unbelief now mean, (2) by considering why contemporary belief in modernity has led to the manipulation of God, and (3) by suggesting how the recovery of God would actually provide freedom from the modernity that has captured much of the evangelical Church.

Believers and Unbelievers

There is, to be sure, a notoriety that goes with proclaiming oneself to be an unbeliever. As a matter of fact, it is almost impossible to be considered a serious thinker in the modern world without passing through a ritual of disaffection with belief. Why is this so? The answer seems to lie, at least partly, in our belief in progress. As we look to the past, even the most recent past, we express our deep disenchantment with it because in doing so we imagine that we are disengaging ourselves from the infancy that is behind us; as we look to the future, we express our disaffection with life as it is because we imagine that it is only by dispensing with its terms and conditions that we will be enabled to plunge deeper into reality. The moment the bubble of progress pops, however, the emptiness of all of this professed disillusionment becomes apparent. There is no infancy out of which we are growing, no maturity toward which we are moving; our attempts to disengage ourselves from the one and to prepare for the other are exercises in futility. Perhaps ever worse than that, these efforts simply reflect the modernity from which we are ostensibly trying to escape, thereby calling the seriousness of the whole into question. So it is that the spirit that parades as unbelief in the modern world in the end turns out to be belief in the modern world.

As I suggested earlier, this strange situation in which belief in modernity hides behind professions of disbelief has come about by the odd ambiguity of the very different phenomenon that we are describing with the word *modern*. If by this term we are thinking about the intellectual developments that began with the Enlightenment, then there is a compelling case for saying that the modern world has now died. Perhaps as early as Nietzsche at the turn of the twentieth century, and certainly by the 1960s, it had become overwhelmingly clear that the Enlightenment project had run out of capital. It had made extravagant promises about life, liberty, and happiness, but in the modern world it had become increasingly difficult to see where those promises were being realized. Thinker after thinker, field after field began to revile the dogmas and results of Enlightenment thinking. Only a very few of these critics turned to Christian belief as an alternative to the failed Enlightenment project, however; most turned instead to what is essentially an Enlightenment landscape stripped of all of its promises, all of its hope, left standing in bleak emptiness. And in Our Time, that world, now characterized as post-modern, has also died.

On the other hand, if by *modern* we mean the shaping of our social environment around cities for the purposes of commerce, the whole linked together by technology and the mass media, then we are now experiencing the high noon of modernity. Because we are living in the nexus of these two meanings of *modern*, Our Time has developed many peculiarities. Since our intellectual world has died, modern life is being defined more by its social processes and cultural environment and less by any ideology. Our increasingly feeble ideas have largely lost the power to shape life; that role has fallen to the impersonal forces of enormous power unleashed by the workings of the modern world. The assertion that disillusionment with the present marks some sort of crest in the next wave of human development is a quaint conceit. It merely marks the recognition that the modern world has died intellectually. And faith in the forward movement of the human spirit is mere illusion. The human spirit is now being moved not by profound thinking but by the experience of living in a metropolis presided over by bureaucracy, tranquilized by television, and awash with the racket of clashing cultures.

It is not because I am world-weary that I believe so little. It is not because I am unaware of the innumerable benefits of the modern world that I reject belief in it. The benefits of modern life are undeniable, and I freely admit to having enjoyed, in measure, its many advantages. It is the deceptions of modernity that I reject.

To speak of deception in this way may seem harsh. It appears to personalize the world and then to imply some sort of conspiracy theory, to suggest that the modern world has cunningly connived to put one over on the unthinking recipients of its bounty. If modernity had at its center this sort of dark human intelligence, it might actually be easier to deal with. But the truth is that the whole system of modern life envelops those who live by it and infuses into them its values in a manner that is entirely impersonal.

Modern experience has the capacity to shape the inner terrain of our lives because it engages us in ways that are intense and unremitting. The interludes of time and space by which the citizens of Wenham lived gave them some sanctuary from the world, but these are now largely gone. The islands of solitude have long since been submerged in the noise, urgency, and clamor of the modern world. We now experience directly the tidal surge of too much information, too many responsibilities, too much change, too many choices, and too many situations over which control has now slipped from our hands almost entirely, all the way from the coldness of the workplace to the pain of broken families. This turbulent surf crashes unremittingly into psyches too small and too fragile to withstand it.

It is in this frantic context, where modernity makes more demands on the self than the self can possibly respond to, that the deceptions are generated. The intensity of the internal experience that constitutes the essence of modernity dazes and distracts us to the point that we are willing to accept it as the true reality. It is here, dazzled by the flash of the new, that the modern individual begins to dismiss even the recent past as valueless, here that the modern soul begins to imagine that it can transcend itself, here that God, who remains outside of modern experience, begins to seem increasingly remote from the urgency of internal experience and hence irrelevant to what is most important in life.

The citizens of Our Time actually believe so little in God because they believe so much in what is modern. I believe so little in the modern world because I believe so much in the Transcendent, in God as sovereign, and in his Word as absolute. I believe in his power to actualize his truth in human life, even in modern human life. I believe in his saving intrusions into this world, in the objective validity of his saving acts in the flesh and bone of our history, in his unbroken control over our destiny, in his power to raise up and to put down civilizations including the world cliche culture that is currently in the making, and I believe in the ultimate collapse of evil in the final unfolding of his purposes. I believe all of these things, and I therefore reject belief in so many of the things to which those who are modern give their solemn assent. This may sound a little like Karl Barth, but in a world now filled with Liberals, sounding a little like Barth has become both a necessity and a virtue.

There is, in fact, a paradox at work here: those who imagine themselves to be on safe terms with modernity are frequently its most servile captives, but those who dissent from it, those who are often the most deeply troubled by it, are those who experience the most freedom from it. This paradox lies at the heart of this book. Evangelicals now stand among those who are on easiest terms with the modern world, for they have lost their capacity for dissent. The recovery of dissent is what is most needed, and the path to its recovery is the reformation of the Church. The requisite dissent arises out of the vision of God in his otherness, and this vision has now largely faded, a fact most obviously evidenced by the disappearance of theology in the evangelical Church.

The Use of God

When Langmead Casserley charged, four decades ago, that modern theology was one of the major causes of unbelief in our world, he could have been speaking for a considerable number of evangelicals, too. First the pietists, then the apostles of relational theology, then the celebrators of self (e.g., Robert Schuller), and now the charismatics — all these have taken turns disparaging this ancient art and accusing it of irrelevance, perhaps of causing harm, and sometimes of producing unbelief. And many of the advocates of church-growth theory assume, as if it were a matter so self-evident as to be beyond discussion, that a church had better not let its theological slip show if it wants to grow. As a matter of fact, its chances for growth might well be enhanced if it has no slip at all.

But there is a difference. Casserley, speaking as a Liberal, mourned what he referred to as theology's "ineptitude" in having squandered its brilliance on a preoccupation with the Bible during the post-Reformation period. He pleaded for a fresh direction in theology that would allow it to recover the philosophical luster it had shown in the patristic and medieval periods. The chorus of evangelical voices that seem to be reiterating his point are in fact doing so from the other side of the theological divide. They are calling for something quite different. They do not merely dismiss modern theology because of its unbelief; they dismiss all theology because of its uselessness. They are not interested in a recovery of any sort. They view theological profundity as an oddity, something irrelevant to the health and well-being of the Church today. Some are even more explicit, asserting that Christianity will become attractive in the world today only to the extent that it is emptied of all theology.

On the face of it, it would seem that two entirely different mindsets must be giving rise to these critiques. From the one comes a critique of the practice of theology; from the other, a rejection of the idea of theology. One wants a better theology; the other seems to want no theology at all.

But appearances are deceiving. In this case, it becomes obvious almost immediately that not all within the evangelical world who express their disaffection with theology are disaffected with *all* theology. They are often unhappy solely with classical evangelical theology, and, whatever their rhetoric, they are really interested in a *different* theology. They want to arrange the three components of any theology — confession, reflection, and wisdom — in a different configuration, typically diminishing the function of the first, eliminating the presence of the second, and transforming the third into uniquely contemporary forms. They want a configuration in which rational knowledge plays a smaller part, in which the sharpness of theological distinctives are softened, and in which any cognitive elements are strained through the sieve of what appears to be "practical," so that what is felt becomes as important as what is known or believed. Theology reconfigured on this model is typically therapeutic: it suggests that Christian faith is mostly about offering wholeness (certainly in spirit and perhaps in body), it suggests that relationships are as important as truth in realizing this wholeness, and it is centered on personal happiness quite as much as righteous-ness. Its advocates want a different look for traditional evangelical faith, but they also want that look to find its place within an ever-widening evangelical firmament.

My point, then, is that even though it may initially appear as if some segments of the evangelical world have set themselves against classical evangelicalism because they are anti-theological, this is not actually the case. The important contrast lies not so much between those who define themselves theologically and those who do not but between two different theologies by which people are defining them-selves. Those who voice dissent with classical evangelicalism at this point do so not because they have *no* theology but because they have a *different* theology. Their theology is centered on a God who is on easy terms with modernity, who is quick to endorse all of the modern evangelical theories about how to grow one's church and how to become a psychologically whole person.

We can only guess how well the apostle Paul might have fared had he sought pastoral employment among evangelicals today, but we would not be risking much to suppose that he would start out with a few strikes against him. Happily, there would be a constituency deeply appreciative of his teaching and service. But he would not be without his critics. Indeed, they might very well be numerous. Some churches would doubtless be delighted that he was willing to support himself and leave more of the church budget for other matters, but the more professionalized congregations would probably be embarrassed by this. Who, they might ask themselves, really wants a cut-rate pastor? Few would warm to his personality, and that would be no small matter. Today, most pastors stand or fall today by their personalities rather than their character. Many would be agitated about his insistence on discipline in the church. Many would be offended by his refusal to grant the legitimacy of each person's private views so long as they were held sincerely. His insistence that truth is given objectively in Christ, not subjectively through private intuition as the pagans thought, would make him sound strangely out of touch. Indeed, his preaching, judged by contemporary standards, would be considered by many a failure because the brief summaries that we have of what he did show no penchant for telling stories at all. Besides, Paul was apparently in the habit of extending his discourses long beyond the twenty minutes to which many churches would limit him. He would probably end up provoking a churchly insurrection — for all the wrong reasons. Few would be able to make much sense of his concern with the connections between New Testament faith and Old Testament promises, because the Old Testament is *terra incognita* in the Church today. His passionately theological mind would get him into trouble on two counts: his preaching would be judged hopelessly irrelevant because its theological focus would put it out of step with modern habits, and his passion would simply prove embarrassing. His vision of God's purposes in the world, one supposes, would probably seem interesting but, in the small world of church life, not really compelling. And so the difficulties would mount. Paul would probably be condemned to flit from place to place, not out of choice but necessity, never finding secure lodging anywhere, his résumé fatally scarred by his many pastoral failures until, abandoned and worn out, he would be left to pass his closing days in a home for the aged.

The contemporary disaffection with classical evangelicalism, not to mention the theology of the Bible, has many expressions and many emphases, not all of which are in agreement with each other, but there can be little question that the shifting of the sands that is under way is of major importance. If it is the case that the intrusion of modernity is so eroding the soil of Christian thinking that the seeds of biblical truth are unable to germinate within it, then we have surely found a cause large enough to explain not only the changing topography of evangelical faith but also the reduction in the capacity of evangelicals to think theologically. This intrusion has been difficult for evangelicals to detect because they tend to consider it quite compatible with the truth of God; indeed, it is frequently identified with the entrée of God himself through the outpouring of his Spirit on Our Time.

This, it has seemed to me, is why theology is dying in the Church. The principal cause is not that we have depleted our store of good methods for constructing theology (although they may be in short supply); the problem is that, without a vision of God as Other, different from and standing over against the modern world, there is no compelling reason to think thoughts about the world that are not essentially modern. In fact, there is no reason to think at all, let alone to think as Christians ought.

Without an audience of those who know the God who stands

outside of the flow of modernity, theology dies as surely as art dies in the absence of art lovers. And the Church should be this audience. It is true that theology has deep and necessary roots in the academy, but its fundamental connection is with the Church. The question, therefore, is whether the Church has a mind for theology. Without this mind, theology cannot take root where by nature and purpose it must take root. There can be no theology worthy of that name that is not a theology *for the Church,* a theology in which the Church actively participates, in which it understands itself to be theology's primary auditor. The Church is the place where biblical knowledge must be learned, developed, and applied. The Church is the context in which God and his Word should receive their most serious thought. This is not to say that theology should not seek to address the academy or the culture. It should. But in the contemporary context, it can do no more than address the academy and the culture from within the academy, because it has been dislodged from its primary location within the Church itself.

Why is this so important? Why should theology not be content simply to think its deep thoughts alone in the learned guild, doing its work only among the scholars? The answer, quite simply, is that the learned guild cannot properly serve as the primary auditor for theology, the wider culture finds it incomprehensible, and theology developed apart from the Church rapidly loses its character. A theology oblivious to the Church as the people of God soon loses a sense of wonder because it is cut off from worship, and it soon loses productive connections to the world because it is not driven by a commitment to service. It will lose its life and character. And, conversely, without theology there can be no Church, because theology holds the key to Christian identity, to Christian continuity, to genuine piety, to serious worship, and to the sort of Christian thought that seeks to bring the import of God's Word into our world.

This should trouble those who have settled down so comfortably with a diminished sense of theology, who do not see through the paper-thin piety that so often passes for godliness today, the empty and childish stories that are served up as sermons from the pulpit week by week in too many evangelical churches, the casual choral singing that masquerades as deep worship in too many services, as if celebrating good feelings were the same thing as rendering to God his due in wonder, love, and adoration. The truth is, though, that where we have emptied ourselves of theology, we have emptied ourselves of Christian seriousness in preaching, worship, piety, thought, and service. Is reform possible in such diminished environs? Is it possible to recover the full-orbed theology of classical Protestantism, in which confession fueled reflection, and confession and reflection combined to produce a wisdom by which God's truth was lived out in the world? Is it any longer possible to reconnect practice to confession and reflection to both? Can the older habits of classical theology be relearned and the habits of the newer theology unlearned? On the face of it, the prospects are bleak.

The internal transformation of evangelical faith which I have attempted to describe in this book is thoroughly in keeping with the cultural transformation of the world by modernization in the present century. Indeed, I have argued that larger cultural changes are principally responsible for the transformation of evangelical theology. The classical orthodoxy from which the new evangelicalism is emerging is no longer at home in contemporary Western culture. And modern culture lends considerable plausibility to the newer evangelicalism even as it denies plausibility to the older orthodoxy. Reform of contemporary evangelicalism will inevitably be opposed by the many vested interests that have become entrenched in the evangelical world and that resonate with the culture. Such people will view reform as unnervingly radical because it would fly in the face of so many of their cultural assumptions. We might be able to get a better sense of the sort of dissonance that would be created by the proposed reform if we look at the matter from another angle.

The vast growth in evangelically minded people in the 1960s, 1970s, and 1980s should by now have revolutionized American culture. With a third of American adults now claiming to have experienced spiritual rebirth, a powerful countercurrent of morality growing out of a powerful and alternative worldview should have been unleashed in factories, offices, and board rooms, in the media, universities, and professions, from one end of the country to the other. The results should by now be unmistakable. Secular values should be reeling, and those who are their proponents should be very troubled. But as it turns out, all of this swelling of the evangelical ranks has passed unnoticed in the culture. It has simply been absorbed and tamed. Aside from Jerry Falwell's aborted attempt from the political Right in the 1980s to roll back the earlier victories scored by the Left, especially during the 1960s, the presence of evangelicals in American culture has barely caused a ripple.

This surely is an odd circumstance. Here is a corner of the religious world that has learned from the social scientists how to grow itself, that is sprouting huge megachurches that look like shopping malls for the religious, that can count in its own society the moneyed and powerful, and yet it causes not so much as a ripple. And its disappearance, judged in moral and spiritual terms, is happening at the very moment when American culture is more vulnerable to the uprooting of some of its cherished Enlightenment beliefs than ever before, because it knows itself to be empty. Thus it is that both American culture and American evangelicalism have come to share the same fate, both basking in the same stunning, outward success while stricken by a painful vacuity, an emptiness in their respective centers. This has produced, in the one, a civilization that has deliberately built itself without religious foundations and imagines God and the supernatural order alike to be irrelevant. In the other it has produced a way of Church life in which God's truth, if one is to judge by the sermons being preached, the books being published, and the journals being blessed by success, seems often to be a stranger to its inner life. As a result, in the one there are no moral absolutes, and in the other there is no theology. This coincidence of spiritual interests will make reform exceedingly difficult.

This is the reason that the word *evangelical* has, by default, been allowed to degenerate into little more than a slogan. Eviscerated of the interests of the older theology, it has lost much of its meaning — although it must be granted that in the contemporary context of modernity, there is a certain convenience to that. The part of the evangelical constituency that has set itself against its past, turning to health or success for emancipation from the classical interest in truth, soon discovers that it has become powerless to offer a vision for the Church or to excite that passion for truth which alone sustains Christian practice in the world. Without this passion, Christian practice does not assert itself against the fallen values of modernity. Without this passion, a moral truce, in effect, is established between Christ and culture. And once the truce is in effect, the word *evangelical* becomes empty.

At the same time this disengagement with the culture occurs, the Church turns in on itself, for once it is without theology, once it is without a center in God's truth, the Church has neither the means nor the desire to look beyond itself. Without this theology, the Church's agenda shrinks to the borders of its own interests. Without this theology, its criterion for success is simply its own success. And where this happens, the same forces of alienation that separate self-absorbed individuals from one another in the culture begin to separate self-absorbed churches from each other in the Christian world. More than that, this self-absorption also separates them from God's larger purposes in the world. Without theology, worshipers have no reason to look beyond themselves, no reason to look out into the world beyond their shores, or even within them, for those who have not yet heard the gospel — except, of course, as they are motivated to produce the sort of church growth that is equated with success. In the absence of theology, the life of the Church becomes hollow, yet this hollowness is so little different from that of modern life that it seems almost normal. And in this wilderness, voices crying about a loss of spiritual integrity are easily not heard.

Here, too, a belief in progress obscures the real nature of things. This belief enables people to suppose that the sort of success that science and technology have delivered in the external world can similarly be had in the inner, spiritual world, that just as the use of technique promises to subdue every external enemy, so a use of technique can subdue all internal enemies. Boredom, unhappiness, the loss of meaning, failed relationships — we can overcome them all simply by discovering a hidden potential within. The promise is that people can become happier, more whole, more actualized, more complete, more fulfilled, and that they will have more of everything they need to be fully satisfied within. But this naive assumption clearly parts company with any sense about the deadly invincibility of evil outside of Christ. We should not be surprised to find such wishful thinking in the secular self movement, but among evangelicals? Nevertheless, the only difference between the secular and evangelical manifestations of the movement is that the former employs a nakedly human technique while the latter employs a technique infused with religious rhetoric.

It may be that evangelicals will never recognize their pious self-absorption for the cultural thing that it is because conformity is a powerful force in the evangelical world, and it quickly stifles lone dissenters. Nevertheless, reality will take its toll. The publicized exodus of various evangelicals into the Roman Catholic and Greek Orthodox churches in recent years is simply a notable symptom of widespread disquiet in the evangelical world. Many ordinary believers are disillusioned with their churches, with their ministers, and with the larger evangelical empire, which has failed in the business of making known the character, acts, will, and purposes of God in the larger society and in embodying these in the kind of service that has the ring of spiritual authenticity about it.

The evangelical world has lost its radicalism through a long process of accommodation to modernity. Tragically, it has lost its traditional understanding of the centrality and sufficiency of God. In its long process or reorganization, it has turned from dependence on God to management of God — which, in this inward-looking and self-confident world has meant domination of God. All too often evangelicals have come to view modernity as value-neutral. They have coopted the techniques that have made the modern world flourish and put them to work in the evangelical world in hopes of making it flourish, too. To the extent that they have thus attempted to manage God, we can be sure that they have been alienated from him. God has never been managed and tamed, either by unbelievers or by believers. God is always angular and will not be made smooth. He is always sovereign over the Church and will not be subject to it or manipulated by it. His apparent smoothness in the evangelical world is the surest sign that it is not his truth that in its purity is driving evangelicalism.

The Recovery of God

God has not been lost, of course, and it is not in this sense that we might think about the need for his recovery. The problem is that all too often he has been lost *to us,* because his truth, which is objective in character, is often lost on us. It does not fit within the modern psyche at all, and it rests uneasily in the modern evangelical psyche.

At moments like this, the customary response to the sense of Christian inadequacy, whether in relation to God or some aspect of the Christian message, has been to call for revival. In the modern period, though, revival has frequently entailed little more than proceeding with business as usual and praying that God will spice it up with some new enthusiasm and effectiveness. This is the legacy of the Finneyite conception of revival as something that can be engineered by the Church with the proper techniques. Working from such assumptions, the Church will almost certainly be inclined to think of its own rejuvenation as self-engineered. But this is simply to apply modernity's solution to a problem that modernity has caused, and that is a dead end. The impotence of the evangelical Church does not stem from inadequate technique or diminished enthusiasm. Where enthusiasm has waned, the malaise is but a symptom of a far deeper and more troubling problem — a problem that is not going to be solved by the Church's efforts at self-regeneration, however fine the religious language in which they are cloaked. What the Church now needs is not revival but reformation.

There are many windows through which we might gain entry to the issues we have been considering in these pages. Why is it that theology is now alienated from the life of the Church? From one angle, the answer is that this is the outgrowth of modern fragmentation in which theology's constituent elements — confession, reflection, and wisdom — have been broken asunder and are now disengaged from one another. From another angle, it can be argued that the displacement of theology is to be explained by the way in which the American character acts upon it, producing on the one hand the current self-absorption of the evangelical world and, on the other, an equally powerful need to conform, a need that is sometimes realized through adaptations to modernity. Then again, the way in which both learning in the academy and pastoring in the Church have become professionalized go a long way toward explaining why theology is no longer granted house room in the Church. All of these are angles on the question and all, I believe, shed some light on it. Yet they do not explain the whole story.

In addition to all of these factors, however, evangelicals have undergone a little-noted revision in their understanding of God — little noted because it is not an explicit part of the current evangelical agenda. Both the earlier Liberalism and the current evangelicalism have made use of culture, but they have done so in different ways. The earlier Liberalism was a deliberate program of adjusting the content of Christian faith to bring it into conformity with the dogmas of culture, on the ground that those dogmas were describing the reality of God as this was reflected in and made known through culture. At the heart of their program, then, was a belief in the immanence of God. Contemporary evangelicalism, because it sees culture as essentially neutral in its values, is also in the process of adapting the contents of Christian faith to cultural dogma, but its program for doing so is haphazard and unconscious. The immanence of God provided the explicit basis of Liberalism but it is only the *implied* basis of evangelicalism. This is why evangelicals do not always recognize the revision in the understanding of God that accompanies this belief; nevertheless, it is present with disconcerting regularity in the practice of evangelical faith. It is there to be seen in the identification that groups have variously made between the kingdom of God on the one hand and America (or the American Way of Life) or social action or other religions or the experiences of the self on the other. None of these adaptations involves a conscious attempt to revise the doctrine of God, but they do all seek to revise reality, and once they have done so, they must then adapt God to fit this revision. And from it all has sprung a way of looking at life that, although religious, is typically at odds with the biblical portrayal of life.

It is not difficult to see that we will arrive at two very different understandings of reality depending on whether we begin with a view of the human being as simply a self or as a human *being*. If we view ourselves as beings made in the image of God, we will recognize in ourselves capacities for God, truth, and goodness — capacities that cannot be meaningfully filled by that which is not divine, not true, not good. As Augustine observed long ago, we will be restless and frustrated until these capacities find their satisfaction in the God for whom they are made. The substitutes that modernity offers, however sweet they may seem initially, will never be adequate. Modernity itself cannot be a sufficient end. We will never be satisfied unless we transcend the world of experience to find the reality that lies behind it.

On the other hand, if we view the human as but a *self,* the world looks entirely different. Thus psychologized, the world appears to have within it the means of its own healing and satisfaction. Access to the riches of modern experience lies not through thought but through *experience*. Truth is displaced by experience, reason by intuition, the universal by the private, the external by the internal — and the result is a way of looking at life that entails substantial modifications of God himself to these modern habits in order to sustain the relevance of the Church. The key modification here involves making God accessible to us through our own selves.

The truth of the matter is that the modern language of psychology often forces upon the biblical idea of the *imago Dei* a set of presuppositions that are profoundly injurious to it. In fact, this is not a language of translation at all; it is a different language altogether, a language that is modern in its interests and perspective on life based on views of sin and God that are substantially different from those of the Bible. And yet this has become the language of the whole modern world, including the little corner of it that calls itself evangelical.

This way of looking at life strikes at the very heart of Christian faith because it strikes at what is authoritative in Christian faith. Christian faith is Christian only to the extent that it has been constituted by the Word of God, the Word that God has made powerful and effective in the reconstituting of sinful life. Christian life is not simply an experience or a private intuition into the meaning of life on a par with other ways of looking at life. No, what makes Christian life Christian is the fact that God has actualized his truth here among the foolish of this world. He leads sinners to see that he stands in his holy purposes over against much of what is taken to be normative in a fallen world. Modern experience does not provide access to God; God alone provides this access. It originates in his grace, is objectively grounded in Jesus Christ, and is open now to moderns not through their experience of themselves but through their acceptance of his revealed truth. It is only the objectivity of this truth — a truth that always stands outside the natural interests and detection of modernity — that can lead us back to Christ.

We can see God's judgment on modernity implied in the biography of Jesus Christ, for this biography is incomprehensible unless it is read as a journey toward the Cross. The Father sent him into the world from eternity, and he came. Assertions of Christ's preexistence and the eternal character of the Father's will are important not simply as quaint additions to the Christmas story or points to bolster the argument that Jesus stands preeminent among the world's religious leaders but because they point to the fact that the dilemmas of life (even of modern life) need to be read against the canvas of eternity. They also help to reveal the depth of God's love in coming so far, in reaching so low. And, when we thus confront the vastness of God's purposes, we receive a measure by which to judge the shallow purpose of our modern life.

It is important to note that the shallowness of modern life derives not from its banality but from its having lost its moral bearings. Our Age, like every age that has preceded it, interrogates the unknown with its own questions — questions that grow out of its needs and interests. Our questions today hardly ever go to the heart of moral reality, because modern life is hardly ever about moral concern. Christ seems to offer little of what this world is asking for. It wants whatever is new; it looks for the next step in the journey of the human spirit. Christ did bring to completion much that was predicted or prophesied in the Old Testament, but he introduced few new ideas, and none that would suggest that the human spirit is embarked on a journey. Rather, he brought access to the world of moral reality from which sinners are alienated, and that is everything. He brought everything in himself, for he is God.

More than that even, Christ brought everything into harmony with the holiness of God. To be sure, this harmony has two entirely different expressions: justification and judgment. In both, the holiness of God comes into its full and awful expression. In the one case, it does so in him who bears the consequences of that wrath on behalf and in the place of those whom he represented; in the other case, it is expressed in the final and awesome alienation of those in whom God's judgment vindicates for all eternity his holiness.

It is this holiness of God, then, without which the Cross of Christ is incomprehensible, that provides the light that exposes modernity's darkness for what it is. For modernity has emptied life of serious moral purpose. Indeed, it empties people of the capacity to see the world in moral terms, and this, in turn, closes their access to reality, for reality is fundamentally moral. God's holiness is fundamental to who he is and what he has done. And the key to it all has been the loss of God's otherness, not least in his holiness, beneath the forms of modern piety. Evangelicals turned from focusing on God's transcendence to focusing on his immanence — and then they took the further step of interpreting his immanence as friendliness with modernity.

The loss of the traditional vision of God as holy is now manifested everywhere in the evangelical world. It is the key to understanding why sin and grace have become such empty terms. What depth or meaning, P. T. Forsyth asked, can these terms have except in relation to the holiness of God? Divorced from the holiness of God, sin is merely self-defeating behavior or a breach in etiquette. Divorced from the holiness of God, grace is merely empty rhetoric, pious window dressing for the modern technique by which sinners work out their own salvation. Divorced from the holiness of God, our gospel becomes indistinguishable from any of a host of alternative self-help doctrines. Divorced from the holiness of God, our public morality is reduced to little more than an accumulation of trade-offs between competing private interests. Divorced from the holiness of God, our worship becomes mere entertainment. The holiness of God is the very cornerstone of Christian faith, for it is the foundation of reality. Sin is defiance of God's holiness, the Cross is the outworking and victory of God's holiness, and faith is the recognition of God's holiness. Knowing that God is holy is therefore the key to knowing life as it truly is, knowing Christ as he truly is, knowing why he came, and knowing how life will end.

It is this God, majestic and holy in his being, this God whose love knows no bounds because his holiness knows no limits, who has disappeared from the modern evangelical world. He has been replaced in many quarters by a God who is slick and slack, whose moral purposes turn out to be avuncular advice that we can disregard or negotiate as we see fit, whose Word is a plaything for those who wish merely to listen to themselves, whose Church is a mall in which the religious, their pockets filled with the coin of need, do their business. We seek happiness, not righteousness. We want to be fulfilled, not filled. We are interested in satisfaction, not a holy dissatisfaction with all that is wrong.

This is why we need reformation rather than revival. The habits of the modern world, now so ubiquitous in the evangelical world, need to be put to death, not given new life. They need to be rooted out, not simply papered over with fresh religious enthusiasm. And they are by this point so invincible that nothing less than the intrusion of God in his grace, nothing less than a full recovery of his truth, will suffice.

In this regard, the death of theology has profound ramifications. Theology is dying not because the academy has failed to devise adequate procedures for reconstructing it but because the Church has lost its capacity for it. And while some hail this loss as a step forward toward the hope of new evangelical vitality, it is in fact a sign of creeping death. The emptiness of evangelical faith without theology echoes the emptiness of modern life. Both have elected to cross over into a world in which God has no place, in which reality has been rewritten, in which Christ has become redundant, his Word irrelevant, and the Church must now find new reasons for its existence.

Unless the evangelical Church can recover the knowledge of what it means to live before a holy God, unless in its worship it can relearn humility, wonder, love, and praise, unless it can find again a moral purpose in the world that resonates with the holiness of God and that is accordingly deep and unyielding — unless the evangelical Church can do all of these things, theology will have no place in its life. But the reverse is also true. If the Church can begin to find a place for theology by refocusing itself on the centrality of God, if it can rest upon his sufficiency, if it can recover its moral fiber, then it will have something to say to a world now drowning in modernity. And there lies a great irony. Those who are most relevant to the modern world are those most irrelevant to the moral purpose of God, but those who are irrelevant in the world by virtue of their relevance to God actually have the most to say to the world. They are, in fact, the only ones who having anything to say to it. That is what Jesus declared, what the Church in its best moments has known, and what we, by the grace of God, can yet again discover.

Selected Bibliography

Adams, E. M. *Philosophy and the Modern Mind: A Philosophical Critique of Modern Western Civilization.* Chapel Hill, N.C.: University of North Carolina Press, 1975.

Adler, Richard P., ed. *Understanding Television: Essays on Television as a Social and Cultural Force.* New York: Praeger, 1981.

Alter, Robert. *The Art of Biblical Narrative.* New York: Basic Books, 1981.

Ammerman, Nancy Tatom. *Baptist Battles: Social Change and Religious Conflict in the Southern Baptist Convention.* New Brunswick, N.J.: Rutgers University Press, 1990.

Anderson, Quentin. *The Imperial Self: An Essay in American Literary and Cultural History.* New York: Alfred A. Knopf, 1971.

Arnold, Matthew. *Culture and Anarchy.* Cambridge: Cambridge University Press, 1932.

Balmer, Randall H. *Mine Eyes Have Seen the Glory: A Journey into the Evangelical Subculture in America.* New York: Oxford University Press, 1989.

Barraclough, Geoffrey. *An Introduction to Contemporary History.* Harmondsworth: Penguin Books, 1967.

Barrett, William E. *Death of the Soul: From Descartes to the Computer.* Garden City, N.Y.: Doubleday, 1987.

_____. *The Illusion of Technique: A Search for Meaning in a Technological Civilization.* Garden City, N.Y.: Doubleday, 1979.

Bell, Daniel. *The Coming of Post-Industrial Society: A Venture in Social Forecasting.* New York: Basic Books, 1973.

_____. *The End of Ideology: On the Exhaustion of Political Ideas in the Fifties.* New York: Free Press, 1960.

Bellah, Robert N. *Beyond Belief: Essays on Religion in a Post-Traditional World.* New York: Harper & Row, 1970.

_____. *The Broken Covenant: American Civil Religion in Time of Trial.* New York: Seabury Press, 1975.

_____ et al. *Habits of the Heart: Individualism and Commitment in American Life.* Berkeley and Los Angeles: University of California Press, 1985.

Berger, Arthur Asa, ed. *Television in Society.* New Brunswick, N.J.: Transaction Books, 1986.

Berger, Peter L. *Facing Up to Modernity: Excursions in Society, Politics, and Religion.* New York: Basic Books, 1977.

_____. *The Heretical Imperative: Contemporary Possibilities of Religious Affirmation.* Garden City, N.Y.: Doubleday, 1980.

_____. *The Precarious Vision: A Sociologist Looks at Social Fictions and Christian Faith.* Garden City, N.Y.: Doubleday, 1961.

_____. *A Rumor of Angels.* Garden City, N.Y.: Doubleday-Anchor, 1970.

Berger, Peter L., Brigitte Berger, and Kellner Hansfried. *The Homeless Mind: Modernization and Modern Consciousness.* New York: Random House, 1979.

Berger, Peter L., and Thomas Luckman. *The Social Construct of Reality: A Treatise in the Sociology of Knowledge.* Garden City, N.Y.: Doubleday, 1966.

Berger, Peter L., and Richard John Neuhaus. *To Empower People: The Role of Mediating Structures in Public Policy.* Washington: American Enterprise Institute for Public Policy Research, 1977.

Berkhof, Hendrikus. *Christ the Meaning of History.* Translated by Lambertus Buurman. Richmond: John Knox Press, 1966.

Berman, Ronald, ed. *Solzhenitsyn at Harvard: The Address, Twelve Early Responses, and Six Later Reflections.* Washington: Ethics and Public Policy Center, 1980.

Bledstein, Burton J. *The Culture of Professionalism: The Middle Class and the Development of Higher Education in America.* New York: W. W. Norton, 1976.

Bloom, Allan. *The Closing of the American Mind: How Higher Education Has Failed Democracy and Impoverished the Souls of Today's Students.* New York: Simon & Schuster, 1988.

Boorstin, Daniel J. *America and the Image of Europe: Reflections on American Thought.* New York: World Publishing, 1966.

_____. *The Americans.* Vol. 2: *The Democratic Experience.* New York: Random House, 1973.

_____. *The Discoverers: A History of Man's Search to Know His World and Himself.* New York: Random House, 1983.

_____. *The Image; or, What Happened to the American Dream.* New York: Atheneum, 1962.

Boyers, Robert, and Robert Orvill, eds. *Psychological Man.* New York: Harper & Row, 1975.

Briggs, Charles Augustus. *History of the Study of Theology*. 2 vols. New York: Scribner's, 1916.

Brittan, Arthur. *The Privatised World*. London: Routledge & Kegan Paul, 1977.

Brogan, D. W. *The American Character*. New York: Alfred A. Knopf, 1944.

Brown, James. *Subject and Object in Modern Theology*. London: SCM Press, 1955.

Brown, Norman O. *Life against Death: The Psychoanalytical Meaning of History*. Middletown, Conn.: Wesleyan University Press, 1959.

Brown, William Adams, et al. *The Education of American Ministers*. 4 vols. New York: Institute of Social and Religious Research, 1934.

Browning, Don S., ed. *Practical Theology: The Emerging Field in Theology, Church, and World*. San Francisco: Harper & Row, 1983.

Brunner, Emil. *Christianity and Civilisation*. 2 vols. New York: Scribner's, 1948-49.

Buber, Martin. *The Eclipse of God: Studies in the Relation between Religion and Philosophy*. 1952. Reprint. New York: Harper & Row, 1965.

Buckley, Jerome Hamilton. *The Turning Key: Autobiography and the Subjective Impulse since 1800*. Cambridge: Harvard University Press, 1984.

Buhle, Paul, ed. *Popular Culture in America*. Minneapolis: University of Minnesota Press, 1987.

Butler, Jon. *Awash in a Sea of Faith: The Christianization of the American People, 1550-1865*. Cambridge: Harvard University Press, 1990.

Calhoun, Arthur W. *A Social History of the American Family*. 3 vols. Cleveland: N.p., 1915-18.

Calhoun, Daniel. *Professional Lives in America: Structure and Aspiration, 1750-1850*. Cambridge: Harvard University Press, 1965.

Carlson, Robert A. *The Quest for Conformity: Americanization through Education*. New York: John Wiley, 1975.

Chadwick, Owen. *From Bossuet to Newman: The Idea of Doctrinal Development*. Cambridge: Cambridge University Press, 1957.

_____. *The Secularization of the European Mind in the Nineteenth Century*. Cambridge: Cambridge University Press, 1976.

Cohen, S. Hennig, ed. *The American Experience: Approaches to the Study of the United States*. Boston: Houghton Mifflin, 1968.

Commager, Henry Steele. *The American Mind: An Interpretation of American Thought and Character since the 1880s*. New Haven: Yale University Press, 1950.

Condry, John. *The Psychology of Television*. Hillsdale, N.J.: Lawrence Erlbaum, 1989.

Cremin, Lawrence A. *The Transformation of the School: Progressivism in American Education, 1876-1957*. New York: Alfred A. Knopf, 1969.

Czitrom, Daniel. *Media and the American Mind: From Morse to McLuhan*. Chapel Hill, N.C.: University of North Carolina Press, 1982.

Davies, Horton. *A Mirror of the Ministry in Modern Novels*. New York: Oxford University Press, 1959.

Dawson, Christopher. *The Crisis of Western Education: With Specific Programs for the Study of Christian Culture*. New York: Sheed & Ward, 1961.

_____. *Religion and the Rise of Western Culture*. Garden City, N.Y.: Doubleday, 1958.

Donnelly, William J. *The Confetti Generation: How the New Communication Technology Is Fragmenting America*. New York: Henry Holt, 1986.

Donohue, William A. *The New Freedom: Individualism and Collectivism in the Social Lives of Americans*. New Brunswick, N.J.: Transaction Publishers, 1990.

Douglas, Ann. *The Feminization of American Culture*. New York: Alfred A. Knopf, 1977.

Dulles, Foster Rhea. *America's Rise to World Power, 1898-1954*. New York: Harper, 1954.

Eisenstein, Elizabeth. *The Printing Press as an Agent of Change*. 2 vols. New York: Cambridge University Press, 1979.

Eliade, Mircea. *Cosmos and History: The Myth of the Eternal Return*. New York: Harper & Row, 1954.

_____. *From Primitives to Zen: A Thematic Sourcebook in the History of Religions*. London: Collins, 1967.

Ellul, Jacques. *The Betrayal of the West*. Translated by Matthew J. O'Connell. New York: Seabury Press, 1978.

_____. *The Humiliation of the Word*. Translated by Joyce Main Hanks. Grand Rapids: William B. Eerdmans, 1985.

_____. *The Technological Society*. Translated by John Wilkinson. New York: Alfred A. Knopf, 1965.

Erikson, Erik H. *Childhood and Society*. New York: W. W. Norton, 1963.

Evans, Gareth R. *Old Arts and New Theology: The Beginnings of Theology as an Academic Discipline*. Oxford: Clarendon Press, 1980.

Farley, Edward. *Theologia: The Fragmentation and Unity of Theological Education*. Philadelphia: Fortress Press, 1983.

Ferré, Nels. *Christian Faith and Higher Education*. New York: Harper, 1954.

Fichter, Joseph. *Religion as an Occupation: A Study in the Sociology of Professions*. Notre Dame, Ind.: University of Notre Dame Press, 1961.

Fiske, John. *Television Culture*. London: Methuen, 1987.

Foucault, Michel. *Discipline and Punish: Birth of the Prison*. Translated by Alan Sheridan. New York: Random House, 1979.

_____. *Madness and Civilization: A History of Insanity in the Age of Reason*. New York: Random House, 1973.

_____. *The Archaeology of Knowledge*. Translated by A. M. Sheridan-Smith. New York: Pantheon Books, 1972.

_____. *The Order of Things: An Archaeology of the Human Sciences*. New York: Vintage Books, 1973.

Frankfort, Henri, Mrs. A. H. Frankfort, John A. Wilson, and Thorkild Jacobsen. *Before Philosophy.* Harmondsworth: Penguin, 1967.

Frei, Hans W. *The Eclipse of Biblical Narrative: A Study in Eighteenth and Nineteenth Century Hermeneutics.* New Haven: Yale University Press, 1974.

Frye, Northrop. *The Modern Century.* Toronto: Oxford University Press, 1967.

Galbraith, John Kenneth. *The Affluent Society.* Boston: Houghton Mifflin, 1958.

Gans, Herbert J. *Popular Culture and High Culture: An Analysis and Evaluation of Taste.* New York: Basic Books, 1975.

Gehlen, Arnold. *Man in the Age of Technology.* Translated by Pat Lipscomb. New York: Columbia University Press, 1980.

Gilkey, Langdon. *How the Church Can Minister to the World without Losing Itself.* New York: Harper & Row, 1964.

_____. *Society and the Sacred: Toward a Theology of Culture in Decline.* New York: Crossroad, 1981.

Gitlin, Todd. *Inside Prime Time.* New York: Pantheon Books, 1985.

Goffman, Erving. *The Presentation of Self in Everyday Life.* Garden City, N.Y.: Doubleday, 1959.

Goodheart, Eugene. *Culture and the Radical Conscience.* Cambridge: Harvard University Press, 1973.

Gouldner, Alvin W. *The Dialectic of Ideology and Technology: The Origins, Grammar, and Future of Ideology.* New York: Oxford University Press, 1982.

Graff, Harvey J. *Literacy and Social Development in the West: A Reader.* New York: Cambridge University Press, 1981.

Greeley, Andrew. *Unsecular Man: The Persistence of Religion.* New York: Schocken Books, 1972.

Green, Garrett, ed. *Scriptural Authority and Narrative Interpretation.* Philadelphia: Fortress Press, 1987.

Habermas, Jürgen. *The Philosophical Discourse of Modernity.* Translated by Frederick G. Lawrence. Cambridge: MIT Press, 1987.

_____. *Theory and Practice.* Translated by John Viertel. Boston: Beacon Press, 1973.

Hadden, Jeffrey K., and Charles E. Swann. *Prime Time Preachers: The Rising Power of Televangelism.* Reading, Pa.: Addison-Wesley, 1981.

Hague, John A., ed. *American Character and Culture in a Changing World: Some Twentieth-Century Perspectives.* Westport, Conn.: Greenwood Press, 1979.

Hanhardt, John G., ed. *Video Culture: A Critical Investigation.* Layton, Vt.: Gibbs M. Smith, 1986.

Harrington, Michael. *The Accidental Century.* New York: Macmillan, 1965.

_____. *The Politics at God's Funeral: The Spiritual Crisis of Western Civilization.* Harmondsworth: Penguin, 1985.

Hart, James D. *The Popular Book: A History of America's Literary Taste.* New York: Oxford University Press, 1950.

Harvey, Van Austin. *The Historian and the Believer: The Morality of Historical Knowledge and Christian Belief.* Philadelphia: Westminster Press, 1981.

Hatch, Nathan O. *The Democratization of American Christianity.* New Haven: Yale University Press, 1989.

Hauerwas, Stanley, and William Willimon. *Resident Aliens: A Provocative Christian Assessment of Culture and Ministry for People Who Know That Something Is Wrong.* Nashville: Abingdon Press, 1989.

Henderson, Katherine, and Joseph Mazzeo, eds. *The Meanings of the Medium: Perspectives on the Art of Television.* New York: Praeger, 1990.

Henry, Carl F. H. *The Christian Mindset in a Secular Society.* Portland: Multnomah Press, 1985.

Hick, John, and Paul F. Knitter, eds. *The Myth of Christian Uniqueness: Toward a Pluralistic Theology of Religions.* Maryknoll, N.Y.: Orbis Books, 1988.

Higham, John, ed. *The Reconstruction of American History.* New York: Harper, 1962.

Hodgson, Peter C. *God in History: Shapes of Freedom.* Nashville: Abingdon Press, 1989.

Hofstadter, Richard. *The American Political Tradition.* New York: Vintage Books, 1957.

_____. *Anti-Intellectualism in American Life.* New York: Vintage Books, 1963.

_____. *Darwinism in American Thought.* New York: George Braziller, 1959.

Holborn, Hajo. *The Political Collapse of Europe.* New York: Alfred A. Knopf, 1951.

Howard, Robert. *Brave New Workplace: America's Corporate Utopias — How They Create Inequities and Social Conflict in Our Working Lives.* New York: Penguin, 1985.

Hughes, Everett C., Barrie Thorne, Agostino DeBaggis, Arnold Gurin, and David Williams. *Education for the Professions of Medicine, Law, Theology, and Social Welfare: A Report Prepared for the Carnegie Commission on Higher Education.* New York: McGraw-Hill, 1973.

Hunter, James Davison. *American Evangelicalism: Conservative Religion and the Quandary of Modernity.* New Brunswick, N.J.: Rutgers University Press, 1983.

_____. *Evangelicalism: The Coming Generation.* Chicago: University of Chicago Press, 1987.

Hutchison, William R. *The Modernist Impulse in American Protestantism.* Cambridge: Harvard University Press, 1976.

_____, ed. *Between the Times: The Travail of the Protestant Establishment in America, 1900-1960.* Cambridge: Cambridge University Press, 1989.

Illich, Ivan, et al. *The Disabling Professions*. New York: Marion Boyars, 1978.

Johnson, Paul. *Modern Times: The World from the Twenties to the Eighties*. New York: Harper & Row, 1983.

Jung, C. G. *Modern Man in Search of a Soul*. Translated by W. S. Dell and Cary F. Baynes. New York: Harcourt, Brace, 1933.

Kelley, Dean M. *Why Conservative Churches Are Growing: A Study in Sociology of Religion*. New York: Harper & Row, 1972.

Kelsey, David H. *The Uses of Scripture in Recent Theology*. Philadelphia: Fortress Press, 1975.

Kerr, Clark. *The Uses of the University*. Cambridge: Harvard University Press, 1963.

Kilpatrick, William Kirk. *Psychological Seduction: The Failure of Modern Psychology*. New York: Thomas Nelson, 1983.

Kliever, Lonnie D. *The Shattered Spectrum: A Survey of Contemporary Theology*. Atlanta: John Knox Press, 1981.

Knitter, Paul F. *No Other Name? A Critical Survey of Christian Attitudes toward the World Religions*. Maryknoll, N.Y.: Orbis Books, 1985.

Kort, Wesley A. *Shriven Selves: Religious Problems in Recent American Fiction*. Philadelphia: Fortress Press, 1972.

Kozol, Jonathan. *Illiterate America*. New York: New American Library, 1985.

_____. *Prisoners of Silence: Breaking the Bonds of Adult Illiteracy in the United States*. New York: Continuum, 1980.

Kraft, Charles H. *Christianity in Culture: A Study in Dynamic Theologizing in Cross-Cultural Perspective*. Maryknoll, N.Y.: Orbis Books, 1981.

Kubey, Robert, and Mihaly Csikszentmihalyi, eds. *Television and the Quality of Life: How Viewing Shapes Everyday Experiences*. Hillsdale, N.J.: Lawrence Erlbaum, 1990.

Kuhn, Thomas. *The Structure of Scientific Revolutions*. 2d ed. Chicago: University of Chicago Press, 1970.

Kuklick, Bruce. *Churchmen and Philosophers: From Jonathan Edwards to John Dewey*. New Haven: Yale University Press, 1985.

Lacey, Michael J., ed. *Religion and Twentieth-Century American Intellectual Life*. Cambridge: Cambridge University Press, 1989.

Lasch, Christopher. *Haven in a Heartless World: The Family Besieged*. New York: Basic Books, 1979.

_____. *The Culture of Narcissism: American Life in an Age of Diminishing Expectations*. New York: W. W. Norton, 1978.

_____. *The Minimal Self: Psychic Survival in Troubled Times*. New York: W. W. Norton, 1984.

_____. *The New Radicalism in America 1889-1963: The Intellectual as a Social Type*. New York: Alfred A. Knopf, 1965.

_____. *The True and Only Heaven: Progress and Its Critics*. New York: W. W. Norton, 1990.

Lears, Jackson. *No Place for Grace: Antimodernism and the Transformation of American Culture, 1880-1920*. New York: Pantheon Books, 1981.

Lemon, Richard. *The Troubled American*. New York: Simon & Schuster, 1971.

Lévi-Strauss, Claude. *The Savage Mind*. Chicago: University of Chicago Press, 1968.

Lindbeck, George A. *The Nature of Doctrine: Religion and Theology in a Postliberal Age*. Philadelphia: Westminster Press, 1984.

Lowery, Sharon A., and Melvin De Fleur, eds. *Milestones in Mass Communication Research: Media Effects*. London: Longman, 1983.

Luckmann, Thomas. *The Invisible Religion: The Problem of Religion in Modern Society*. New York: Macmillan, 1967.

Lyotard, Jean-François. *The Postmodern Condition: A Report on Knowledge*. Translated by Geoff Bennington and Brian Massumi. Minneapolis: University of Minnesota Press, 1984.

MacDonald, Dwight. *Against the American Grain: Essays on the Effects of Mass Culture*. New York: Da Carpo Press, 1952.

McGrath, Alister. *The Genesis of Doctrine: A Study in the Foundations of Doctrinal Criticism*. Oxford: Basil Blackwell, 1990.

Machen, J. Gresham. *Christianity and Liberalism*. New York: Macmillan, 1923.

Machlup, Fritz, et al. *The Production and Distribution of Knowledge in the United States*. Princeton: Princeton University Press, 1962.

MacIntyre, Alasdair. *After Virtue: A Study in Moral Theory*. Notre Dame, Ind.: University of Notre Dame Press, 1981.

_____. *Against the Self-Images of the Age: Essays on Ideology and Philosophy*. New York: Schocken Books, 1971.

_____. *Secularization and Moral Change*. London: Oxford University Press, 1967.

McKenzie, John L. *The Civilization of Christianity*. Chicago: Thomas More Press, 1986.

McLoughlin, William J. *Patterns of Professional Education*. New York: G. P. Putnam, 1960.

McLuhan, Marshall. *The Gutenberg Galaxy: The Making of Typographic Man*. Toronto: University of Toronto Press, 1962.

_____. *Understanding Media: The Extensions of Man*. New York: McGraw-Hill, 1964.

Maritain, Jacques. *Reflections on America*. New York: Scribner's, 1958.

Marsden, George M. *The Evangelical Mind and the New School Presbyterian Experience: A Case Study of Thought and Theology in Nineteenth-Century America*. New Haven: Yale University Press, 1970.

_____. *Fundamentalism and American Culture: The Shaping of Twentieth-Century Evangelicalism, 1870-1925*. New York: Oxford University Press, 1980.

_____. *Reforming Fundamentalism: Fuller Seminary and the New Evangelicalism.* Grand Rapids: William B. Eerdmans, 1987.

Martin, David. *A General Theory of Secularization.* New York: Harper, 1978.

_____. *The Religious and the Secular: Studies in Secularization.* New York: Schocken Books, 1969.

_____. *Tongues of Fire: The Explosion of Protestantism in Latin America.* Oxford: Basil Blackwell, 1990.

Martin, David, John Mills, and W. S. F. Pickering, eds. *Sociology and Theology: Alliance and Conflict.* New York: St. Martin's Press, 1980.

Marty, Martin E. *Religion and Republic: The American Circumstance.* Boston: Beacon Press, 1987.

_____. *Righteous Empire: The Protestant Experience in America.* New York: Dial Press, 1970.

Mascall, E. L. *The Secularization of Christianity: An Analysis and Critique.* New York: Holt, Rinehart, & Winston, 1965.

Metz, Johannes Baptist. *Faith in History and Society.* Translated by David Smith. New York: Seabury Press, 1979.

Miller, David Leroy. *The New Polytheism: Rebirth of the Gods and Goddesses.* New York: Harper & Row, 1974.

Miller, Perry. *The Life of the Mind in America: From the Revolution to the Civil War.* New York: Harcourt, Brace & World, 1965.

Molnar, Thomas. *The Pagan Temptation.* Grand Rapids: William B. Eerdmans, 1987.

Moore, R. Laurence. *Religious Outsiders and the Making of Americans.* New York: Oxford University Press, 1987.

Morgan, Edmund S., ed. *The American Revolution: Two Centuries of Interpretation.* Englewood Cliffs, N.J.: Prentice-Hall, 1965.

Mumby, Frank Arthur, and Ian Norrie. *Publishing and Bookselling: A History from the Earliest Times to the Present Day.* 5th ed. New York: R. R. Bowker, 1974.

Mumford, Lewis. *The Culture of Cities.* New York: Harcourt, Brace, 1938.

_____. *The Myth of the Machine.* 2 vols. 1934. Reprint. New York: Harcourt, 1970, 1971.

Neuhaus, Richard John. *The Naked Public Square: Religion and Democracy in America.* Grand Rapids: William B. Eerdmans, 1984.

_____, ed. *Unsecular America.* Grand Rapids: William B. Eerdmans, 1986.

Newbigin, Lesslie. *Foolishness to the Greeks: The Gospel and Western Culture.* Grand Rapids: William B. Eerdmans, 1986.

Newcomb, Horace, ed. *Television: The Critical View.* 3d ed. Oxford: Oxford University Press, 1982.

Newman, John Henry. *The Idea of a University.* New York: Longmans, 1947.

Niebuhr, H. Richard. *Christ and Culture.* New York: Harper, 1951.

_____. *The Social Sources of Denominationalism.* Cleveland: World Publishing, 1957.

Niebuhr, H. Richard, Wilhelm Pauck, and Francis P. Miller. *The Church against the World*. Chicago: Willet, Clark, 1935.

Niebuhr, H. Richard, Daniel Day Williams, and James M. Gustafson. *The Advancement of Theological Education*. New York: Harper, 1957.

Niebuhr, H. Richard, and Daniel Day Williams, eds. *The Ministry in Historical Perspective*. New York: Harper, 1956.

Nisbet, Robert A. *History of the Idea of Progress*. New York: Basic Books, 1979.

_____. *The Sociological Tradition*. New York: Basic Books, 1966.

_____. *Tradition and Revolt: Essays Historical, Sociological, and Critical*. New York: Vintage Books, 1970.

_____. *Twilight of Authority*. New York: Oxford University Press, 1977.

Noble, David W. *Historians against History: The Frontier Thesis and the National Covenant in American Historical Writing since 1830*. Minneapolis: University of Minnesota Press, 1965.

Noll, Mark. *Between Faith and Criticism: Evangelicals, Scholarship, and the Bible in America*. San Francisco: Harper & Row, 1982.

Novak, Michael. *Democracy and Mediating Structures: A Theological Inquiry*. Washington: American Enterprise Institute for Policy Research, 1977.

Oleson, Alexandra, and John Voss, eds. *The Organization of Knowledge in Modern America, 1860-1920*. Baltimore: The Johns Hopkins University Press, 1979.

Olson, Alan M., Christopher Parr, and Debra Parr, eds. *Video Icons and Values*. Albany: State University of New York, 1990.

Ong, Walter J. *Interfaces of the Word: Studies in the Evolution of Consciousness and Culture*. Ithaca, N.Y.: Cornell University Press, 1977.

_____. *The Presence of the Word: Some Prolegomena for Cultural and Religious History*. New Haven: Yale University Press, 1967.

Orr, James. *The Christian View of God and His World as Centering in the Incarnation*. New York: Scribner's, 1897.

Packard, Vance. *A Nation of Strangers*. New York: David McKay, 1972.

Pannenberg, Wolfhart. *Jesus — God and Man*. Translated by Lewis L. Wilkins and Duane A. Priebe. Philadelphia: Westminster Press, 1977.

Parsons, Talcott. *Essays in Sociological Theory*. New York: Free Press, 1954.

_____, and Gerald Platt. *The American University*. Cambridge: Harvard University Press, 1973.

Passmore, John. *The Perfectibility of Man*. New York: Scribner's, 1970.

Palen, John J. *The Urban World*. 3d ed. New York: McGraw-Hill, 1987.

Pinnock, Clark H. *A Wideness in God's Mercy: The Finality of Jesus Christ in a World of Religions*. Grand Rapids: Zondervan, 1991.

Polanyi, Michael. *Knowing and Being*. Edited by Marjorie Greene. Chicago: University of Chicago Press, 1969.

_____. *Personal Knowledge: Towards a Post-Critical Philosophy*. Chicago: University of Chicago Press, 1958.

Post, Albert. *Popular Freethought in America, 1825-1850.* 1943. Reprint. New York: Octagon Books, 1943.

Potter, David M. *History and American Society: Essays of David M. Potter,* edited by Don E. Fehrenbacher. New York: Oxford University Press, 1975.

_____. *People of Plenty: Economic Abundance and the American Character.* Chicago: University of Chicago Press, 1954.

Quebedeaux, Richard. *By What Authority? The Rise of Personality Cults in American Christianity.* San Francisco: Harper & Row, 1982.

Resnick, Daniel P., ed. *Literacy in Historical Perspective.* Washington: Library of Congress, 1983.

Reynolds, David S. *Faith in Fiction: The Emergence of Religious Literature in America.* Cambridge: Harvard University Press, 1981.

Rieff, Philip. *The Triumph of the Therapeutic: Uses of Faith after Freud.* New York: Harper & Row, 1968.

_____, ed. *On Intellectuals: Case Studies.* Garden City, N.Y.: Doubleday, 1970.

Riegler, Gordon A. *Socialization of the New England Clergy, 1800-1860.* Philadelphia: Porcupine Press, 1979.

Riesman, David. *Individualism Reconsidered and Other Essays.* New York: Free Press, 1954.

Riesman, David, et al. *The Lonely Crowd: A Study of the Changing American Character.* Revised ed. New Haven: Yale University Press, 1961.

Reventlow, Henning G. *The Authority of the Bible and the Rise of the Modern World.* Translated by John Bowden. Philadelphia: Fortress Press, 1984.

Rogow, Arnold A. *The Dying of the Light: A Searching Look at America Today.* New York: G. P. Putnam, 1975.

Roof, Wade Clark. *Community and Commitment: Religious Plausibility in a Liberal Protestant Church.* New York: Elsevier North-Holland, 1978.

Roof, Wade Clark, and William McKinney. *American Mainline Religion: Its Changing Shape and Future.* New Brunswick, N.J.: Rutgers University Press, 1987.

Roozen, David A., William McKinney, and Jackson W. Carroll. *Varieties of Religious Presence: Mission in Public Life.* New York: Pilgrim Press, 1984.

Rorty, Richard. *Philosophy and the Mirror of Nature.* Princeton: Princeton University Press, 1979.

_____. *Consequences of Pragmatism: Essay, 1972-1980.* Minneapolis: University of Minnesota Press, 1982.

Russell, Jeffrey Burton. *The Devil: Perceptions of Evil from Antiquity to Primitive Christianity.* Ithaca, N.Y.: Cornell University Press, 1977.

_____. *Mephistopheles: The Devil in the Modern World.* Ithaca, N.Y.: Cornell University Press, 1986.

Schaefer, William D. *Education without Compromise: From Chaos to Coherence in Higher Education.* San Francisco: Jossey-Bass, 1990.

Schaff, Philip. *America: A Sketch of its Political, Social, and Religious Character.* Edited by Perry Miller. Cambridge: Harvard University Press, 1961.

Schlesinger, Arthur M. *Paths to the Present.* New York: Macmillan, 1949.

Schlesinger, Arthur M., and Morton White. *Paths of American Thought.* Boston: Houghton Mifflin, 1963.

Schneider, Herbert Wallace. *Religion in Twentieth-Century America.* Cambridge: Harvard University Press, 1952.

Scholes, Robert, and Robert Kellogg. *The Nature of Narrative.* London: Oxford University Press, 1966.

Schuller, David S., Merton P. Strommen, and Milo L. Brekke, eds. *Ministry in America.* San Francisco: Harper & Row, 1980.

Schultze, Quentin J. *Televangelism and American Culture: The Business of Popular Culture.* Grand Rapids: Baker Book House, 1991.

Schweitzer, Albert. *The Decay and Restoration of Civilization.* London: Adam and Charles Black, 1955.

Scott, Donald M. *From Office to Profession: The New England Ministry, 1750-1850.* Philadelphia: University of Pennsylvania Press, 1978.

_____. *Pastors and Providence: Changing Ministerial Styles in Nineteenth-Century America.* Evanston, Ill.: Seabury-Weston Theological Seminary, 1975.

Sell, Alan P. F. *Theology in Turmoil: The Roots, Course, and Significance of the Conservative-Liberal Debate in Modern Theology.* Grand Rapids: Baker Book House, 1984.

Shils, Edward. *The Intellectuals and the Powers and Other Essays.* Chicago: University of Chicago Press, 1972.

_____. *The Constitution of Society.* Chicago: University of Chicago Press, 1982.

Skolnick, Arlene, and Jerome H. Skolnick, eds. *Family in Transition: Rethinking Marriage, Sexuality, Child Rearing, and Family Organization.* 3d ed. Boston: Little, Brown, 1980.

Smart, James D. *The Strange Silence of the Bible in the Church: A Study in Hermeneutics.* Philadelphia: Westminster Press, 1970.

Smith, Gary Scott. *The Seeds of Secularization: Calvinism, Culture, and Pluralism in America, 1870-1915.* Grand Rapids: Christian University Press, 1985.

Smith, Huston. *Beyond the Post-Modern Mind.* New York: Crossroad, 1982.

Spengler, Oswald. *The Decline of the West: Form and Actuality.* Translated by Charles Francis Atkinson. New York: Alfred A. Knopf, 1929.

Stanley, Manfred. *The Technological Conscience: Survival and Dignity in an Age of Expertise.* New York: Free Press, 1978.

Stark, Rodney, and William S. Bainbridge. *The Future of Religion: Secularization, Revival and Cult Formation.* Berkeley and Los Angeles: University of California Press, 1985.

Stewart, Edward C. *American Cultural Patterns: A Cross-Cultural Perspective.* Pittsburgh: Regional Council for International Education, 1971.

Stout, Harry S. *The New England Soul: Preaching and Religious Culture in Colonial New England.* New York: Oxford University Press, 1988.

Stout, Jeffrey. *The Flight from Authority: Religion, Morality, and the Quest for Autonomy*. Notre Dame, Ind.: University of Notre Dame Press, 1981.

Sweet, Leonard I., ed. *The Evangelical Tradition in America*. Macon, Ga.: Mercer University Press, 1984.

Sykes, Stephen. *The Identity of Christianity: Theologians and the Essence of Christianity from Schleiermacher to Barth*. Philadelphia: Fortress Press, 1984.

Szasz, Thomas. *The Myth of Psychotherapy: Mental Healing as Religion, Rhetoric, and Repression*. Garden City, N.Y.: Doubleday-Anchor, 1978.

Taylor, George Rogers. *The Transportation Revolution, 1815-1860*. Edited by H. David et al. New York: Harper, 1968.

Tocqueville, Alexis de. *Democracy in America*. Edited by J. P. Mayer; translated by George Lawrence. Garden City, N.Y.: Doubleday, 1969.

Toulmin, Stephen. *Cosmopolis: The Hidden Agenda of Modernity*. New York: Free Press, 1990.

Tracy, David. *The Analogical Imagination: Christian Theology and the Culture of Pluralism*. New York: Crossroad, 1985.

_____. *Blessed Rage for Order: The New Pluralism in Theology*. New York: Seabury Press, 1975.

Turner, James. *Without God, without Creed: The Origins of Unbelief in America*. Baltimore: The Johns Hopkins University Press, 1986.

Van Alstyne, Richard W. *The Rising American Empire*. Oxford: Basil Blackwell, 1960.

Veysey, Laurence. *The Emergence of the American University, 1870-1910*. Chicago: University of Chicago Press, 1965.

Warren, Sidney. *American Freethought, 1860-1914*. New York: N.p., 1943.

Weaver, Richard M. *Ideas Have Consequences*. Chicago: University of Chicago Press, 1948.

Weber, Max. *Economy and Society: An Outline of Interpretive Sociology*. Edited by Guenther Roth and Claus Wittich. Berkeley and Los Angeles: University of California Press, 1978.

_____. *The Protestant Ethic and the Spirit of Capitalism*. Translated by A. M. Henderson and Talcott Parsons. New York: Oxford University Press, 1947.

_____. *The Sociology of Religion*. Translated by Ephraim Fischoff. Boston: Beacon Press, 1963.

_____. *The Theory of Social and Economic Organization*. Translated by Talcott Parsons. New York: Scribner's, 1947.

Whyte, William H., Jr. *The Organization Man*. New York: Simon & Schuster, 1956.

Wiebe, Robert H. *The Opening of American Society: From the Adoption of the Constitution to the Eve of Disunion*. New York: Vintage Books, 1985.

Wiles, Maurice. *The Making of Christian Doctrine: A Study in the Principles of Early Doctrinal Development*. London: Cambridge University Press, 1967.

Williams, Peter W. *Popular Religion in America: Symbolic Change and the Modernizing Process in Historical Perspective.* Urbana, Ill.: University of Illinois Press, 1989.

Wilson, Bryan R. *Contemporary Transformations of Religion.* Oxford: Oxford University Press, 1976.

_____. *Religion in Secular Society.* Baltimore: Penguin Books, 1969.

Wilson, John. *Religion in American Society: The Effective Presence.* Englewood Cliffs, N.J.: Prentice-Hall, 1978.

Wuthnow, Robert. *The Restructuring of American Religion: Society and Faith since World War II.* Princeton: Princeton University Press, 1990.

_____. *The Struggle for America's Soul: Evangelicals, Liberals, and Secularism.* Grand Rapids: William B. Eerdmans, 1989.

Wright, G. Ernest. *God Who Acts: Biblical Theology as Recital.* London: SCM Press, 1952.

_____. *The Old Testament against Its Environment.* London: SCM Press, 1960.

Yankelovich, Daniel. *New Rules: Searching for Self-Fulfillment in a World Turned Upside Down.* New York: Random House, 1981.

Znaniecki, Florian. *The Social Role of the Man of Knowledge.* New York: Harper & Row, 1968.

Index

316